ACTS

The Hodder Bible Commentary

Edited by Lee Gatiss

ACTS

MARTIN C. SALTER

HODDER &
STOUGHTON

The Hodder Bible Commentary
Series Editor: Lee Gatiss

First published in Great Britain in 2024 by Hodder & Stoughton
An Hachette UK company

I

The Hodder Bible Commentary: Acts copyright © Martin C. Salter 2024

The right of Martin C. Salter to be identified as the Author of the Work has
been asserted by him in accordance with the Copyright, Designs
and Patents Act 1988.

A CIP catalogue record for this title is available from the British Library

Hardback ISBN 9781473694965
ebook ISBN 9781473695146

Typeset in Bembo Std and Utopia by
Palimpsest Book Production Ltd, Falkirk, Stirlingshire

Printed and bound in Great Britain by Clays Ltd, Elcograf S.p.A.

Hodder & Stoughton policy is to use papers that are natural, renewable
and recyclable products and made from wood grown in sustainable
forests. The logging and manufacturing processes are expected to
conform to the environmental regulations of the country of origin.

Hodder & Stoughton Ltd
Carmelite House
50 Victoria Embankment
London EC4Y 0DZ

www.hodderfaith.com
www.hodderbiblecommentary.com

Contents

Series Preface

The unfolding of your words gives light.
(Psalm 119:130)

The Hodder Bible Commentary aims to proclaim afresh in our generation the unchanging and unerring word of God, for the glory of God and the good of his people. This fifty-volume commentary on the whole Bible seeks to provide the contemporary church with fresh and readable expositions of Scripture which are doctrinally sensitive and globally aware, accessible for all adult readers but particularly useful to those who preach, teach and lead Bible studies in churches and small groups.

Building on the success of Hodder's NIV Proclamation Bible, we have assembled as contributors a remarkable team of men and women from around the world. Alongside a diverse panel of trusted Consultant Editors, they have a tremendous variety of denominational backgrounds and ministries. Each has great experience in unfolding the gospel of Jesus Christ and all are united in our aim of faithfully expounding the Bible in a way that takes account of the original text, biblical theology, the history of interpretation and the needs of the contemporary global church.

These volumes are serious expositions – not overly technical, scholarly works of reference but not simply sermons either. As well as carefully unpacking what the Bible says, they are sensitive to how it has been used in doctrinal discussions over the centuries and in our own day, though not dominated by such concerns at the expense of the text's own agenda. They also try to speak not only into a white, middle-class, Western context (for example), as some might, but to be aware of ways in which other cultures hear and need to hear what the Spirit is saying to the churches.

As you tuck into his Word, with the help of this book, may the glorious Father 'give you the Spirit of wisdom and revelation, so that you may know him better' (Ephesians 1:17).

Lee Gatiss, Series Editor

Consultant Editors

The Series Editor would like to thank the following Consultant Editors for their contributions to the Hodder Bible Commentary:

Shady Anis (*Egypt*)
Kirsten Birkett (*UK*)
Felipe Chamy (*Chile*)
Ben Cooper (*UK*)
Mervyn Eloff (*South Africa*)
Keri Folmar (*Dubai*)
Kerry Gatiss (*UK*)
Kara Hartley (*Australia*)
Julian Hardyman (*Madagascar*)
Stephen Fagbemi (*Nigeria*)
Rosanne Jones (*Japan*)
Henry Jansma (*USA*)
Samuel Lago (*USA*)
Andis Miezitis (*Latvia*)
Adrian Reynolds (*UK*)
Peter Ryan (*Australia*)
Sookgoo Shin (*South Korea*)
Myrto Theocharous (*Greece*)

Acknowledgments

I am grateful to the many people who have enabled me to write this commentary. The Grace Community Church family here in Bedford have given me the time to study and write. The Tyndale House library has allowed me access to resources for research. Many friends have commented on various parts of the manuscript. Lee Gatiss has offered much helpful advice at various stages and has provided great resources from others. My family have been a constant support, showing interest and encouragement. And anything good here is from the Lord's empowering and illuminating Spirit helping me to see the beauty of the gospel. All of the errors are my own.

Abbreviations

ABC	*Africa Bible Commentary* (Grand Rapids: Zondervan, 2006)
ACCS	Ancient Christian Commentary on Scripture
BDAG	Walter Bauer, Frederick W. Danker, W. F. Arndt and F. W. Gingrich. *Greek-English Lexicon of the New Testament and Other Early Christian Literature* (3rd edition; Chicago: University of Chicago Press, 2000)
CBQ	*Catholic Biblical Quarterly*
HTR	*Harvard Theological Review*
JPT	*Journal for Pentecostal Theology*
JSNT	*Journal for the Study of the New Testament*
LNTS	*Library of New Testament Studies*
LXX	Septuagint
NovT	*Novum Testamentum*
NPNF	*Nicene and Post-Nicene Fathers*
OT	Old Testament
PTMS	*Princeton Theological Monogram Series*
RCS	*Reformation Commentary on Scripture.* Specifically, New Testament Volume 6 edited by Esther Chung-Kim and Todd R. Hains, *Acts* (Downers Grove: InterVarsity Press, 2014)
SABC	*South Asia Bible Commentary: A One-Volume Commentary on the Whole Bible*, edited by Brian Wintle (Grand Rapids: Zondervan, 2015)
SBL	Society of Biblical Literature
TDNT	*Theological Dictionary of the New Testament.* 10 volumes, eds Gerhard Kittel and Gerhard Friedrich. Translated by Geoffrey W. Bromiley (Grand Rapids: Eerdmans, 1964–76)
TynBul	*Tyndale Bulletin*

Introduction to Acts

The book of Acts can be summarised in just three words: *God's unstoppable mission*. The narrative covers the first three decades of the numeric and geographic expansion of Jesus's first followers. As readers, we observe Jesus ascend to heaven and pour out his Spirit, and we wait with bated breath to see what will become of this fledgling movement of followers. Luke charts the miracles; the social care; the spread of the word and the growth of the church; the persecution, opposition and trials.

One writer notes, 'Taken simply as a tale of adventure, it is by far the most action-packed book in the New Testament.'[1] But of course, it is so much more. As we reach the end of the book, the apostle Paul has reached the capital of the Empire. Though he is chained, the word is not. God's unstoppable mission keeps going to the end and invites us to become the next instalment, witnessing to the transforming power of the risen Lord.

The book of Acts gives the contemporary reader great confidence that wherever we are and whatever we face, the one enthroned in heaven is still at work, through his people, empowered by his Spirit, to transform lives. In this brief introduction we are going to look at some of the main issues and themes before we move into the commentary on the text.

1. Author and date

The earliest tradition of the church claims that Luke, the doctor and co-worker of Paul (Colossians 4:14; Philemon 24), was the author of both the third Gospel and the book of Acts.[2] Luke himself was not an apostle nor an eyewitness to the resurrection, but he was a close travelling

---

[1] Jaroslav Pelikan, *Acts* (Grand Rapids: Brazos, 2005), 24.
[2] Irenaeus, *Against Heresies* 3.14.1. David G. Peterson, *Acts of the Apostles* (Nottingham: Apollos, 2009), 1.

companion of Paul.[3] This connection likely gave him access to other apostles who were able to inform his account. This makes him a reliable source in recounting the story of the early church.

As to when Luke wrote his account, we cannot be completely certain. There are, however, some clues to help us. For example, Luke makes no mention of the outcome of Paul's trial, the increased persecution of Christians under Nero or the Jewish war culminating in the destruction of the Temple in Jerusalem in AD 70. There is therefore a strong case to be made for dating Luke's account to a period before all these events, and shortly after Paul's Roman imprisonment – AD 62–4.[4]

However, a number of other scholars date Acts to the AD 70s or 80s, based on the material in Luke 21 which appears to refer to the events of AD 70.[5] This would require us to read Luke 21 with the perspective that the events described had already occurred, which is by no means certain. If this were the case, it would seem strange to find no other mention of these events in the rest of Luke–Acts. As Darrell Bock concludes, 'Either Acts is written so much after AD 70 that these issues are no longer worth noting . . . or it is written before it. On balance, the latter is more likely.'[6]

2. Audience and purpose

The primary addressee of Luke's two-volume work was an individual described as 'most excellent Theophilus' (Luke 1:3; Acts 1:1). He is one who has already received some measure of teaching (Luke 1:4), and Luke's account is designed to provide greater certainty. The work therefore has both apologetic and didactic intent.

Luke's self-stated aim in his two-volume work is to provide Theophilus with 'certainty' concerning the things he had been taught.[7] Luke is at pains to demonstrate he has carefully investigated and ordered his material (Luke 1:1–4).[8] Given Luke's emphases, the 'certainty' would appear to be around the message of salvation and the legitimacy of the Gentile

---

[3] See the 'we' passages in Acts 16:10; 20:5; 21:1; 27:1.

[4] Peterson, *Acts*, 5.

[5] For example, Ben Witherington III, *The Acts of the Apostles: A Socio-Rhetorical Commentary* (Grand Rapids: Eerdmans, 1998), 61.

[6] Darrell L. Bock, *Acts* (Grand Rapids: Baker Academic, 2007), 27.

[7] Robert Maddox, *The Purpose of Luke–Acts* (Edinburgh: T&T Clark, 1982), 183–6.

[8] Luke Timothy Johnson, *The Gospel of Luke* (Collegeville: Liturgical Press, 1991), 28.

mission.[9] We can see this in the repeated summary statements regarding the spread of the word, or the repeated portrayal of the legal innocence of 'the Way'. Luke is providing an *apologia* for Christianity. He is keen to demonstrate that the Gentile church is not a dangerous sect, but rather emerged 'in continuity from a faithful and restored Israel'.[10]

One way Luke provides assurance to his readership is through repetition, or what has been termed 'functional redundancy'.[11] Repetition highlights significant events or messages. We see this most notably in the conversion accounts of Paul (Acts 9; 22; 26) and Cornelius (Acts 10; 11; 15) and the call to Gentile mission (Acts 13:46; 18:6; 28:28). In this way, Luke further demonstrates the legitimacy of 'the Way' to both Jewish and Gentile audiences.

Another key feature of Luke's narrative is his summary statements, charting the progress of the word. Growth and persecution walk hand in hand through the account. Luke's summary statements appear in the following places:

- Acts 6:7 – 'so the word of God spread'
- Acts 9:31 – 'the church throughout Judea, Galilee and Samaria enjoyed a time of peace and was strengthened . . . it increased in numbers'
- Acts 12:24 – 'the word of God continued to spread'
- Acts 16:5 – 'the churches were strengthened in the faith and grew daily in numbers'
- Acts 19:20 – 'the word of the Lord spread widely and grew in power'

These statements in part advance the plotline, but they also demonstrate that God's hand was upon the church to advance the mission and protect against opposition.[12] Luke's main interest in the selection and ordering of his material is the ministries of Peter and Paul, and the expansion of the church from Jerusalem to the ends of the earth.[13]

---

[9] Martin C. Salter, *The Power of Pentecost* (Eugene: Wipf and Stock, 2012), 64.

[10] Johnson, *Luke*, 30

[11] R. D. Witherup, 'Functional Redundancy in the Acts of the Apostles', *JSNT* 48 (1992): 67–86.

[12] Steven M. Sheeley, *Narrative Asides in Luke–Acts* (Sheffield: JSOT Press, 1992), 137–76.

[13] Eckhard J. Schnabel, *Acts* (Grand Rapids: Zondervan, 2012), 30.

In summary, Luke's concern is with all that Jesus is continuing to do and teach, through his church empowered by the Holy Spirit (Acts 1:1–8). The apostolic message is credible, urgent and inclusive. Salvation is for all, in fulfilment of Israel's Scriptures.[14] It extends to the poor, the sick, the possessed, the outcast and those previously excluded.[15] The church, in the power of the Spirit, is fulfilling the vocation given to Israel to be a light to the nations.

3. Structure and outline

Acts 1:8 provides us with the major structural outline that the book follows. The disciples were to wait in Jerusalem until they received the Holy Spirit. They were then to be witnesses in Jerusalem, Judea and Samaria, and to the ends of the earth. We can trace this movement through Acts as follows:

- Acts 1–7: in Jerusalem
- Acts 8–9: in Judea and Samaria
- Acts 10–28: to the ends of the earth

The third section can be further divided into ever-expanding missionary circuits which start and finish (mostly) in Antioch.

- Acts 13–14: First missionary circuit
- Acts 16–18: Second missionary circuit
- Acts 19–21: Third missionary journey ending in Jerusalem
- Acts 22–8: From Jerusalem to Rome – the custody narratives

As can be seen, a significant amount of space is given to the custody narratives which run from Paul's arrest in Jerusalem (Acts 22) to the end of the book as Paul awaits trial before Caesar (Acts 28). Commentators debate the reason why so much space is devoted to Paul's trial and accompanying speeches. As already noted, Luke is keen to demonstrate the innocence of 'the Way' for his readership. In addition, we note the truth of Paul's statement to the churches in Lystra, Iconium and Antioch: 'We must go through many hardships to enter the kingdom of God'

---

14 Bock, *Acts*, 24.
15 Witherington, *Acts*, 71.

(Acts 14:22). The Christian life is not triumphalist, devoid of sickness, suffering or persecution. Believers in every place should expect trials and opposition if they are standing faithfully for Christ.

Around one-third of the material in Acts is given over to speeches.[16] Peter delivers eight speeches; Paul delivers nine speeches; and other speeches are given by Stephen (7:2–53), James (15:13–21) and other officials.[17] The speeches serve to provide the reader not just with historical events, but also with the theology of the gospel. Luke is both a historian and a theologian.[18] He is not merely recounting historical events but also intends his narrative to have an impact in evangelising and discipling others.

4. Major themes

God's sovereign purpose and plan

The plan and purpose of God features prominently in the book, driving the narrative forward. This is in continuity with the opening of Luke's Gospel where we see mention of 'waiting for the consolation of Israel' (Luke 2:25) and 'looking forward to the redemption of Jerusalem' (Luke 2:38). On several occasions we see reference to the plan/purpose (boulē) as evidence of the divine hand behind the events of the narrative.

On the day of Pentecost, Peter speaks of Jesus's death occurring in fulfilment of God's 'deliberate plan [boulē] and foreknowledge' (Acts 2:23). In Acts 4:28, as the believers pray on the release of Peter and John from custody, they too refer to Jesus's death: 'They did what your power and will [boulē] had decided beforehand should happen.' God's sovereign purpose enables the believers to have confidence as they continue to speak boldly in Jesus's name. In Paul's farewell to the Ephesian elders, he assures them that he has not failed to declare to them 'the whole will [boulēn] of God' (Acts 20:27). In Acts 21, Paul receives a prophecy from Agabus of the trouble that awaits him in Jerusalem. He reiterates his resolution to go, to which those with Paul said, 'The Lord's will be done' (Acts 21:14). Elsewhere, the little Greek word dei ('it is necessary')

---

[16] Bock, Acts, 20.

[17] J. Bradley Chance, Acts (Macon: Smyth & Helwys, 2007), 9.

[18] See I. Howard Marshall, Luke: Historian and Theologian (Grand Rapids: Zondervan, 1970).

appears twenty-eight times in Luke–Acts to demonstrate the present fulfilment of God's plan and purpose.[19]

God is portrayed as the almighty ruler of all creation, to whom allegiance is owed. He is described in the following ways: the one who 'made the heavens and the earth' (Acts 4:24; 14:15); 'the earth is [his] footstool' (Acts 7:49); he 'made the world and everything in it . . . he made all the nations . . . he marked out their appointed times' (Acts 17:24, 26). He is the King of kings and the Lord of lords, and there is no other name under heaven by which men may be saved (Acts 4:12). The God of Israel is also the God of the nations. And we see repeatedly that the God of the whole earth desires the good news to be taken to the whole earth (Acts 1:8; 3:25; 13:47). As Squires notes, the 'scope of this divine plan is cosmic and universal'.[20]

As we read Luke's summary statements concerning the spread of the word, we see the divine hand directing the events. As Bock says, 'At key junctures God enables, directs, protects, and orchestrates.'[21] This all lends credence to Luke's *apologia* for the identity and mission of Jesus and the early church as the gospel is taken to the Gentiles. As Chris Green notes, God is the one 'who plans and guides the route the gospel takes from Jerusalem to the ends of the earth, and if Acts has a hero at all, it is God'.[22] We may wish to go further (as the next sections will argue) and say that the hero of Acts is God – Father, Son, and Holy Spirit. As Squires puts it, the 'plan of God is an important way by which Luke nurtures and equips the church of his time for its God-given task'.[23]

Jesus Christ – risen and exalted

For the attentive reader of Acts, what is particularly striking is Jesus's ubiquitous presence throughout the narrative. The opening chapters (even the opening words) set the scene for Jesus's active and present rule. In Acts 1:1 Luke speaks of 'all that Jesus began to do and teach'. This immediately implies that Jesus, in Acts, is continuing to 'do and teach', albeit from

---

[19] Charles H. Cosgrove, 'The Divine ΔEI in Luke-Acts', *NovT* 26 (1984): 174.

[20] John Squires, 'The Plan of God in the Acts of the Apostles', in *Witness to the Gospel: The Theology of Acts*, eds I. H. Marshall and D. G. Peterson (Grand Rapids: Eerdmans, 1998), 37.

[21] Bock, *Acts*, 7.

[22] Chris Green, *The Word of His Grace: A Guide to Preaching and Teaching from Acts* (Leicester: InterVarsity Press, 2005), 10.

[23] Squires, 'The Plan of God', 39.

heaven.[24] In Acts 1 we see Jesus's ascension into heaven, and the events and speech of Acts 2 inform the reader of Jesus's current place and status. Peter's speech on the day of Pentecost tells us that Jesus is risen and exalted to the right hand of God (Acts 2:32–3). Peter's conclusion is, 'God has made this Jesus, whom you crucified, both Lord and Messiah' (Acts 2:36).

As the narrative progresses, we see repeatedly that Jesus is no absent king, enthroned but distant from his people. The first Christian martyr, Stephen, sees Jesus standing at the right hand of God (Acts 7:55–6). Jesus appears to Paul at various points in his own journey, promising his presence with him (Acts 9:3–6; 18:9–10; 23:11).

Jesus is described as the one who will restore all things at the eschaton (Acts 3:21) and who will also be the judge of all (Acts 17:31). There is therefore an urgency in calling people to repent and turn to him as the one who has power to condemn and acquit.

At numerous points, the name 'Lord' is used interchangeably to refer to God and Jesus.[25] The one enthroned at the right hand of the Father is no less than God the Son, fully divine and worthy of worship. Chris Green is right in observing the following: 'To put it starkly, Luke claims to be writing not the Acts of the Apostles, nor even the Acts of the Holy Spirit, but volume two of the Acts of Jesus.'[26]

The Holy Spirit (and the spirit world)

The Holy Spirit is clearly a key character in Acts, but we must also note the wider context of a spiritual realm if we are to understand Luke's portrayal of him and his work. It is worth recalling Luke's wider purpose – to provide 'certainty' to his reader.[27] The Spirit proves himself to be the true Spirit of God amid the other spiritual forces at work in the Graeco–Roman world. The Spirit speaks, fills, acts upon and empowers the main characters in the advance of the narrative.[28]

Just as the Spirit gave miraculous conceptions to Elizabeth and Mary

---

[24] Alan J. Thompson, *The Acts of the Risen Lord Jesus: Luke's Account of God's Unfolding Plan* (Downers Grove: Apollos, 2011), 48.

[25] Acts 2:34–6; 9:5; 10:36; 16:31–2; 20:21.

[26] Green, *The Word of His Grace*, 14.

[27] William H. Shepherd Jr., *The Narrative Function of the Holy Spirit as a Character in Luke–Acts* (Atlanta: Scholars Press, 1994); Ju Hur, *A Dynamic Reading of the Holy Spirit in Luke–Acts* (Sheffield: Sheffield Academic Press, 2001).

[28] David J. Bosch, *Transforming Mission: Paradigm Shifts in the Theology of Mission* (Maryknoll: Orbis, 1991), 115.

(Luke 1–2), so too he brings forth the birth of the new covenant community (Acts 2). The Spirit empowered Jesus's ministry and he empowers the ministry of Jesus's eyewitnesses. At each new junction in the narrative (geographical and social), the Spirit brings fresh empowerment as the orchestrator of the mission. George Bonnah says, 'The Holy Spirit directs, determines and legitimates almost all that the narrator writes about in the Acts of the Apostles.'[29] The Spirit points away from himself and towards Jesus as the risen and exalted Messiah.

We can see this most clearly in the early chapters of Acts. At Pentecost the Spirit descends upon Jesus's apostles. They are then empowered to be witnesses to the gospel, and the work of the Spirit is multifaceted. The Holy Spirit enables them to speak with great boldness (Acts 4:8, 31). He empowers ministries of compassion (Acts 6:5). The Spirit strengthens and encourages the church (Acts 9:31). The Holy Spirit directs and even blocks missionary endeavour (Acts 13:2; 16:6). The Spirit warns of hardship (Acts 20:23). And the Holy Spirit appoints overseers (Acts 20:28).

At this point we must also consider the other spiritual forces at work that appear to compete with the Spirit of God. We see such encounters with Simon the sorcerer (Acts 8:9–24); Elymas the sorcerer (Acts 13:6–12); the girl with the python spirit (Acts 16:16–23); and the seven sons of Sceva (Acts 19:11–20). At each point there is a threat to the gospel from another spiritual force.

In the ancient world it was easy to group all spiritual forces together. Magic and miracle were dangerously close to one another in the syncretistic culture of Luke's day.[30] Luke's concern is to bring clarity where there may have been confusion. Magicians – portrayed as 'diabolical agents – are the perfect vehicle for Luke to illustrate Satan's impotence in the period after Jesus's exaltation to glory', as Susan Garrett puts it.[31] Luke, with his skilful characterisation of magic (in its source, efficacy and motive), demonstrates that Christ has bound the 'strong man' (Luke 11:21–2) and therefore magic is to be repudiated and Christ's name extolled (Acts 19:17–19).

Readers are left in no doubt that the source of magic is the devil. The efficacy of magic, while real, is no match for the power of the risen Christ.

[29] George K. A. Bonnah, *The Holy Spirit: A Narrative Factor in the Acts of the Apostles* (Stuttgart: Verlag Katholisches Bibelwerk GmbH, 2007), 265.

[30] Daniel Marguerat, 'Miracle and Magic in the Acts of the Apostles', in *Magic in the Biblical World*, ed. Todd Klutz (London: T&T Clark, 2003), 100–101.

[31] Susan R. Garrett, *The Demise of the Devil: Magic and the Demonic in Luke's Writings* (Minneapolis: Fortress, 1989), 2.

The motive of magic is one of self-promotion and self-interest. The Holy Spirit is the only one who can bring real healing, life and transformation.

At this point it is worth providing a general comment on the role of the miraculous in Acts. At numerous points in the narrative we see the apostles perform signs and wonders, we see examples of prophecy and tongues-speech, and we see angelic appearances. Since the rise of Pentecostalism in the twentieth century, many have seen such things as desirable and normative for the church today. However, we must remember the unique position of the apostles as eyewitnesses to the resurrected Christ. The signs and wonders authenticated them, as Paul makes clear in 2 Corinthians 12:12. The miracles performed mirror those done by Jesus, and demonstrate them to be his authorised witnesses.[32] In the history of God's redemptive work we see clusters of miracles at significant moments – Moses and the Exodus, the ministries of Elijah and Elisha, and around Jesus and his apostles. Therefore, we need to be careful to read the narrative within its redemptive historical context, recognising the unique authority of the apostles.[33]

Similarly, it will be argued that tongues-speech serves a particular purpose for Luke in authenticating both the apostolic witness and, in the post-Pentecost narrative, mission to controversial people groups. Many of the things recorded serve to demonstrate the fulfilment of Joel 2:28–32 cited in Acts 2:17–21. Prophecy, too, serves a purpose for the church in the era before the apostolic teachings are written down and circulated, later becoming canonical. We must remember that in the first three decades of the church's life they were without the collected writings that we call the New Testament. It is notable that in the post-apostolic era the command of Paul in the pastoral epistles is to teach the things passed on by the apostles. We will explore these themes more fully at the relevant points in the commentary.

The church – Jews and Gentiles

One of the distinctive differences between Luke's Gospel and Acts is the birth of the church. That small band of disciples explodes at Pentecost and, with Jesus ascended into heaven, organises itself around the apostles as a new *ekklesia*. As Bosch notes:

---

[32] See, for example, Luke 5:17–26 with Acts 3:6 and 14:10 or Luke 7:11–17 with Acts 9:40 and 20:10.

[33] For more on this see Salter, *The Power of Pentecost*, 39–58.

> There is no church in Luke's gospel, only 'disciples' . . . One might
> say that what distinguishes Acts from the gospel is the church . . .
> The Lordship of Christ is not exercised in a vacuum but in the
> concrete historical circumstances of community which lives under
> the direction of the Spirit.[34]

The early chapters of Acts provide two summaries of the life of the early
church (Acts 2:42–7; 4:32–7). We are provided with a picture of a church
devoted to the apostles' teaching, to fellowship, to prayer and to the breaking
of bread. They exercise radical generosity in meeting the needs of one
another. We see the church tackling serious immorality (Acts 5:1–10) and
structuring itself to meet the needs of the community (Acts 6:1–7).

It is impossible to read Acts without perceiving the tension that runs
throughout between Jew and Gentile. As the gospel reaches into Samaritan
then Gentile territory, the relationships between these groups become
strained, requiring apostolic intervention (Acts 8:14–17; 11:1–18; 15:1–33).

Perhaps most significantly we see Gentiles welcomed into the church,
with the conversion story of Cornelius taking up two whole chapters.
Things are not entirely straightforward, however, as Jewish and Graeco–
Roman cultures clash. In Acts 15 we see the church wrestling over the
issue of circumcision and how Jewish Law ought to be applied to Gentile
converts. The Jerusalem consultation (and the accompanying letter to the
churches) is one of the most significant moments in the book. The early
Christian leaders did not want to make it difficult for Gentiles turning
to God, yet they wanted these Gentiles to exercise sensitivity towards the
new Jewish brothers and sisters in Christ (Act 15:19–21).

It is important to note that Luke does not see the church as the replacement
for Israel as the people of God. Rather, he sees the ingrafting of Gentiles as
the fulfilment of God's plan for Israel.[35] It is because the Messiah has come
to bring restoration and refreshing that Israel can fulfil her vocation to be a
light to the nations. The new covenant people of God are thus made up of
Jew and Gentile, united by the Spirit under the Lordship of Christ.

As the mission grew, churches were planted and Paul and Barnabas
appointed elders in every church (Acts 14:23). In Acts 20, we see Paul
charge the elders of the church at Ephesus. They were to be the overseers
in the absence of the apostle. Their role was to preserve the apostolic
teaching. This is how the church was to be provided for and protected

---

[34] Bosch, *Transforming Mission*, 121.
[35] Chance, *Acts*, 18.

in the post-apostolic era. Thus the organic and organised elements of ecclesial life are both seen as important.

Acts presents a picture of a dynamic movement of disciples, not without difficulties but distinctive in their countercultural boldness and compassion. They met in the Temple courts and house to house (Acts 2:46). They broke bread in homes and organised themselves under deacons and elders.[36] The large and the small, and the organic and organised, were all part of the life of the early church as they sought to encourage one another and bear witness to those around them. They understood themselves to be local communities on mission for Christ.[37]

The mission

One of the big themes in the book of Acts is that of mission. Jesus's first followers were instructed to be his witnesses (Acts 1:8), something the early churches took seriously. Bosch notes, 'The noun "witness(es)" (*martyrs/martyres*) occurs thirteen times in Acts but only once in Luke's gospel . . . In Acts, "witness" becomes *the* appropriate term for "mission."'[38]

We can see from Acts that the theme of mission or 'witness' is broad and varied. Goheen states, 'Witness defines the people of God in the entirety of their lives – all of life is witness!'[39] It clearly involved their verbal witness and preaching (Acts 2:14–39; 4:31; 8:4). It involved the strategic planting of churches (Acts 14:21–8). It also involved deeds of compassion (Acts 6:1–7; 9:36–9). And it also involved a countercultural way of living which attracted the favour and interest of those around them (Acts 2:47). With the pouring out of God's Spirit, the 'witness' become democratised – something the whole community was drawn into, everyone playing their part.[40]

We also see variety in the apostolic approach to preaching, Paul being the most obvious example. In Pisidian Antioch he gave a history of God's dealings with Israel (Acts 13:16–41). In Athens he appealed to the God of creation (Acts 17:22–31). This sensitive contextualisation is a distinctive feature of the mission which reaches priests and slave girls. It is a good

---

[36] Acts 2:46; 6:1–7; 14:23.

[37] Acts 2:47; 4:29–31; 5:13–14; 6:7.

[38] Bosch, *Transforming Mission*, 117.

[39] Michael W. Goheen, *A Light to the Nations: The Missional Church and the Biblical Story* (Grand Rapids: Baker Academic, 2011), 128.

[40] Richard B. Hays, *The Moral Vision of the New Testament* (New York: HarperOne, 1996), 121.

reminder to us to think carefully about how we can best reach our own communities with the good news of Jesus Christ.

Transformed people came together to form a new community – the church, a group with a constantly outward orientation that refused to be drawn in on itself. The church is constantly looking out at the needs of the least and the lost. Mission is an 'ecclesial enterprise' and every believer a 'missionary'.[41]

Salvation and the gospel

The word 'salvation' (*sōzō*) has a range of meanings in Acts, including rescue, healing and the bringing of eternal life, with the latter being the most common.[42] The most striking feature of this message of salvation is that it is a free gift, given in grace, received by faith (Acts 15:11). Nothing needs to be added to earn salvation. Repentance and faith are all that is required (Acts 2:38; 16:31). As we have noted, this message was for Jew and Gentile alike (Acts 11:14). There were no boundaries as to who may receive the gift.

This was the basic apostolic message of salvation – repent and believe for the forgiveness of your sins. This is still the church's message today. Peterson states, 'Salvation is essentially status reversal for Luke. The kingdom of God displaces other kingdoms, drawing Jews and Gentiles, even social outcasts, into a new community around Jesus.'[43] Nearly one hundred years ago C. H. Dodd identified five elements that are common in the apostolic gospel:[44]

- It is the age of fulfilment (Acts 2:16; 3:18; 13:26)
- Achieved by the life, death and resurrection of Jesus (Acts 2:23; 4:10–11; 10:39–40; 13:28–30)
- Who is now exalted to the right hand of the Father (Acts 2:32–6; 3:15; 5:31–2; 10:40–41)
- And will one day return as judge (Acts 3:20–21; 17:31)
- So repent and believe (Acts 2:38; 3:19; 5:31; 10:43; 13:39; 17:30)

---

[41] Bosch, *Transforming Mission*, 121.

[42] With reference to eternal life see Acts 2:21, 40, 47; 4:12; 11:14; 15:1, 11; 16:30–31. With reference to physical healing see Acts 4:9; 14:9. With reference to rescue from danger see Acts 27:20, 31.

[43] David Peterson, 'Luke's Theological Enterprise', in *Witness to the Gospel*, eds. Marshall and Peterson, 523.

[44] C. H. Dodd, *The Apostolic Preaching and Its Development* (London: Hodder and Stoughton, 1936).

Green's summary of the message overlaps and simplifies Dodd's. The repeated elements identified are 'you killed him, God raised him, we saw him, so repent'.[45] This is the core of the gospel message that is adapted to different audiences. The apostolic preaching was characterised by boldness and the call for response. Thompson describes the apostolic preaching as 'response oriented' rather than 'response driven'. They were not adapting the message to get a favourable response; indeed, the response was often mixed, yet a clear call to repentance was a critical element in the faithful preaching of the gospel.[46]

It is sometimes suggested that atonement theology is absent from the book of Acts. While it is true that the resurrection, ascension and exaltation of Christ are prominent, it is not true to say there is no reference to the atoning death of Christ. In Acts 8:32–5 Philip helps the Ethiopian eunuch understand that Isaiah 53 was about the atoning death of Christ. In Acts 20:28 Paul describes God's church as 'bought with his own blood', which strongly suggests redemption through substitutionary atonement. Further, language of Christ setting us free from sin and justifying us (Acts 13:38–9) and the necessity of his suffering (Acts 17:3) would also point to Jesus's atoning death being a key part of the apostolic preaching. An emphasis on the resurrection does not imply that the message of the cross was not present or prominent. Further, Paul's writings suggest it would have occupied an important place within the speeches, of which we only have summaries, for example, 1 Corinthians 2:2.

It is also worth noting that the gospel and conversion were not for Luke a purely individualistic act of commitment. As one friend recently commented, the gospel is not merely fire insurance! Conversion drew the convert into the life of the community and involved a radical change of life.[47] As Marshall notes, 'Whereas the gospel is often understood to be the good news of salvation, it includes the announcement of God's judgment, a call to repentance, and a programme for a new life for the "saved" that may sharply challenge their former, sinful way of life.'[48] Salvation for Luke is not simply a 'ticket to the sky when you die' but a whole-of-life transformation in the community of the saved.[49]

---

[45] Green, *The Word of His Grace*, 26–9.

[46] Thompson, *The Acts of the Risen Lord Jesus*, 96–7.

[47] Bosch, *Transforming Mission*, 119.

[48] I. Howard Marshall, 'Luke's Social Gospel: The Social Theology of Luke–Acts', in *Transforming the World*, eds. Jamie A. Grant and Dewi A. Hughes (Nottingham: Apollos, 2009), 113.

[49] I am indebted to N. T. Wright for the phrase 'ticket to the sky when you die', though I cannot remember where I first heard him use it.

Ethics

Marshall notes the social and ethical elements built into the new life created by the gospel. These include the sharing of possessions, care for the needy, preaching and healing, and financial generosity.[50] One of Luke's distinctive interests is in the needs of and concern for the poor defined in socio-economic terms.[51]

Luke's interest in ethics is linked closely to his understanding of mission. Mission is not simply gospel proclamation but includes the outworking of the transformed lives of the community.[52] Hays notes, 'The *power* of the apostles' "testimony to the resurrection of the Lord Jesus" is linked directly by Luke to the community's economic sharing (Acts 4:32–5). The testimony is credible because the evidence of God's power is palpable in the community's life.'[53]

Luke's depiction of the community's attitude towards money and possessions in particular draws on Old Testament ideals of justice and generosity. Particularly striking is the statement in Acts 4:34, that 'there was no needy person among them'. This is almost a direct quote from Deuteronomy 15:4. Here is an idealised portrait in miniature of the renewed Israel fulfilling its God-given vocation. The church's 'economic relations are a practical and symbolic medium for displaying and enacting Luke's central message of the dawning of a new age'.[54]

It should be noted that this is not a 'programme' of social mission, but rather 'the social implications of the gospel'.[55] Luke is not presenting a vision of the church interested only in social action without any need for gospel proclamation. Proclamation and ethics belong together for the people of God in their witness to the transforming power of the risen Christ. As Hays describes it, the church 'turns the world upside down

---

[50] Marshall, 'Luke's Social Gospel', 114–16. See Acts 2:44–5; 6:1–4; 9:36–9; 11:27–30; 19:11–12.

[51] Bosch, *Transforming Mission*, 119.

[52] For more on this see Martin C. Salter, *Mission in Action: A Biblical Description of Missional Ethics* (Nottingham: Apollos, 2019).

[53] Hays, *Moral Vision*, 125.

[54] Stephen Barton, 'Money Matters: Economic Relations and the Transformation of Value in Early Christianity', in *Engaging Economics: New Testament Scenarios and Early Christian Reception*, eds. Bruce W. Longenecker and Kelly D. Liebengood (Grand Rapids: Eerdmans, 2009), 49.

[55] Marshall, 'Luke's Social Gospel', 120.

not through armed revolution but through the formation of the church as a counter-culture, an alternative witness-bearing community'.[56]

Persecution and suffering

Luke's Gospel presented Jesus as man destined to suffer (Luke 24:27), and the disciples too must follow in the Master's footsteps as they seek first the kingdom, deny self, take up their cross and follow him. In Acts we see multiple episodes of imprisonment, trial, beating, being chased out of town and even martyrdom.[57] The apostles in particular continually live in the shadow of death as they remain faithful to Christ.[58]

The weaving together of growth and suffering cautions the modern Christian against living in an 'over-realised eschatology' where we think all the promises of kingdom victory can be had now. The book of Acts shows us that suffering and gospel progress walk hand in hand together. Hays says, 'The apostolic hardships of the Acts narrative can be read as the fulfilment of Jesus's call to surrender everything and take up the cross in order to follow him . . . Despite the power unleashed . . . Luke does not minimize suffering.'[59]

As Thompson observes, 'The Lord reigns and is accomplishing his saving purposes, yet his reign remains contested, the fulness of the kingdom is still "not yet".'[60] As Paul said when he revisited the churches he had previously planted, 'We must go through many hardships to enter the kingdom of God' (Acts 14:22).

———

The attentive reader of Acts will find themselves challenged, encouraged, even inspired to persevere in 'running the race' of faith. While hardships await, the presence of God – Father, Son, and Holy Spirit – gives the church great confidence to be bold and courageous in bearing witness to the risen Lord. The task of 'witness' remains urgent, but Jesus is still active, through his church, empowered by his Holy Spirit. And the word of God continues to spread . . .

---

[56] Hays, *Moral Vision*, 128.
[57] For some of these see Acts 5:18; 7:58; 12:1–5; 16:22–4; 17:10–15; 22:33.
[58] Bosch, *Transforming Mission*, 123.
[59] Hays, *Moral Vision*, 122.
[60] Thompson, *The Acts of the Risen Lord Jesus*, 55.

New Beginnings

ACTS 1

1. Commission and ascension • Acts 1:1–14

Acts 1:1–3: The ongoing work

Jesus taken up into heaven

1 In my former book, Theophilus, I wrote about all that Jesus began to do and to teach **2** until the day he was taken up to heaven, after giving instructions through the Holy Spirit to the apostles he had chosen. **3** After his suffering, he presented himself to them and gave many convincing proofs that he was alive. He appeared to them over a period of forty days and spoke about the kingdom of God.

'In my former book, Theophilus, I wrote about all that Jesus began to do and to teach . . .' (Acts 1:1).

These opening words set the scene for Luke's second volume and tell us what we ought to expect as readers.

Theophilus is a name also mentioned at the start of Luke's first volume (Luke 1:3). We know almost nothing about him. His name means 'loved by God', but this is not necessarily an indication he was already a Christian.[1] He may have been a seeker; he could have been young in faith seeking clearer understanding.[2] He apparently had some interest in Luke's work, and it is possible Luke saw him as a potential sponsor, an official of rank, who could enable his work to be taken before a greater audience.[3]

Luke reminds Theophilus that in his former book he had spoken of that which Jesus 'began' (*ērxato*) to do and to teach. Luke–Acts is a unity,

---

[1] Marshall thinks Theophilus was probably a Christian and Luke's work is intended to give him and others a reliable account of the beginning of Christianity. See I. Howard Marshall, *Acts* (Leicester: InterVarsity Press, 1980), 56.

[2] Witherington, *Acts*, 106.

[3] Peterson, *Acts*, 102.

with both parts narrating the ministry of Jesus, on earth and from heaven. The contrast between the two parts is not between the ministry of Jesus and the ministry of the church, but, as John Stott put it, 'between two stages of the ministry of the same Christ'.[4]

In this second volume, Luke will report all that Jesus is *continuing* to do, from the right hand of the Father, by the power of his Holy Spirit, through the community of his followers.[5] The book of Acts is not merely an account of the growth and spread of the church. It is an account of the acts of the risen Lord seen in the remarkable spread of the gospel through the Graeco–Roman world.

Admittedly, 'The Acts of the Apostles' is a much snappier title than 'The Acts of the Risen Jesus, through his Apostles, by the power of his Holy Spirit', but the latter would be a more accurate description. It is an important reminder to us that the source, power and efficacy of our endeavours comes not from ourselves, but from our living Lord Jesus who is still at work today, advancing his mission through his church.

John Stott notes that this opening verse sets Christianity apart from every other world religion: 'These [other religions] regard their founder as having completed his ministry during his lifetime; Luke says Jesus only began his.'[6]

Luke highlights the multiple post-resurrection appearances of Jesus to his disciples over a forty-day period, giving 'many convincing proofs that he was alive'. Paul also mentions the post-resurrection appearances in 1 Corinthians 15:3–8 and will later remind King Agrippa that the events of Jesus's life, including his death and resurrection, were 'not done in a corner' (Acts 26:23–6). Luke wants his audience to be assured that his account is historically credible, there are 'many convincing proofs', and what we are about to read is not myth or fable, but history. There are solid grounds for faith in Christ. The Jesus who really lived is the same Jesus who really lives.

It is also worth noting that Jesus's resurrection is an affirmation, not a denial, of the physical body. This is not a platonic escape from the physical to a higher realm. Neither is it a reincarnation or transmigration of the

---

[4] John Stott, *The Message of Acts* (Leicester: InterVarsity Press, 1990), 32.

[5] Witherington suggests it is over-pressing the verb, *ērxato*, since it could be translated simply as 'all that Jesus did and taught'. Grammatically this is correct but, given the contextual and rhetorical prominence of the ascension and Pentecost, it seems Luke intends his audience to see the ministry of the church as the continuation of Jesus's work from heaven, in the power of his Spirit. See Witherington, *Acts*, 9–10.

[6] Stott, *Acts*, 34.

soul. While this idea may be popular in some cultures, Jesus demonstrates that resurrection is nothing less than the renewal and glorification of our physical bodies.[7]

Acts 1:4–8: Power to witness

4 On one occasion, while he was eating with them, he gave them this command: 'Do not leave Jerusalem, but wait for the gift my Father promised, which you have heard me speak about. **5** For John baptised with[a] water, but in a few days you will be baptised with[a] the Holy Spirit.'

6 Then they gathered round him and asked him, 'Lord, are you at this time going to restore the kingdom to Israel?'

7 He said to them: 'It is not for you to know the times or dates the Father has set by his own authority. **8** But you will receive power when the Holy Spirit comes on you; and you will be my witnesses in Jerusalem, and in all Judea and Samaria, and to the ends of the earth.'

_____

a 5 Or *in*

Verse 4 sets the expectation that carries the narrative towards Pentecost. Jesus tells his followers to wait in Jerusalem for 'the gift my Father promised'. Just as John baptised with water, so the disciples are to be baptised with the Holy Spirit. It is another indicator of the dynamic nature of Luke's work. The Holy Spirit will be a central character in the narrative driving the mission forward. The Spirit will enable signs and wonders (2:19), cause believers to speak with boldness (4:31), help the church to administer compassion (6:3), lead and guide individuals (8:29), encourage the church (9:31), begin (and prevent!) new missionary initiatives (13:2; 16:6) and establish elders over the church (20:28). The Holy Spirit is mentioned more than fifty times in the book of Acts. The Spirit is not an added extra to the life of the Christian or the church but is the life-giving power who births and animates the church. He is a divine person, not merely some sort of impersonal force. A Christian or a church without the Spirit is an oxymoron.

However, these verses do raise a question as to the possibility of being a Christian without the Holy Spirit. Are we meant to see the disciples as unregenerate pre-Pentecost?[8] And if they are already regenerate, is this

---

[7] Babu Immanuel Venkataraman, 'Acts', in *SABC*, 1453.

[8] Verses that suggest a pre-Pentecost regeneration on the part of the disciples are as follows: Matthew 8:26; 16:16–17; John 6:44; John 17:8, 12. It is hard to believe that they had come thus far without the regenerating work of the Spirit.

'baptism in the Spirit' a second blessing as in Pentecostal theology? At this stage we should note the Spirit is clearly at work before the Day of Pentecost, and we must affirm that, post Pentecost, 'becoming a Christian' and 'baptism in the Spirit' are synonymous.[9] The New Testament does not teach a second-blessing or post-conversion baptism in the Spirit. The Day of Pentecost, as we shall see, rather inaugurates a new and fuller blessing on the church in fulfilment of Joel's prophecy. Joel speaks of a day when the Spirit would be personally and permanently present to every believer. Pentecost is a unique and unrepeatable event in the history of God's redemptive plan, and not something the contemporary church should seek to repeat. We will explore this again as we encounter subsequent Spirit baptisms in the book of Acts.[10]

In verse 6 the disciples ask Jesus a question: 'Lord, are you at this time going to restore the kingdom to Israel?' What do they understand or expect in asking this question? Calvin said their question contained almost as many errors as words.[11] Yet the question is surely correct. Acts 1:3 has told us that Jesus was teaching about the kingdom of God. He spoke frequently of the kingdom in the Gospel (Luke 4:43; 7:28; 10:9; 12:31; 17:21). He described the kingdom as being 'near' (Luke 10:9, 11; 21:31). And Jesus has just conquered death itself. The question is surely a natural one – 'Are you now going to restore the kingdom?'[12]

The misunderstanding in the question is in continuing to think of the kingdom as a political and ethnic entity – 'Are you now going to restore the kingdom to *Israel*?' It seems the disciples understood Jesus's teaching on the kingdom to be about restoring something like the Davidic kingdom – a place of political power, wealth and status, with a Davidic king on the throne and the Romans expelled from their occupation. It is this understanding that Jesus corrects.

---

[9] In the Old Testament we can see the work of the Spirit, empowering for service, in the following places: Exodus 31:3; Deuteronomy 34:9; Judges 14:6; Psalm 51:11. The Old Testament looked forward to a day when the Spirit would be given to all with a new power (Numbers 11; Jeremiah 31; Ezekiel 36; Joel 2). For evidence that the work of regeneration and 'baptism in the Spirit' are synonymous in the New Testament, see Romans 6:4; 1 Corinthians 12:13; Colossians 2:11–12; Titus 3:5.

[10] For more on this issue, see the discussion in Wayne Grudem, *Systematic Theology: An Introduction to Biblical Doctrine* (Leicester: InterVarsity Press, 1994), 763–87.

[11] John Calvin, *The Acts of the Apostles* (repr. Grand Rapids: Baker, 1998), 43.

[12] Spencer notes, 'Restoration hopes were deeply rooted in classical prophecies of Israel's future and closely tied to the sacred space of Jerusalem/Zion' (see Isaiah 2:2–4; Micah 4:1–8; Zechariah 8:20–23. Cited in Peterson, *Acts*, 109.

He begins by reminding them it is not for them to know the times or dates the Father has set.[13] This is a timely warning for those who wish to indulge in eschatological speculation. 'The secret things belong to the LORD' (Deuteronomy 29:29), and these things are for the Father alone to know.

In Jesus's answer we see that kingdom restoration is most certainly on the agenda, but perhaps not in the way they are expecting. Exactly how or when the fullness of kingdom restoration will come is not for them to know. 'But you will receive power . . . and you will be my witnesses.' This is not a change of topic, but rather an answer to the question. They may not know the times or dates, but in the meantime they have a role to play in the unfolding plan of kingdom restoration.

When the Spirit comes, they will be witnesses (*martyres*). The meaning of 'witness' can include the sense of providing a legal testimony, or attestation.[14] As we move through the book of Acts, we will see that 'witness' will occur through both words and deeds. Later, *martyros* came to have an association with those who lost their lives on account of their testimony.[15]

In one sense, the apostolic testimony is unique – they were first-hand witnesses of the resurrection. They have a unique authority, which is why we take their testimony, as found in Scripture, with utmost seriousness. Yet as they pass on the story of Jesus, each subsequent generation takes up the call to proclaim the message. It is worth noting the obvious here – they are described as 'my witnesses' – the church witnesses to Christ. While our stories are always personal, he is the centre and the hero. It is his story before it is mine. Here also is a reminder both of the necessity of gospel proclamation and of the cost that such proclamation may bring. Many of these 'witnesses' did indeed lose their lives on account of their testimony. To be a part of God's mission is exciting, but it can also be incredibly costly, as many around the world and throughout history can testify.

As Jesus commissions them, he wants to cause them to 'think upon this triumph which they hoped to have been so nigh at hand'.[16] It is only the resurrection of Christ (and the hope it provides) and the power of the Spirit that enable the church to keep speaking of Christ and his kingdom. Without a humble dependence on the 'power from on high'

---

[13] See also Matthew 24:35–7; Mark 13:32.

[14] Matthew 18:16; Mark 14:63; Hebrews 10:28.

[15] Revelation 2:13; 3:14.

[16] Calvin, *Acts*, 48.

(Luke 24:49) and a conscious submission to *his* agenda, the church will lose its passion and power for witness.

The believers will speak of all Jesus said and did, and in so doing, little by little, the kingdom reign of the Lord Jesus grows, as its life-transforming power reaches further into the darkness. We must remember that the church is not the kingdom, and the kingdom is not the church, but the kingdom reign of Christ expands as he uses the church as his Spirit-empowered means in bearing witness to him. The church is the recipient and instrument of kingdom blessing and power. The church is much more than a merely social phenomenon, yet we must be careful to recognise that the full blessings of the kingdom are both now *and* not yet.[17]

We must beware of the extremes of over-spiritualising or over-politicising the kingdom. It is not established by military force or political coercion. It grows as individual lives are transformed by the power of the Spirit. Yet it will have social implications as kingdom values encounter secular values.[18] The gospel of the kingdom requires Christians and churches to recognise that while the kingdom is not established by force, the power of God's kingdom rule can (and should) have transformative power over individuals and the societies in which they live.

We ought not to rush past the significance of Jesus's commission in verse 8. For those first Jewish apostles, the idea of mission beyond the borders of Israel would have been surprising, if not shocking. In the Old Testament, mission is seen as predominantly centripetal – the nations will come to Israel as they see the attractiveness of her way of life (see Deuteronomy 4:5–8). There are notable exceptions (e.g., Jonah), but generally the outsider would come to Israel, rather than the other way round. In practice, mission did not largely figure in the reality of Israel's life, and a deep loathing of Gentiles was not uncommon – something Roman occupation did nothing to dispel. The idea of centrifugal mission to the ends of the earth would have taken some processing – a fact seen in the church's reaction to the conversion of Cornelius's household (Acts 10–11) and disputes over Gentile converts seen in Acts 15. It is tempting to pride ourselves on having moved beyond such racial blinkers, but the doctrine of indwelling sin should remind us of our own bias (conscious or unconscious) against the very people towards whom God would have us reach out. This will be a theme we return to through the narrative.

---

[17] For more on this, see Herman N. Ridderbos, *The Coming of the Kingdom* (Philipsburg: P&R, 1962).
[18] Stott, *Acts*, 42.

The reference to Jerusalem, Judea and Samaria and the ends of the earth (1:8) provides the structural outline for the book of Acts. In Acts 1–7 we see the witness of the apostles in Jerusalem. In Acts 8–12 the believers are scattered throughout Judea and Samaria. And in Acts 13–28 we see the mission expanding, ultimately arriving with Paul in Rome at the end of the book.[19] In one sense, of course, Rome is not the 'ends of the earth'. But in another sense – the sense of political centre – all roads lead to Rome. At the start of Luke's Gospel, Caesar issues his decree to take a census of 'the entire Roman world' (Luke 2:1). At the start of Acts, Jesus issues his decree that news of him would reach the 'ends of the earth' (1:8).[20] To take the gospel to the power-centre of the Empire really could be seen as the gospel expanding to the ends of the earth. Rome does not exhaust the reference to 'the ends of the earth', but it can certainly be seen as a remarkable fulfilment of the promise.[21]

Acts 1:9–11: Jesus taken up to heaven

9 After he said this, he was taken up before their very eyes, and a cloud hid him from their sight.

10 They were looking intently up into the sky as he was going, when suddenly two men dressed in white stood beside them. **11** 'Men of Galilee,' they said, 'why do you stand here looking into the sky? This same Jesus, who has been taken from you into heaven, will come back in the same way you have seen him go into heaven.'

The disciples must have had many questions, but Luke tells us at this point Jesus is taken from them as he ascends into heaven and is hidden from

---

[19] David Pao argues that the 'kingdom restoration' motif in Acts is a fulfilment of the 'new Exodus' as prophesied by Isaiah. This would involve '(1) the dawn of salvation upon Jerusalem; (2) the reconstitution and reunification of Israel [Judea and Samaria] . . . (3) the inclusion of Gentiles within the people of God'. See David W. Pao, *Acts and the Isaianic New Exodus* (Grand Rapids: Baker Academic, 2000), 95.

[20] James M. Scott draws out some of the political geographical horizons in Luke's work in his essay, 'Luke's Geographical Horizon', in *The Book of Acts in Its Graeco-Roman Setting*, eds. David W. J. Gill and Conrad Gempf (Grand Rapids: Eerdmans, 1994), 483–544.

[21] Tannehill sees an allusion here to Isaiah 49:6, which would give the 'ends of the earth' an ethnic as well as a geographical flavour. It would be the fulfilment of God's promise to glorify his Servant by restoring his people and bringing salvation to the ends of the earth. Robert C. Tannehill, *The Narrative Unity of Luke–Acts, Volume 2: The Acts of the Apostles* (Minneapolis: Fortress Press, 1994), 17.

their sight.[22] As Chris Green notes, 'God's glory was frequently masked by cloud, as at Mount Sinai (Exodus 19:9 etc.); in the tabernacle (Leviticus 16:2); and in the temple (1 Kings 8:10).'[23] Jesus's ascent in the cloud is a picture of his exaltation to glory – to the right hand of the Father. It is not a space you or I could go and find with a suitably advanced spacecraft. It is a realm of glorious rule and providential care.[24] Jesus is not abandoning his followers; he is entering into operational command from the throne room of heaven.[25]

As the disciples stare, wondering what just happened, two men, presumably angels from the description of their dress (see Luke 24:4; Acts 10:30), assure them that this same Jesus will one day return in the same way they have seen him go. As Marshall notes, 'The promise of the parousia forms the background of hope against which the disciples are to act as the witnesses to Jesus.'[26] These verses assure us of the personal return of the eternal and glorified Son. The personal return of Christ is the comfort and the challenge that motivate the church's mission. As with 1:6–7, the gazing speculation into the unknown is not the task of Jesus's followers. As we await the eschatological 'ends of the earth', we engage in our mission to the geographical 'ends of the earth'. That is the concern of the church in the period between Jesus's ascension and return.

As Stott notes, the error of 1:6 was too earthly, and the error of 1:10 was too heavenly – one a politicist; the other a pietist. The remedy: 'Witness to Jesus in the power of the Spirit, with all that this implies of earthly responsibility and heavenly enabling.'[27]

---

[22] Witherington notes there is no necessary conflict in ascension accounts between Luke 24 and Acts 1. The purpose in each is slightly different, and the recapitulation and expansion in Acts 1 serves his narrative purpose and conforms to rhetorical convention. Witherington, *Acts*, 107–8.

[23] Green, *The Word of His Grace*, 45.

[24] There are various opinions on how we understand the ascension. To speculate much beyond the data of Scripture is unwise. The emphasis in Jesus's ascension relates more to his function than his location. For more, see Louis Berkhof, *Systematic Theology* (London: Banner, 1959), 350–53.

[25] Calvin is keen to note the bodily absence of Jesus against those who wish to see his bodily presence in the Lord's Supper. While the person of the Word is omnipresent according to his divinity, Acts 1:11 is clear – his body is now in heaven, until the day he returns. Calvin, *Acts*, 51.

[26] Marshall, *Acts*, 62.

[27] Stott, *Acts*, 51.

Acts 1:12–14: Together in prayer

Matthias chosen to replace Judas

12 Then the apostles returned to Jerusalem from the hill called the Mount of Olives, a Sabbath day's walk[b] from the city. **13** When they arrived, they went upstairs to the room where they were staying. Those present were Peter, John, James and Andrew; Philip and Thomas, Bartholomew and Matthew; James son of Alphaeus and Simon the Zealot, and Judas son of James. **14** They all joined together constantly in prayer, along with the women and Mary the mother of Jesus, and with his brothers.

_____

b 12 That is, about 5/8 mile or about 1 kilometre

The apostles returned to Jerusalem from the Mount of Olives to the place they were staying.[28] Luke names the apostles, eleven in number, with the notable absence of Judas Iscariot, preparing the way for the narrative to follow.

Luke reports their devotion in prayer and the presence of other women, Mary the mother of Jesus, and his brothers. Whether we would describe ourselves as 'complementarian' or 'egalitarian', we should not miss the presence and participation of Jesus's female followers. It is easy to 'baptise' our own practice as the biblical ideal, without examining ways in which we've fallen short or gone beyond the data of Scripture. Though the women are not apostles by the criteria applied in Acts 1:21–6, they play a significant role in the life of the community.

The description in verse 14 of them 'joined together constantly in prayer' speaks of their devotion and what Peterson describes as their 'exemplary unity'.[29] It is often assumed, based on 1:13 and 2:2, that the location of their prayer is the place where they are staying. However, given Luke 24:53 and Acts 3:1, it is possible, perhaps likely, that the 'prayer' refers to the set times of prayer in the Temple. One of the striking things in the early chapters of Acts is the community's continuity with the Jewish practices. Just as the Reformation was an attempt at reform, not escape, from the established church, so the early church understood themselves to be in continuity with, and indeed the fulfilment of, Israel's story.

The importance and centrality of prayer in the life of the apostles and the early church is a reminder of the need for constant dependence on

_____

[28] A 'Sabbath day's walk' equated to around three-quarters of a mile or 1.2km. Marshall, *Acts*, 62.

[29] Peterson, *Acts*, 117–18, note 64.

God in his mission. The apostles understood the need for prayer to be a central part of their life together. The church today must do likewise.[30] It is also interesting to note how unity and prayer walk hand in hand. The church over the last two millennia has found many ways to divide. Sometimes this has been sadly necessary, but at other times division has crept in, which must grieve our Lord. Here is a glimpse, and one we shall see again, of the God-glorifying power and beauty of the church united on her knees.

2. Restoring the Twelve • Acts 1:15–26

At this point in the narrative, the expectant waiting for the gift of the Spirit is interrupted by an episode which, at first glance, may seem of questionable relevance or importance. However, as we will see, the reconstitution of 'the Twelve' is an important part of the story Luke is recounting.

15 In those days Peter stood up among the believers (a group numbering about a hundred and twenty) **16** and said, 'Brothers and sisters,[c] the Scripture had to be fulfilled in which the Holy Spirit spoke long ago through David concerning Judas, who served as guide for those who arrested Jesus. **17** He was one of our number and shared in our ministry.'

18 (With the payment he received for his wickedness, Judas bought a field; there he fell headlong, his body burst open and all his intestines spilled out. **19** Everyone in Jerusalem heard about this, so they called that field in their language Akeldama, that is, Field of Blood.)

20 'For,' said Peter, 'it is written in the Book of Psalms:

' "May his place be deserted;
    let there be no one to dwell
    in it,"[d]

and,

' "May another take his place of
        leadership."[e]

21 Therefore it is necessary to choose one of the men who have been with us the whole time the Lord Jesus was living among us, **22** beginning from John's baptism to the time when Jesus was taken up from us. For one of these must become a witness with us of his resurrection.'

23 So they nominated two men: Joseph called Barsabbas (also known

---

[30] Calvin notes, 'the hastiness of our petitions is a corrupt, yea a hurtful plague' (*Acts*, 58).

26

as Justus) and Matthias. **24** Then they prayed, 'Lord, you know everyone's heart. Show us which of these two you have chosen **25** to take over this apostolic ministry, which Judas left to go where he belongs.' **26** Then they cast lots, and the lot fell to Matthias; so he was added to the eleven apostles.

c 16 The Greek word for *brothers and sisters* (*adelphoi*) refers here to believers, both men and women, as part of God's family; also in 6:3; 11:29; 12:17; 16:40; 18:18, 27; 21:7, 17; 28:14, 15.
d 20 Psalm 69:25
e 20 Psalm 109:8

In verse 15 we see Peter standing up among the believers – a larger group than that mentioned in 1:14, numbering around 120. The remainder of the chapter describes a brief speech of Peter followed by the selection of a replacement for Judas. This, says Peter, is all in fulfilment of Scripture. The speech begins by reminding the hearers of the words spoken by the Spirit through David concerning Judas. As an aside, it is worth simply noting here the high view of Scripture held by the first followers of Jesus. These were not just the words of King David, but also the words of the Holy Spirit.

Before citing the scriptures he has in mind, Peter reminds his hearers of Judas's share in the ministry, and his role in the betrayal of Jesus. In verses 18–19 Luke inserts a historical note regarding the fate of Judas. With the money he received he purchased a field. In that place his body fell and burst open, spilling his intestines. As a consequence, this place came to be known as the 'Field of Blood'.

Many have pointed out the discrepancy here between this account of Judas's death and the account given in Matthew 27:3–8. In Matthew's account we are told that it was the chief priests who purchased the field, and that Judas had gone away and hung himself. Here in Acts 1, it seems it is Judas who buys the field, and there is no mention of hanging.

Commentators suggest it is quite possible and plausible to harmonise the accounts here.[31] Whether the formal transaction is done by Judas or, as Matthew suggests, the chief priests, it is still the money paid to Judas for his betrayal that buys the field. The hanging and the 'fall' may both describe Judas's end. The Greek phrase, *prēnēs genomenos*, is translated in the NIV as 'fell headlong.' It is possible it could also be translated as he 'became swollen'.[32] Either way, it is possible that a body that has been hanging for a period of time will eventually distend and break down,

---

[31] See, for example, Stott, *Acts*, 55–6.
[32] Peterson, *Acts*, 124.

leading to its rupture and the spilling of the intestines. This would make good sense of the two accounts. It seems implausible for someone simply to fall over and burst open, spilling their intestines. The graphic description given by Luke accentuates the grim end of the wicked. Matthew and Luke are describing the same event, but from different points in the timeline. There is therefore no contradiction in the accounts. The emphasis in both accounts is on the wickedness of Judas and the tragic end that befalls the evildoer.[33] Luke inserts Judas's demise here, rather than at the end of his Gospel, to demonstrate how the Scriptures are fulfilled and God's plans are not thwarted.[34]

In verse 20, Peter cites the writings of David referred to in 1:16. Psalm 69:25 says, 'May his place be deserted; let there be no one to dwell in it,' and Psalm 109:8 says, 'May another take his place of leadership.' The conclusion (verse 21) is that it is necessary to choose another to take the place of Judas. This is the proper and necessary fulfilment of Scripture.

One important question in our interpretation of Acts concerns the use of Old Testament texts. We repeatedly see the apostles relate the events happening around them to the fulfilment of Old Testament scriptures. It is worth briefly considering their approach in order to understand how they view the events of their day. This particular example is fairly typical of the apostolic hermeneutic which we shall see repeated.

The question revolves around the sense in which Psalm 69:25 and Psalm 109:8 are being fulfilled. In both psalms, David speaks of his enemies as those who surround and oppose him, seeking to do him harm. It would be difficult to argue that David understood these to be an explicit reference to Judas, a figure that lay a thousand years after him. The sense of both psalms is more general. There are enemies who oppose God's anointed king, and David prays that God would deliver him and overcome those who oppose. Yet Peter is clear – the events surrounding Judas's betrayal, death and replacement are the fulfilment of that which David spoke about in Psalms 69 and 109.

To understand this way of reading the Old Testament texts we need to remember Jesus's teaching to his disciples in Luke 24:

---

[33] In the Old Testament, an ignominious death is often indicative of great evil – for example, Goliath (1 Samuel 17), Saul (1 Samuel 31), Absalom (2 Samuel 18), Jezebel (2 Kings 9), Haman (Esther 7), and in Acts itself we have Herod (Acts 12). What is sobering here is that it befalls one who walked so closely with Jesus.
[34] Robert. W. Wall, 'Acts', in *New Interpreter's Bible, Volume X* (Nashville: Abingdon, 2002), 48–9.

And beginning with Moses and all the Prophets, he explained to them what was said in all the Scriptures concerning himself. (Luke 24:27)

He said to them, 'This is what I told you while I was still with you: everything must be fulfilled that is written about me in the Law of Moses, the Prophets and the Psalms.' (Luke 24:44)

Jesus taught his followers that the entirety of the Old Testament pointed towards him as its climax and fulfilment. This does not mean that every single word or phrase was about Jesus, but the trajectory of Israel's story was irresistibly moving towards him as the goal. The apostles do not read Judas as the fulfilment of Psalms 69:25 and 109:8 because that was David's intent, but because they now read all of the Old Testament through the lens of Jesus's fulfilment of Israel's story. They are employing what Peter Enns has described as a 'Christo-telic' hermeneutic.[35] Peter looks around and sees the Davidic King ascended to his throne, the enemies silenced and overcome, and the necessity of re-establishing the Twelve as necessary elements in restoring the kingdom. Hence the replacement of Judas is not simply recruiting an extra pair of hands. It is the symbolic restoration of God's covenant community and its vocation to the nations, in fulfilment of Scripture.

This obviously raises a question around our own interpretation of the Old Testament. Are we permitted to replicate the apostolic hermeneutic? It seems to me that the principle of reading the Old Testament through a 'Christo-telic' lens is surely correct, given Luke 24:27, 44. However, we still need to exercise great care in employing all the tools of responsible exegesis, including paying attention to genre, context, authorial intent, etc. There are many helpful tools available to help us grow and develop in our hermeneutical skill and awareness.[36]

As we consider the rest of Peter's speech, we see the necessary qualifications given in 1:21–2. The man must have been present with the group from the beginning, and a witness to the resurrection. Again, it is worth noting here that if we want to use biblical terminology in a way

---

[35] Peter Enns, 'Fuller Meaning, Single Goal', in *Three Views of the New Testament Use of the Old Testament*, eds Walter C. Kaiser Jr, Darrell L. Bock and Peter Enns (Grand Rapids: Zondervan, 2008), 167–217.
[36] For example, see Craig G. Bartholomew, *Introducing Biblical Hermeneutics* (Grand Rapids: Baker Academic, 2015); Grant R. Osborne, *The Hermeneutical Spiral* (Downers Grove: IVP Academic, 2006).

that respects its original meaning and context, we have to say that the term 'apostle' should only be used of those who were eyewitnesses to the resurrection of Christ. These men had a unique experience, calling and authority, and using the term 'apostle' of church leaders today has the potential to confuse.

Two men are nominated – Joseph and Matthias. As in 1:14, we observe the central role of prayer in the life of the community. The prayer appeals to the Lord who knows the heart, an echo of 1 Samuel 16:7, and a reminder of the importance of character over gifting. After they have committed the decision to the Lord in prayer, they cast lots, with the lot falling to Matthias.

Casting lots is a method used in the Old Testament for making decisions.[37] However, as the narrative progresses beyond Pentecost we find statements like, 'it seemed good the Holy Spirit and to us . . .' (Acts 15:28). As Peterson observes, 'There are no further examples of such decision making in NT.'[38] In this instance we stand at a historically unique moment in between the ascension of Jesus and the coming of the Spirit. Given the uniqueness of the circumstances, we should not conclude that casting lots would be an appropriate method for decision making in the life of the church today.

The restoration of the Twelve signifies the beginning of the restoration of Israel (see 1:6–8; 3:19–21; Luke 2:25, 38).[39] The Twelve were now to be the new tribal heads and judges of Israel restored.[40] As Wall states, 'The group's return to its full complement heralds the apostles' inspired roles as agents of God's plan to restore the "twelve tribes of Israel."'[41] To the reader acquainted with Israel's story it is hard not to see various Old Testament echoes in play. Just a few weeks prior, the Passover meal has been eaten, the darkness has descended, the lamb has been slain and the death of the firstborn has come. Yet out of that darkness deliverance has dawned. The Davidic King has overcome. The prophet like Elijah has ascended. Israel is being redeemed and restored. And now this redeemed new 'Israel' is awaiting the fiery leading of God's presence with them.

As Turner notes, the early chapters of Acts bring together the fulfilment

---

[37] See Leviticus 16:8; Numbers 26:55; 33:54; 34:13; 36:2; Joshua 18:6–10; 1 Chronicles 24:5, 31; 25:8–9; 26:13–14.

[38] Peterson, *Acts*, 128–9.

[39] Arie Zwiep, *Judas and the Choice of Matthias* (Tübingen: Mohr Siebeck, 2004), 159–79.

[40] See Luke 22:30. Tannehill, *Narrative Unity*, 22.

[41] Wall, 'Acts', 48.

of Mosaic and Davidic Christologies.[42] We might add Elijah and see Jesus as prophet, priest and king *par excellence*, carrying Israel's vocation and hope to fulfilment. All that has been promised is beginning to come true. The inauguration of the kingdom has happened; its restoration is under way; one day its consummation will come. The reader should be in no doubt – the plans, purposes and promises of the Lord are on their way to being fulfilled, and no power or force of evil will ultimately be able to derail the divine purpose. The disciples now need to wait until the promised gift of the Spirit comes, and their mission begins in earnest.

---

[42] M. M. B. Turner, *Power from on High: The Spirit in Israel's Restoration and Witness in Luke–Acts* (Sheffield: Sheffield Academic Press, 1996), 279.

2

The Day of Pentecost

ACTS 2

1. The Spirit comes • Acts 2:1–13

In Acts 1:4–5, the risen Lord Jesus had commanded his disciples not to leave Jerusalem but to wait for the promised gift of the Holy Spirit. This gift would serve to empower his followers to be witnesses in Jerusalem, Judea and Samaria, and to the ends of the earth (1:8). Having restored the Twelve in 1:15–26 we now come to the moment when the promised gift is to be given. God the Son has ascended; now God the Spirit is to descend so that those present on earth are empowered to witness.

The Holy Spirit comes at Pentecost

2 When the day of Pentecost came, they were all together in one place. **2** Suddenly a sound like the blowing of a violent wind came from heaven and filled the whole house where they were sitting. **3** They saw what seemed to be tongues of fire that separated and came to rest on each of them. **4** All of them were filled with the Holy Spirit and began to speak in other tongues[a] as the Spirit enabled them.

5 Now there were staying in Jerusalem God-fearing Jews from every nation under heaven. **6** When they heard this sound, a crowd came together in bewilderment, because each one heard their own language being spoken. **7** Utterly amazed, they asked: 'Aren't all these who are speaking Galileans? **8** Then how is it that each of us hears them in our native language? **9** Parthians, Medes and Elamites; residents of Mesopotamia, Judea and Cappadocia, Pontus and Asia,[b] **10** Phrygia and Pamphylia, Egypt and the parts of Libya near Cyrene; visitors from Rome **11** (both Jews and converts to Judaism); Cretans and Arabs – we hear them declaring the wonders of God in our own tongues!' **12** Amazed and perplexed, they asked one another, 'What does this mean?'

13 Some, however, made fun of them and said, 'They have had too much wine.'

---

a 4 Or *languages*; also in verse 11
b 9 That is, the Roman province by that name

Luke tells us that it was the day of Pentecost, when a violent wind came from heaven and blew through the house where they were staying. The noise, wind and fire were all part of Old Testament theophanies alerting us to the presence of God. Tongues of fire came to rest on each person. All of them were filled with the Holy Spirit and began to speak in other languages.

As Barrett notes, Pentecost was celebrated fifty days after Passover, and in the Old Testament was the Feast of Weeks.[1] This was a harvest festival and later came to be associated with the giving of the Law at Sinai.[2] Israel had emerged from her slavery in Egypt. The Passover lamb had been slain, the tyrant had been overcome, they had passed through the waters and were on their way to the Promised Land. When Israel came to the foot of Mount Sinai, Exodus 19:18 tells us YHWH descended on the mountain in fire. The Law was given. The people were to be a kingdom of priests bearing witness to the nations through their distinctive lives (see Exodus 19:6; Deuteronomy 4:5–8). The fire of God would continue to lead them on their journey to the Promised Land (Exodus 40:38).

It is not difficult to see why a number of commentators see Acts 2:1–13 as a new Sinai.[3] It is fifty days since Christ, the Passover Lamb, has been killed. His death released people not from slavery to Egypt, but from slavery to sin. The new life comes as people pass through the waters of baptism. The fire of God descends, establishing a kingdom of priests. The Law is written now not on tablets of stone but on the tablets of human hearts. And the believing community journeys on, led by the fire, towards the Promised Land.

The phenomenon that would have most shocked an early Jewish hearer would be the fact that the fire of God had now come, not upon

---

[1] Barrett, *Acts*, 111. See Exodus 23:16; 34:22; Numbers 28:26; Leviticus 23:15–21; Deuteronomy 16:9–12.

[2] Witherington, *Acts*, 131. Chrysostom sees a connection between the harvest festival and the harvest of souls that was about to happen. See Francis Martin (ed.), *Acts*, in ACCS 5 (Downers Grove: IVP Academic, 2006), 20.

[3] For more detail on the evidence for the Sinai allusion, see Salter, *The Power of Pentecost*, 28–32. Scott Spencer describes Acts 2:1–13 as a Sinai *déjà vu*. See Scott F. Spencer, *Journeying Through Acts* (Peabody: Hendrickson, 1994), 42. Johnson similarly concludes, 'Nowhere is the same cluster of symbols found all together except in the Septuagint's description of Sinai.' See Luke Timothy Johnson, *The Acts of the Apostles* (Collegeville: Liturgical Press, 1992), 46. This interpretation goes back at least as far as Augustine (See *Acts* in ACCS 5:20). Those less persuaded include Barrett, *Acts*, 111–12; Darrell L. Bock, *Proclamation from Prophecy and Pattern: Lucan Old Testament Christology* (Sheffield: Sheffield Academic Press, 1987), 182–3.

a mountain, or in the Tabernacle/Temple, but upon the people. At Sinai the people were not to go near or touch the mountain, but now the fire of God has come near and touched them. The fire is not hovering above a holy place (i.e., the mountain in Exodus 19 or the Tabernacle in Exodus 40), but the people now seem to become this holy place in which God makes his dwelling (see 1 Peter 2:4–10).

Acts 2:1–13 is depicting a new Exodus. Redemption has come and now this 'kingdom of priests' are empowered to be a witness to the nations. The once-for-all cleansing achieved by Christ's death on the cross makes it possible for God's empowering presence not just to be with them, but also to be within them. This will make the critical difference in the vocational success of the believing community.

We noted in 1:5, and will continue to see throughout Acts, that the people of God are utterly dependent on the Spirit to enable and empower their missional efforts. Success will not depend on human ingenuity, courage or luck, but will come through the emboldening of God's presence within them. One of the most vital things for the church to affirm is her complete dependence on God's Spirit for her existence, life, sustenance and mission. Without this we will all too easily become discouraged in the face of difficulty, or proud if we enjoy success (however we have defined it). Without a humble and prayerful dependence on God's Spirit we will put our hope in the latest programme, leadership course, communications strategy, big personality or any number of other things. I recently heard of a pastor proclaiming that churches that fail to develop an online strategy will die. At the time he made this claim, the church was growing fastest in Iran, where persecution is severe. This is not to disparage planning, strategy and many other useful tools and resources. All of these can be useful in their place, so long as we remember Paul's words: 'I have been crucified with Christ and I no longer live, but Christ lives in me' (Galatians 2:20).

As the disciples begin to speak in new languages, a large crowd gathers. Since it is the time of the festival, there are many people in Jerusalem. Luke describes them as being from 'every nation under heaven' and his list in 2:9–10 gives the sense of people present from every point on the compass. Tannehill suggests the list is not meant to be exhaustive but rather representative of the 'intended scope of the mission'.[4] The mission begins in Jerusalem, but already we see a glimmer of its power to reach the 'ends of the earth'.

The crowd are described as being 'in bewilderment' as each hears their

---

[4] Tannehill, *Narrative Unity*, 27.

own language being spoken. The list of places demonstrates this isn't just an ability to speak a slightly different regional dialect, but a completely different language. The crowd's description of the disciples as 'Galileans' further highlights the unlikeliness of them having learned these different languages. It may have been a slightly reproachful way of drawing attention to their lack of formal education – they were considered unschooled and uncultured people who somehow had the ability to speak in many different languages.[5] God delights to use the foolish things to shame the wise.[6] We are often drawn to the articulate, intelligent and impressive communicators, yet God often uses the proverbial 'Galilean' to accomplish his purposes.[7] The glory is always his and never ours.

This is clearly a miracle that brings people divided by language together. Some have seen this as a reversal of Babel.[8] At Babel, God judged man's self-exalting pride (Genesis 11:1–9). He dispersed and divided people by confusing their language. Here we see people from 'every nation under heaven' brought back together by a divine act that unifies. As Stott notes, 'At Babel earth proudly tried to ascend to heaven, whereas in Jerusalem heaven humbly descended to earth.'[9] Here is a parody of Babel – the nations are gathered with the intention of scattering them again to the ends of the earth.[10]

The languages (*glōssa*) described here are human languages that were able to be understood by the people from their various regions. The ability to speak in other languages is an appropriate sign foreshadowing the Gentile mission.[11] This does raise the question of the relationship between tongues-speech in Acts and that described by Paul in 1 Corinthians 12–14. In Acts the languages seem to be recognisable human languages, whereas in 1 Corinthians there is a suggestion that they are not and therefore require

---

[5] Witherington, *Acts*, 136.

[6] 1 Corinthians 1:27.

[7] As Chrysostom says, 'the uncouth rustic has overcome them all'. *Acts*, in ACCS 5:25.

[8] Barrett, *Acts*, 112.

[9] Stott, *Acts*, 68.

[10] Joel B. Green, '"In Our Own Languages": Pentecost, Babel, and the Shaping of Christian Community in Acts 2:1–13', in *The Word Leaps the Gap: Essays in Scripture and Theology in Honor of Richard B. Hays*, eds. J. Ross Wager, C. Kavin Rowe, A. Katherine Grieb (Grand Rapids: Eerdmans, 2008), 208–13.

[11] Craig S. Keener, 'Why Does Luke Use Tongues as a Sign of the Spirit's Empowerment?' in *JPT* 15.2 (2007): 182–4.

interpretation.[12] Often, in contemporary Pentecostalism, tongues-speech is identified with the latter rather than the former. Further, tongues-speech is seen as the sign of a 'baptism in the Spirit' subsequent to conversion. However, we should note that what is happening in Acts 2 is the description of a unique moment in the fulfilment of God's redemptive historical plan and therefore should not be seen as prescriptive for contemporary Christian experience.[13] There is clearly something unrepeatable about this unique moment in redemptive history.

As interpreters of narrative we need to be careful in differentiating the descriptive from the prescriptive. I would argue that Acts 2 gives us the fulfilment of Old Testament prophecy concerning the last days and the coming of the Spirit. It is not evidence of the normal Christian experience of Spirit-baptism or speaking in tongues. The apostles occupied a unique point in the unfolding plan of salvation. They had already received the Spirit (John 20:22), but this was an empowering in fulfilment of Scripture that initiated the mission to the ends of the earth. 1 Corinthians 12:13 makes clear that Spirit-baptism happens at conversion and is not a subsequent post-conversion blessing for only some Christians. Acts 2 does not support the idea of a normative 'baptism in the Spirit' subsequent to conversion, evidenced by tongues-speech, as something available for Christians today. We will return to consider some of these issues again as we encounter other 'fillings' of the Spirit in the narrative. A careful understanding of Luke's depiction of the Spirit as a central character will help us to understand how we interpret and apply the Spirit's work to our lives today. It is also worth saying that much confusion could be avoided if we were to stop conceiving of the Spirit as if he were like petrol put into a car – something we needed to keep topping up – and instead consider him a person in relationship with his people.

The content of the believers' speech is described by the crowd as the 'wonders of God' (ta megaleia tou theou). Peterson suggests that, given the content of Peter's sermon, the 'wonders' must refer to the

---

[12] See 1 Corinthians 14:27. This is a debatable point, in truth, but space precludes further exploration.

[13] Marshall notes that language of 'baptising' (1:5; 11:16), 'filling' (2:4), 'pouring' (2:17f; 10:45) and 'receiving' (10:47) are synonymous, and that there is no New Testament usage of a subsequent 'baptism of the Spirit' for the person who is already a Christian believer. Pentecost is not the description of normative Christian experience, but the fulfilment and inauguration of the new covenant era, established by the death, resurrection and ascension of Christ, and prophesied by Joel. See Marshall, Acts, 69; Grudem, Systematic Theology, 763–84.

exaltation of Jesus and the pouring out of his Spirit.[14] They ask, 'What does this mean?'

While some dismiss them as drunk, Peter explains the meaning of these events to the watching crowd.[15] Almost before the disciples have begun the mission, they, like their master, face opposition from those quick to rationalise and discredit.[16] With the passing of centuries, some things do not change.[17] This reminds us that the miracles alone will not be sufficient. Ultimately it will not be some kind of 'power evangelism' that will bring conviction and conversion, but the inward work of the Spirit, through the proclamation of the gospel.

The interpreter must make their choice regarding the degree to which they see Pentecost as a new Sinai within a new Exodus motif, or tongues-speech as a reversal of Babel. What Peter is about to make clear is critical for every generation of believers. Pentecost, in a nutshell, means that the Jesus who was crucified is Lord and Messiah, and the only appropriate response is repentance (2:36–8).

2. The events explained • Acts 2:14–40

The speeches in Acts provide us with summaries of what would have been longer addresses – Acts 2:40 tell us as much. To read Acts 2:14–40 takes just a few minutes. It seems likely Peter would have spoken for longer, but here Luke records the main contours and emphases of Peter's address. The speeches in Acts occupy around one-third of the total material. Witherington suggests the reason for the large amount of speech material is because the growth of the church is 'carried forward in the main by evangelistic preaching'.[18] If this is correct, it is a good reminder that evangelistic preaching is the means by which God grows his church. We should never be embarrassed by this or quick to seek new methods to reach and influence, as useful as these may be. God uses what older theologians have termed the 'ordinary means of grace'

---

[14] Peterson, *Acts*, 137.

[15] Bede observes that if they were drunk it was not with 'old wine' but with 'the new wine of spiritual grace', alluding to Jesus's parable. *Acts*, in ACCS 5:26.

[16] Marshall, *Acts*, 67.

[17] 'Hereby it appeareth how monstrous as well the sluggishness, as also the ungodliness of men is, when Satan hath taken away their mind.' Calvin, *Acts*, 81.

[18] Witherington, *Acts*, 118.

(ministry of word and sacrament) to grow and sustain his church.[19] Any move away from this in the search of greater relevance or efficacy will not be a step forward.

This speech is undoubtedly one of the best known in Acts, alongside Paul's address to the Areopagus in Acts 17. It is a speech that connects three separate but related events by means of three Old Testament citations. They are the coming of the Spirit (Joel 2), the resurrection of Christ (Psalm 16) and the ascension and enthronement of Christ (Psalm 110). These three events together, predicted in the Old Testament and fulfilled by Christ, are evidence of the truthfulness of his claims, the efficacy of his work and the ushering in of the 'last days'. The speech concludes with an appeal based on Deuteronomy 32:5 to repent, be baptised and 'save yourselves from this corrupt generation' (2:40). If they will repent, they too will receive the gift of the Holy Spirit. An astonishing three thousand people were added to their number that day.

The fulfilment of prophecy (Acts 2:14–21)

Peter addresses the crowd

14Then Peter stood up with the Eleven, raised his voice and addressed the crowd: 'Fellow Jews and all of you who live in Jerusalem, let me explain this to you; listen carefully to what I say. **15**These people are not drunk, as you suppose. It's only nine in the morning! **16**No, this is what was spoken by the prophet Joel:

17 ' "In the last days, God says,
　　I will pour out my Spirit on all
　　　people.
　　Your sons and daughters will
　　　prophesy,
　　your young men will see visions,
　　your old men will dream
　　　dreams.

18 Even on my servants, both men and
　　　women,
　　I will pour out my Spirit in those
　　　days,
　　and they will prophesy.
19 I will show wonders in the heavens
　　　above
　　and signs on the earth below,
　　blood and fire and billows of
　　　smoke.
20 The sun will be turned to darkness
　　and the moon to blood
　　before the coming of the great and
　　　glorious day of the Lord.
21 And everyone who calls
　　on the name of the Lord will be
　　　saved."ᶜ

_____
ᶜ 21 Joel 2:28-32

_____
[19] Westminster Larger Catechism Q. 154.

Peter begins the speech by appealing to the crowd to listen carefully, refuting the charge of drunkenness, since it is only nine o'clock in the morning. The events witnessed are the fulfilment of that which was prophesied by Joel. The prophesy begins with the phrase, 'In the last days . . .' This refers to the eschatological fulfilment of the Old Testament promises. It is not, as is sometimes thought, just concerned with events surround Christ's *parousia*, but is a period that covers the time from the incarnation to the return of Christ. Many in the first century understood the phrase to refer to an imminent end of all things. However, the New Testament makes clear that the 'last days' is the period in which Jesus is building his church before his final return.[20] We occupy those same last days.

The promise is for the pouring out of the Spirit on all people:

Your sons and daughters will prophesy,
your young men will see visions,
your old men will dream dreams.

Even on servants, male and female, the Spirit will come, and they will prophesy.[21] In the Old Testament, the Spirit had come on particular individuals for specific seasons, offices or tasks. Moses had prayed for the day when all would have the Spirit (Numbers 11:29). This is the fulfilment of Moses's wish. Now all of God's people, not just some of his people, have the Holy Spirit within them. Dreams and visions were all part of the prophetic activity in the Old Testament.[22] Joel foresaw a day when all people would have access to, and understanding of, the Word of God, and an empowerment to speak given by the Spirit.

All words have a semantic range, and so require careful interpretation. Prophecy in the Old Testament was a wide-ranging phenomenon including declarative praise, preaching of the Law and prediction of events to come.[23] In the New Testament we also find a range of meaning with language of 'prophecy/prophesy'. There is the narrower sense of

---

[20] See 2 Timothy 3:1; Hebrews 1:2; James 5:3; 2 Peter 3:3. Salter, *Power of Pentecost*, 3.
[21] These verses should not be used as support for debates around the ordination of women. The point is the democratisation of the Spirit, not specific ministry roles. Notice the decision of Acts 1:21–6 was not reneged upon.
[22] Peterson, *Acts*, 141. See, for example, Isaiah 1:1; Ezekiel 1:1; Daniel 1:17; Zechariah 10:2.
[23] There are the 'professional prophets' (Amos 7:14), teachers (Malachi 4:4), leaders of music and singing (1 Chronicles 25:1–8), messengers of God (1 Kings 22:14). See J. Lindblom, *Prophecy in Ancient Israel* (Oxford: Blackwell, 1963), 218.

prophecy – the gift of an individual – and a broader sense – that which is given to all believers. Within Acts we encounter individuals with a special gift of prophecy (Acts 11:27; 21:10), and we have Joel's statement that *all* shall prophesy.[24]

Are all prophets? Yes and no. In the narrow sense we have to say 'no'. There are individuals gifted to bring revelation from God. These people are often listed alongside apostles in the New Testament.[25] Such gifting, and the authoritative revelation that accompanied it, died out with the apostles.[26] Yet in a broader sense we would have to say 'yes'. There is that sense in which, in the era of the new covenant, every believer has the sort of access, by the illuminative work of the Spirit, to the revelation of God that was once only enjoyed by a very few.[27] That same Spirit empowers believers to speak of this apostolic truth, as witnesses to the good news of the gospel. In this sense we are all prophets. By his Spirit we now know him and make him known.[28]

It is worth saying, however, that we need to be careful in our use of language. For me to describe myself as a 'prophet' is in one sense true, but in another not true. Given the potential for confusion, we are best to explain our usage carefully to ensure we are not putting ourselves on a par with the New Testament 'apostles and prophets' who possessed a unique authority.

For Joel, the idea that all God's people would prophesy speaks of a new way in which every member of God's family would know his Word, would understand his truth and would be equipped to proclaim it to others.

In 2:19–20, a number of signs and wonders are described using imagery of blood, fire, smoke, the darkening of the sun and the moon being turned to blood. All of these things must happen 'before the coming of the great and glorious day of the Lord'. This imagery is associated in the Old Testament with both the Exodus and prophetic speech which signifies

---

[24] Schweizer distinguishes between general dynamic endowment by the Spirit on all, and the animistic endowment on individuals for particular tasks. E. Schweizer, 'πνεῦμα', in *TDNT* 1:506.

[25] 1 Corinthians 12:28–9; Ephesians 2:20; 3:5; 4:11; Revelation 18:20.

[26] This is an area of ongoing and often vigorous debate. Those interested could read John R. W. Stott, *Baptism and Fullness* (Downers Grove: InterVarsity Press, 1964); Wayne Grudem (ed.) *Are Miraculous Gifts for Today? Four Views* (Leicester: InterVarsity Press, 1996).

[27] Calvin says that 'all men shall be endued with spiritual wisdom, even to the prophetical excellency'. *Acts*, 87.

[28] Stott, *Acts*, 74.

political convulsion.[29] Some have tied some of these signs to the death of Jesus – the darkening of the sun being the most obvious connection (Luke 23:44–5). However, it would seem preferable to consider how this imagery is used in the Old Testament and by the prophets themselves. They would often connect these sorts of cosmic portents to political upheaval (see Isaiah 13:9–13; Ezekiel 32:7–8; Amos 8:9). Employing this sort of imagery is a way of saying that the powers that have set themselves against God will be overthrown. If that were the case, then Peter's citation of Joel 2:30–32 would show that the powers have been vanquished and a new order has been established, with a new king on the throne. This would make good sense of what initially looks like a clumsy transition to the resurrection and ascension of Jesus. In other words, the blood, fire, smoke and darkness are not things yet future, but things that have already happened as Jesus has triumphed over his enemies to lead a new exodus liberation.[30]

In verse 21, Peter reminds his hearers that there is still time to call on the name of the Lord and be saved. Peter is about to introduce a staggering application of Joel's prophecy as he explains who exactly the Lord is – the one on whose name people must call.[31]

Ascended and exalted (Acts 2:22–36)

22 'Fellow Israelites, listen to this: Jesus of Nazareth was a man accredited by God to you by miracles, wonders and signs, which God did among you through him, as you yourselves know. 23 This man was handed over to you by God's deliberate plan and foreknowledge; and you, with the help of wicked men,[d] put him to death by nailing him to the cross. 24 But God raised him from the dead, freeing him from the agony of death, because it was impossible for death to keep its hold on him. 25 David said about him:

' "I saw the Lord always before me.
  Because he is at my right hand,
  I will not be shaken.
26 Therefore my heart is glad and my
    tongue rejoices;
  my body also will rest in hope,
27 because you will not abandon me
    to the realm of the dead,
  you will not let your holy one
    see decay.
28 You have made known to me the
    paths of life;
  you will fill me with joy in your
    presence."[e]

---

[29] Stott, *Acts*, 75.
[30] For a fuller discussion, see Salter, *Power of Pentecost*, 13–17.
[31] Green, *The Word of His Grace*, 50.

29 'Fellow Israelites, I can tell you confidently that the patriarch David died and was buried, and his tomb is here to this day. 30 But he was a prophet and knew that God had promised him on oath that he would place one of his descendants on his throne. 31 Seeing what was to come, he spoke of the resurrection of the Messiah, that he was not abandoned to the realm of the dead, nor did his body see decay. 32 God has raised this Jesus to life, and we are all witnesses of it. 33 Exalted to the right hand of God, he has received from the Father the promised Holy Spirit and has poured out what you now see and hear. 34 For David did not ascend to heaven, and yet he said,

'"The Lord said to my Lord:
   'Sit at my right hand
35 until I make your enemies
   a footstool for your feet.' "**f**

36 'Therefore let all Israel be assured of this: God has made this Jesus, whom you crucified, both Lord and Messiah.'

---

d 23 Or *of those not having the law* (that is, Gentiles)
e 28 Psalm 16:8-11 (see Septuagint)
f 35 Psalm 110:1

Peter moves from the citation of Joel as an explanation for that which the crowd has witnessed to an explanation of where (or better who) this has come from. Peter mentions the miracles, wonders and signs God did among them, through Jesus. He then refers to the death of Jesus, with two interesting details. The first is that 'you' put him to death. Of course, many in the crowd would not have been in Jerusalem fifty days earlier, but perhaps some of those listening had a more active involvement. The Jewish people, represented by their leaders, had sought his death. And there is, of course, that sense in which all of us must bear responsibility. There is a real sense in which my sin is the cause of his death.

The second interesting detail is that Peter says this happened according to 'God's deliberate plan and foreknowledge'. The crucifixion was not an unfortunate accident, or an evil that had gotten out of control. Jesus's mission was to die. It was part of God's sovereign plan that he should die for our sins. The providence of God was in no way frustrated by the death of the Son. Here we must affirm the mysterious sovereign power and purpose of God. His ways are higher than our ways, and here we see perhaps the greatest example of how God can intend good while others intend evil (see Genesis 50:20). The Son is not an unwilling victim suffering under an abusive Father. There is no division in the will of the triune God. He came willingly, knowing what lay before him, to give his life; such was his great love for us. And yet humans are held responsible for the wicked things they do. It is no less wicked because it was all part of God's sovereign plan. This is one of the great mysteries – divine sovereignty and human responsibility. The Bible teaches both, and so we must hold on to both in reverent humility.

Peter's main interest is less in the crucifixion than in what follows. The majority of his speech is given to the resurrection and its implications. In verse 24 we see that 'God raised him from the dead . . . because it was impossible for death to keep its hold on him.' How so? Because this is what David had spoken about him in Psalm 16:8–11. Here is another fascinating statement. Did David know that he was speaking not about himself but about the Messiah when he wrote Psalm 16:10? It seems to us unlikely. The context of the psalm and David's prayer is very much centred on his own troubles and his own hope that God will not abandon him. As we noted in commenting on the use of Psalm 69:25 and Psalm 109:8 in Acts 1:20, it is a Christo-telic view of the Old Testament that enables Peter to say David was speaking of the Davidic Messiah to come. Jesus, in his resurrection, demonstrates the fullness of the Father's commitment to his Messiah – he will not abandon him to the realm of the dead; he will not let him see decay. His resurrection is the testimony of the Father's approval of the Son as the faithful Servant and Messiah.

Peter drives his point home by noting that David is, in fact, dead. David was appealing to God's promise given in 2 Samuel 7:10–16 that he would place one his descendants on the throne. David knew that God would not let his dynasty die, and so his psalm is not just about his own life but also about his dynasty. Jesus is the fulfilment of that which David saw. God raised this Jesus from the dead and Peter says, 'We are all witnesses of it' (2:32).

Peter moves from resurrection to exaltation, which is crucial for the direction of his argument. Jesus has not just returned from the dead but has also ascended to the Father. He is now exalted at the Father's right hand and has poured out the Spirit, resulting in the phenomena witnessed by the crowd (2:33). Peter's final citation is from Psalm 110:1:

> The Lord said to my Lord:
>   'Sit at my right hand
> until I make your enemies
>   a footstool for your feet.'

The conclusion to Peter's speech comes in verse 36: 'Therefore let all Israel be assured of this: God has made this Jesus, whom you crucified, both Lord and Messiah.' The person who had been despised, rejected, mocked, insulted, beaten and crucified was not just another dangerous revolutionary to be silenced. He is God the Son. In raising him from the dead, God the Father speaks his verdict of approval on the work of the Son. And this same Jesus did not just overcome death and make a few appearances. He ascended. He took his place at the right hand of the Father. He is on the throne. He is the Lord over every human, in every place, at every moment. As Joel had prophesied, now is the time to call on the name of the Lord and be saved.[32]

The response (Acts 2:37–40)

37 When the people heard this, they were cut to the heart and said to Peter and the other apostles, 'Brothers, what shall we do?'

38 Peter replied, 'Repent and be baptised, every one of you, in the name of Jesus Christ for the forgiveness of your sins. And you will receive the gift of the Holy Spirit. 39 The promise is for you and your children and for all who are far off – for all whom the Lord our God will call.'

40 With many other words he warned them; and he pleaded with them, 'Save yourselves from this corrupt generation.'

The crowd understands the enormity of what they have seen and heard. Luke records them as being 'cut to the heart', and they respond with the question of what they must do. Peter replies, 'Repent and be baptised, every one of you, in the name of Jesus Christ for the forgiveness of your sins. And you will receive the gift of the Holy Spirit' (2:38).

Repentance means to turn – to turn from sin and to turn towards God. A right response will require more than a change of mind about Jesus, or feelings of regret or sadness. Peterson describes repentance as 'a radical reorientation of life with respect to Jesus'.[33] Many today think that becoming a Christian is a matter of praying a prayer, or attending church a bit more regularly, or trying to be a better person. We need to see, and communicate, that repentance is nothing less than turning our whole selves over to Christ as our saviour and our Lord. Robert Wall gives a powerful summary of the gospel call: 'He offers no helpful hints on living a more fulfilling life, no useful projects to work on, no

---

[32] Acts 2:36 cannot be used in support of adoptionist Christologies. It is clear from Luke's Gospel that Jesus is to be seen as the Lord well before his ascension and exaltation. See Luke 1:76; 2:11; 3:4; 6:5; 20:42–3.

[33] Peterson, *Acts*, 154.

feel-good platitudes; rather, he calls people to conversion.'[34] There is no shortage of people offering self-help pseudo-spirituality in the world. The only thing that will truly transform individuals and cultures is the true confession of Jesus Christ as Lord.

Alongside Peter's call to repentance is the call to baptism. Baptism in the New Testament is presented as a cleansing, as a death and resurrection with Christ, and as the pledge of a good conscience.[35] The symbolism depicts transformation into a new life as a part of God's new family. It is the initiatory rite into the believing community and is associated with repentance, forgiveness of sins and the reception of the Spirit in Christian conversion.[36] It is undertaken by those who have made a personal commitment to Christ as their personal Saviour and Lord. It also seems that, where possible, faith and baptism ought not be separated by significant periods of time. Repentance and baptism belong together.[37]

Peter then makes reference to the gift of the Spirit, which presumably refers to the empowering presence witnessed by the crowd. In terms of dogmatic theology, we should note that the regenerating work of the Spirit precedes faith, and it may appear that Peter sees a different *ordo salutis* than Paul. In experience, however, these things are part of the nexus of events that happen at conversion and are normally experienced contemporaneously. The experience of Spirit reception is only known after the Spirit has awakened us to his presence in our lives. We need not see any necessary contradiction between Peter and Paul or between biblical studies and systematic theology. We see again, as we have noticed before, that the Spirit is the '*sine qua non* for being a Christian, not merely a means by which one gets a spiritual booster shot subsequent to conversion', as Witherington puts it.[38]

Peter assures his listeners that the promise extends to them, their children and all who are far off. Some have detected here an argument for paedobaptism – 'The promise is for you and your children.' It is argued that we have here a restatement of the genealogical principle given to

---

[34] Wall, *Acts*, 70.

[35] Ephesians 5:26; Romans 6:3–4; 1 Peter 3:21.

[36] Robert H. Stein, 'Baptism in Luke–Acts', in *Believers Baptism: Sign of the New Covenant in Christ*, eds Thomas R. Schreiner and Shawn D. Wright (Nashville: B&H, 2006), 35–66.

[37] For the reader interested in different views on baptismal practice, see John H. Armstrong (ed.) *Understanding Four Views on Baptism* (Grand Rapids: Zondervan, 2009).

[38] Witherington, *Acts*, 140.

Abraham in the old covenant (Genesis 17:7). However, baptist interpreters would note two things.[39] First, the content of the promise states that it is given for those who will repent. The promise is not, 'Repent and you and your children will receive forgiveness and the Spirit.' The promise is, 'If *you* repent you receive forgiveness and the Spirit.' *That* promise is for your children. Second, note that the scope of the promise includes 'all who are far off'. It seems untenable to claim the genealogical principle for immediate children then exclude those who are far off. Even if we thought the 'far off' only referred to multiple generations within the same family (which is unlikely), not many in practice would work this sort of theology out to grandchildren, great grandchildren and beyond.[40] As a Credobaptist, I can concede there are good arguments for paedobaptism, but Acts 2:39 is not one of them.[41]

With many other words Peter pleads with the crowd. He paraphrases Deuteronomy 32:5 as a rhetorical appeal for his hearers to see themselves of part of a 'corrupt generation' from which they need saving. Stott observes, 'Peter was not asking for private and individual conversions only, but for a public identification with other believers. Commitment to the Messiah implied commitment to the Messianic community, that is, the church.'[42] The appeal of the gospel is urgent and serious. We are not inviting people to join our social group or community projects. It is not to be presented as a 'take it or leave it' option among many other legitimate choices. We are calling people, with utmost seriousness, to turn from death to life. Peter gives us an example of preaching that is rooted in Scripture, points to Jesus, calls for response, proceeds with logic and persuades with passion.

---

[39] The term 'baptist' here refers to Credobaptist convictions, rather than denominational affiliation.

[40] Given Acts 1:8; 2:17, 21, 39, it would seem most plausible to see 'all who are far off' as including not just Jews in distant lands, but also the Gentiles who are far off (see also Ephesians 2:13, 17). Marshall, *Acts*, 82.

[41] A much better case can be found in David Gibson's article, '"Fathers of Faith, My Fathers Now!": On Abraham, Covenant, and the Theology of Paedobaptism', in *Themelios* 40.1, www.thegospelcoalition.org/themelios/article/fathers-of-faith-my-fathers-now-on-abraham-covenant-theology-paedobaptism (accessed 23 August 2023).

[42] Stott, *Acts*, 78–9.

3. The new community • Acts 2:41–7

41 Those who accepted his message were baptised, and about three thousand were added to their number that day.

The fellowship of the believers

42 They devoted themselves to the apostles' teaching and to fellowship, to the breaking of bread and to prayer. **43** Everyone was filled with awe at the many wonders and signs performed by the apostles. **44** All the believers were together and had everything in common. **45** They sold property and possessions to give to anyone who had need. **46** Every day they continued to meet together in the temple courts. They broke bread in their homes and ate together with glad and sincere hearts, **47** praising God and enjoying the favour of all the people. And the Lord added to their number daily those who were being saved.

Many Bible translations put a section break after verse 41. However, Luke's summary regarding those who responded (2:41) would more naturally belong to the wider summary statement, ending at 2:47.[43] Summaries appear at various points in Acts and serve to demonstrate the 'irresistible progress' of the word.[44]

The summary, beginning with verse 41, records a staggering three thousand people converted in a single day. It is an astonishing testimony to the power of the risen and exalted Christ that he can work through these apparently unimpressive Galileans to transform so many hearts. This is the work Jesus is continuing to do from heaven (see 1:1). The believers' work as witnesses has now truly begun.[45]

In verse 42 we see four elements that were central in the life of the early church – devotion to the apostles' teaching, fellowship, the breaking of bread, and prayer. Many have seen here something of a paradigm for the church in subsequent generations. It is worth briefly considering each of these in turn.

---

[43] Barrett, *Acts*, 159.

[44] Barrett, *Acts*, 160. See also 4:32–7; 5:12–16.

[45] Witherington notes there is good evidence that the Temple precincts could accommodate that number of people, and there were pools nearby in which many baptisms could have happened. *Acts*, 156.

The apostles' teaching

The apostles were those who had been with Jesus during his earthly ministry and had witnessed first-hand his resurrection (1:21–2). They were those closest to Jesus, and those to whom he had given instruction (1:2). They possessed a unique authority to teach as instructed by Christ. Today we find the body of the apostolic teaching in the documents of the New Testament. If we wish to devote ourselves to the apostles' teaching, we need to devote ourselves to the study and teaching of Scripture. Sadly, many church leaders today use the Bible as if it were a springboard to launch them into their own ideas. Little attention is paid to careful exegesis, word studies, contexts, logical flow or authorial intent. Some think they can pick and choose the bits they like, having moved beyond that which they consider outdated or irrelevant. Others think that a seven-minute homily will sustain hungry sheep for another week of living for Christ. Some preachers sound more like self-help gurus who sprinkle a Bible verse in here and there, among a whole host of other market-place ideas. Similar dangers exist for those who lead Bible study groups, or those who teach children and young people. If the church wishes to be healthy, to grow, to equip and to reach others, it must diligently devote itself with utmost seriousness to the apostolic teaching as revealed in the New Testament documents. As we will see when we arrive at Acts 6:2–4, this will require a significant amount of time and attention on the part of church leaders, and it is a critical part of their ministry from which they must not be distracted.

In addition, Stott notes that devotion to the apostles' teaching immediately follows the outpouring of the Spirit. There was no sense that human teachers were now unnecessary because the Spirit had come, or that the filling of the Spirit led to a new mystical experience separate from the apostles' teaching.[46] Occasionally, people have unhelpfully described a division between so-called 'Holy Spirit churches' and 'Bible churches'. Yet, the New Testament is clear – a Holy Spirit church *is* a Bible church, and a Bible church *is* a Holy Spirit church. The Spirit is the Spirit of Truth. What God has joined together, let no one separate!

Fellowship (koinonia)

This 'fellowship' is deeper than mere association. The word is used to refer to our fellowship with God himself (1 Corinthians 1:9). It is used to describe a depth of feeling towards one another (2 Corinthians 8:4).

---

[46] Stott, *Acts*, 82.

It is used to describe a participation with another (1 Corinthians 10:16). Fellowship is much more than social acquaintance. It is a deep commitment to and affection for one another. We can see this in 2:44–6 as the believers share possessions and meals.

Conversion is never merely an individual experience. It brings us into a new family, and our faith is developed through corporate and communal means. Paul describes the church as being like a body in which the various parts are all valuable and needed (1 Corinthians 12:12–26). The individual should never say they have no need of the church, and the church should never act as though it has no need of the individual. More-individualistic cultures may miss out on the rich blessings that the *koinonia* would give. Too often faith is individualistic, even consumerist.

Churches can become places where particular people are valued while others are marginalised. Perhaps particularly gifted people are drawn into the inner circle of leadership, invested in and given opportunities. Meanwhile, others, less impressive to our eyes, are ignored, never receiving invitations to fellowship or leadership. The church must always be a community of *koinonia* – a community of radical inclusiveness that recognises our need for corporate, communal, 'body life' together. If this is something that sounds alien to your context, or you fear your church has become a sort of social club, it is worth reflecting on how you might recapture a more meaningful sense of fellowship.

The breaking of bread

There has been debate as to whether Luke is here describing ordinary meals shared by the believers or whether he intends a reference to the Lord's Supper. The words used for the 'breaking of bread' (*tē klasei tou artou*) are used in the New Testament to refer to both the Lord's Supper and ordinary meals.[47] It appears that over time the 'breaking of bread' was understood to be the Lord's Supper (as described in Acts 20:7–11 and 1 Corinthians 11). The context of Acts 2 suggests that the 'breaking of bread' may have been a regular meal including some prayer and praise, and possibly some teaching also. Perhaps what we have here is an early form of the Lord's Supper which became more formalised over time.[48] Taking the food and the fellowship together should make us reflect. If

---

[47] See Matthew 14:19; 26:26; Luke 22:19; 24:30; Acts 20:7–11; 27:35; 1 Corinthians 11:24.
[48] Witherington describes this as a 'primitive way of alluding to the Lord's Supper'. *Acts*, 161.

our church life consists of almost no time to eat together, and our Lord's Supper has become an overly formalised consumption of a tiny piece of bread and a sip of wine once every few months, are we missing some of the blessing God has for us?

Prayers

The use of the plural here is deliberate. The NIV says 'prayer', but the noun is in the plural (*proseuchais*). As suggested when discussing Acts 1:14, and seen explicitly in 3:1, this may well refer to the set times of prayer in the Temple.[49] At this point, the early believers still see themselves as being in continuity with Judaism. Jesus is the climax of their covenant story. It is only as the persecution increases that a more marked separation occurs. This reference to 'the prayers' is not so much a commitment to the personal 'quiet time' (as it has been called), but rather to the set corporate times of prayer.

Words like 'religion' or 'ritual' can often be met with suspicion. Yet this was a key part of the early church's life together. Often our personal prayer lives are sporadic and perfunctory. We think a few minutes at the start of the day will tick the box and alleviate our guilt. Of course, Jesus instructed us to pray in private also, and not to babble on like the pagans (Matthew 6:6–7). He rebuked those who made of show of lengthy eloquent prayers (Mark 12:40). Our Father in heaven knows what we need before we ask him. Yet many of us would benefit from devoting more time and thought to our prayer lives.

Some enjoy their personal prayer time but are happy to neglect meeting with others to pray as something extra and unnecessary. Of course, we aren't saved by attending prayer meetings, but there is something important about the corporate body of the church devoting itself to times of prayer. Count Ludwig von Zinzendorf (1700–60) initiated the Moravian hundred years of 24/7 prayer.[50] This may seem an extreme example, and one that can engender its own sort of legalism, but we would do well to remember the words of E. M. Bounds: 'Talking to men for God is a great thing, but talking to God for men is greater still.'[51]

It is unclear from verse 43 whether 'everyone' refers to the community of believers or to the Jewish community more broadly. The NIV

---

[49] Peterson, *Acts*, 162.

[50] See Richard F. Lovelace, *Dynamics of Spiritual Life* (Downers Grove: InterVarsity Press, 1979), 35–7.

[51] E. M. Bounds, *E. M. Bounds on Prayer* (repr. Peabody: Hendrickson, 2006), 115.

describes the 'awe' (*phobos*) that came upon those who saw the signs and wonders performed by the apostles. The semantic range of *phobos* includes a sense of reverent fear (hence the translation 'awe'). The signs and wonders are not circus tricks for entertainment or adulation, but bring awe, conviction and repentance. The phrase 'signs and wonders' (*sēmeia kai terata*) appears nine times in Acts, and almost exclusively in Jewish contexts, with its last appearance coming in Acts 15:12. Of course, miracles happen beyond Acts 15, but 'signs and wonders' seems to have been a particularly evocative phrase for those in and around Jerusalem – an echo of the first Exodus, and testimony to the new Exodus unfolding before their eyes.[52] Signs and wonders are also linked particularly to the apostles as Jesus's specially chosen witnesses. In that sense they serve a legitimising function to authenticate Christ's chosen apostles.[53] Again, this is not to say that miracles cannot happen today, but simply to observe that we need to exercise caution, recognising the uniqueness of the apostles and their place in redemptive history.[54] Signs and wonders seem to have served a particular function in accrediting Jesus's eyewitnesses, and we ought not therefore make the 'signs and wonders' of the apostolic era normative for subsequent generations.

In verses 44–5 we see the believers sharing possessions and meeting need as it arose in the community. Some have seen here an idealised portrait of a communal society and sought to replicate it in their own contexts. What we have here is a description of their life which included radical generosity, not a proscription on the owning of personal property, a point we will return to in seeking to understand Acts 5:1–11.[55] That said, let us not miss how radical this generosity must have been. It is easy for individuals to step into the snare of materialism, seduced by a world and a media that portray a picture of the good life in material terms. It is easy to think that our happiness and security are achieved through acquiring

---

[52] For the connection of the phrase 'signs and wonders' to the first Exodus, see Exodus 11:9–10; Deuteronomy 6:22; 7:19; 11:3; 28:46; 29:2; Psalm 78:43; 135:9; Jeremiah 32:20.

[53] Peterson, *Acts*, 162. Peterson claims the miracles confirm both the teaching and status of the apostles. Fitzmyer states, 'What revealed the heavenly accreditation of Jesus [2:22] is now used by Luke to confirm the heavenly approbation of the apostles' testimony.' J. A. Fitzmyer, *The Acts of the Apostles* (New York: Doubleday, 1998), 271.

[54] For more on this, see Salter, *Power of Pentecost*, 52–6.

[55] Peterson describes their sharing as 'voluntary and occasional . . . Here was no primitive "communism", but a generous response to particular problems in their midst.' *Acts*, 163.

money and possessions. Consequently, we can develop a tight grip on such things, and a closed heart towards those in need. Churches, too, can become inward looking, concerned to protect their own interests, and fail to release resources to other ministries in need. Acts 2:44 provides no justification for communism, but it certainly challenges our materialism.[56]

Daily they met together in the Temple courts, and broke bread in their homes. Again, we have a reference to the value of shared meals. It is unclear whether we are to understand that all three thousand met every day, or whether we should understand that every day groups of believers could be found in the Temple courts. It is an interesting window on the life of the early church. Historically, some have sought to emphasise the meeting in homes and seen here a command to plant house churches. Sometimes larger churches are looked down upon as somehow less pure than these smaller house churches. And sometimes large churches have been dismissive of small churches or house churches, believing that their large church is somehow more blessed or important in the kingdom. What we see in Acts 2:46 is both things happening together. It seems there were larger gatherings in the Temple courts and smaller gatherings in private homes. It did not have to be either one or the other. It was possible for the early church to be both large and small. They organised themselves such that they had larger and smaller gatherings, and these things together developed their growth in depth and number.

It is interesting to note in verse 47 that the life of this early community of Jesus followers were 'enjoying the favour of all the people. And the Lord added to their number daily those who were being saved.'[57] This 'favour' (*charis*) would not last; persecution was not far away. It is worth reading this statement in the context of Scripture's wider testimony. Sometimes the godly will face persecution, shame and disgrace if they are distinctive (Luke 6:26; Acts 14:22; 2 Timothy 3:12). Sometimes their distinctiveness will win favour (Matthew 5:16; 1 Timothy 3:7; 1 Peter 2:12). To some, the church will be the aroma of death; for others, the aroma of life (2 Corinthians 2:16). The distinctive life of the believing community will bring both responses. We need to be prepared to respond to both. We ought to be careful of judging other churches based on the response of the world around them. It is all too easy to think that a church enjoying 'favour' has sold out, or that a church enduring trial has failed to be

---

[56] Green, *Acts*, 53.
[57] Calvin says, 'The faithful did so behave themselves, that the people did full well like of them for their innocency of life.' *Acts*, 133.

culturally sensitive. Our task is to be godly and distinctive. God's sovereign work will bring a variety of responses.

This first summary statement demonstrates that it was not just the proclamation of the apostles, but also the distinctive life of the believing community that was a significant part of its mission and witness. This is what elsewhere has been termed 'missional ethics'.[58] It is not just the content of our speech, but also the lived reality of our faith that communicates to the watching world. Sound theology and faithful gospel preaching are critical, but without a community that demonstrates the transforming power of grace, the words alone can sound hollow. The community must inhabit and enact the message for its full power to be displayed. This is not just the task of individual Christians, but also something for local churches to consider. How is our life together, as God's redeemed people, bearing witness to our local community? It may draw opposition. It may win favour. But it ought not be invisible.

Stott notes four crucial relationships seen here that characterised the early church. They were related to the apostles, in submission to their teaching. They were related to one another in fellowship and practical care. They were related to God in prayer and praise. They were related to the world in bearing witness to the risen Christ.[59] Acts 2:41-7 provides us with a summary that is encouraging, inspiring and challenging in equal measure as we seek to live out our communal life, dependent on the Spirit, bearing witness to the world.

---

[58] See Martin C. Salter, *Mission in Action: A Biblical Description of Missional Ethics* (Nottingham: Apollos, 2019).
[59] Stott, *Acts*, 87.

3

Times of Refreshment

ACTS 3

1. The healing of a lame man • Acts 3:1–10

Peter heals a lame beggar

3 One day Peter and John were going up to the temple at the time of prayer – at three in the afternoon. **2** Now a man who was lame from birth was being carried to the temple gate called Beautiful, where he was put every day to beg from those going into the temple courts. **3** When he saw Peter and John about to enter, he asked them for money. **4** Peter looked straight at him, as did John. Then Peter said, 'Look at us!' **5** So the man gave them his attention, expecting to get something from them.

6 Then Peter said, 'Silver or gold I do not have, but what I do have I give you. In the name of Jesus Christ of Nazareth, walk.' **7** Taking him by the right hand, he helped him up, and instantly the man's feet and ankles became strong. **8** He jumped to his feet and began to walk. Then he went with them into the temple courts, walking and jumping, and praising God. **9** When all the people saw him walking and praising God, **10** they recognised him as the same man who used to sit begging at the temple gate called Beautiful, and they were filled with wonder and amazement at what had happened to him.

The section running from Acts 3–7 can be seen as a development of 2:41–7. In the following chapters we see the following elements already encountered in that first summary passage:

- Signs and wonders (3:1–10; 5:12–16)
- Teaching and preaching (3:11–26; 4:8–12; 5:25–32)
- Fellowship, prayer and worship (4:23–30)
- Stewardship of possessions (4:32–6; 6:1–6)

We also see in this section growth in both adherence of new believers and persecution by the religious authorities. Just as Jesus himself had

seen favour and opposition, so too his followers must endure the same.[1]
Growth and persecution walk hand in hand through the book of Acts. As
the church increases in number, so the persecution escalates in severity,
right up until we see the first martyr (Acts 7). Beyond this we see the
dispersal of the church beyond Jerusalem to Judea and Samaria (Acts 8:1
in fulfilment of Acts 1:8).

Stott notes that it is in this section we see the other unseen actor in
the narrative.[2] If Christ is the one enthroned in heaven, we also see Satan
(named in Acts 5:3) attempting to destroy the advance of the kingdom.
Luke is reminding his readers that in addition to the narrated characters
and events (in the foreground, so to speak), there are unseen actors at
work. The church is to remain on mission, confident of the rule of Jesus,
made manifest by the work of his Spirit, but all the while aware of the
enemy at work behind historical events.[3]

The church should not become overly obsessed with the devil as if he
were equal to God, and be tempted to see demons around every corner.
Neither should the church become functionally atheist in its consideration
of the demonic forces at work in the world. Jesus reigns and nothing
will thwart his purposes and plans, yet Satan is a real foe, on the prowl,
desiring to devour (see 1 Peter 5:8).

Following the summary of Acts 2:41–7, we have here the first specific
instance of the 'signs and wonders' described in 2:43. Just as in Acts 2,
we see a miraculous event followed by Peter's explanation in the form
of evangelistic preaching.

In verse 1, Luke describes one afternoon when Peter and John are
going up to the Temple for the set time of prayer. They encounter a man
described as 'lame from birth'.[4] He is being carried to the Temple gate
called 'Beautiful', where he would sit and beg.[5] The association between

---

[1] As Jesus himself had predicted: Luke 6:22–6; 12:11; 21:12–3. Stott, *Acts*, 89.

[2] Stott, *Acts*, 88.

[3] See Ephesians 6:10–20.

[4] Literally 'lame from his mother's womb'. The 'ninth hour' is around 3 p.m. Their
attendance at Temple prayers is a reminder that Christianity grew out of Judaism,
with Jesus as the fulfilment of the Jewish story. It is only as persecution intensifies
that a more obvious break becomes necessary. See Witherington, *Acts*, 173.

[5] The precise location of the gate is debated, but it is clearly part of the Temple
area. Most commentators opt for the Nicanor gate situated at the eastern entrance
to the Temple precincts. It is described by Josephus as made of Corinthian brass,
covered in silver and gold. Stott, *Acts*, 90. Josephus, *Wars* V. 5.3.

worship, piety and almsgiving was longstanding.[6] It is possible that some may have considered their almsgiving as part of their worship, or the means through which they might earn favour with God. This would have been a good place for the man to request help, and worshippers should have been positively disposed to his request.[7]

As Peter and John approacd the Temple gate, the lame man asks them for money (verse 3). Peter and John stop, requesting of the man, 'Look at us!' As he gives them his attention, Peter says to him, 'Silver and gold I do not have, but what I do have I give you. In the name of Jesus Christ of Nazareth, walk' (verse 6). Luke tells us that they take him by the hand and lift him to his feet. He is instantly and completely healed (verse 7).

The power that the apostles possess is not to be found in wealth or status. They are not part of the powerful and influential Sanhedrin, who are about to become key characters in the next section of Luke's account. They do not have wealth, as Peter tells the man. In the world's eyes the apostles are unimpressive. They have no status, wealth or reputation. What they do have is the powerful presence of the risen Lord at work by his Holy Spirit.

The invocation of the 'name' is not to be seen as a sort of magical incantation. It is rather the declaration of where the power for the efficacious healing resides – namely in the risen, living and active Lord Jesus, present with the apostles by his Spirit. The healing of this man, unable to walk since birth, is complete and instant. This is not the temporary healing of a bad back, as is sadly sometimes seen with charlatan television evangelists. This is complete and instant healing of a man who has been disabled from birth. The man joins Peter and John in the Temple courts, walking, leaping and praising God. This man is clearly known to many since, when they see him, they are filled with wonder and amazement.

This is the first of a number of miracles that are similar in kind to those performed by Jesus in his ministry on earth.[8] The miracles do two things. First, they serve to legitimise Jesus's apostles as true witnesses to his resurrection.[9] Second, they show that although Jesus is now ascended into heaven, he is continuing to work through his apostles, evidenced by

---

[6] Wall, *Acts*, 77.

[7] See Deuteronomy 26:12; Proverbs 21:13.

[8] See, for example, Luke 5:17–26; 7:11–17; 8:44 and Acts 5:15; 9:40.

[9] It is interesting to note that in the post-apostolic era, sickness was to be dealt with by calling the elders to pray and anoint with oil (James 5:14), suggesting that the signs and wonders were primarily the authenticating signs of Jesus's apostles.

the miracles being performed in Jesus's name. Again, the book of Acts is showing us what Jesus continues to do and teach (Acts 1:1).

The lame man would previously have been excluded from the Temple courts on account of his disability (see Leviticus 21:17–20), but now his restoration is a sign of a much greater work God is doing, as we will see in Peter's explanation (3:19–21). The boundaries of Israel are being redrawn and expanded as those previously kept on the outside are brought in as part of the restoring of the kingdom (see Luke 7:21–2; Acts 1:6–8).[10] The miracles in Acts (and the Gospels) are more concerned with that which they signify, rather than the events themselves. Isaiah 34–35 prophesied a day when the Lord would uphold Zion's cause against her foes. When God delivered them from their enemies, they would see the 'lame leap like a deer' (Isaiah 35:6). The day of deliverance has come.

One of the things we will see in the next few chapters is the surprising identity of those enemies that God is overthrowing. It is not the Roman overlords in their occupation of Jerusalem. It is in fact the Jewish authorities that have crucified Jesus who will persecute his apostles, and who have taken their stand against the Lord (4:26). The forces that oppose God's people will not be allowed to triumph. It is a sobering warning to those, with all their power, who thought they were on God's side but actually turn out to be opposed to him.

In our own contexts, it is often those who claim local religious authority who most vehemently oppose the gospel, perhaps because they have the most to lose. There are those who would claim to be followers of Jesus who would deny his bodily resurrection, deny his personal return and deny the parts of his teaching they deem unpalatable. They are not faithful teachers of God's word, but rather the enemies of Jesus who, without repentance, will find themselves ultimately overthrown.

2. The significance of the healing • Acts 3:11–26

Peter speaks to the onlookers

11 While the man held on to Peter and John, all the people were astonished and came running to them in the place called Solomon's Colonnade. 12 When Peter saw this, he said to them: 'Fellow Israelites, why does this surprise you? Why do you stare at us as if by our own power or godliness we had made this man walk? 13 The God of Abraham, Isaac and Jacob, the God of our fathers, has glorified his servant Jesus. You

---

[10] Wall, *Acts*, 77.

handed him over to be killed, and you disowned him before Pilate, though he had decided to let him go. **14** You disowned the Holy and Righteous One and asked that a murderer be released to you. **15** You killed the author of life, but God raised him from the dead. We are witnesses of this. **16** By faith in the name of Jesus, this man whom you see and know was made strong. It is Jesus' name and the faith that comes through him that has completely healed him, as you can all see.

17 'Now, fellow Israelites, I know that you acted in ignorance, as did your leaders. **18** But this is how God fulfilled what he had foretold through all the prophets, saying that his Messiah would suffer. **19** Repent, then, and turn to God, so that your sins may be wiped out, that times of refreshing may come from the Lord, **20** and that he may send the Messiah, who has been appointed for you - even Jesus. **21** Heaven must receive him until the time comes for God to restore everything, as he promised long ago through his holy prophets. **22** For Moses said, "The Lord your God will raise up for you a prophet like me from among your own people; you must listen to everything he tells you. **23** Anyone who does not listen to him will be completely cut off from their people."[a]

24 'Indeed, beginning with Samuel, all the prophets who have spoken have foretold these days. **25** And you are heirs of the prophets and of the covenant God made with your fathers. He said to Abraham, "Through your offspring all peoples on earth will be blessed."[b] **26** When God raised up his servant, he sent him first to you to bless you by turning each of you from your wicked ways.'

---

[a] 23 Deut. 18:15,18,19
[b] 25 Gen. 22:18; 26:4

The miracle understandably draws a crowd, which provides the occasion for Peter's second speech. The focus of Peter's speech is similar to that of his first speech on the day of Pentecost.[11] In both, he appeals to the events witnessed as evidence that Jesus truly is God's Messiah, and the people must turn to him in repentance to receive forgiveness of sins.[12] While it would have been easy (maybe tempting) for Peter to take the adulation and start his own 'The Apostle Peter Ministries', he is quick to point away from himself, and away from the miracle, to the author and the significance of the miracle. Again, without wishing to labour the point, today's televangelists, with their named ministries, pseudo-miracles, expensive clothes, seven-figure salaries and private jets seem a long way

---

[11] See Barrett, *Acts 1–14*, 189.
[12] Green, *The Word of His Grace*, 60, helpfully demonstrates the similarities and development in the early speeches.

from the humble fisherman who was so keen to point away from himself and point people instead to Jesus. How often do we see examples of ministries more intent on glorifying themselves than glorifying the Son?

Peter's speech begins and ends with reference to Abraham, the father of the Jewish faith. It was with Abraham that God made a covenant to make his descendants as numerous as the stars in the sky, to bless him, and through him to bring blessing to the world (Genesis 12:1–3). Peter claims, 'God's intention to bless Israel and all the nations through Abraham's offspring is fulfilled through the glorification of Jesus as the Servant of the Lord.'[13]

Peter moves quickly from his initial reference to the patriarchs to make clear that the God of Abraham, Isaac and Jacob – the God of the Jews – has glorified Jesus. As in 2:23, he wastes little time in telling the crowd that they are responsible for the Messiah's death – 'You handed him over . . . You disowned [him] . . . You killed the author of life' (verses 13–15). Peter could certainly not be accused of 'scratching itching ears' or seeking popularity.

Peter emphasises the heinousness of the crime by drawing attention to Jesus's identity as God's 'servant', the 'Holy and Righteous One' and the 'author of life'.[14] Peter compounds their guilt by reminding them that they requested a murderer be spared, while Jesus was crucified. The rhetorical force is undeniable. They released a murderer while committing the most grievous of all murders. They took life from the author of life. But God raised him from the dead, and it is faith in the name of *this* Jesus that has brought healing to the man born lame.[15]

Peter appeals to the crowd that their ignorance can be forgiven if they repent and turn to God, 'that times of refreshing may come from the Lord'. It may be tempting to think Peter is softening his polemic with reference to their 'ignorance'. However, ignorance is often used in Scripture to refer to a wilful hardening of the heart, and as such his audience are fully culpable for their sin.[16] This is not the ignorance of

---

[13] Peterson, *Acts*, 171.

[14] The Greek term *paida* ('servant') could mean 'servant' or 'son' here. Either way, it emphasises the special relationship that existed between God and his 'servant' Jesus. If the idea of 'servant' is to the fore, it would fit with the Servant of Isaiah 52:13–14, raised up and highly exalted.

[15] It is unclear whether the faith exercised is that of Peter and John or of the lame man. Given there is no explicit reference to any exercise of faith by the lame man, the former is to be preferred.

[16] See, for example, Ephesians 4:18; 1 Peter 1:14; 2 Peter 2:13.

the person who has never heard the name Jesus. This is the ignorance of those who saw and rejected.

The reference to 'times of refreshing' speaks of the last days and all the blessings that were to come.[17] This no doubt included the gift of the Spirit, but would have included, within a Jewish understanding of eschatology, peace, abundance, justice, health, restoration and prosperity.[18] Witherington has observed that in Luke's eschatology three things are of critical importance. First, the last days are an 'age for decision' regarding Jesus. Second, ignorance can no longer be overlooked. Third, knowing the first two things is crucial, but knowing the timings of the 'concluding eschatological events' is not.[19] People today often spend too much time on the third of these things in unhealthy speculation about events and times that are not ours to know. The church needs to give itself to the first and the second of these things as we await the second coming.

Peter appeals to the crowd to listen to Jesus, the prophet Moses spoke of in Deuteronomy 18:18–20, with the warning that any who fail to listen to him will be cut off from the community of the covenant people. All the prophets from Samuel onward have foretold these days.[20] Peter pleads with his audience as those who are 'heirs of the prophets and of the covenant God made with your fathers' (verse 25).

The Jewish nation has a special relationship with God as heirs of the prophets and those with whom God has made a covenant. Their Messiah has come to them first, and it is critical they do not miss their Messiah and all he brings. While Israel had a special part in God's plans, by virtue of their election and the covenant God made with them, we need to be careful about our understanding of this relationship today. It is true the message was to go to Israel first. However, once Israel had rejected the message it went to the Gentiles. Paul is clear that the children of Abraham are those who have faith (Romans 4:11–12). Israel's story is fulfilled in Jesus and now it is those who are in union with him who are heirs of the promises (Galatians 3:1–29). There are not 'two distinct plans for the

---

[17] The phrase itself is not found in the OT, but it seems to refer perhaps to the Holy Spirit as the first gift, and all the subsequent blessing to come at the culmination of the last days.

[18] See Isaiah 2:1–4; 60:1–7; 61:1–7; 65:20–25; Micah 4:1–5; Zechariah 9:9–10:12. See Walter Brueggemann, *Hopeful Imagination: Prophetic Voices in Exile* (Philadelphia: Fortress, 1986).

[19] Witherington, *Acts*, 186.

[20] Here is another example of the Christo-telic hermeneutic employed by Jesus's apostles.

two different groups of people'.[21] As Peterson notes, 'Only those who acknowledge Jesus as the key to their future will prove to be "heirs of the prophets and of the covenant God made"'.[22]

Special ministries set up to reach the Jewish people today should, in principle, be no different from ministries set up to reach Africa, Asia, Europe or Latin America. Ministries based on the understanding that ethnic Israel are today privileged, or that Israel's response will somehow usher in the second coming, are misguided. The worldwide church is the fulfilment of God's universal purposes, as given to Abraham in Genesis 12:1–3. The promises for the restoration of Zion are fulfilled in, and applied to, Christ and his seed, which includes Jew and Gentile, brought together into one new humanity (Ephesians 2:12–18). There is no support for those who advocate Zionist theologies in Acts 3:25–6.[23]

The speech calls the people to see Jesus as the climax of God's covenant promises and the fulfilment of the prophetic hopes for the Messiah. He is the one through whom God will bring refreshing and restoration. The urgent call is for repentance and a turning back to God. Acts 4 will show us the beginnings of the Jewish authorities' response to Peter's message.

From one perspective, the healing of the man is one isolated incident of the Spirit-empowered apostles bearing witness to the risen Christ. Another way of looking at this scene is to see the man as an example in microcosm of what Jesus has begun to do for all creation, and what he will do for any who will turn to him.[24] As Wall observes, 'The healed man is the herald of a broken and battered creation's being made whole again.'[25] His perfect restoration is about more than just a need or desire for physical healing. It is about the refreshing and restoration Christ would bring to any unclean outsider who sees their need and stretches out their hand. What Jesus offers is not money or status, but the sort of healing that admits us into his heavenly courts. And what God has done

---

[21] To quote Grudem in his rebuttal of Lewis Sperry Chafer's dispensational view. See Grudem, *Systematic Theology*, 860.

[22] Peterson, *Acts*, 172.

[23] This is a much wider debate incorporating other key passages, such as Romans 9–11. For more on this debate, see Grudem, *Systematic Theology*, 859–63; Herman Bavinck, *Reformed Dogmatics*, ed. John Bolt; trans. John Vriend (Grand Rapids: Baker Academic, 2008), 4:664–72.

[24] Bede goes further and compares the man's condition to that of Israel as a whole, spiritually lame, unable to take hold of the sacrifice provided. They needed healing even more than the beggar did. Bede, *Acts*, in ACCS 5:39.

[25] Wall, *Acts*, 82.

for the one is a glimpse of what he is doing for many, and indeed will do for the whole cosmos (see Romans 8:22–5).

It is worth remembering where all of this is taking place. The Jewish people are streaming into the Temple courts as the place of sacrifice where they find their own cleansing, healing and forgiveness for their sin. Yet here is this lame man, outside the Temple courts, made whole by the name of Jesus. For a first-century Jewish person, the idea that salvation could be found outside the Temple provision would have been scandalous, yet here stands (literally) this man, a symbol of the restorative power released by the crucified author of life, who has the authority to wipe out sins.

As in Acts 2:14–40 we see the intent of the apostolic preaching – to point people to Jesus and to call for repentance. Peter's sermons to Jewish audiences always contain elements of Israel's story since their faith is to be rooted in God's salvific and redemptive dealings with them. Yet his preaching never stops at merely recounting historical facts. It always moves towards the call to repentance. Preaching must never become a history lecture. It must always sense the presence of the risen Lord, at work by his Spirit. And it must always sense the eschatological urgency that calls for action. Anything less has failed to grasp the enormity of the 'last days' in which we live, and the life-transforming power of the risen Christ.

4

The Opposition Begins

ACTS 4

Thus far, in the book of Acts, we have seen remarkable events in the birth and growth of the church. Jesus has ascended to heaven, his Spirit has been poured out, many have believed and a man born lame has been healed. Apart from some mocking in 2:13, the church appears to be on an upward trajectory in winning converts and favour.

At this point the narrative takes a sobering turn. The opposition from the Jewish leaders will escalate through the next four chapters. We will see warning and threats in 4:18–21, physical beating in 5:40, and ultimately the first Christian martyr in 7:58. Over the course of the next few chapters we will also see threats to the church not only from those who oppose, but also from satanic attack (5:3), and internal sin and conflict (5:1–11; 6:1–7).

Jesus warned his followers that they would face persecution for following him (Luke 21:12–19), and now they are beginning to be confronted with that painful reality. And yet, the gospel continues to advance, and people continue to be added to their number (4:4; 5:14; 6:7). Persecution and growth walk hand in hand throughout Luke's narrative. It serves as a reminder, a challenge and an encouragement to endure hardship in serving the Lord.

1. Before the Sanhedrin • Acts 4:1–22

As Peter and John were speaking with the people, they found themselves arrested, imprisoned and facing trial for their actions. This is the first of a number of trials in the book of Acts where the ruling authorities are opposed to the apostolic message concerning the Lordship of Jesus.

Acts 4:1–4: A great disturbance and great growth

Peter and John before the Sanhedrin

4 The priests and the captain of the temple guard and the Sadducees came up to Peter and John while they were speaking to the people. **2** They were greatly disturbed because the apostles were teaching the people, proclaiming in Jesus the resurrection of the dead. **3** They seized Peter and John and, because it was evening, they put them in jail until the next day. **4** But many who heard the message believed; so the number of men who believed grew to about five thousand.

The miracle performed by Peter and John had evidently drawn significant attention. We are told that a group of priests and Sadducees came, along with the captain of the Temple guard, to confront Peter and John.[1] The reference to them 'speaking to the people' perhaps suggests that Peter's speech had finished and a more informal dialogue was in progress.

It is interesting to note that the thing that captured the primary attention of the priests and Sadducees was not so much the healing of the lame man as the content of their teaching – 'proclaiming in Jesus the resurrection of the dead'. It is this teaching which appears to have caused most alarm. The verb translated as 'greatly disturbed' (*diaponoumenoi*) has the sense of distress or annoyance. It is the same verb used to express Paul's distress at the slave girl in Acts 16:18. On Good Friday the Jewish leaders must have thought they had rid themselves of Jesus and his followers. The last thing they wanted was a resurgence of his influence. Luke does not tell us whether their alarm was owing to their belief that the teachings of Jesus were false, or perhaps because they now had cause to fear that they were true. Here is a narrative ambiguity that invites the reflection of the reader.[2]

Since it was by now evening (further evidence that Peter and John may have been there some time), they imprisoned Peter and John overnight to await further questioning the following day. The action appears somewhat extreme and indicates the irrational, possibly fearful, opposition of the Jewish leaders to the apostles. We can feel a sense of injustice before the trial has even begun.

---

[1] Peterson, *Acts*, 187, notes the captain of the Temple guard was 'the highest ranking priest after the high priest. He assisted the high priest in the performance of his ceremonial duties and was the chief of police in the temple area, with the power to arrest.'

[2] The Sadducees did not believe in a general resurrection from the dead, but it seems the greater alarm was caused by the mention of the name of Jesus.

Luke closes this opening scene with the report that 'many who heard the message believed; so the number of men who believed grew to about five thousand'.[3] This is something we see repeated numerous times throughout the book of Acts – the messengers may be detained, but the message is not. The laity here see what the leaders cannot. The sign cannot be denied or suppressed. The meaning of the miracle is clear to many. Jesus really is alive, ruling and reigning from the right hand of the Father. Only wilful unbelief on the part of the Jewish leaders sustains their increasing hatred and opposition.

Christians are never promised justice and fairness in this life – much of that must be left with God (see Romans 12:19). And opposition often takes unjust and irrational forms. Sometimes the only course of action for the godly is to entrust oneself 'to him who judges justly' (1 Peter 2:23). We should not suppose this will be easy, nor should we simply passively accept injustice. However, we ought not be surprised if irrational and unjust opposition comes our way.

Acts 4:5–12: A uniquely powerful 'name'

5 The next day the rulers, the elders and the teachers of the law met in Jerusalem. **6** Annas the high priest was there, and so were Caiaphas, John, Alexander and others of the high priest's family. **7** They had Peter and John brought before them and began to question them: 'By what power or what name did you do this?'

8 Then Peter, filled with the Holy Spirit, said to them: 'Rulers and elders of the people! **9** If we are being called to account today for an act of kindness shown to a man who was lame and are being asked how he was healed, **10** then know this, you and all the people of Israel: it is by the name of Jesus Christ of Nazareth, whom you crucified but whom God raised from the dead, that this man stands before you healed. **11** Jesus is

'"the stone you builders rejected,
which has become the
cornerstone."[a]

12 Salvation is found in no one else, for there is no other name under heaven given to mankind by which we must be saved.'

_____

a 11 Psalm 118:22

_____

[3] Peterson, *Acts*, 188, notes that if 'men' 'means only males, the total number of believers, including women and children, will have been much larger. However, as noted in connection with 1:16, females are included with males in some NT uses of this Greek word.'

Verse 5 leads us to believe that Peter and John had created quite a stir as the 'priests and . . . Sadducees' have now become the 'rulers, the elders and the teachers of the law' – in short, the Sanhedrin. This group would have consisted of seventy-one members, presided over by the high priest. They would have sat in a semicircle, and Peter and John would have been placed in the centre.[4] It is perhaps hard for us to imagine just how intimidating this must have felt for Peter and John. As a reader we may ponder how we might have reacted in such a situation. Those named as part of the Sanhedrin include Annas, Caiaphas, John and Alexander. Although nothing is known regarding John and Alexander, we have already met Annas and Caiaphas in the Gospels at the trial of Jesus (John 18:13–28). It is an ominous detail as we see 'the apostles were arraigned before the same court that tried and condemned Jesus'.[5]

The presenting issue, it seems, was not whether the miracle had really occurred (see 4:16), but by what power they had performed the sign. In response, Peter delivers a speech which appears to be shorter than those delivered in Acts 2:14–39 and 3:12–26, but is no less direct.[6] 'Filled with the Holy Spirit', he replied that the act of kindness towards the lame man had been performed 'by the name of Jesus Christ of Nazareth'. For rhetorical bite he added, 'whom you crucified but whom God raised from the dead'. This was the third time Peter employed such a formula (Acts 2:23–4; 3:15). The God these Jewish leaders claimed to serve had raised and exalted the Jesus they tried and crucified. It was in his name the man had been healed. This should have served as a serious warning to the continued use of threats and trials against the followers of Jesus, but the Jewish leaders seem blind to this fact.

To ensure the Jewish leaders would draw the appropriate conclusion, Peter cited Psalm 118:22 – 'the stone you builders rejected, which has become the cornerstone'. There are a number of differences in the precise wording of Peter's quotation of Psalm 118:22, which shows Peter's primary concern was not with exact replication of the quotation but rather with its significance and meaning. Significantly, however, he

---

[4] Stott, *Acts*, 96. Commentators differ as to the extent of the judicial powers possessed by the Sanhedrin. Whatever their exact nature, we can see, looking back to the trial of Jesus, and forward in Acts, they are a group who respond in severe terms to any threat to their power.

[5] Peterson, *Acts*, 189.

[6] Here we see fulfilled Jesus's promise to his disciples given in Luke 12:12; 21:15.

does appear to very deliberately add 'you', emphasising their guilt in the rejection of Jesus.[7]

In the conclusion of his brief defence, Peter asserted, 'Salvation is found in no one else, for there is no other name under heaven given to mankind by which we must be saved.'[8] Eckhard Schnabel notes, 'The negative formulation "in no one else" . . . placed at the beginning of the sentence for emphasis, expresses the exclusive nature of salvation through Jesus.'[9] The one rejected by the Jewish leaders is their only hope of salvation. It will not be enough for the Jewish leaders to claim their position, status, heritage or even God's long-standing covenant with Israel. God had sent his Son. Salvation is found in him and in him alone. The one they had despised, beaten and spat upon is the one before whom they must bow the knee if they wish to find salvation.

It is not uncommon today for people to believe in pluralism – the idea that there are many roads up the mountain of salvation. Each one must follow their own path, but we will all reach the top in the end. Peter's statement firmly shuts the door on such a belief. The pluralist belief is, of course, in itself an assertion about the way of salvation. It was the missiologist Lesslie Newbigin who said:

> There is an appearance of humility in the protestation that the truth is much greater than any one of us can grasp, but if this is used to invalidate all claims to discern the truth it is in fact an arrogant claim to a kind of knowledge which is superior to the knowledge which is available to fallible human beings.[10]

Despite the often difficult and painful consequences, we must hold on to Peter's statement that there is only one name by which mankind may be saved – the name of Jesus. The apostolic witness is crystal clear. Salvation

---

[7] It is noteworthy that Jesus, too, teaching in the Temple courts, cited Psalm 118 in conclusion to the parable of the tenants. His usage went on to include a warning of judgment to any who reject God's cornerstone (see Luke 20:9–19).

[8] Barrett notes that 'salvation' in Acts can have a broad and narrow meaning. In its broad sense it means deliverance, which can include things like physical healing (Acts 4:9) and deliverance from danger (27:20, 31). The word is most often used in a theological sense of being delivered both from and for – from the judgment to come on a perverse generation (2:40) and for a relationship with God and his people (2:47). Barrett, *Acts 1–14*, 231.

[9] Eckhard J. Schnabel, *Acts* (Grand Rapids: Zondervan, 2012), 242.

[10] Lesslie Newbigin, *The Gospel in a Pluralist Society* (London: SPCK, 1979), 170.

is found in no one else. By virtue of his resurrection and exaltation, he is the fountain from which all blessing flow.

John Calvin, commenting on Acts 4:12 in his *Institutes,* says the following:

> We see that our whole salvation and all its parts are comprehended in Christ [Acts 4:12] . . . If we seek strength, it lies in his dominion . . . If we seek redemption, it lies in his passion; if acquittal, in his condemnation . . . if newness of life, in his resurrection; if immortality, in the same . . . In short, since rich store of every kind of good abounds in him, let us drink our fill from this fountain, *and from no other.*[11]

Acts 4:13–22: Who is really in charge?

13 When they saw the courage of Peter and John and realised that they were unschooled, ordinary men, they were astonished and they took note that these men had been with Jesus. **14** But since they could see the man who had been healed standing there with them, there was nothing they could say. **15** So they ordered them to withdraw from the Sanhedrin and then conferred together. **16** 'What are we going to do with these men?' they asked. 'Everyone living in Jerusalem knows they have performed a notable sign, and we cannot deny it. **17** But to stop this thing from spreading any further among the people, we must warn them to speak no longer to anyone in this name.'

18 Then they called them in again and commanded them not to speak or teach at all in the name of Jesus. **19** But Peter and John replied, 'Which is right in God's eyes: to listen to you, or to him? You be the judges! **20** As for us, we cannot help speaking about what we have seen and heard.'

21 After further threats they let them go. They could not decide how to punish them, because all the people were praising God for what had happened. **22** For the man who was miraculously healed was over forty years old.

The Jewish leaders were clearly surprised by the courage of Peter and John, noting they were 'unschooled, ordinary men'.[12] Here is another sign that should have driven these leaders towards the truth of Peter's

---

[11] John Calvin, *Institutes of the Christian Religion,* edited by John T. McNeill, translated by Ford Lewis Battles, two volumes (Philadelphia: Westminster Press, 1960) 2.16.19. Emphasis mine.

[12] Literally 'unlettered' men (*agrammatoi*). 'Courage' or 'boldness' (*parrēsian*) is something that characterised the apostolic preaching and something for which they prayed (4:29, 31; 9:27; 13:46; 14:3; 18:26; 19:8; 26:26). Marshall, *Acts,* 101.

testimony, but instead seemed to drive them further away. Like Pharaoh in the days of Moses, the more evidence they saw, the more their hearts were hardened. Robert Wall observes how the risen Lord uses the 'unschooled' and 'ordinary'. It is easy to be impressed with educational backgrounds, institutions and qualifications. These things can be useful and beneficial and have been for many. However, we must note that the Bible's emphasis falls on the spiritual authority that comes as a result of the Spirit's work, evidenced by character and gifting. We need to be wary of overlooking some and preferring others because we have placed too much confidence in certain institutions, colleges, camps, pathways and qualifications.[13] Character, gifting and a Spirit-given boldness is more to be treasured and sought than an expensive education or influential connections.

Remarkably, Luke reports how the Jewish leaders were unable to say anything owing to the presence of the man who had been healed. They sent Peter and John out of the Sanhedrin in order to confer.[14] The Jewish leaders acknowledged, 'Everyone living in Jerusalem knows they have performed a notable sign, and we cannot deny it.' It seems neither would they accept that to which it pointed. Their desire was to suppress the further spread of this Jesus movement, so they determined to warn the apostles to speak no longer in the name of Jesus.

This 'behind closed doors' insight serves to remind us of the importance of prayer and dependence on the work of God's Spirit. These leaders were presented with evidence of Jesus's identity via the miracle of the lame man's healing and the transformation of 'ordinary men' into bold and eloquent preachers. Yet it was not enough to open their blind eyes to the truth. They were still bent on suppression. Evidence alone, without the work of God's Spirit, is unable to bring conviction and conversion.

Having summoned Peter and John to deliver their verdict, Peter appeals to a higher court. To paraphrase, Peter said, 'You want to play the judges? Then judge for yourselves – should we obey you or God?' Peter protested that they simply 'cannot help speaking about what we have seen and heard'. Disobedience of authorities is something Christians need to consider very carefully. Ordinarily the New Testament commands

---

[13] Wall, *Acts*, 92.
[14] Some commentators wonder how Luke would have known what happened behind closed doors. Stott, *Acts*, 98, suggests the possibility that Paul may well have heard from Gamaliel the substance of their deliberations.

Christians to submit to human authorities, even when they act in ways that are unfair or unjust (Romans 13:1–7; 1 Peter 2:13–20). However, when the authority in question demands that we act in such a way as to be in clear disobedience of God's commands, we are duty-bound to refuse. Christians need to walk this line carefully. Civil disobedience should not be undertaken lightly. However, on rare occasions, where submission to a human authority would require a clear and obvious disobedience to the Lord, we must respectfully but determinedly refuse, aware that further unjust sanctions may have to be borne.[15] We must regularly pray that God would give us the strength to endure in such trials. If we are not personally facing such trials ourselves, we must pray for those brothers and sisters facing persecution today as they seek to remain faithful to the Lord. We must pray that God would give them wisdom and courage in knowing how to respond to persecution and injustice.

After issuing further threats, they released Peter and John. The NIV translation states, 'They could not decide how to punish them.' A more literal translation would be, 'They could find no way to punish them.' It may have been they had no legal basis to punish them, further illustrating the unjust nature of the whole process. Alternatively, they dared not punish them for fear of the crowd. This second view would fit with Luke's comment in the second half of verse 21.[16] While the apostles resolved to fear God, not man, the Sanhedrin stood in stark contrast, further compounding their guilt.

In this sobering and dramatic scene, we see three different candidates for the role of 'judge and jury'. There are the Jewish rulers who reject their message (though they cannot reject the sign) and order their silence. There is the crowd, many of whom see the sign, accept the message and praise God. And then there is Peter's clear sense of the only audience that really matters – God himself. Peter is not swayed by the praise of the crowd or the threats of the Sanhedrin. He knows that his first allegiance is to the God who raised his friend and Lord to be the cornerstone. He is the one to be worshipped and obeyed. He is the only one in whom salvation is found.

---

[15] For a much fuller discussion of this issue, see Calvin, *Institutes* 4.20
[16] Barrett, *Acts 1–14*, 238.

2. The prayer of the believers • Acts 4:23–31

The believers pray

23 On their release, Peter and John went back to their own people and reported all that the chief priests and the elders had said to them. 24 When they heard this, they raised their voices together in prayer to God. 'Sovereign Lord,' they said, 'you made the heavens and the earth and the sea, and everything in them. 25 You spoke by the Holy Spirit through the mouth of your servant, our father David:

'"Why do the nations rage
and the peoples plot in vain?
26 The kings of the earth rise up
and the rulers band together
against the Lord
and against his anointed one.b"c

27 Indeed Herod and Pontius Pilate met together with the Gentiles and the people of Israel in this city to conspire against your holy servant Jesus, whom you anointed. 28 They did what your power and will had decided beforehand should happen. 29 Now, Lord, consider their threats and enable your servants to speak your word with great boldness. 30 Stretch out your hand to heal and perform signs and wonders through the name of your holy servant Jesus.'

31 After they prayed, the place where they were meeting was shaken. And they were all filled with the Holy Spirit and spoke the word of God boldly.

_____

b 26 That is, Messiah or Christ
c 26 Psalm 2:1,2

Previously, in Acts 2:42, Luke reported how the early Christians 'devoted themselves to the apostles' teaching and to fellowship, to the breaking of bread and to prayer'. Here, in Acts 4:23–31, we see an example of the community's devotion to prayer, as a response to the opposition from the Jewish leaders.[17]

Their response to their first encounter with serious opposition is striking. Peter and John had been detained, interrogated and threatened. It must have felt intimidating to face the same group that had tried and condemned Jesus. Upon their release, Peter and John reported everything

_____

[17] Some have seen here a second Pentecost (for example, Venkataraman, *SABC*, 1462). However, it should be noted that this prayer occurs in response to persecution, there is no mention of tongues-speech here, there are no outsiders present, and no conversions and baptisms. The dissimilarities to Pentecost outweigh the similarities seen in the shaking of the building and the empowering through the Spirit's filling. The latter element will repeat, but Pentecost itself was unrepeatable within the scheme of redemptive history.

to 'their own people'.[18] At this point they did not come up with a new strategy or campaign. Perhaps surprisingly to us, they did not even pray for the persecution to stop. Rather, they immediately responded by raising their voices to heaven in prayer.[19] I remember hearing the story of one pastor praying for another in a context of persecution. The first pastor prayed for the persecution to stop. The second pastor immediately stopped him and said, 'We don't ask for the persecution to stop because we know that with it comes refining and growth. We rather ask that God would give us strength and courage to faithfully endure.'

Their prayer expressed confidence in God's sovereignty and an appeal to see more of God's power at work, through his emboldening power in their speech and his miraculous power to perform healings, signs and wonders.[20] They desired to see more of what had begun in the early of chapters of Acts, and they knew they would need more of God's enabling presence and power at work in their lives. Here is a wonderful example of prayerful confidence in God's sovereignty in the face of persecution.

Their prayer begins by addressing God as 'Sovereign Lord'. The Greek term (*despota*) is not commonly used to refer to God in Scripture, but when it is employed, it speaks of his authority as the Lord over all things.[21] The context supports this as the next phrase affirms God as the creator of the heavens and earth and all that is in them.

God's Lordship over creation is further affirmed in the citation of Psalm 2:1–2 which speaks of God's authority over all nations, not just Israel. Psalm 2 is a fitting psalm for the believers to cite as it affirms God's control over enemies and his ultimate victory over opposition. In the psalm, David acknowledges the nations that rage, plot and take their stand against God's anointed (Psalm 2:1–3). In the wider context of the

---

[18] Wall, *Acts*, 91, suggests that it is to the rest of the apostles they return, rather than the believers more widely. However, the majority view is that a larger group than just the Twelve were present. We are probably not meant to understand the five thousand gathered in one place, but a significant number of believers including the remaining ten apostles. See, for example, Barrett, *Acts 1–14*, 242–3.

[19] The word 'together' (*homothymadon*) expresses their unity. Marshall, *Acts*, 103.

[20] The prayer shows us concern to both worship and witness. Wall, *Acts*, 93.

[21] Witherington, *Acts*, 201. In the Septuagint (LXX) of the Old Testament it is found in Genesis 15:2, 8; Isaiah 1:24; 3:1; Jeremiah 1:6; 4:10; Daniel 9:8, 15–16. In the New Testament it is used of God in Luke 2:29; 2 Timothy 2:21; 2 Peter 2:1; Jude 4; Revelation 6:10. It can also be used of human masters (1 Timothy 6:1–2; Titus 2:9; 1 Peter 2:18).

psalm, which is not cited here but is surely in mind, we see God laughs at their feeble attempts to dethrone him (Psalm 2:4). Further, he rebukes the nations for their rebellion, as he has installed his king on Zion. The installed king is the Son, the nations are the Son's inheritance, and any opposition will be dashed to pieces (Psalm 2:4–9). In the face of very real opposition, we can see why the early believers would have turned to this psalm to give them comfort, confidence and courage in the Sovereign Lord's power and purpose.

In verse 27 they apply Psalm 2 to their own historical situation. Herod, Pilate, the Gentiles and the people of Israel had conspired against 'your holy servant Jesus, whom you anointed'. There are two things here worth noting. First, the believers are clearly applying the language of the 'anointed' to Jesus. The Greek translation (Septuagint) of Psalm 2:2 uses the noun *christou* for the 'anointed', and here in Acts 4:27 the believers use the related verb *echrisas* with reference to Jesus. In its original context, Psalm 2 would have been understood as referring to David as the anointed king installed on God's holy hill. Here, the believers understand that its fulfilment comes in Jesus as the king and Son *par excellence*. He is the anointed king, enthroned by the Father, set to inherit the nations. And opposition to him will be met with God's judgment.

The second thing worth noting here is the use of Psalm 2 *against* Israel. It is striking that the 'people of Israel' (*laois Israēl*) are included now in the group that opposes the Lord and faces his judgment.[22] Again, in its original context this psalm would have been a comfort to Israel in the face of the nations who would seek to destroy them. Yet here it is used against Israel (or at least against her religious leaders) to condemn them as those that oppose, and risk being dashed to pieces. It is difficult, in reading the citation of the psalm, not to also think of the end of the psalm which calls those who oppose Jesus to kiss the Son and take refuge in him (Psalm 2:12).

In verse 28 we see a further expression of confidence in God's sovereign plan – their plot against Jesus was all part of God's plan. It was his power and will that had decided what would happen. It is worth simply noting here that the early Christians, it seems, would reject more recent theological accounts of God's sovereignty that would deny his knowledge of or involvement in historical events. Acts 4:28 would seem to be a problem for both the Arminian and the open theist, since the future is not only

---

[22] Witherington, *Acts*, 202.

known to God, but also directed by his power and will.[23] Throughout Scripture, God's absolute sovereignty, rather than being used to negate the need for prayer, is always used as the inspiration for confidence in prayer.

In view of God's sovereign hand over events and circumstances, the believers requested that God would enable them to speak the word 'with great boldness' (see 4:13). They understood the need not just to speak to God, but also to speak for God as witnesses to the resurrected Lord Jesus. This was their primary mission, as it is for us today.

They also requested that God would continue to stretch out his hand to heal and perform signs and wonders. They had seen the power of the miraculous events in Acts 2 and 3 to draw many people to faith. As discussed when we were examining Acts 2, whether the miraculous gifts are for today is a debatable point. Nevertheless, we should all affirm that God can still perform miracles. Crucially we, like the first followers of Christ, should be interested in what the miracles point to, not simply the miracles in themselves. The speeches show us that the point of the miracles is to bear witness to the living Lord Jesus. We should be wary of ministries or theologies that seem more interested in the miracles than the one to whom they point.[24]

As in Acts 2:2 there is a physical phenomenon (the place was shaken) that accompanied their praying, and their prayer was swiftly answered as they were 'filled with the Holy Spirit and spoke the word of God boldly'.[25] We should see the subsequent Holy Spirit 'fillings' in Acts as special empowerment and enablement for the task, rather than thinking of the Spirit continually coming and going to and from the believers.

Richard Lovelace in his *Dynamics of Spiritual Life* laments the loss of serious prayer in the modern church.[26] Often prayer is tacked on to the end of a Bible study and given minimal time in our gatherings. Our prayers are often concerned solely with the circumstances of our week, and not enough taken up with kingdom concerns. Churches that would

---

[23] Calvin, *Acts*, 187. For a fuller discussion on the relationship between the doctrine of God as creator and providence, see John Webster, 'On the Theology of Providence', in *God Without Measure, Volume 1: God and the Works of God* (London: T&T Clark, 2016), 127–41.

[24] For a fuller discussion in this area, see Stott, *Acts*, 100–4.

[25] Chrysostom notes the phenomenon of 'shaking' and its Old Testament associations with the awesome presence of the Lord (Judges 5:5; Psalm 46:6; 77:18; 99:1; Amos 9:5; Micah 1:4; Nahum 1:5). He concludes, 'The place was shaken, and that made them all the more unshaken.' Chrysostom, ACCS 5:54.

[26] See Richard F. Lovelace, *Dynamics of Spiritual Life* (Downers Grove: InterVarsity Press, 1979), 153–8.

see a renewal and awakening of their spiritual lives need to take seriously the example of the early Christians in their fervency and urgency in kingdom-centred prayer.

We also see the early church's commitment to personal evangelism. This is not to reduce our definition and understanding of mission down to the verbal proclamation of certain elements of the gospel. The rest of Acts will show us we need a broad understanding of terms like salvation, gospel and mission. Nevertheless, there is a clear 'ultimacy' about speaking boldly of the Lord Jesus.[27] Many of us are nervous of what others will think of us. Many of us feel like failures in this area. We need to ask the Lord in faith that he would give us the boldness to speak for him where the opportunity presents itself. We do not wish to be insensitive Bible-bashing bulldozers. But I suspect this is not the tendency of many of us. Lord, grant us boldness to speak, trusting in your sovereignty.

3. Care in the community • Acts 4:32–7

The believers share their possessions

32 All the believers were one in heart and mind. No one claimed that any of their possessions was their own, but they shared everything they had. **33** With great power the apostles continued to testify to the resurrection of the Lord Jesus. And God's grace was so powerfully at work in them all **34** that there was no needy person among them. For from time to time those who owned land or houses sold them, brought the money from the sales **35** and put it at the apostles' feet, and it was distributed to anyone who had need.

36 Joseph, a Levite from Cyprus, whom the apostles called Barnabas (which means 'son of encouragement'), **37** sold a field he owned and brought the money and put it at the apostles' feet.

Here we see the second summary statement in the book of Acts (the first being in 2:42–7). There are some similarities to Luke's earlier report, as well as some differences. The section serves to summarise the situation following the initial round of persecution, and to transition into the events of 5:1–11.

---

[27] Christopher Wright uses the idea of 'ultimacy' in discussing the relationship between word and action. Both are necessary, but there is a certain ultimacy about proclamation. See Christopher J. H. Wright, *The Mission of God* (Downers Grove: IVP Academic, 2006), 318–19.

In 4:32 the believers (described as a 'multitude' – *plēthous*) are described as being 'one in heart and mind' (*ēn kardia kai psychē mia*). Their early trials have served to draw them together in closer unity. The reference to 'heart and mind' may echo Deuteronomy 6:5. In this summary we see the early Christians presented as living in fulfilment of the Law, loving God and loving neighbour (Luke 10:27–37).[28] Luke shows us the compelling beauty in the unity of the church.

As in Acts 2:42–7, we see the believers sharing possessions to meet need, and the apostles continuing to testify with great power to the resurrection of the Lord Jesus.[29] Just as they had enjoyed the favour (*charis*) of the people in 2:47, so Luke describes how the *charis* of God was powerfully at work in them all.[30] God's transformative power is made manifest in their concern for and generosity towards one another.

In verse 34, Luke records that there was 'no needy person among them'. This could be an allusion to Deuteronomy 15:4 where a similar phrase is used, including the same word in the LXX to describe the 'poor/needy' (*endeēs*). Deuteronomy 15 anticipated a time when Israel had taken possession of the land. If they obeyed God they would find blessing, including provision for the poor and needy. Israel's exemplary ethic would lead to international influence (Deuteronomy 15:6) if they remained faithful to the Lord. It may be that Luke is utilising the ethical ideal of Deuteronomy 15 and applying it to the 'new Israel' in Acts 4:32–7.[31] They are fulfilling the vocation of the elect to be a witness to the nations in word and deed. Witherington observes that friendship in the Graeco–Roman world often involved reciprocity between equals. Here, Luke is portraying a contrast society or counterculture in which the wealthy give to the needs of the poor expecting nothing in return.[32] Their generosity is a picture of God's generosity towards us in the gospel.

Luke informs the reader that the provision for need came from the sale of property or land. The owners chose to give some or all of the money to the apostles to be distributed to anyone who had need.[33] As Luke transitions towards the incident with Ananias and Sapphira, he informs

---

[28] Wall, *Acts*, 96; Witherington, *Acts*, 206.

[29] The 'great power' (*dynamei megalē*) would seem to be a reference to the signs and wonders already mentioned in 2:43.

[30] Wall, *Acts*, 96.

[31] Peterson, *Acts*, 205.

[32] Witherington, *Acts*, 205.

[33] Luke is here anticipating the need for others to help in the administration of such resources that will be seen in Acts 6:1–6. Marshall, *Acts*, 109.

us of a man named Joseph, a Levite from Cyprus (also called Barnabas), who sold a field and gave the proceeds to the apostles for distribution. Barnabas will play a much fuller role in Luke's narrative as it progresses. It is the first time we see the ministry beginning to spread out beyond the activity of the twelve apostles.

As with Luke's previous summary statement, we see a strikingly attractive picture of the early church. In this second summary, three things are mentioned: their unity, their testimony and their generosity, with an emphasis on the latter.

It is a sad feature of many churches today that we seem to be only good at one of these things. Some churches have a deep sense of unity among one another. They enjoy being together and offer genuine support to one another. Yet their passion for outward testimony has dwindled, and their generosity to the needy is lacking. Other churches may be known for their gospel testimony, their teaching, training and resources. Perhaps they are considered 'preaching centres' and they develop evangelistic resources for other churches. This is wonderful work for which to be thankful. However, these churches can easily have a superficial sort of unity, and perhaps even consider generosity to the needy a distraction from what they consider to be the main business of gospel testimony. Still other churches are known for their care for the poor and their programmes of practical support and social action. Yet they devote little effort or attention to internal unity and, though they are handing out bread, they have lost the urgency to be handing out the bread of life.

From Luke's account, we can see that a healthy church will continually be working at all three of these things as part of their life together and gospel witness – unity, testimony and generosity. It is a powerful summary that encourages us all to reflect on our own situations and the areas where we need to be prayerfully seeking progress.

5

Internal and External Threat

ACTS 5

In Acts 5, Luke continues with the twin themes of opposition and growth. Previously, in Acts 4, we saw the initial opposition from the Sanhedrin which culminated in a warning. In Acts 5 the warning will become a physical flogging (5:40). In addition to the escalation in the opposition from their Jewish opponents, we see spiritual opposition with the mention of Satan in 5:3 – their battle is not just against flesh and blood.[1] The community of believers will face increased pressures, both internal and external, as Luke's narrative progresses. Nevertheless, the word continues to spread and many more are added to their number (5:14, 42).

1. Ananias and Sapphira • Acts 5:1–11

Ananias and Sapphira

5 Now a man named Ananias, together with his wife Sapphira, also sold a piece of property. 2 With his wife's full knowledge he kept back part of the money for himself, but brought the rest and put it at the apostles' feet.

3 Then Peter said, 'Ananias, how is it that Satan has so filled your heart that you have lied to the Holy Spirit and have kept for yourself some of the money you received for the land?

4 Didn't it belong to you before it was sold? And after it was sold, wasn't the money at your disposal? What made you think of doing such a thing? You have not lied just to human beings but to God.'

5 When Ananias heard this, he fell down and died. And great fear seized all who heard what had happened. 6 Then some young men came forward, wrapped up his body, and carried him out and buried him.

7 About three hours later his wife

---

[1] Calvin says, 'Satan had invented a shift to get into that holy company, and that under the colour of such excellent virtue; for he hath wonderful wiles of hypocrisy to insinuate himself. This way doth Satan assault the Church, when as he cannot prevail by open war.' *Acts*, 194.

came in, not knowing what had happened. **8** Peter asked her, 'Tell me, is this the price you and Ananias got for the land?'

'Yes,' she said, 'that is the price.'

9 Peter said to her, 'How could you conspire to test the Spirit of the Lord? Listen! The feet of the men who buried your husband are at the door, and they will carry you out also.'

10 At that moment she fell down at his feet and died. Then the young men came in and, finding her dead, carried her out and buried her beside her husband. **11** Great fear seized the whole church and all who heard about these events.

Acts 5:1–11 presents us with one of the more disturbing episodes in the book of Acts. It shows us that the church is not (and has never been) a perfect institution. The reality of Luke's account gives greater historical credence to his report. Luke is not seeking to cover up sin but presents these new believers, warts and all.

Acts 5:1 introduces a couple, apparently members of the believing community, who lie about money they received from a property sale – money they in turn laid at the apostles' feet. As a consequence, they are struck dead, and great fear seized the whole church. On first glance it appears an extremely harsh sentence given the nature of their crime. As readers we need to slow ourselves down and try to understand what is happening in this episode. Augustine once said that if we struggle to understand a text, then we're faced with one of three options: a problem with the manuscript, a problem with the translation or a problem with self.[2] Often our problem with these difficult texts falls into the last category. This reminds us to approach God's word not seeking to master it, but rather to have it master us.

In verse 2, Luke alludes to the joint deception at work: 'With his wife's full knowledge he kept back part of the money for himself.' As Tannehill notes, this was a 'calculated deception'.[3] The surprise comes in verse 3. Peter, rather than thanking them for their generous gift, confronted them: 'How is it that Satan has so filled your heart that you have lied to the Holy Spirit and have kept for yourself some of the money you received for the land?' Their actions, far from being sacrificial and generous, have a satanic origin.

As Peterson notes, we must see the diabolical presence at work here

---

[2] Augustine, *Letter to Jerome* 82.3. Cited at www.newadvent.org/fathers/1102082.htm (accessed 24 August 2023).

[3] Tannehill, *Narrative Unity*, 79.

if we are to make sense of the severity of the judgment.[4] The description of Satan having 'filled your heart' had only previously been used by Luke in reference to Judas (Luke 22:3).[5] This is no minor misdemeanour, but a diabolical betrayal aimed at harming God's redeemed community. If Satan can invade the heart of Ananias, it threatens the 'one heart' of the community mentioned in 4:32.[6] The reader sensitive to the whole canon of Scripture cannot help but think back to Genesis 3 here. Here is a husband and wife, standing at the infancy of God's creative blessings on his new humanity, tempted by Satan, and facing death as the consequence of sin.[7] This story is not just about greed and duplicity, but about 'an invasion of the community of the Spirit by the powers of darkness'.[8] This is why the judgment must be swift and total.

In verse 4, Peter explains the nature of their sin: 'You have not lied just to human beings but to God.' It is important to note here that their sin was not keeping the money from the sale of the property. Peter makes clear that the property belonged to them before it was sold, and the money was at their disposal after it had been sold. The early church did not impose some sort of communism, and neither did they denounce the ownership of private property. The property belonged to Ananias and Sapphira and so did the proceeds of its sale. The gift to the community was voluntary not mandatory.[9]

The problem was made clear by Peter in verses 3–4. Twice he condemned Ananias and Sapphira for lying – in verse 3 they had lied to the Holy Spirit, and in verse 4 Peter told them they had 'not lied just to human beings but to God'.[10] The problem was not in retaining the proceeds of the sale; it was in the deliberate intent to deceive.

Luke does not record their motive in doing this. Perhaps they wanted others to see them as generous benefactors. Maybe they sought a position of status or leadership in the group. Did they want to ingratiate themselves with the apostles? There is a reason why Jesus instructed his followers that the left hand should not know what the right hand gives (Matthew 6:3).

---

[4] Peterson, *Acts*, 208.

[5] Witherington, *Acts*, 215.

[6] Tannehill, *Narrative Unity*, 79.

[7] Peterson, *Acts*, 209.

[8] Witherington, *Acts*, 215.

[9] Witherington, *Acts*, 216; Stott, *Acts*, 109, cites Bengel: 'The sin of Achan and that of Ananias were in many respects similar, at the beginning of the churches of the Old and New Testament respectively.'

[10] It is worth noting here Peter ascribes deity to the Holy Spirit. Calvin, *Institutes* 1.13.15.

The temptation towards sinful motives, even in our generosity, is great. Their deceit threatened the integrity of the community in its infancy, and therefore had to be met with swift justice.

As Peter finished his condemnation of their act, Ananias fell down and died. Three hours later, Sapphira returned and attempted to continue the lie, not knowing what had happened. Peter had denounced Ananias for lying, and here he expanded on the nature of the sin by asking Sapphira, 'How could you conspire to test the Spirit of the Lord?' Testing the Lord had brought a divine rebuke for Israel in the Old Testament.[11] The Spirit whose presence animated and inspired the early church could not turn a blind eye to the high-handed attempt to deceive. In Numbers 15:22–30, provision was made to atone for the person who sinned unintentionally and repented. However, the person who sinned 'defiantly' had to be cut off from the people.

Acts 5:1–11 is not advocating a return to the Mosaic Law, but rather demonstrating the seriousness of holiness in the life of the early church. In verse 10 Sapphira too fell down and died.[12] Peter's prophetic announcement of judgment is owing to his authority as an apostle, and is therefore unique.[13] Luke tells us in verse 11 that 'great fear seized the whole church and all who heard about these events'.

How are we to understand and interpret this shocking event in the life of the early church? Perhaps a clue to understanding this event lies in a similarly shocking incident seen in Joshua 7.[14] As Israel stood on the verge of the promised land, YHWH had instructed the people to 'devote to destruction' (herem) anything that would turn their hearts away from following the Lord (Deuteronomy 7:1–6). This herem was to include the inhabitants of the land, the altars, sacred stones, Asherah poles and idols. Israel were to be a people 'holy to the Lord' and anything that threatened their purity would threaten their relationship with God and their vocation to be a light to the nations. Integrity and purity were critical to their existence as God's chosen and holy people.

---

[11] See Exodus 17:2; Numbers 14:22; Deuteronomy 6:16; 33:8.

[12] Some commentators seek to find a naturalistic explanation for these events. Perhaps the shock of exposure caused a heart attack. This seems unnecessary. The narrative is clear that, whatever the precise cause of death, it was an active judgment of God on them both for their sin. Paul seems to allude to something similar in 1 Corinthians 5:1–11.

[13] David R. McCabe, *How to Kill Things with Words: Ananias and Sapphira under the Prophetic Speech-Acts of Divine Judgement (Acts 4.32–5.11)* (LNTS 454; London: T&T Clark, 2011), 222.

[14] Witherington, *Acts*, 213.

Shortly after taking possession of Canaan, the story of Achan is recounted (Joshua 7). Achan and his family had taken some of the forbidden 'devoted things' and buried them under his tent. The verb translated as 'kept back' (*enosphisato* – Acts 5:2–3) is rare, occurring only in two other places in Scripture, one of which is in the Greek translation (Septuagint) of Joshua 7:1.[15] His sin had jeopardised the whole community, and therefore he and his family had to be destroyed along with the items they had taken. As with Acts 5, Joshua 7 strikes us as severe, but it was critical for the people of God in their infancy to see the importance of integrity and purity. Without this, their worship and witness were compromised. As soon as Ananias and Sapphira had devoted the profit to the Lord, it was his property they were stealing, and their deception compounded their guilt.

In short, the passage is really about purity, not property. The people of God, in the infancy of their existence, needed to see just how serious moral purity was in the service of God. If his presence were to go with them, and if they were to continue to enjoy his grace upon them (4:33), there was no room for the toleration of high-handed sin.

It's a sobering reminder to us that our moral purity is more important to God than our gifts, experience, wealth or work ethic. How can we expect the Spirit of God to bless us if we continue in deliberate sin? This episode reminds us that threats to the church can come from both outside and inside – from the world, the flesh and the devil.[16] Thankfully we are justified by grace, not works, but we should never cheapen grace or expect God's blessing if we continue in sin.

Of course, we need to be careful not to adopt a view of God that portrays him as some sort of heavenly snack dispenser – if I put the right thing in then I'll get the good stuff out. Providence teaches us that sometimes righteous people suffer, and sometimes the wicked prosper. None of this is an excuse for us to take lightly our own pursuit of purity. God does not require us to lead lives of sinless perfection – that would be impossible this side of glory. We need to regularly come to him in confession and repentance, genuinely seeking a greater conformation to the likeness of Christ. Purity and integrity matter hugely to our walk and witness.

In addition, this passage, in demonstrating the importance of the purity of church, reminds us of the necessity of church discipline. John

---

[15] Marshall, *Acts*, III.
[16] Tannehill, *Narrative Unity*, 79.

Stott notes in his commentary that while this event is highly unusual, the church is still called to remove from its membership those who sin defiantly and who refuse to repent.[17] Not all sin should lead to excommunication, but public high-handed sin needs to be publicly addressed. Stott observes that some churches are too lax while others are too severe. Jesus left us a model of how such things should be dealt with (Matthew 18:15–20). Penitent sinners should be dealt with graciously, always aiming at their restoration. Yet where we find the sort of thing we see here – public, high-handed, unrepented-of sin – we should act to preserve the purity of God's church, for the sake of her walk and her witness.[18]

2. Further growth and healings • Acts 5:12–16

The apostles heal many

12 The apostles performed many signs and wonders among the people. And all the believers used to meet together in Solomon's Colonnade. 13 No one else dared join them, even though they were highly regarded by the people. 14 Nevertheless, more and more men and women believed in the Lord and were added to their number. 15 As a result, people brought those who were ill into the streets and laid them on beds and mats so that at least Peter's shadow might fall on some of them as he passed by. 16 Crowds gathered also from the towns around Jerusalem, bringing those who were ill and those tormented by impure spirits, and all of them were healed.

Here is the third summary statement so far in Acts. Again, there is some overlap with the summary statements seen in 2:42–7 and 4:32–7. Luke mentions the signs and wonders performed by the apostles, their unity in worship and the continued growth of the early church.

It is interesting to note in verses 13–14 the dynamic between those that did not dare to join them and the 'more and more' who believed and were added to their number. It seems there was a growing tension between the Jewish leaders and the early Christians. People were aware of what the Jewish leaders thought and so feared to join. However, we are told that among the people, the believers were 'highly regarded' and many did in fact join the church. The power of God's Spirit to draw

---

[17] See, for example, Matthew 18:15–20; 1 Corinthians 5:1–5.
[18] See Stott's excellent paragraph on this in *Acts*, 112.

people to himself was greater than the power of the Sanhedrin to deter. This encourages us to keep bearing faithful witness to Christ in word and deed, whatever the opposition we face. The power of God to draw people to himself is greater than any power or authority around us that would seek to discredit the gospel or dissuade the inquirer.

In verses 15–16 Luke reports people laying the sick in the streets that Peter's shadow might fall upon them. Luke does not tell us whether these attempts were successful. However, he does inform us that people from the surrounding towns brought the sick and possessed to the apostles and all of them were healed.[19] Here is a further indication that satanic opposition is being overcome in the name of Jesus.[20] The message is getting out from Jerusalem into Judea (see Acts 1:8). It is a remarkable summary statement which demonstrates the authenticity and authority of the apostles as eyewitnesses to the risen Jesus. He performed similar signs in his own ministry, and now his power is clearly at work in his apostles (see Luke 6:17–19). Here is further evidence of what Jesus is continuing to do and teach from the right hand of the Father (see Acts 1:1).

3. Increased persecution • Acts 5:17–42

Acts 5:16 and 5:41–2 form an *inclusio* around the second trial incident. In 5:16 Luke reports the increased crowds and in 5:42 we see the apostles' unceasing ministry in the Temple courts and house to house. Within the narrative of the second trial, we see a number of elements that have already appeared or will appear again in Acts. We see a miraculous release from detention, reminding us that God's word cannot be chained (5:19–20; see 12:1–10; 16:25–8). We see the repeated warning not to speak in Jesus's name and the apostles' assertion that they must obey God rather than man (5:40; see 4:18–20). Coupled with the apostles' right fear of God we see the Sanhedrin's fear of man (5:26; compare 4:21). Peter again speaks of their guilt in crucifying Jesus, and his exaltation to the right hand of the Father (5:30–31; compare 2:23–4; 3:15; 4:10). The new elements here are Gamaliel's interjection and the flogging of the apostles.

---

[19] The reference to the miraculous powers of Peter reminds us that the 'signs and wonders' were performed by the apostles as Jesus's chosen eyewitnesses, not by the community more broadly.
[20] Wall, *Acts*, 99.

Gamaliel's pragmatism may have prevented a more severe punishment for the moment, but the jealousy and fury mentioned in 5:17 and 33 anticipate further escalation in the persecution.

Acts 5:17–24: Arrest and escape

The apostles persecuted

17 Then the high priest and all his associates, who were members of the party of the Sadducees, were filled with jealousy. 18 They arrested the apostles and put them in the public jail. 19 But during the night an angel of the Lord opened the doors of the jail and brought them out. 20 'Go, stand in the temple courts,' he said, 'and tell the people all about this new life.'

21 At daybreak they entered the temple courts, as they had been told, and began to teach the people.

When the high priest and his associates arrived, they called together the Sanhedrin – the full assembly of the elders of Israel – and sent to the jail for the apostles. 22 But on arriving at the jail, the officers did not find them there. So they went back and reported, 23 'We found the jail securely locked, with the guards standing at the doors; but when we opened them, we found no one inside.' 24 On hearing this report, the captain of the temple guard and the chief priests were at a loss, wondering what this might lead to.

The arrest and escape is almost comical as we see the bewilderment of the high priest and his associates. In verse 17 Luke switches his attention from the crowds back to the Temple authorities, describing their jealousy of the apostles. The term, translated in the NIV as 'jealous' (*zēlos*) can be positive or negative. It is used positively to describe the zeal of Phinehas, God's own jealousy for his name, and Paul's ardent concern for the church.[21] It can also be used negatively of strife and jealousy between people.[22] Within the context of Acts, it would seem clear it is the latter in view.[23] The Sanhedrin have already shown they fear men more than God (4:21; 5:26). In 5:33 we will see their fury and desire to kill the apostles. In 6:13 we will see they accept the testimony of false witnesses. And in 6:54–8:1 their fury will finally boil over into fatal violence against Stephen.

Their zeal is not for the Lord but is rather for the protection of their own name and reputation in the face of the apostles' growing popularity and persistent condemnation of their murder of Jesus. Luke does not

---

[21] LXX Numbers 25:11; LXX Deuteronomy 29:19; 2 Corinthians 11:2.

[22] Romans 13:13; 1 Corinthians 3:3; 2 Corinthians 12:20.

[23] Bock, *Acts*, 238, describes their reaction as being about 'power politics'.

specify what exactly they are jealous of, but we may guess it is related to the newfound attention and authority the apostles enjoy with the crowds. It reminds us of those three great temptations of the Christian: money, sex and power. Power is subtle and deceitful. It is easy to believe we have no struggle and temptation in this area, until we see someone else being admired or having the sort of attention and influence we think we ought to have. Jealousy is a symptom of a deeper sin, a thirst for that which someone else has – in this case influence, respect and authority. A jealousy orientated towards the wrong object can mask a sort of pride which tragically has its own power to blind us to our need for humility and repentance.

In verse 19 we see the first of a series of miraculous escapes in the book of Acts. This is one of Luke's narrative devices that demonstrates the inability of opponents to chain the word of God. This will be important as Luke concludes the book of Acts with Paul under house arrest. The spread or growth of the gospel is one of Luke's favourite themes (see 6:7; 12:24; 19:20). He wants his readers to be both comforted and challenged that whatever our situation we can have confidence that God uses his word to do his work. It is easy to feel downcast and defeated by our own weakness or external pressure or opposition. But the power lies not with us, nor with the world, but with God and his gospel. As Paul reminds the Corinthians, we simply plant the word, for that is our job – it is God that will make it grow (1 Corinthians 3:6).

At daybreak, the apostles were once again in the Temple courts, teaching the people (verse 21). The Sanhedrin assembled themselves in verse 21 for a second interrogation of the apostles, only to find the prison cell empty. More remarkably, the doors were locked and the guards on duty, further emphasising the miraculous nature of their escape. They are described as 'at a loss' (*diēporoun*). The same term was used of the disciples when they found an empty tomb (Luke 24:4), and of the crowds on the day of Pentecost (Acts 2:12). It will appear again when Peter has his vision in Acts 10:17. In those other occurrences those who are perplexed find new revelation. Here it leads to a greater blindness.

Occasionally we may meet people who will say something like, 'If only I could see the miracles that happened during the time of Jesus or the early church, then I would believe.' The continued blindness of the Sanhedrin sadly refutes this idea. Our hearts are more important than our eyes when it comes to truly beholding Jesus.

Acts 5:25–40: Further questioning and the advice of Gamaliel

25 Then someone came and said, 'Look! The men you put in jail are standing in the temple courts teaching the people.' 26 At that, the captain went with his officers and brought the apostles. They did not use force, because they feared that the people would stone them.

27 The apostles were brought in and made to appear before the Sanhedrin to be questioned by the high priest. 28 'We gave you strict orders not to teach in this name,' he said. 'Yet you have filled Jerusalem with your teaching and are determined to make us guilty of this man's blood.'

29 Peter and the other apostles replied: 'We must obey God rather than human beings! 30 The God of our ancestors raised Jesus from the dead – whom you killed by hanging him on a cross. 31 God exalted him to his own right hand as Prince and Saviour that he might bring Israel to repentance and forgive their sins. 32 We are witnesses of these things, and so is the Holy Spirit, whom God has given to those who obey him.'

33 When they heard this, they were furious and wanted to put them to death. 34 But a Pharisee named Gamaliel, a teacher of the law, who was honoured by all the people, stood up in the Sanhedrin and ordered that the men be put outside for a little while. 35 Then he addressed the Sanhedrin: 'Men of Israel, consider carefully what you intend to do to these men. 36 Some time ago Theudas appeared, claiming to be somebody, and about four hundred men rallied to him. He was killed, all his followers were dispersed, and it all came to nothing. 37 After him, Judas the Galilean appeared in the days of the census and led a band of people in revolt. He too was killed, and all his followers were scattered. 38 Therefore, in the present case I advise you: leave these men alone! Let them go! For if their purpose or activity is of human origin, it will fail. 39 But if it is from God, you will not be able to stop these men; you will only find yourselves fighting against God.'

40 His speech persuaded them. They called the apostles in and had them flogged. Then they ordered them not to speak in the name of Jesus, and let them go.

Undeterred by these miraculous events, the captain of the Temple guard rearrested the apostles and brought them before the Sanhedrin (verse 26). The previous encounter is recalled along with their warning: 'We gave you strict orders not to teach in this name' (verse 28). Their frustration is evident by the mention of their 'strict orders' (*parangelia parēngeilamen* – literally 'an order we ordered') and the additional statement, 'You have filled Jerusalem with your teaching and are determined to make us guilty of this man's blood.' It is an intriguing accusation. They clearly were responsible (along with the Roman authorities) for Jesus's death. Are they now trying to lay blame at the feet of the Romans, or – perhaps more likely – do they consider themselves innocent, since in their view Jesus's death was a just punishment? They are clearly unnerved by both the rapid spread of the apostolic teaching and the miracles, though they seem unable to respond properly to either.

One of the great offences of the gospel today is the idea that we may bear any guilt before a holy God. We would like to believe that we are basically moral and upstanding people whom God would accept. Any notion that we might be guilty before him is difficult to admit. Yet, if we are to accept the good news of Jesus the Saviour, we need to understand the bad news of human beings as guilty sinners before a holy God.

In reply, Peter reiterated his statement from Acts 4:18–20 – they were always obliged to obey God rather than man (verse 29). Further, Peter reasserted their guilt. They did kill Jesus by hanging him on a cross. This seems an allusion to Deuteronomy 21:23, which refers to the cursed state of the person who has been hanged (see also Galatians 3:13).[24] The leaders' failure to see the deeper reality of the curse that rested on Jesus and themselves prevented them from seeing their need of repentance and salvation. Yet God exalted him as 'Prince and Saviour'. The term translated as 'prince' (*archēgon*) was also used in 3:15 in describing Jesus as the 'author' of life. The 'author of life' is also Israel's 'Prince and Saviour'. Peter informed his hearers that Jesus's mission was to bring Israel to repentance. Is there even here an implicit invitation if only the leaders of Israel would listen? Peter again reiterated the fact that the apostles were witnesses of the events, as was the Spirit, by whom they were able to speak and work wonders.

Having heard this, the members of the Sanhedrin are described as being furious (*dieprionto*; see 7:54), desiring to put them to death (verse 33). At this point we see a fascinating intervention by a Pharisee named Gamaliel. Paul names Gamaliel as his instructor in Acts 22:3. Gamaliel, having put the apostles outside, appeals for moderation. He cites two historical instances of uprisings (led by Theudas and Judas the Galilean) which, in time, came to nothing.[25] His conclusion in verses 38–9 has caused some debate. He counsels his fellow members to leave the apostles

---

[24] Wall, *Acts*, 106.

[25] For further historical backgrounds to these movements, see Peterson, *Acts*, 225.

alone. If the movement is of human origin, it will fail. However, if it is from God, then they will be unable to oppose it and will find themselves opposing God himself. As Stott notes, this is not quite as wise as it might sound, since sometimes in God's providence evil prospers in the short run while the good and godly suffer. The 'Gamaliel principle is not a reliable index to what is from God and what is not'.[26]

Commentators disagree as to whether Gamaliel is in some measure sympathetic to the early Christians, or whether he is simply being a pragmatist confronted with their growing popularity.[27] Is he a sympathetic seeker or a skilful politician? Luke's narrative gives little away. This may be one of those narrative ambiguities that invites the reader to consider their own response. Will we be one who finds pragmatic grounds for sidelining the claims of Jesus, or might we be the sympathetic hearer drawn closer to consider his teaching. It will be one of Gamaliel's students (Paul) who will show us that even the most zealous opponent can change their mind, find forgiveness and find their whole life transformed by the risen Lord.

Gamaliel's intervention gave a temporary reprieve, but not without a painful and humiliating flogging (verse 40).[28]

Acts 5:41–2: The unstoppable word

41 The apostles left the Sanhedrin, rejoicing because they had been counted worthy of suffering disgrace for the Name. **42** Day after day, in the temple courts and from house to house, they never stopped teaching and proclaiming the good news that Jesus is the Messiah.

---

[26] Stott, *Acts*, 118.

[27] Barrett describes him as a 'good Pharisee' who is willing to 'wait and see' (*Acts 1–14*, 281). Witherington thinks it is clear that Luke is presenting Gamaliel in a favourable light (*Acts*, 233). Personally, I am less convinced. Johnson makes a persuasive case that Gamaliel is seeking to keep the peace among the people but is no more persuaded than the others that Jesus is any more credible than Theudas or Judas. *Acts*, 99–103. See also John A. Darr, 'Irenic or Ironic? Another look at Gamaliel before the Sanhedrin (Acts 5:33–42)', in *Literary Studies in Luke–Acts: Essays in Honor of Joseph B. Tyson*, eds Richard P. Thompson and Thomas E. Phillips (Mercer University Press: Macon, 1998), 121–39.

[28] This may have been the forty lashes minus one prescribed in Deuteronomy 25:3. Bock suggests it would have been done across the back and chest with a three-stranded leather strap, leaving the subject seriously injured. Bock, *Acts*, 252. Marshall suggests that some even died from such a punishment. *Acts*, 124.

Remarkably, Luke reports how the apostles rejoiced, having been 'counted worthy of suffering disgrace for the Name' (verse 41). Those of us who know little of physical persecution must always remember to be in prayer for the persecuted church, that they too may know joy in the sufferings. It is hard for us to imagine, but critical to pray for. Having been released, they pay little heed to the orders of the Sanhedrin as they continue 'day after day, in the temple courts and from house to house' to teach and proclaim the good news that Jesus is the Messiah.

As Witherington notes, the apostles 'win by losing'.[29] This is Luther's 'theology of the cross' versus the 'theology of glory'. The theologian of glory loves power, wisdom and status. Yet God is known and manifested through the suffering and shame of the cross. It is the 'way of the cross' that looks foolish to the world yet is the ultimate manifestation of God's glory. The church must never lose this perspective of rejoicing in disgrace.[30] As Witherington puts it, the 'suffering and even death of disciples, like that of their Master, doesn't lead to the squelching of the Jesus movement, it leads to its success and expansion'.[31]

Venkataraman also notes here the apostles' non-violent resistance.[32] They submit to their arrest and even their flogging, yet they still speak at every opportunity. It is a noteworthy feature of their encounter with opposition that they do not resort to using the weapons of the world. Instead, they entrust themselves to 'him who judges justly' (1 Peter 2:23).

This brief summary gives us a snapshot of the life and structure of the early church. It appears that larger groups gathered in the Temple courts and smaller gatherings were held in homes. If we also consider the summaries from 2:42–7, 4:32–5 and 5:12–16, we can see that proclamation, prayer, mutual care and fellowship, and signs and wonders were all significant parts of the community's life. Their rapid growth and the increased persecution may explain why their times together were a mix of 'temple courts and from house to house'.

Today it is easy to find strong opinions on the size and structure of churches. Some are strong advocates of the attractional power of the large crowd ('temple courts'). Others think small house churches more faithfully represent the early church's pattern of life ('house to house').

---

[29] Witherington, *Acts*, 229.
[30] See Martin Luther, 'The Heidelberg Disputation', xx-xxi in *Luther: Early Theological Works* (London: SCM, 1962), 290–91.
[31] Witherington, *Acts*, 229.
[32] Venkataraman, 'Acts', in *SABC*, 1464.

It is noteworthy that throughout Acts we see little in the way of hard prescription on such matters.

While there is ecclesiological gold to be mined in the book of Acts, we need to be careful that we are not over-prescriptive. It seems there was a degree of freedom that enabled early Christian communities to respond to their own particular contexts within the constraints of the circumstances and resources at hand. This is a point we shall return to as we progress through Luke's account. At this point it is simply worth acknowledging that ecclesiological preference is not the same as biblical mandate, and we need to be careful not to make our interpretation of Scripture bear more weight than it can carry. The history of global Christianity would suggest that, at different times and in different places, the models of 'temple courts' and 'house to house' (or a mix of the two) have both proved to be used by God. We ought therefore to be slow to judge someone else's different approach to this issue.

What is clear is that the power and presence of God continues to accompany his church, bringing gospel growth out of even the most challenging of circumstances.

6

Growth and Grief

ACTS 6:1–8:3

In Acts 6 we see two further obstacles to the growth of the word, one internal and one external. In Acts 4–5 we observed the escalation of persecution from warning to beating. As we move forward in the narrative, we shall see further escalation in the martyrdom of Stephen. We also noted in Acts 5 the threat to the community from within through the corruption of Ananias and Sapphira. Luke recorded the satanic forces at work in this event, from which we may infer that Satan stands behind all the various oppositions the church faces (5:3).[1]

Here, in chapter 6, we see another threat from within, related to the distribution of food. Acts 3–7 show us the power of the world, the flesh and the devil in their attempt to hinder the advance of the gospel. However, we also see in these chapters that the word continues to spread, and the church continues to grow despite the outward and inward struggles. These post-Pentecost chapters equip the church with a sense of both reality and confidence.

1. Grumbling over food • Acts 6:1–7

The choosing of the seven

6 In those days when the number of disciples was increasing, the Hellenistic Jews[a] among them complained against the Hebraic Jews because their widows were being overlooked in the daily distribution of food. 2 So the Twelve gathered all the disciples together and said, 'It would not be right for us to neglect the ministry of the word of God in order to wait on tables. 3 Brothers and sisters, choose seven men from among you who are known to be full of the Spirit and

---

[1] Calvin describes this incident also as part of the 'subtleties of Satan'. *Acts*, 230. Stott describes this attack as 'the cleverest of the three' – the three being persecution, corruption and distraction. *Acts*, 120. The apostles demonstrate in this section not just a sensitivity to the Holy Spirit, but also an alertness to the schemes of Satan.

wisdom. We will turn this responsibility over to them [4] and will give our attention to prayer and the ministry of the word.'

[5] This proposal pleased the whole group. They chose Stephen, a man full of faith and of the Holy Spirit; also Philip, Procorus, Nicanor, Timon, Parmenas, and Nicolas from Antioch, a convert to Judaism. [6] They presented these men to the apostles, who prayed and laid their hands on them.

[7] So the word of God spread. The number of disciples in Jerusalem increased rapidly, and a large number of priests became obedient to the faith.

In verse 1, Luke introduces the problem to the reader. As the number of disciples was increasing, a dispute arose between the Hellenistic Jews and the Hebraic Jews, with the former claiming that 'their widows were being overlooked in the daily distribution of food'. Here we see an example of the self-sacrificial generosity described in the summary statements of Acts 2:42–7 and 4:32–5. We also see here that those statements should not be read as some sort of utopian ideal. Luke does not shy away from the reality that the early church's life together had some real struggles as they grew together. I remember hearing an old preacher once say, 'There is no perfect church, and if you find one, don't join it, as you'll spoil it.' It's always tempting to believe that the grass is greener in someone else's church. This side of heaven there will always be struggles and tensions over all sorts of issues. Church leaders do well to see (and help their people to see) that this is the ordinary Christian life, learning and growing together, side by side.

This particular difficulty within the church was dangerous for three reasons. First, and most obviously, people were being neglected in the caregiving of the church. They had already exemplified the Deuteronomy 15 ideal – no needy persons – and so any person neglected was a problem. Their social concern for the needy was not seen as an irrelevant distraction from the real business of gospel proclamation. Rather, the care of the needy was so important it needed a solution. Meeting material need could not be ignored or dismissed. It was an integral part of what it meant to be the renewed people of God, living in the power of God's Spirit, fulfilling her vocation to be a light for the world, to the glory of God and for the sake of the nations.[2]

---

[2] See Alan J. Thompson, *One Lord, One People: The Unity of the Church in Acts in its Literary Setting* (LNTS; London: T&T Clark, 2008), 94. We can also see God's concern for the care of the most vulnerable in passages such as Leviticus 19; 25; Deuteronomy 16; 26; Isaiah 1; 10; Jeremiah 7; 22; Ezekiel 22; Micah 6; Malachi 3. See also Wall, *Acts*, 111. Moreover, Luke's Gospel has shown us God's concern for the vulnerable: see Luke 2:36–8; 4:24–6; 7:12; 18:1–8; 21:2–3.

Second, we see that a particularly concerning part of this tension was not just in meeting a need, but also in resolving a tension rooted in differing ethnic identities.[3] The gospel has power to bring people of different ethnicities together into the one family of Christ (Ephesians 2:11–22). A failure to address this issue may have undermined or undone the transforming and unifying power of the gospel.[4] This would have been catastrophic for the community commissioned to go to the ends of the earth. This is an ever-present danger facing the church in every generation. It is all too easy to see the needs of people similar to ourselves, and to miss or even overlook others. This happens with social status, gender and ethnicity. The church must be at the forefront of identifying and addressing such tensions, particularly within the church. This requires much humility and frequent repentance as we acknowledge the ways in which we all too easily notice the needs of some more than others. Ethnic divisions have plagued the history of the church and have significant power, if unaddressed, to hinder and undermine the church's good news of inclusivity for every tribe and tongue and nation. This problem needed urgent action.

The third danger here can be seen by observing one particular word Luke employs. In verse 1 he uses the Greek word *gongysmos* ('complained'). This word appears just eight times in the Greek translation of the Old Testament (five times in Exodus 16; twice in Numbers 17). In Exodus 16, just weeks after leaving Egypt, the whole community grumbled against their leaders, wishing they could be back in Egypt where they had food. As a result, God provided food for them, in the form of the manna and quail. In Numbers 17 we see the story of God causing Aaron's staff to bud. It is an act done in response to the constant grumbling of Israel against Moses and Aaron – in particular the incident from the previous chapter with the rebellion of Korah, Dathan and Abiram (Numbers 16). Both of these incidents of grumbling threatened the existence of God's people. The grumbling and division in these cases required divine intervention to prevent disaster. When Luke uses this rare term for the Hellenists 'grumbling', we as readers ought to see just how high the stakes are at this point. This could have meant the beginning of the end of the community still in its infancy, without the right sort of intervention.

---

[3] Witherington presents an extended discussion regarding the identity of the 'Hellenists' and the likely origins of the tensions that may have existed between the groups. See Witherington, *Acts*, 240–47.

[4] Marshall suggests that there may even be the danger of a division at this point into two separate groups of Christians – an early church split based on cultural differences. *Acts*, 125.

What is interesting in this passage is the response to the grumbling. Unlike in Exodus 16 or Numbers 17 we do not see either miraculous provision of food or miraculous attestation of the leaders. Nor do we see Peter and the apostles rebuke the Hellenistic Jews for grumbling. As one writer has said, we don't see an Acts 6 problem addressed with an Acts 5 solution![5] We may not have been surprised if Peter made another speech, appealing to those Old Testament wilderness years, encouraging the people to stop grumbling against one another.

The Twelve here demonstrate something critically important for the ongoing health of the mission. They exercise insightful leadership.[6] Notably, the problem as presented is not met with rebuke. Rather, Peter and the other apostles see the issue as one of logistics – they recognise the changing size dynamics and new challenges that often accompany growing churches. Correct diagnosis was critical to an effective solution.

In verse 2 they gather the disciples and begin with a clear understanding and articulation of their own particular responsibility: 'It would not be right for us to neglect the ministry of the word of God in order to wait on tables.' Ministers of the word should not be distracted by every call on their attention. Their unique responsibility cannot be delegated or pushed to one side. Gospel ministers must ensure they give significant time to the preparation and delivery of faithful word ministry, and to prayer. Many of us are drawn to leaning on our elbows, pouring over our books. We should equally be on our knees, praying for fruit from our labour in teaching. Stott notes, 'If [Satan] could preoccupy the apostles with social administration, which though essential was not their calling, they would neglect their God-given responsibilities to pray and to preach, and so leave the church without any defence against false doctrine.'[7]

But notice what they do not say. They do not say, 'It would not be right for *the church* to neglect the ministry of the word of God in order to wait on tables.' They do not view compassion ministries as a distraction for the church, and something with which the church should not get involved. And they do not view 'waiting on tables' as somehow inferior to the ministry of the word. Rather, they see compassion ministries as something that they, the Twelve, should not get involved with. That was

[5] Ray Evans, *Ready, Steady, Grow: Equipping Today's Gospel Churches* (Nottingham: InterVarsity Press, 2014), 61–81.
[6] For an excellent analysis of the leadership seen in Acts 6:1–7, see Evans, *Ready, Steady, Grow*, 61–81.
[7] Stott, *Acts*, 120.

not their calling or ministry. They had to devote themselves to the ministry of the word and prayer (6:4). Yet the issue was so important that they were determined to find a good solution to the problem. Any church leader that appeals to Acts 6:1–7 as evidence that the church should not concern itself with social action has completely missed the point. The church should be involved in such ministries, and it is the leaders' responsibility to find a way to make it happen, while not neglecting their particular responsibility to minister the word and pray.

In verse 3 they encourage the believers to identify and appoint seven men, 'full of the Spirit and wisdom', and the Twelve would give them the responsibility for addressing the problem. Three things are worth noting here. First, the process of appointment involves the whole community. It is not just the Twelve who appoint another seven. It is the community who together recognise those whom God has given – 'full of the Spirit and wisdom'. It is too early in the life of the church to view this as an enshrined and developed form of congregational government. Nonetheless, it is suggestive to all church leaders. Whatever model of church government is in use, it seems the voice of the congregation should play a significant role.[8]

Second, these leaders are to be men of character. The task appears to be mainly material and administrative. Yet we can never neatly divide spiritual and material need. These leaders needed a level of spiritual maturity to minister to physical needs. As we will see in Acts 7–8, at least two of these men seem to have been able evangelists also (see 7:8–10; 8:5–8). We see in the appointment of these leaders that character trumps competence every time.

Third, these leaders are empowered. The responsibility is entrusted to them. They are not micromanaged by the Twelve, and this is not mere delegation of an unwelcome menial task. Leadership requires genuine empowerment of others to take responsibility in significant ministry areas. Too many leaders try to hold on to power. Here the Twelve model the sort of leadership that truly empowers others in a task.[9]

Many have debated whether we should see the seven as the first

---

[8] Calvin notes the importance of the role of the laity and the public laying on of hands in establishing office bearers. These two elements (seen in Acts 6) demonstrate the unity of the church and the solemnity of the office. *Institutes* 4.3.15-16.
[9] Land notices the diffusion of power and authority from the apostles to the community and to the newly appointed deacons. See Darin H. Land, *The Diffusion of Ecclesiastical Authority: Sociological Dimensions of Leadership in the Book of Acts* (PTMS 90; Eugene: Pickwick, 2008), 152–67.

deacons. It is true that the noun and verb form for 'deacon' (*diakonia/diakoneo*), are used (6:1, 2, 4). However, it is also true that the seven are never actually referred to as 'deacons'. Interestingly, the Twelve describe their own ministry as a *diakonia* of the word (verse 4). It seems that what is described here is a group of people who fulfil a particular ministry task that in time would be more formally recognised as an office (see Philippians 1:1; 1 Timothy 3:8–13). It would perhaps be better to view the seven as 'proto-deacons' whose ministry would play a significant part in shaping and formalising what was later recognised as an office within the church.[10]

The proposal of the Twelve pleased the group and they appointed the seven men, who included, it would seem, Greek speakers and one Gentile convert.[11] The apostles prayed and laid hands on them, further signifying the importance of this ministry.[12] The result of the wise leadership of the Twelve is reported in verse 7: 'So the word of God spread. The number of disciples in Jerusalem increased rapidly, and a large number of priests became obedient to the faith.'[13] Even those most opposed in previous chapters (the priests) are being drawn into the community of faith. God is powerful to save those who look most opposed and least likely to come to him. We may wonder how the conversion of priests in significant numbers would have appeared to the Temple authorities. What might their reaction be in the chapters that follow?

It is worth noting here the missional significance of the church's compassion ministry. Whether outsiders witnessed or benefited from such ministries is a debatable point. It seems that outsiders would have at the very least witnessed large-scale and radical caregiving, and that some of the boundary lines at this stage may have been blurred. Therefore, it is

---

[10] It is interesting that many modern commentators dismiss any idea that Luke is describing the office of deacons here, whereas this view was commonplace in the history of the church. See Chrysostom, *Homilies*, in ACCS 5:70; Ammonius, *Catena*, in ACCS 5:71; Calvin, *Acts*, 229; Calvin, *Institutes* 4.3.9.

[11] Peterson, *Acts*, 234–5.

[12] Peterson notes that the laying on of hands is 'associated with the giving of the Spirit in 8:17–19; 19:6, and with healing in Luke 13:13; Acts 9:12, 17'. *Acts*, 235. It is clear from 6:3 that the seven already possessed the Spirit, but the laying on of hands seems to be linked to an appointment to task and may explain why we begin to see men outside the apostolic group perform signs and wonders (see Acts 2:43; 4:33; 5:12; 6:8; 8:6–7).

[13] More literally 'the word of God grew' (*ēuxanen*). This sort of summary statement will appear again in 9:31; 12:24; 16:5; 19:20.

likely that outsiders too would have benefited from the generosity and care of the community.[14] We have already noted that at least Philip and Stephen have evangelistic impact in Acts 7–8. Here is another example of word and deed belonging and working together. It is the whole life of the people of God, engaged in holistic mission, which is used by God to reach many and grow his church. The church must always hold these elements together if she is to be a God-glorifying and missionally effective outpost of the kingdom.

Stott's concluding reflection on this passage is both provocative and challenging:

> We do a great disservice to the church whenever we refer to the pastorate as 'the ministry'. . . . This use of the definite article implies that the ordained pastorate is the only ministry there is. But *diakonia* is a generic word for service . . . All Christians without exception, being followers of him who came 'not to be served, but to serve', are themselves called to ministry, indeed to give their lives in ministry . . . We need to recover this vision of the wide diversity of ministries to which God calls his people.[15]

This passage is a striking portrait of the challenges faced by the early church and their response to them. We see a church serious about tackling issues of social justice and compassion, exercising wise and insightful leadership, while not losing focus on the necessity of the ministry of word and prayer.

What a rare and unusual picture of a church that combines excellence in all three areas – ministry, compassion and leadership. This is surely a challenge to us today who may be good at one or two of these. The challenge to be a church in which these things are held together within the emphases of concern and ministry remains a difficult one. Yet the word spreads, and the number of disciples increases where mission, leadership, compassion, the word and prayer are held together.

---

[14] For more on this, see Salter, *Mission in Action*, 207; I. Howard Marshall, 'Luke's Social Gospel: The Social Theology of Luke–Acts', in *Transforming the World: The Gospel and Social Responsibility*, eds Jamie A. Grant and Dewi A. Hughes (Nottingham: InterVarsity Press, 2009), 125.

[15] Stott, *Acts*, 122.

2. The first martyr • Acts 6:8–8:3

Here we see the third escalation in the external opposition. The threats of 4:21 became a beating in 5:40, and here in this next section we shall hear more of Stephen (introduced in 6:5), the first Christian martyr.

In addition, the next few chapters will introduce the counterpoint to the increase in persecution. We shall observe the beginnings of the mission beyond Jerusalem as we see three remarkable witnesses (Stephen, Philip and Peter – Acts 7–8, 10) and three remarkable conversions (the Ethiopian eunuch, Saul and Cornelius – Acts 8–10).[16]

Acts 6:8–15: Stephen is opposed

Stephen seized

8 Now Stephen, a man full of God's grace and power, performed great wonders and signs among the people. **9** Opposition arose, however, from members of the Synagogue of the Freedmen (as it was called) – Jews of Cyrene and Alexandria as well as the provinces of Cilicia and Asia – who began to argue with Stephen. **10** But they could not stand up against the wisdom the Spirit gave him as he spoke.

11 Then they secretly persuaded some men to say, 'We have heard Stephen speak blasphemous words against Moses and against God.'

12 So they stirred up the people and the elders and the teachers of the law. They seized Stephen and brought him before the Sanhedrin. **13** They produced false witnesses, who testified, 'This fellow never stops speaking against this holy place and against the law. **14** For we have heard him say that this Jesus of Nazareth will destroy this place and change the customs Moses handed down to us.'

15 All who were sitting in the Sanhedrin looked intently at Stephen, and they saw that his face was like the face of an angel.

In Acts 6:5 Stephen is described as a man 'full of faith and of the Holy Spirit'. Here in 6:8 Stephen is further described as a 'man full of God's grace and power' and we are told he 'performed great wonders and signs among the people'. The powerful witness of Stephen drew attention from a group called the Synagogue of the Freedmen.[17] They began to argue

---

[16] Stott, *Acts*, 125.

[17] Wall, *Acts*, 121, describes these men as part of a religious movement within diaspora Judaism. They were likely Roman citizens and may thus have held some kind of political influence.

with Stephen, but they were unable to stand up against 'the wisdom the Spirit gave him'. This reminds us of Jesus's words in Luke 21:15 and anticipates the Spirit-given speech he was about to deliver.

Since they were unable to match him in debate, the opponents of Stephen stirred up others to accuse him of blaspheming against Moses (a reference to the Law) and against God.[18] Having dragged him before the Sanhedrin – the third time we've seen this court in action – false witnesses are produced who accuse him of speaking against the Temple and the Law. Luke is clear who the real criminals are here. Specifically, they accuse him of having said that Jesus of Nazareth would 'destroy this place and change the customs Moses handed down to us'. Before we hear Stephen's reply, Luke gives a tantalising detail: 'his face was like the face of an angel'. This may be a way of linking Stephen to Moses (see Exodus 34:29), thus making him, not his opponents, the right interpreter of Moses.[19]

Acts 7:1–53: Stephen's speech

Stephen's speech to the Sanhedrin

7 Then the high priest asked Stephen, 'Are these charges true?'

2 To this he replied: 'Brothers and fathers, listen to me! The God of glory appeared to our father Abraham while he was still in Mesopotamia, before he lived in Harran. 3 "Leave your country and your people," God said, "and go to the land I will show you."[a]

4 'So he left the land of the Chaldeans and settled in Harran. After the death of his father, God sent him to this land where you are now living. 5 He gave him no inheritance here, not even enough ground to set his foot on. But God promised him that he and his descendants after him would possess the land, even though at that time Abraham had no child. 6 God spoke to him in this way: "For four hundred years your descendants will be strangers in a country not their own, and they will be enslaved and ill-treated. 7 But I will punish the nation they serve as slaves," God said, "and afterwards they will come out of that country and worship me in this place."[b] 8 Then he gave Abraham the covenant of circumcision. And Abraham became the father of Isaac and circumcised him eight days after his

---

[18] Barrett, *Acts 1–14*, 334, notes these are new charges, not brought previously against the Twelve.
[19] Wall, *Acts*, 123. Wall argues that Stephen's speech is a 'midrash on the biblical traditions of Moses for the "last days"'. There is also evidence of Luke shaping the speech around conventions of rhetoric.

birth. Later Isaac became the father of Jacob, and Jacob became the father of the twelve patriarchs.

9 'Because the patriarchs were jealous of Joseph, they sold him as a slave into Egypt. But God was with him 10 and rescued him from all his troubles. He gave Joseph wisdom and enabled him to gain the goodwill of Pharaoh king of Egypt. So Pharaoh made him ruler over Egypt and all his palace.

11 'Then a famine struck all Egypt and Canaan, bringing great suffering, and our ancestors could not find food. 12 When Jacob heard that there was grain in Egypt, he sent our forefathers on their first visit. 13 On their second visit, Joseph told his brothers who he was, and Pharaoh learned about Joseph's family. 14 After this, Joseph sent for his father Jacob and his whole family, seventy-five in all. 15 Then Jacob went down to Egypt, where he and our ancestors died. 16 Their bodies were brought back to Shechem and placed in the tomb that Abraham had bought from the sons of Hamor at Shechem for a certain sum of money.

17 'As the time drew near for God to fulfil his promise to Abraham, the number of our people in Egypt had greatly increased. 18 Then "a new king, to whom Joseph meant nothing, came to power in Egypt".c 19 He dealt treacherously with our people and oppressed our ancestors by forcing them to throw out their newborn babies so that they would die.

20 'At that time Moses was born, and he was no ordinary child.d For three months he was cared for by his family. 21 When he was placed outside, Pharaoh's daughter took him and brought him up as her own son. 22 Moses was educated in all the wisdom of the Egyptians and was powerful in speech and action.

23 'When Moses was forty years old, he decided to visit his own people, the Israelites. 24 He saw one of them being ill-treated by an Egyptian, so he went to his defence and avenged him by killing the Egyptian. 25 Moses thought that his own people would realise that God was using him to rescue them, but they did not. 26 The next day Moses came upon two Israelites who were fighting. He tried to reconcile them by saying, "Men, you are brothers; why do you want to hurt each other?"

27 'But the man who was ill-treating the other pushed Moses aside and said, "Who made you ruler and judge over us? 28 Are you thinking of killing me as you killed the Egyptian yesterday?"e 29 When Moses heard this, he fled to Midian, where he settled as a foreigner and had two sons.

30 'After forty years had passed, an angel appeared to Moses in the flames of a burning bush in the desert near Mount Sinai. 31 When he saw this, he was amazed at the sight. As he went over to get a closer look, he heard the Lord say: 32 "I am the God of your fathers, the God of Abraham, Isaac and Jacob."f Moses trembled with fear and did not dare to look.

33 'Then the Lord said to him, "Take

off your sandals, for the place where you are standing is holy ground. **34** I have indeed seen the oppression of my people in Egypt. I have heard their groaning and have come down to set them free. Now come, I will send you back to Egypt."**g**

35 'This is the same Moses they had rejected with the words, "Who made you ruler and judge?" He was sent to be their ruler and deliverer by God himself, through the angel who appeared to him in the bush. **36** He led them out of Egypt and performed wonders and signs in Egypt, at the Red Sea and for forty years in the wilderness.

37 'This is the Moses who told the Israelites, "God will raise up for you a prophet like me from your own people."**h** **38** He was in the assembly in the wilderness, with the angel who spoke to him on Mount Sinai, and with our ancestors; and he received living words to pass on to us.

39 'But our ancestors refused to obey him. Instead, they rejected him and in their hearts turned back to Egypt. **40** They told Aaron, "Make us gods who will go before us. As for this fellow Moses who led us out of Egypt – we don't know what has happened to him!"**i** **41** That was the time they made an idol in the form of a calf. They brought sacrifices to it and revelled in what their own hands had made. **42** But God turned away from them and gave them over to the worship of the sun, moon and stars. This agrees with what is written in the book of the prophets:

' "Did you bring me sacrifices and
offerings
for forty years in the wilderness,
people of Israel?
43 You have taken up the tabernacle
of Molek
and the star of your god
Rephan,
the idols you made to worship.
Therefore I will send you into
exile"**j** beyond Babylon.

44 'Our ancestors had the tabernacle of the covenant law with them in the wilderness. It had been made as God directed Moses, according to the pattern he had seen. **45** After receiving the tabernacle, our ancestors under Joshua brought it with them when they took the land from the nations God drove out before them. It remained in the land until the time of David, **46** who enjoyed God's favour and asked that he might provide a dwelling-place for the God of Jacob.**k** **47** But it was Solomon who built a house for him.

48 'However, the Most High does not live in houses made by human hands. As the prophet says:

49 ' "Heaven is my throne,
and the earth is my footstool.
What kind of house will you build
for me?
says the Lord.
Or where will my resting place
be?
50 Has not my hand made all these
things?"**l**

51 'You stiff-necked people! Your hearts and ears are still uncircumcised.

You are just like your ancestors: you always resist the Holy Spirit! **52**Was there ever a prophet your ancestors did not persecute? They even killed those who predicted the coming of the Righteous One. And now you have betrayed and murdered him - **53**you who have received the law that was given through angels but have not obeyed it.'

a 3 Gen. 12:1
b 7 Gen. 15:13,14
c 18 Exodus 1:8
d 20 Or *was fair in the sight of God*
e 28 Exodus 2:14
f 32 Exodus 3:6
g 34 Exodus 3:5,7,8,10
h 37 Deut. 18:15
i 40 Exodus 32:1
j 43 Amos 5:25-27 (see Septuagint)
k 46 Some early manuscripts *the house of Jacob*
l 50 Isaiah 66:1,2

Stephen's speech is the longest in the book of Acts.[20] It serves as a defence against the two particular charges he was faced with: 'speaking against this holy place and against the law' (6:13).[21] The speech charts the course of Israel's history to demonstrate two things. First, God's presence with his people has never been confined to one specific holy place.[22] To think in such terms would be to limit God's presence and purpose in ways he himself had not.[23] Second, Israel's track record in obeying the Law should give caution to anyone who thinks they alone have understood and obeyed its intent and trajectory. These twin emphases can be seen in the following two tables:

PERSON(S)	PLACES	DIVINE PRESENCE
Abraham (7:2)	Mesopotamia (7:2)	'The God of glory appeared' (7:2)
	Harran (7:4)	'God spoke to him' (7:6)
Joseph (7:9)	Egypt (7:9)	'But God was with him' (7:9)

[20] Bock, *Acts*, 276.
[21] Tannehill, *Narrative Unity*, 84–5; Green, *The Word of His Grace*, 64.
[22] Stott, *Acts*, 139, describes Israel's God as a 'pilgrim God, who is not restricted to any one place'.
[23] Green suggests Stephen's speech is concerned with 'theological geography'. His summary of the main contours of Stephen's speech is excellent. *The Word of His Grace*, 64–7.

Patriarchs (7:11–16)	Egypt (7:14–15) Shechem (7:16)	God is getting ready to fulfil his promise to Abraham (7:17)
Moses (7:20–44)	Egypt (7:20–8) Midian (7:29–34)	God appears to Moses in the burning bush (7:30–34) – 'holy ground' (7:33)
Israel (7:35–44)	Wilderness (7:36) Sinai (7:38) Canaan (7:45) Exile (7:43)	'the angel who spoke to him [Moses] on Mount Sinai' (7:38) 'the nations God drove out' (7:45)
David and Solomon (7:45–7)	'the land' (7:45)	'enjoyed God's favour' (7:46)
	heaven and earth (7:49)	'heaven is my throne, and the earth is my footstool . . .' (7:49–50)

Incident of rebellion against God
Patriarchs rejected Joseph – 7:9
Moses rejected by the Israelites – 7:25–8
'This is the same Moses they had rejected' – 7:35
'Our ancestors refused to obey him' [Moses] – 7:39
The golden calf incident – 7:40–42
Further idolatry – 7:43
Resisting the Spirit, persecuting the prophets, killing God's Messiah – 7:51–3

We can see most of the space within the speech is given over to the life of Moses. This makes sense given the charge that Stephen was blaspheming against Moses and speaking against the Law. The main emphases of the speech demonstrate that most of God's historical covenantal dealings happened outside the land (therefore God cannot be confined to the Temple), and Israel's history in relation to God's Law is one of rejection and disobedience. Any charge against Stephen misunderstood both the

Temple as symbolic of God's presence and the Law as pointing towards the need for the Messiah.[24]

The punchline of the speech is seen in Acts 7:48–53 where Stephen directly answers the two charges: 'the Most High does not live in houses made by human hands' (verse 48), and, 'you who have received the law that was given through angels but have not obeyed it' (verse 53).

He describes his accusers as being 'stiff-necked' with uncircumcised hearts. In this way they are no better than the generations of Israel in the past who rejected Moses, disobeyed God's Law and resisted God's Spirit. It is they, not Stephen, who have blasphemed against God in their own misunderstanding of his presence and his Law. They have persecuted the prophets, killed those who predicted the coming of the Messiah and killed the Son of God now enthroned at the right hand of the Father (7:51–3). As Stephen reaches the climax of his speech, he has turned the tables on his opponents.[25] It is not he who is on trial before them, but rather they who are on trial before God. Stephen is critical of neither the Temple nor the Law, but rather he is critical of the leaders who have disobeyed God's Law and attempted to restrict God's presence to the Temple.[26]

Acts 7:54–8:3: Stephen is stoned to death

The stoning of Stephen

54 When the members of the Sanhedrin heard this, they were furious and gnashed their teeth at him. 55 But Stephen, full of the Holy Spirit, looked up to heaven and saw the glory of God, and Jesus standing at the right hand of God. 56 'Look,' he said, 'I see heaven open and the Son of Man standing at the right hand of God.'

57 At this they covered their ears and, yelling at the top of their voices, they all rushed at him, 58 dragged him out of the city and began to stone him. Meanwhile, the witnesses laid their coats at the feet of a young man named Saul.

59 While they were stoning him, Stephen prayed, 'Lord Jesus, receive my spirit.' 60 Then he fell on his knees and cried out, 'Lord, do not hold this sin against them.' When he had said this, he fell asleep.

---

[24] Green, *The Word of His Grace*, 67.

[25] Tannehill states, 'His speech is not calculated to secure acquittal on the charges; instead, he turns the charges into an indictment of his audience.' *Narrative Unity*, 85.

[26] Witherington, *Acts*, 261–4. This is perhaps the most significant step thus far in the separation of the early church from Judaism.

8 And Saul approved of their killing him.

The church persecuted and scattered

On that day a great persecution broke out against the church in Jerusalem, and all except the apostles were scattered throughout Judea and Samaria. **2** Godly men buried Stephen and mourned deeply for him. **3** But Saul began to destroy the church. Going from house to house, he dragged off both men and women and put them in prison.

The members of the Sanhedrin are described by Luke as 'furious' as they 'gnashed their teeth at him'.[27] At this point Stephen saw a vision of Jesus, standing at the right hand of the Father in heaven. At this they dragged him out and began to stone him. As Stott observes, the Romans had removed the Jews' right of capital punishment. Here they heap further guilt upon themselves with a 'mob-lynching'.[28] We are introduced to a young man named Saul who is holding the coats. Stephen, in words reminiscent of Jesus (Luke 23:46, 34), says, 'Lord Jesus, receive my spirit,' and, 'Lord, do not hold this sin against them.'[29] At this he fell asleep. And Saul approved of their killing him. As readers, we know that God will hear Stephen's prayer, at least as far as Saul is concerned.

Following the martyrdom of Stephen, 'a great persecution broke out against the church'. Luke tells us that 'all except the apostles were scattered throughout Judea and Samaria' (8:1). Here is one of those verses that is double-edged. On the one hand, the scattering of the church would make an initial reader wonder if this would be the death-knell of the church. On the other hand, we recall Jesus's words in Acts 1:8: 'you will be my witnesses in Jerusalem, in all Judea and Samaria, and to the ends of the earth'. Here is the fulfilment, albeit by unexpected means, of Jesus's commission given in 1:8. Tannehill states, 'Here again there is an ironic turn. The efforts of the Sanhedrin to halt the preaching of the word . . . result in the spread of the word in Judea, Samaria, and Antioch.'[30] Green notes that God's chosen people were once again about to find themselves

---

[27] The words translated as 'furious' could be more literally translated as 'cut to the heart' (*dieprionto tais kardiais*).

[28] Stott, *Acts*, 142.

[29] Witherington, *Acts*, 253, enumerates the parallels between the trials of Stephen and Jesus – the trial before the Sanhedrin, false witnesses, charge of blasphemy, committal of spirit and intercession for enemies. Stephen is a righteous sufferer, as was Jesus.

[30] Tannehill, *Narrative Unity*, 101.

in the wilderness outside the land.[31] Given Stephen's speech, that now seems not a disaster, but part of God's plan for the nations.

Saul is attempting to destroy the church, imprisoning men and women. Again, for the reader familiar with where the story is heading, it is hard to avoid a wry smile, knowing it will be the same man who will perhaps do more to build the church than any of the other apostles. God is working in painful and surprising ways to advance the kingdom. Luke 'introduces a pattern of events that will be repeated in other contexts: rejection in one place becomes the opportunity for people elsewhere to receive the gospel and become part of the messianic community'.[32]

There are a number of things here in this section, from Acts 6:8 to 8:3, that are worth noting in our understanding and application. The following list is not intended to be prescriptive or exhaustive. These are simply twelve things worth drawing out of this rich section.

First, and most obviously, God's purposes for the salvation of humanity do not begin at the incarnation. Stephen's recounting of salvation history demonstrates God's purposes to bring blessing to all humanity through his election of the seed of Abraham. The fulfilment of the Abrahamic covenant is the event to which the rest of biblical history points. Hermeneutically, we read the Bible as one story charting God's plan and purpose to bless the nations through Abraham's seed.

Second, God's purposes can take strange and unexpected turns. If anyone is commended in Stephen's speech, it is those outside the covenant people. It is the Egyptians who treat Joseph and Moses well. It is in unexpected places that God meets with people like Abraham, Joseph and Moses. God uses persecution and figures like Saul to advance the gospel. The course of biblical history repeatedly demonstrates that 'God moves in a mysterious way, his wonders to perform'.[33]

Third, God is present with his people and is not confined to certain places or persons. Any notion that God was confined to the Temple was simply mistaken. Sometimes people today still think of God's presence as being especially tied to particular buildings, or holy sites, or even a

---

[31] Green, *The Word of His Grace*, 68.

[32] Peterson, *Acts*, 275.

[33] William Cowper (1731–1800), 'God Moves in a Mysterious Way' (public domain).

special class of professional ministers. Stephen's speech disabuses us of such theologies.

Fourth, the presence and work of the Spirit did not begin at Pentecost. Stephen condemns his listeners as they are just like their ancestors: 'you always resist the Holy Spirit' (7:51). The Spirit had been at work throughout Israel's history to lead, anoint, empower and bring God's word to the prophets. Pentecost brings a democratisation of the Spirit, and initiates his personal permanent presence with every believer, but we must not think that pre-Pentecost the Spirit had not been present with God's people.

Fifth, the promise of the Messiah did not begin with the latter prophets. In 7:37 Stephen refers to Deuteronomy 18:15 – the promise that God would raise up a prophet like Moses. Just as Israel of old had rejected Moses, so the Jewish leaders of Stephen's day had rejected the 'prophet like [Moses]'. Jesus had told his own disciples that the entire Old Testament pointed towards his coming (Luke 24:27, 44). The whole trajectory of God's plan of salvation had been heading towards the coming of God the Son.

Sixth, God's holiness must be held in dynamic tension with his presence. He is both transcendent and immanent. He is present to care for individuals in the Old Testament and yet he is awesome in his holiness. Believers do well to maintain the tension between God's personal presence and his holy transcendence.

Seventh, the judgment of God sometimes involves giving people over to their sin. In 7:42 Stephen claims God 'gave them over to the worship of the sun, moon and stars', citing Amos 5:25–7 as evidence. Those with persistently hard hearts are sometimes left in their sin – this is its own sort of temporal judgment. Paul says something similar in Romans 1:24.

Eighth, God's patience with stubbornness is an undeserved mercy. It is striking that God drove out the nations before Israel in the conquest, despite their rejection of him and of Moses. It is a gracious providence that stays his hand of judgment, which by rights could fall on anyone at any time.

Ninth, it is possible to resist the Holy Spirit. We do it all the time. Reformed theology rightly, in my view, affirms 'irresistible grace'. This is the idea that when God determines to regenerate an individual by the power of his Spirit, his will is invincibly done. However, that is not to say that human beings do not regularly and often push back against the work of his Spirit. Stephen condemns his hearers for just that in 7:51.

Yet, when God determines to work regeneration in an individual, such a work is irresistible.[34]

Tenth, sacraments are outward signs of inward realities. Stephen rebukes his audience for having 'hearts and ears . . . still uncircumcised' (7:51). Circumcision was an outward sign that pointed to the need for a circumcised heart (see Deuteronomy 10:16; 30:6). This was always intended to be the case, and the new covenant brought the fulfilment of that which is described in Deuteronomy 30:6.[35]

Eleventh, Jesus is not just our priest but also our judge. Jesus is described in the early chapters of Acts as both sitting (2:34) and standing (7:56). Often in the New Testament the imagery of sitting is used to demonstrate the completed or finished work of Jesus as priest.[36] His sacrifice has paid the price and so his work is finished. The imagery of standing, seen here in 7:56, speaks of Jesus as judge. It is a reminder of the need to come to Jesus the priest, lest we find ourselves facing Jesus as our judge.

Twelfth, even murderers can find forgiveness. Readers of Luke's narrative cannot help but think ahead as we see the description of Saul in 8:1. We know God is going to transform and use this man greatly. Even a murderer, who stands utterly opposed, can find forgiveness and transformation, and be used greatly of God.

I realise that no preacher wants twelve points for a Sunday sermon. The above is not intended to provide an outline for such a task. They are simply theological observations drawn out of the text. For the preacher or Bible study leader I would suggest that focus should remain on key areas that may be drawn out in some of the above.

In short, we see the holy and transcendent God, present with his people, often in surprising ways. He is at work to fulfil his purposes by the work of the Spirit and the Son. God's mission is about his word and his people, not buildings and traditions. His patience and his holiness call for immediate response. Stephen's listeners had already made up their minds, but for us as readers, Luke confronts us with the reality of who

---

[34] Donald MacLeod notes, 'the Latin word *irrestibilis*, as used in the phase "irresistible grace", does not mean "non-resistible" but "invincible"'. See Donald MacLeod, *Christ Crucified: Understanding the Atonement* (Nottingham: InterVarsity Press, 2014), 127, note 41.

[35] For more on this subject, see Martin Salter, 'The Abrahamic Covenant in Reformed Baptist Perspective', *Themelios* 40.1 (2015), www.thegospelcoalition. org/themelios/article/the-abrahamic-covenant-in-reformed-baptist-perspective (accessed 25 August 2023).

[36] For example, see Hebrews 1:3; 8:1; 10:12; 12:2.

God is and what he has done in Jesus. We must respond to his invitation; we must no longer resist his Spirit. We must, like Stephen, behold the Son, and find forgiveness in him. We may even be called to suffer as God works to advance the gospel through unexpected means. God is the hero of the story, and no one can thwart his purposes – a theme we shall see repeated as Luke's narrative progresses.

7

Unexpected Converts

ACTS 8:4–40

The escalation in persecution seen through Acts 3–7 culminated in the martyrdom of Stephen. As a result, the church was scattered from Jerusalem to Judea and Samaria. This was the unexpected fulfilment of the risen Lord Jesus's commission in Acts 1:8. Having been introduced to Stephen and Philip in Acts 6:5, we saw Stephen's story in Acts 6:8–7:59.

As we reach the next section of Luke's narrative, we see the development of Philip's story through Acts 8:4–40.[1] He, like Stephen, is a man who is empowered by the Spirit to perform signs and speak with persuasive power. In Acts 8 we continue to see the gospel advancing into new spaces – spaces that to a first-century Jewish reader may have been seen as 'unclean' – a theme that will re-emerge in Acts 10. We see this in the advance into Judea and Samaria, the encounter with Simon the sorcerer and Philip's meeting with the Ethiopian eunuch.[2] These surprising movements of the Spirit prepare us for more surprising conversions to come in Acts 9–10.

1. 'The Great Power of God' • Acts 8:4–25

Philip in Samaria

4 Those who had been scattered preached the word wherever they went. **5** Philip went down to a city in Samaria and proclaimed the Messiah there. **6** When the crowds heard Philip and saw the signs he performed, they all paid close attention to what he said. **7** For with shrieks, impure spirits came out of many, and many who were paralysed or lame were healed. **8** So there was great joy in that city.

Simon the sorcerer

9 Now for some time a man named Simon had practised sorcery in the city and amazed all the people of Samaria. He boasted that he was someone

---

[1] Acts 21:8 suggests that Luke may have got his material here from Philip directly.
[2] Witherington, *Acts*, 280, dates these events as being around the late 30s AD.

great, **10** and all the people, both high and low, gave him their attention and exclaimed, 'This man is rightly called the Great Power of God.' **11** They followed him because he had amazed them for a long time with his sorcery. **12** But when they believed Philip as he proclaimed the good news of the kingdom of God and the name of Jesus Christ, they were baptised, both men and women. **13** Simon himself believed and was baptised. And he followed Philip everywhere, astonished by the great signs and miracles he saw.

14 When the apostles in Jerusalem heard that Samaria had accepted the word of God, they sent Peter and John to Samaria. **15** When they arrived, they prayed for the new believers there that they might receive the Holy Spirit, **16** because the Holy Spirit had not yet come on any of them; they had simply been baptised in the name of the Lord Jesus. **17** Then Peter and John placed their hands on them, and they received the Holy Spirit.

18 When Simon saw that the Spirit was given at the laying on of the apostles' hands, he offered them money **19** and said, 'Give me also this ability so that everyone on whom I lay my hands may receive the Holy Spirit.'

20 Peter answered: 'May your money perish with you, because you thought you could buy the gift of God with money! **21** You have no part or share in this ministry, because your heart is not right before God. **22** Repent of this wickedness and pray to the Lord in the hope that he may forgive you for having such a thought in your heart. **23** For I see that you are full of bitterness and captive to sin.'

24 Then Simon answered, 'Pray to the Lord for me so that nothing you have said may happen to me.'

25 After they had further proclaimed the word of the Lord and testified about Jesus, Peter and John returned to Jerusalem, preaching the gospel in many Samaritan villages.

Following the persecution and scattering (Acts 8:1), Luke informs us that those scattered preached the word wherever they went. It is easy to skip over this statement without noticing two important things. First, the early Christians understood that a significant part of their mission was to spread the good news about the gospel. The Christian faith is first and foremost news and needs to be proclaimed. The scattered believers of Acts 8 would reject the saying, often misattributed to St Francis of Assisi, 'Preach the gospel at all times; if necessary use words.'[3] It is like saying, 'Feed people at all times; if necessary use food!' Second, the preaching of the word is not the preserve of the apostles, or a specially qualified,

---

[3] There is no evidence that St Francis ever said this despite it often being quoted, and in fact his own emphasis on preaching is evident in *Regula non bullata* (1221).

set-apart or gifted class of Christians. It seems the earliest Christians understood that they *all* had a responsibility to evangelise, even if some had a specific gift.

Philip went to a city in Samaria. We may recall Jesus's conversation with the Samaritan woman (John 4) or his story of the good Samaritan (Luke 10:25–37) to remind ourselves of the hostility that existed between Jews and Samaritans. For many first-century Jews, Samaria was considered 'unclean'. The Samaritans had 'sold out' following the Assyrian occupation hundreds of years earlier.[4] They had intermarried and adopted Assyrian idolatry into their worship. They had begun to worship God in different places and different ways. The providence of God and prompting of the Spirit had taken Philip to a people that were considered little better than Gentiles. It is a reminder to us of the sorts of people God reaches. They may not be, by the world's standards, the most popular or admirable. Yet God calls us, and the Spirit moves us, towards the least and the lost.

Philip performed many signs, including exorcisms and healings. Here again we see the motif of the 'unclean' in Luke's description of the spirits (*pneumata akatharta* = 'unclean spirits') which Philip drove out. The people 'paid close attention to what he said', and Luke tells us that 'there was great joy in that city'. Philip, like Jesus and the apostles, performed notable signs.[5] Such signs are evidence that Philip stands in continuity with Jesus and the apostles, as signified by their laying on of hands in Acts 6:6. The signs give credibility to the message as it is taken into a new area. As we have noted before in discussing Acts 2:42–7, we ought to be careful about inferring from this the continuity of 'signs and wonders' ministries beyond the infancy of the church and the generation of Jesus and the apostles.

In Acts 8:9–24 we are told of one particular incident that occurred in Philip's ministry in a city in Samaria. Luke reports the competing ministry of a man named Simon, who 'had practised sorcery in the city and amazed all the people of Samaria'.[6] Simon is not what we might term an illusionist, deceiving people with sleight of hand. His interest

---

[4] 'The Samaritans were not popular among the Jews, as they were despised for being unfaithful and of mixed ancestry, and they were treated as defecting half-breeds.' Bock, *Acts*, 324.

[5] Luke 4:35; 5:18; 7:22–3; Acts 3:2; 5:16.

[6] Simon is described as doing *mageuōn* ('magic' or 'sorcery') and being *megan* ('great'). It's possible there is a play on words here. One can certainly see how the *magos megas* would sell tickets!

in the power of the Holy Spirit (8:18–19) is evidence that Simon's own power has a demonic spiritual origin.[7]

It is worth pausing here to note the reality of the occult. Some believers do not think about the very real power of the occult. We believe the stories of Jesus's miracles and see evidence of the miraculous in our lives and the lives of others. We recognise the wonderful things God is doing around the world and give thanks. Yet we may tend to think of the occult as somehow less real. We may not take seriously the work of the devil and the demons. We may dismiss such things as unreal. Yet the Bible is clear that Satan and his forces are a real and powerful force, active in our world to destroy and devour.[8] We have seen thus far in Acts Satan's attempts to derail the spread of the good news through persecution, deception and division. Here we see a more explicit contest of power, as the work of the devil has already taken hold in the city through Simon the sorcerer.[9]

It is, of course, possible to become overly fascinated with the demonic and see such things around every corner. We can become excessively interested in things like deliverance ministries, and there have been some real abuses in some parts of the church in this area. In the West I suspect this is not our danger. For Christian brothers and sisters in other parts of the world, however, they know all too well the power of the local shaman or witchdoctor. Christians ought to be aware, informed and prepared to think about how to engage with the forces of evil whenever and wherever we encounter them.[10]

Luke tells us that Simon himself boasted that he was someone great, and the people of the city described him as 'the Great Power of God'. Luke is setting his story up to see whose power is greater.[11] Simon's power is evident, but how can it compare to the power of the one at work through Philip? As Luke recounts the story, it turns out to be no

---

[7] Garrett describes magic in Acts as 'satanic power actualised'. Cited in Peterson, *Acts*, 283.

[8] 2 Corinthians 4:4–6; Ephesians 6:12–13; 1 Peter 5:8.

[9] We shall see similar encounters in Acts 13:4–12 and 19:11–20.

[10] Some works to consider in this area include Michael S. Heiser, *The Unseen Realm* (Bellingham: Lexham, 2015); C. S. Lewis, *The Screwtape Letters* (repr. London: Collins, 1979); Thomas Brooks, *Precious Remedies Against Satan's Devices* (Puritan Paperbacks; repr. Edinburgh: Banner of Truth, 2000).

[11] Hans Josef-Klauck, *Magic and Paganism in Early Christianity*, trans. Brian McNeill (Edinburgh: T&T Clark, 2000), 18–19.

contest.[12] In verse 12 we see that when Philip proclaims the good news of the kingdom of God and the name of Jesus Christ, the people follow him instead and are baptised, both men and women. Philip does not consider himself to be someone great, but rather it is the one who is working in him who is great.

Remarkably Simon himself believes and is baptised. He follows Philip everywhere, astonished by the signs and the miracles. Here we see in Acts what may be observed in the Gospels. When the powers of Satan and his demons come up against the power of Jesus, they must bow in submission. This is why Christians reject any form of good/evil dualism – as if there could be some kind of battle between good and evil. The truth is that although the personal forces of evil set themselves against God, there is no battle or war in the sense that we might understand it. Satan and the demons act only by permission, and their ultimate defeat, though delayed, is beyond doubt.[13]

Having heard of Philip's ministry in Samaria, Peter and John come to pray for the new believers. More specifically, Peter and John pray that the new believers might receive the Holy Spirit, 'because the Holy Spirit had not yet come on any of them; they had simply been baptised in the name of the Lord Jesus'. Peter and John pray for them, place their hands upon them and they receive the Holy Spirit. There are a number of things worth noting at this point.

First, we must acknowledge from the wider testimony of Scripture that faith is preceded by regeneration, which is a work of the Spirit.[14] Therefore this reception of the Spirit must be seen as the gift of his personal and permanent presence and should not be taken as the complete absence of his work prior to this moment.

Second, we must ask why there is a delay in the giving of the Spirit. We see a similar phenomenon in Acts 10:44–6 and 19:1–6. It seems that wherever we find new (and perhaps controversial) people groups, there is a more public evidence of their conversion described. Given the historic tensions between Jews and Samaritans, it was important that the apostles

---

[12] Some see a link here to Moses and the Egyptian magicians. Just as the power at work in Moses was greater than that at work in Pharaoh's magicians, so too the power at work in Philip is greater than the power at work in Simon. This observation might strengthen the case for seeing Acts as a sort of 'new Exodus' narrative. Bock, *Acts*, 329.

[13] Grudem, *Systematic Theology*, 415–19.

[14] John 1:12–13; 3:5; 1 Corinthians 2:16; 2 Corinthians 5:17; Ephesians 2:1–10; Titus 3:5. Calvin, *Institutes* 3.1–2.

of Jerusalem should be eyewitnesses (even instruments) of the gift of the Holy Spirit to the Samaritans.[15]

Third, the laying on of hands by the apostles gives further credibility to this new group of people who at this point would have been seen by some as outside the covenantal boundary.[16]

Fourth, this event should not be seen as a subsequent Pentecost. That event was an unrepeatable fulfilment of Scripture. While this event has a similar function in the miraculous accreditation of those to whom God's Spirit is given, it is not a simple repeat of Pentecost, but rather an extension of the Pentecost blessing.

Fifth, this event, unique as it is, does not set down a pattern for Christian conversion, whereby one may become a believer and receive a subsequent gift of the Spirit.[17] As has been argued above, this event, like those in Acts 10 and 19, is unique and unrepeatable, related to a particular set of historical circumstances.

At this point, the narrative takes an unexpected turn. We have already seen the dangers that money presented to the new community (Acts 5:1–11), and here it is repeated. Simon, seeing the gift of the Holy Spirit administered through the laying on of hands by the apostles, attempts to purchase this power, as if that were possible. He wants status and power, and he will use money to obtain it.[18] The term 'simony' refers to the practice of seeking ecclesiastical preferment or power in exchange for money, and is derived from this incident. It is so different from the ministry of Jesus, who shunned possessions and went to the humiliation of the cross. As followers, we have to decide whether we want the broad road of power, wealth and influence or the narrow Calvary Road of suffering and humiliation. Wherever we see so-called power ministries wrapped up with financial reward, influence, status and power, there is a good indication that the origin is not divine but demonic.

Peter rebukes Simon for his actions, warning him of the very real

---

[15] Jervell describes this as a 'special legitimization' given the potential controversy of Samaritan inclusion. Cited in Bock, *Acts*, 332. So too Witherington, *Acts*, 289, and Peterson, *Acts*, 287. It is possible, even likely, that tongues-speech was the visible evidence of Spirit reception, though Luke makes no explicit mention here.

[16] V. J. Samkutty, *The Samaritan Mission in Acts* (London: T&T Clark, 2006), 211–14.

[17] There is no evidence here that would support either the Pentecostal view of a second blessing or the Catholic and Anglican rites of confirmation (see Barrett, *Acts 1–14*, 400). Stott has an excellent discussion of this issue in *Acts*, 151–9.

[18] Tannehill, *Narrative Unity*, 106–7, describes the 'dangers the mission must avoid': to seek to be seen as 'great', and the corrupting influence of money.

danger that he might perish if he does not repent. Peter urges him to 'repent of this wickedness and pray to the Lord in the hope that he may forgive you for having such a thought in your heart. For I see that you are full of bitterness and captive to sin.'

One of the questions raised by Luke's account is whether we should see Simon's conversion as genuine or spurious. On the one hand, he had 'believed and was baptised' (verse 13), and Luke does not tell us explicitly that his profession was false. Yet Luke gives a number of clues that Simon's profession of faith may not have been what it seemed. Luke does not tell us explicitly that Simon himself had received the gift of the Spirit, simply that he had observed it (verses 15–17). Peter informed Simon that he currently stood in the place of perishing (verse 20) and was in need of repentance (verse 22).[19]

Peter said to Simon, 'You have no part or share in this ministry.' That could mean no part of share in the ministry of laying on hands, but that seemed to be confined to the apostles anyway. It is possible, and perhaps more likely, that he would have no share in the blessings of the word – i.e., salvation.[20] The words for 'part' (*meris*) and 'share' (*klēros*) are used elsewhere to refer to the inheritance that is salvation.[21] Further, the word translated 'ministry' in the NIV more literally means 'word' (*en tō logō toutō*). It seems more likely, then, to see Simon's lack in reference to the inheritance that comes from the word – the word being the message of the good news. Peter also described Simon as still 'captive to sin' (*syndesmon adikias* – literally in 'bonds of unrighteousness') which would lend further support to Simon being as yet unregenerate.

Finally, Simon's response suggests he had misunderstood the gospel offer. He asked Peter to pray for him, and his appeal was so that nothing bad may happen to him. He desired to avoid punishment, rather than seek genuine pardon. It appears from Luke's narrative that Simon is an example of someone who made an initial profession of faith, but his confession is revealed to be dishonest.[22] Although Luke gives the reader hints regarding Simon's status, his character is somewhat ambiguous, which

---

[19] Perhaps more literally 'your silver and you with it can go to hell (*apōleian*)'. Ambrose notes that even though Simon is in gross error, the offer of repentance and forgiveness is still held out even to him. ACCS, 5:94.

[20] Barrett, *Acts 1–14*, 414.

[21] For *meris* see Luke 10:42; Colossians 1:12. For *klēros* see Acts 26:18; Colossians 1:12.

[22] Witherington, *Acts*, 288–9, offers a similar list of hints that we should view Simon as unconverted. Peterson, *Acts*, 289–90, also shares the view that Simon was not truly converted.

provides the reader an opportunity to ponder their own response to the message and its call for repentance.[23]

So was Philip wrong to baptise him? No, for baptism is administered upon a credible profession of faith. It is sadly often the case that people make a very believable profession of repentance and belief, yet in time prove themselves to be false. The nature of the visible church is mixed. It will, this side of heaven, contain both true and false believers.[24] The church must work to try to maintain her purity as best as she is able. Yet Simon's story reminds us that this will never be perfectly attainable this side of the new creation. It is a reminder that the church should exercise due caution in admitting people to the membership of the body, recognising that not every profession will be genuine. That said, the church must also be careful not to make the bar for baptism and membership too high. What is required is a *credible* profession of faith, and we must recognise that that will take different forms for different persons. This is an area of church life that requires much sensitivity, care, discernment and wisdom.

In verse 25, Luke gives a mini summary, stating that after further proclamation of the word, Peter and John returned to Jerusalem, preaching in many Samaritan villages. The word had spread not just to one Samaritan city, but to many Samaritan villages. The gospel is beginning to cross boundary lines and reach 'unclean' places. Luke is once again showing the reader the power of God and the call to the church. In the meantime, the church must faithfully proclaim the message, going to the least and the lost. We must resist the seduction and corruption of worldly riches, recognising the spiritual battle that lies behind these things. God's providential ordering is all the power the church requires, even in the face of persecution, and the Lord will bless faithful proclamation and the pursuit of purity.

2. The Ethiopian eunuch • Acts 8:26–40

Philip and the Ethiopian

26 Now an angel of the Lord said to Philip, 'Go south to the road – the desert road – that goes down from Jerusalem to Gaza.' 27 So he started out, and on his way he met an Ethiopian[a] eunuch, an important official in charge of all the treasury of the Kandake (which

---

[23] Bock, *Acts*, 336.

[24] See Gregg R. Allison, *Sojourners and Strangers: The Doctrine of the Church* (Wheaton: Crossway, 2012), 161–8.

means 'queen of the Ethiopians'). This man had gone to Jerusalem to worship, **28** and on his way home was sitting in his chariot reading the Book of Isaiah the prophet. **29** The Spirit told Philip, 'Go to that chariot and stay near it.'

30 Then Philip ran up to the chariot and heard the man reading Isaiah the prophet. 'Do you understand what you are reading?' Philip asked.

31 'How can I,' he said, 'unless someone explains it to me?' So he invited Philip to come up and sit with him.

32 This is the passage of Scripture the eunuch was reading:

'He was led like a sheep to the
slaughter,
and as a lamb before its shearer
is silent,
so he did not open his mouth.
33 In his humiliation he was deprived
of justice.
Who can speak of his
descendants?
For his life was taken from the
earth.'**b**

34 The eunuch asked Philip, 'Tell me, please, who is the prophet talking about, himself or someone else?' **35** Then Philip began with that very passage of Scripture and told him the good news about Jesus.

36 As they travelled along the road, they came to some water and the eunuch said, 'Look, here is water. What can stand in the way of my being baptised?' **[37]** **c 38** And he gave orders to stop the chariot. Then both Philip and the eunuch went down into the water and Philip baptised him. **39** When they came up out of the water, the Spirit of the Lord suddenly took Philip away, and the eunuch did not see him again, but went on his way rejoicing. **40** Philip, however, appeared at Azotus and travelled about, preaching the gospel in all the towns until he reached Caesarea.

---

a 27 That is, from the southern Nile region
b 33 Isaiah 53:7,8 (see Septuagint)
c 37 Some manuscripts include here *Philip said, 'If you believe with all your heart, you may.' The eunuch answered, 'I believe that Jesus Christ is the Son of God.'*

If Simon was a man of 'power' who turned out to be disingenuous, in Philip's next encounter we meet another powerful outsider (8:27) who is a genuine seeker, and whose inclusion is as surprising as that of the Samaritans in the previous episode. Many have noted that in some ways the Ethiopian eunuch is even further removed from the people of God than Cornelius (Acts 10), who is often seen as the first Gentile convert.[25] The difference between the two is that the Ethiopian is returning home, where he will likely be the only convert. Cornelius, however, is the first

---

[25] Witherington, *Acts*, 290, argues this narrative could be a sort of foreshadowing of the gospel progressing towards the ends of the earth, more of which will be seen as the narrative unfolds.

localised and situated Gentile convert. His conversion leads to the formation of local churches in Gentile territory, in relationship with the church
in Jerusalem.[26] Both stories illustrate the power of God and the gospel to
reach previously unreached places.

The passage begins with the angelic command to Philip that he
should go to 'the desert road – that goes down from Jerusalem to Gaza'.
The mission continued to be divinely driven forward. On his way he
met an Ethiopian eunuch who is described as 'an important official in
charge of all the treasury of the Kandake (which means "queen of the
Ethiopians")'. Luke informs us that this man was returning home after
visiting Jerusalem to worship (verse 27).

There are three factors of interest in Luke's description of this man.
First, he is a high-ranking government official. The story of the conversion of a man like this is just the sort of story a man like Theophilus
needs to hear.[27] The gospel can reach people from any social class or
status. Second, he is an Ethiopian – an African man from the edge of
the known world.[28] He is, ethnically speaking, a Gentile and, as such, an
outsider to the Jewish religion, though he clearly has an earnest interest
in Judaism, by virtue of his possession of a copy of an Isaiah scroll, and
his pilgrimage to Jerusalem. Third, he is described as a eunuch, a fact
that would have prevented him from becoming a proselyte in the fullest
sense.[29] Those who served in royal courts were often eunuchs.[30] Jesus
described three categories of eunuchs: those born that way, those forced
to be eunuchs, and those who choose to be eunuchs for the kingdom
of heaven (Matthew 19:12). The Ethiopian likely fell into the second
category. In Old Testament terms (Deuteronomy 23:1) such a man would
have been excluded from the assembly of the Lord. So while he is not
what Bock terms a 'pure Gentile', neither can he be seen as a proselyte
in the fullest sense.[31]

As a non-Jew and a eunuch, he must have been acutely aware of being
seen as an unclean outsider as he worshipped at the Temple precincts

---

[26] Barrett, *Acts 1–14*, 421.

[27] Bock, *Acts*, 347.

[28] Tannehill, *Narrative Unity*, 108. Luke's identification of Ethiopia (*Aithiops*) is
probably modern-day Sudan (Bock, *Acts*, 341).

[29] Barrett, *Acts 1–14*, 420. To become a full proselyte would have required circumcision, an act impossible for a eunuch.

[30] Other examples can be seen in 2 Kings 9:32; 20:18; Esther 2:3, 14–15; 4:4–5;
6:14; 7:9.

[31] Bock, *Acts*, 338.

in Jerusalem. He may have worshipped in the Court of the Gentiles.[32] Peterson describes him as someone on the 'fringes of Judaism'.[33] His presence may have been tolerated, but he must have felt like an unwelcome outsider. As Green notes, 'This man had pressed as close as he could to entering the temple, the symbol of God's presence and mercy, but was banned.'[34]

It is worth pausing to reflect on how easy it is for groups of worshippers to make those who are unlike the majority feel like unwelcome outsiders. It can happen through little things like the sideways glance, being seated at the back of church or simply being ignored. I've even known someone to 'tut' at a visitor with a crying baby. It is always a beneficial exercise to consider how your church welcomes outsiders.

As the man travelled home in his chariot, he was reading from the prophet Isaiah. Scrolls were expensive to produce and purchase so his possession of a copy of the Isaiah scroll is further indication of both his wealth and his earnest interest.[35] Philip approached the chariot and asked the man if he understood what he was reading (verse 30). The eunuch immediately confessed his ignorance: 'How can I . . . unless someone explains it to me?'

This perhaps further illustrates the distance at which he was forced to worship at the Temple in Jerusalem. He would have had no access to the teachers or teaching of the Law. Philip was perhaps the first Jewish person to reach across the boundary of 'clean/unclean' to share the gospel with this enquirer.

It is worth us remembering that sometimes people are overtly hostile to the gospel. At other times people are much more sensitive, keen to find out more. We tend to think that nobody would ever want to sit down and read the Bible with us. Yet the Ethiopian eunuch reminds us that there are those who desire to enquire and are eager to have someone explain the Scriptures side by side.

Luke informs us of the passage the man was reading – Isaiah 53:7–8. The passage is taken from Isaiah's fourth Servant Song. It is likely that in quoting a few lines, Luke intends us to see the whole of the Servant

---

[32] Peterson, *Acts*, 294.

[33] Peterson, *Acts*, 291. This is another reason why the conversion of Cornelius is more significant for Luke's narrative since Cornelius is a man with no ties to Judaism.

[34] Green, *The Word of His Grace*, 71.

[35] Bock, *Acts*, 342. Bock suggests the scroll was probably 8 to 12 inches in width and anywhere from 16.5 to 145 feet long.

Song to be in view (Isaiah 52:13–53:12).[36] It describes the Servant led like a sheep to the slaughter, who in his humiliation was deprived of justice, and who in death left countless descendants.[37] Throughout the history of the church, Isaiah 53 has been viewed as a key Old Testament text predicting the suffering and atoning death of Jesus Christ.[38] The previous verses of Isaiah 53 describe how he was:

> . . . pierced for our transgressions,
>   he was crushed for our iniquities;
> the punishment that brought us peace was on him,
>   and by his wounds we are healed.

We can see how Philip could begin with this passage to explain the good news about Jesus (8:35; Luke 24:27, 44). The death and resurrection of Jesus are always at the core of the gospel presentation. Without understanding these foundational elements, repentance and faith will always seem confusing. Only when we understand who Jesus is, and what he has done, will we be ready to turn and trust in him.

One can't help but wonder if Philip worked a few more inches down the scroll to Isaiah 56:3–8:

> Let no foreigner who is bound to the LORD say,
>   'The LORD will surely exclude me from his people.'
> *And let no eunuch complain,*
>   *'I am only a dry tree.'*
> *For this is what the Lord says:*
> *'To the eunuchs who keep my Sabbaths,*
>   *who choose what pleases me*
>   *and hold fast to my covenant –*
> *to them I will give within my temple and its walls*
>   *a memorial and a name*

---

[36] Peterson, *Acts*, 295.

[37] Green, *The Word of His Grace*, 71, notes how the description of the Servant stands in contrast to the earlier description of Simon Magus: 'great . . . boasted . . . amazed . . . Great Power'. Luke is showing us that the true power lies in the way of the Suffering Servant – despised, rejected and humiliated.

[38] Jewish interpretation of Isaiah's 'Servant' identified him in a variety of ways, including the nation as a whole, the prophet himself, one (or a group of) Israel's leaders or the coming Messiah. It is the last of these that Philip connects to Jesus. Jeremias, *TDNT* 5:682–700.

better than sons and daughters;
I will give them an everlasting name
 that will endure forever.
And foreigners who bind themselves to the LORD
 to minister to him,
to love the name of the LORD,
 and to be his servants,
all who keep the Sabbath without desecrating it
 and who hold fast to my covenant –
these I will bring to my holy mountain
 and give them joy in my house of prayer.
Their burnt offerings and sacrifices
 will be accepted on my altar;
for my house will be called
 a house of prayer for all nations.'
The Sovereign LORD declares –
 he who gathers the exiles of Israel:
'I will gather still others to them
 besides those already gathered.'[39]

As Witherington notes, 'Nothing hindered the eunuch from being a full-fledged follower of the one in whom Isaiah's promises were being fulfilled in the present, even though he could not be a full-fledged Jew.'[40]

It appears their conversation lasted long enough for Philip to explain baptism as the necessary response of faith. When they came to some water, the eunuch asked if he could be baptised. Philip baptised the man and then was immediately taken away, appearing again at Azotus and preaching the gospel in 'all the towns until he reached Caesarea', where we later find him having made his home (verse 40; compare 21:8).[41] The reference to the Spirit of the Lord suddenly taking Philip away is reminiscent of the prophet Elijah.[42] Luke intends us to see these early Christian leaders and evangelists as standing in the same line as the Old Testament prophets. They have been rejected and persecuted, but the authority with which they speak is evidence that God is with them and their words are true.

---

[39] My emphasis.
[40] Witherington, *Acts*, 296.
[41] Peterson notes that the Spirit 'taking hold' of Philip need not necessarily imply supernatural transportation but could mean the Spirit directed Philip. Either way it is clearly the Spirit's leading that takes Philip to Azotus. Peterson, *Acts*, 297.
[42] See 1 Kings 18:12; 2 Kings 2:16.

Meanwhile the Ethiopian eunuch 'went on his way rejoicing'. We do not hear of him again in the narrative. Presumably he returned to the Kandake and continued his work.

The story is reminiscent of Elisha's meeting with Naaman in 2 Kings 5. Philip, like Elisha, stands in continuity with the Spirit-anointed leader who has commissioned him (see 2 Kings 2 and Acts 6). Naaman, like the eunuch, is an important official in the royal household (2 Kings 5:1). Naaman would also be seen as an unclean outsider by virtue of his ethnicity and his leprosy. Naaman finds healing by undergoing his own sort of baptism (2 Kings 5:14). Naaman, like the Ethiopian eunuch, must return to the royal household and live out his new-found faith alone in a pagan context.[43]

If it is right to see an echo here of 2 Kings 5, there are two key things to draw out. First, as already noted, Philip stands with the prophets and apostles as a Spirit-anointed servant of the Lord. The miraculous events that surround his life and his powerful speech are all evidence that Philip is truly sent by the Lord, and his message about the good news of the Lord Jesus is true. The signs and wonders and angelic commands are not typical or normative. Rather, they serve to accredit the first generation of Jesus's followers as they take the gospel from Jerusalem to Judea and Samaria and to the ends of the earth.

Second, the Ethiopian eunuch's conversion, baptism and return are also to be seen as unique in their circumstance. Ordinarily, baptism is a church ordinance administered by the ordained office-bearers of a local church.[44] Baptism is an initiation into a local body of believers.[45] This is the understanding that developed over time in the early church.

There are occasional reports of people baptising their friends in a local

---

[43] Brodie suggests Luke is employing 'rhetorical imitation' in using the Old Testament sources. It should be asserted that Luke is not inventing stories based on the Old Testament narratives but is rather echoing them for rhetorical purposes – namely accrediting Philip as a prophet of God. Brodie also suggests that Simon the Sorcerer may parallel Gehazi in 2 Kings 5 in his greed for money. See Thomas L. Brodie, 'Towards the Unravelling of Rhetorical Imitation of Sources in Acts: 2 Kgs 5 as One Component of Acts 8, 9–40', in *Biblica* 67.1 (1986): 41–67. Witherington is right to describe Luke's writing as an 'echo' of the Elijah–Elisha cycle. Witherington, *Acts*, 292.

[44] Mark E. Dever, 'Baptism in the Context of the Local Church', in *Believer's Baptism: Sign of the New Covenant in Christ*, eds. Thomas R. Schreiner and Shawn D. Wright (Nashville: B&H, 2006), 329–52.

[45] 1 Corinthians 12:13. Thomas R. Schreiner, 'Baptism in the Epistles: An Initiation Rite for Believers', in Schreiner (ed.), *Believer's Baptism*, 67–96.

river, or even in a bath or backyard swimming pool. After all, they say, 'What can stand in the way of my being baptised?' (Acts 8:36).

The short answer is, 'The elders of a local church who deem your profession not to be credible.' The situation in Acts 8 is unique and gives no warrant for spontaneous baptisms occurring outside the God-given 'ordinary means of grace' – the word and sacrament administered under the authority of the ordained office-bearers of a local church.

Additionally, we should note here that there is no mention of how much water was available and whether baptism ought to be by immersion or sprinkling. The normative mode of baptism, it would seem, given the symbolism of burial and cleansing seen elsewhere, should ordinarily be by total immersion.[46] What this passage does show is the importance of baptism in the early church. It was not seen as an optional extra for keen Christians. It was a command of the Lord Jesus and his apostles for all those who would obediently follow him.[47]

In summary, Luke's brief account of Philip's ministry teaches a number of things. First, we see the word of God continuing to spread beyond Jerusalem and into Judea and Samaria in fulfilment of Acts 1:8. God in his sovereign power continues to drive forward his mission unstoppable. This gives us great confidence that nothing can stand in the way of his sovereign purposes.

Second, we see Philip and his message about Jesus further accredited through his remarkable deeds and persuasive speech. The signs are evidence that point to the truth and reality of Jesus's atoning death, resurrection, ascension and the pouring out of the Holy Spirit.

Third, we see the gospel reaching beyond not just geographical boundaries, but also ethnic boundaries. The gospel of grace is now for all people, whatever their ethnicity, class or caste. The church must reflect this and actively fight against systems or attitudes that discriminate.

Fourth, the gospel also reaches the people and places once considered unclean. The Lord is building his 'house of prayer' and it will be for all nations (Isaiah 56:7). The gospel message is for anyone and everyone regardless of their background. As Peter said, 'Everyone who calls on the name of the Lord will be saved' (Acts 2:21). The Ethiopian eunuch is further evidence of that claim. We must consider how we can reach the full variety of people in our communities, and beware of favouring certain people groups over others.

---

[46] See Acts 22:16; Romans 6:3–4; Colossians 2:11–12; 1 Peter 3:21.
[47] Matthew 28:19; Acts 2:38.

Fifth, Luke shows us the value of word-ministry to the crowds (8:10–12) and one to one. We see the necessity of both preaching and personal evangelism. Both are used by God in advancing his gospel. Churches must consider how they can train people to use both of these important means in our evangelistic endeavours.

In Acts 9–10 we will see two more remarkable conversions as the word of God continues to spread to seemingly impossible places. All of this should give the modern church much encouragement as we see the power of God at work to overcome all obstacles. And her radical inclusivity should itself be a compelling witness to the transforming, unifying and reconciling power of the gospel of grace.

8

An Unlikely Convert

ACTS 9

Following the martyrdom of Stephen and the persecution of the church instigated by Saul (8:2–3), Luke has narrated the continued advance of the gospel, including some surprising conversions of those previously considered outsiders or unclean. These have included the Samaritan villages (8:9–25) and the Ethiopian eunuch (8:26–40). As we come to Acts 9–10, we see two more conversions, perhaps even more surprising than those observed in chapter 8.[1] The word of God continues to spread and the risen Jesus, by the power of the Spirit, continues to be powerfully at work overcoming various hurdles.[2]

1. Saul's Damascus Road encounter • Acts 9:1–31

Acts 9:1–9: Saul meets the risen Jesus

Saul's conversion

9 Meanwhile, Saul was still breathing out murderous threats against the Lord's disciples. He went to the high priest **2** and asked him for letters to the synagogues in Damascus, so that if he found any there who belonged to the Way, whether men or women, he might take them as prisoners to Jerusalem. **3** As he neared Damascus on his journey, suddenly a light from heaven flashed around him. **4** He fell to the ground and heard a voice say to him, 'Saul, Saul, why do you persecute me?'

---

[1] Witherington describes Saul's conversion as one of, if not the, most important event Luke describes, given its significance in opening up the Gentile mission. Paul himself will recall his conversion in Acts 22 and 26. Witherington provides a helpful discussion of the alleged discrepancies between the three accounts in Acts and the details in Paul's letters, arguing that what we see here are summaries including particular salient points for a purpose. There is therefore no necessary contradiction between the various accounts. See Witherington, *Acts*, 302–15.

[2] Bock estimates that the story of Saul's conversion probably occurs somewhere between one and three years after Jesus's death. *Acts*, 349.

5 'Who are you, Lord?' Saul asked. 'I am Jesus, whom you are persecuting,' he replied. **6** 'Now get up and go into the city, and you will be told what you must do.'

7 The men travelling with Saul stood there speechless; they heard the sound but did not see anyone. **8** Saul got up from the ground, but when he opened his eyes he could see nothing. So they led him by the hand into Damascus. **9** For three days he was blind, and did not eat or drink anything.

The reintroduction of Saul into the narrative correlates well with Luke's description in 8:3: 'Saul began to destroy the church. Going from house to house, he dragged off both men and women and put them in prison.' And here in 9:1, 'Meanwhile, Saul was still breathing out murderous threats against the Lord's disciples.' If we were reading this for the very first time, we might well expect to read another account of persecution of the church, maybe even martyrdom.

Saul requested letters from the high priest (probably Caiaphas) addressed to synagogues in Damascus so that, if he found any followers of 'the Way' (*tēs hodou*), he might take them as prisoners to Jerusalem (verse 2).[3] This is the first time Christian disciples have been referred to as followers of 'the Way'. The phrase will occur five more times in Acts (19:9, 23; 22:4; 24:14, 22). It likely has both soteriological and ethical overtones.

The zeal of Saul is evident in his willingness to travel significant distances to persecute the Christians. Damascus lay 135 miles north of Jerusalem and was a significant city, a commercial centre, with a large Jewish population.[4] The earliest disciples, some having already fled from Jerusalem, must have feared for their lives. If we can imagine ourselves as first readers, we would wonder if this spelled the end for the church.

There are many small communities of believers today who live with similar fear and the threat of violence. It is a comfort to know the 'bigger story' that God can and does grow his church amid persecution. Yet we must not underestimate the challenge of remaining faithful under such conditions. Those of us who enjoy greater freedoms must find ways to support those in such situations – through prayer, through financial support, through justice advocacy, through support of organisations working to help. It is easy for those who do not suffer direct

---

[3] Witherington, *Acts*, 315.
[4] Barrett, *Acts 1–14*, 447.

persecution to remain comfortably uninformed and inactive with regard to the persecuted church.[5]

As we imagine ourselves into the situation Luke describes, Acts 9:3 must stand as one of the most surprising turning points in the whole of Acts. Saul, the zealous persecutor of the church, is suddenly stopped in his tracks as a 'light from heaven flashed around him'. Witherington notes that light or lightning is a regular feature of Old Testament theophanies (Exodus 19:6; 2 Samuel 22:15; Ezekiel 1:28), but here it is used of a Christophany, highlighting the divinity of Jesus. It also provides echoes of Old Testament narratives which depict the commissioning of significant characters.[6]

As he lay on the ground, blinded, he heard a voice: 'Saul, Saul, why do you persecute me?'

Saul inquired as to the identity of the speaker: 'Who are you, Lord?'[7]

The reply: 'I am Jesus, whom you are persecuting.'

Here is yet another reminder that Jesus's ascension does not take him 'backstage' away from the action and oblivious to events. Stephen saw Jesus standing at the right hand of God (7:56), and now Saul has heard him speak. As we observed in the opening verse of Acts, Luke intends to show us what Jesus is *continuing* to do and teach from heaven (see 1:1). He is still an active character in the narrative, driving the action forward.

Also noteworthy here is Jesus's identification with the persecuted. He claims that Saul is persecuting *him*. As readers we may have thought that it was the church being persecuted. Such is the connection between Jesus and his followers that to persecute them *is* to persecute him.[8] Some of these ideas become more theologically developed in Paul's own writings. The idea of 'faith-union' by the Spirit (Romans 8), the head and the body (1 Corinthians 12), the spiritual temple (1 Peter 2), the vine and the branches (John 15) all depict the real connection that exists between Jesus and his church. It is a spiritual union, but it is no less real for that. The persecuted church is never alone. Their pain is felt by the rest of the body, including the head of that body. This does not lessen the pain, but it brings comfort and courage to trust Jesus in dark places.

---

[5] Organisations like Open Doors do excellent work in this area and its website has lots of information, resources and ways to find out more and get involved: www.opendoors.org (accessed 25 August 2023).

[6] Witherington, *Acts*, 316.

[7] The term 'Lord' (*kyrie*) can be a term of respectful address (e.g., 'sir' or 'master') and is not necessarily a confession of faith in the identity of Jesus, though that is certainly not far away for Saul.

[8] See Matthew 25:34–45.

Having been confronted by the risen Jesus, Saul was commanded to get up and go into the city (of Damascus) where he would be told what to do. His travelling companions were startled – they heard the sound but did not see anyone.[9] Saul, blinded by the light, was led by his companions to the city of Damascus. Luke tells us he was blind for three days, during which time he did not eat or drink anything.[10] As Stott notes, Christ arrested Saul, before he could arrest any of the disciples.[11]

Acts 9:10–19a: Saul meets Ananias

[10] In Damascus there was a disciple named Ananias. The Lord called to him in a vision, 'Ananias!'

'Yes, Lord,' he answered.

[11] The Lord told him, 'Go to the house of Judas on Straight Street and ask for a man from Tarsus named Saul, for he is praying. [12] In a vision he has seen a man named Ananias come and place his hands on him to restore his sight.'

[13] 'Lord,' Ananias answered, 'I have heard many reports about this man and all the harm he has done to your holy people in Jerusalem. [14] And he has come here with authority from the chief priests to arrest all who call on your name.'

[15] But the Lord said to Ananias, 'Go! This man is my chosen instrument to proclaim my name to the Gentiles and their kings and to the people of Israel. [16] I will show him how much he must suffer for my name.'

[17] Then Ananias went to the house and entered it. Placing his hands on Saul, he said, 'Brother Saul, the Lord – Jesus, who appeared to you on the road as you were coming here – has sent me so that you may see again and be filled with the Holy Spirit.' [18] Immediately, something like scales fell from Saul's eyes, and he could see again. He got up and was baptised, [19] and after taking some food, he regained his strength.

Meanwhile, Luke takes us to a man named Ananias – a disciple from Damascus to whom the Lord spoke in a vision. This double-vision (Saul and Ananias) will correspond to the double-vision of Cornelius and Peter in Acts 10, further emphasising both the importance of the event

---

[9] Bock, *Acts*, 351, suggests the companions of Saul heard the sound and saw the light, but did not hear the voice or see Jesus. The Christophany was a public event, but the revelation was to Saul alone.

[10] Bock suggests his blindness was not a punishment but rather a sign that he had seen the glory of the Lord. The fact he did not eat or drink may be seen as the prayer and fasting of the penitent as he awaited the further instruction promised in verse 6. See Bock, *Acts*, 359.

[11] Stott, *Acts*, 170.

and God's control over the events.[12] Ananias was instructed to go to the house of Judas on Straight Street to meet a man from Tarsus named Saul.[13] Ananias, unsurprisingly was more than a little concerned, having heard reports of Saul and all the harm he had done in Jerusalem. The Lord sometimes calls us to difficult places and situations – places that require courage and trust. We can only imagine how Ananias felt – stomach churning, heart racing – as he turned down Straight Street and knocked on the door of Judas.

Jesus in the vision gave assurance to Ananias: 'This man is my chosen instrument to proclaim my name to the Gentiles and their kings and to the people of Israel. I will show him how much he must suffer for my name.'[14] It must have been a huge surprise for Ananias to hear of Saul having been appointed by the risen Jesus to take the gospel to the Gentiles. Saul must have seemed perhaps the least likely man on the face of the earth to do such a task. The disciple-murderer had become a disciple-maker. God moves in a mysterious way. He often uses the least-expected or least-obvious people to accomplish great things in his name and power. In this case, God can save even the chief persecutor of the church.

Ananias was obedient to a difficult call. How must he have felt as he uttered his opening words, 'Brother Saul (*Saoul adelphe*)'? The man who had once been an enemy was now a 'brother'. We may never face a situation as stark as this, but perhaps some of us will. How easy would we find it to call someone, once an enemy and persecutor of the church, now transformed, 'brother' or 'sister'. In some ways, Ananias utters the most beautiful words in all of Acts with his fraternal welcome of a man once an enemy of Christ and his church: '*Saoul adelphe*'.

As Ananias obeyed Jesus's command, something like scales fell from Saul's eyes and his sight returned. His literal and spiritual blindness were overcome. He got up and was baptised, which presumably included the filling with the Holy Spirit spoken of in verse 17.

---

[12] See Genesis 41:32.

[13] Tarsus was a significant city and a seat for the Roman governor. This detail tells us Saul had been a diaspora Jew, and it will also provide important context for Saul's return in 9:30 and his appeal to Caesar as a Roman citizen later in Luke's narrative. Bock, *Acts*, 360.

[14] The inclusion of 'the people of Israel' reminds us we should not think of Paul as apostle to the Gentiles exclusively, as also does his subsequent practice of going to synagogues first. Rhetorically, of course, it is striking that Gentiles are mentioned before Israel, signifying the narrative turn towards Gentiles and Gentile regions in fulfilment of Acts 1:8. Wall, *Acts*, 152.

Acts 9:19b–22: Saul's ministry begins

Saul in Damascus and Jerusalem
Saul spent several days with the disciples in Damascus. **20** At once he began to preach in the synagogues that Jesus is the Son of God. **21** All those who heard him were astonished and asked, 'Isn't he the man who caused havoc in Jerusalem among those who call on this name? And hasn't he come here to take them as prisoners to the chief priests?' **22** Yet Saul grew more and more powerful and baffled the Jews living in Damascus by proving that Jesus is the Messiah.

After this, Luke tells us that Saul spent several days with the disciples in Damascus and almost immediately began to preach in the synagogues, to the astonishment of those present. One can imagine the confusion, maybe suspicion, among the people who heard him. Yet, says Luke, 'Saul grew more and more powerful and baffled the Jews living in Damascus by proving that Jesus is the Messiah.'

Saul's transformation was dramatic. His intimate knowledge of the Jewish Scriptures, as a student of Gamaliel (see Acts 22:3), coupled with his meeting with the risen Jesus on the Damascus Road, enabled him to now interpret the Scriptures afresh, empowered by the Spirit, to see Jesus as the climax of Israel's covenantal history.

The narrative of Saul's conversion should prompt a few reflections. First, we see that God really can convert anyone, no matter how opposed. Conversion is not a matter of mere persuasion, reason or argument – it is the irresistible power of God's sovereign grace to transform and enable us to see Jesus. This provides us with the encouragement to keep bearing witness to him even in the most barren places and seasons.

Second, we should not attempt to make Paul's experience normative. Every conversion story is different. Some people's stories sound like a kind of 'Damascus Road' experience – the light went on and everything changed in an instant. Other people seem to come more slowly. Others have grown up hearing the good news and never doubted. We should be wary of expecting every story to be the same or of ranking some testimonies as somehow better than others. Each conversion story is a miracle, however dramatic or otherwise it may appear to us.

Third, Saul's call was unique. He was to be the apostle to the Gentiles. While all Christians can and should find ways to witness to the Lord Jesus, it will look different for each of us, given our own particular blend of gifting, experience, understanding and opportunity. We need to be sensitive to Luke's intent with his narrative if we are to understand how we apply it to our own situations. Description is not necessarily prescription. The triune God is ultimately the hero of the narrative. We need to keep finding our trust and confidence in him, and sensitively discerning lessons for our own lives.

Acts 9:23–31: Saul meets the apostles

23 After many days had gone by, there was a conspiracy among the Jews to kill him, 24 but Saul learned of their plan. Day and night they kept close watch on the city gates in order to kill him. 25 But his followers took him by night and lowered him in a basket through an opening in the wall.

26 When he came to Jerusalem, he tried to join the disciples, but they were all afraid of him, not believing that he really was a disciple. 27 But Barnabas took him and brought him to the apostles. He told them how Saul on his journey had seen the Lord and that the Lord had spoken to him, and how in Damascus he had preached

fearlessly in the name of Jesus. 28 So Saul stayed with them and moved about freely in Jerusalem, speaking boldly in the name of the Lord. 29 He talked and debated with the Hellenistic Jews,[a] but they tried to kill him. 30 When the believers learned of this, they took him down to Caesarea and sent him off to Tarsus.

31 Then the church throughout Judea, Galilee and Samaria enjoyed a time of peace and was strengthened. Living in the fear of the Lord and encouraged by the Holy Spirit, it increased in numbers.

_____

a 29 That is, Jews who had adopted the Greek language and culture

In verse 23, Luke's narrative turns again as Saul the persecutor became Saul the persecuted. He now found himself on the receiving end of zealous Jews who conspired to kill him. He made a midnight escape (verse 25) and remarkably returned to the place where his reception was unlikely to be warm – Jerusalem.[15]

It is worth noting in passing that the church in Jerusalem, having been decimated in Acts 8:1, appears to have begun to grow again in Acts 9:26. The disciples were afraid, suspicious that Saul was not really a disciple. At this point Barnabas re-entered the story (the 'son of encouragement' from Acts 4:36) and took Saul to the apostles. Amid the preaching and

_____

[15] Bock addresses the question of Paul's time in Arabia (Galatians 1:17) and how to reconcile the apparent discrepancy. It seems likely that Luke is quite deliberate in not giving every chronological detail, but rather providing a summary of the key events in his narrative. See Bock, *Acts*, 363–4.

the miracles, Barnabas appeared as a man with significant influence through his generosity and kindness. It is not just the preachers who are significant for Luke (as we will see in the next section – 9:32–43). The humble 'friend of sinners' has a crucial part to play. While Saul does (and will) take centre stage, the supporting cast of Barnabas and Ananias are in some ways equally heroic in this chapter. Without their contribution, what may have become of Saul? God uses all sorts of people, with all sorts of giftings, in his purposes.

Having been accepted by the apostles, Saul remained in Jerusalem. 'speaking boldly in the name of the Lord'. One can only imagine the mixed reception he must have encountered, and his courage to keep speaking for Jesus. In verse 29 we hear of him debating with Hellenistic Jews – they too wanted to kill him. And so the believers took him to Caesarea and sent him off to Tarsus.

Here is courage combined with wisdom. Saul's obedience to Jesus's commission sees him speaking in situations that were dangerous – we see this repeated. Yet we also see the wisdom to leave a situation and go elsewhere as necessity and opportunity arose. It is surely one of the hardest tightropes to walk to know when to courageously speak whatever the consequences and when to quietly remove oneself to 'live to fight another day', so to speak. Some of us lack courage. Some of us lack wisdom. Awareness of our own weaknesses will help us take another difficult step along that tightrope.

Luke summarises in verse 31 the peace and growth the church enjoyed at this time, 'living in the fear of the Lord and encouraged by the Holy Spirit'.[16] The murderous threats of Acts 9:1 have become peace, strengthening and increase. It really is a quite remarkable summary statement given all that has happened in chapters 7–9. The witness commanded in Acts 1:8 to Jerusalem, Judea and Samaria has borne fruit by the continued active presence of the risen Jesus and the power of the Holy Spirit.

---

[16] The word 'church' (*ekklēsia*) is used here in the singular to refer to the three regions. This is a reminder that though local churches are individual and separate, there is also an important sense in which there is one church, united in its service of the Lord Jesus. This small observation reminds us of the importance of unity and interdependence among true churches.

2. Peter heals Aeneas and raises Dorcas • Acts 9:32–43

Aeneas and Dorcas

32 As Peter travelled about the country, he went to visit the Lord's people who lived in Lydda. **33** There he found a man named Aeneas, who was paralysed and had been bedridden for eight years. **34** 'Aeneas,' Peter said to him, 'Jesus Christ heals you. Get up and roll up your mat.' Immediately Aeneas got up. **35** All those who lived in Lydda and Sharon saw him and turned to the Lord.

36 In Joppa there was a disciple named Tabitha (in Greek her name is Dorcas); she was always doing good and helping the poor. **37** About that time she became ill and died, and her body was washed and placed in an upstairs room. **38** Lydda was near Joppa; so when the disciples heard that Peter was in Lydda, they sent two men to him and urged

him, 'Please come at once!'

39 Peter went with them, and when he arrived he was taken upstairs to the room. All the widows stood round him, crying and showing him the robes and other clothing that Dorcas had made while she was still with them.

40 Peter sent them all out of the room; then he got down on his knees and prayed. Turning towards the dead woman, he said, 'Tabitha, get up.' She opened her eyes, and seeing Peter she sat up. **41** He took her by the hand and helped her to her feet. Then he called for the believers, especially the widows, and presented her to them alive. **42** This became known all over Joppa, and many people believed in the Lord. **43** Peter stayed in Joppa for some time with a tanner named Simon.

In Acts 9:32, Luke turns the camera from Saul (who will return in 11:25) back on to Peter, who was travelling and visiting the Lord's people living in Lydda.[17] In this section we see Peter perform two significant miracles, the purpose of which will be considered in due course.

The first miracle in this section is reminiscent of the healing miracle performed in Acts 3:1–10 and of Jesus's healing miracle in Luke 5:17–26. Luke introduces us to a man named Aeneas who was paralysed and had been bedridden for eight years.[18] As in Acts 3:6, Peter heals the man with an appeal to the power of Jesus Christ. This account of the healing of a

---

[17] Lydda and Joppa were in the coastal region of Judea. The believers may have been scattered in the persecution of Acts 8:1 or have been converted through the preaching of Philip in the nearby regions. Lydda was twenty-five miles from Jerusalem, and Joppa another twelve miles further on. Peterson, *Acts*, 319–20.

[18] The phrase *ex etōn oktō katakeimenon epi krabattou* could indicate that he had been bedridden for eight years or bedridden since the age of eight. Witherington, *Acts*, 329.

paralysed man provides the reader with further evidence of the truth of the apostolic message. In an earlier section of this chapter (9:3–16), we saw the double-vision (Saul and Ananias) used to confirm the divine origin of the events (see Genesis 41:32). In the Old Testament, two witnesses were required to give credibility to an accusation.[19] The double-miracle serves to give credibility to the apostles and their message about the Lord.

Peter's statement to Aeneas, 'Jesus Christ heals you,' is a reminder that it was not so much the apostle performing the miracle as the risen Lord Jesus performing the miracle *through* him, as an appointed eyewitness.[20] Here is further evidence that Jesus Christ is risen, active and present in the events of Luke's narrative. The miracles always point beyond themselves to the truth of the message about Jesus. We can see this from verse 35: 'All those who lived in Lydda and Sharon saw him and turned to the Lord.' When miracles become and end in themselves, or are used to draw attention towards the worker (or their ministry), we must wonder as to the motive, origin and efficacy of such works.

The second miracle in this section takes place in Joppa. We hear of a disciple named Tabitha (Dorcas in Greek) who is described as 'always doing good and helping the poor'.[21] In verse 39, the widows showed Peter the clothes she had made. It would be easy to pass over these details and move on to the miracle of verses 40–41, yet Luke has included them for a reason.

A distinctively Lucan concern is for the poor, and he is particularly interested in those characters who exercise care or concern for the marginalised. This is one of his favourite themes. We can see this Lucan emphasis in the following episodes:

- Jesus's synagogue sermon in Nazareth which announced 'good news to the poor' (Luke 4:18)
- The Sermon on the Plain: 'Blessed are you who are poor, for yours is the kingdom of God' (Luke 6:20)
- The report to John: 'Good news is proclaimed to the poor' (Luke 7:22)

---

[19] Deuteronomy 17:6; 19:15.

[20] See Acts 1:8.

[21] She is literally 'full of good works and alms' (*plērēs ergōn agathōn kai eleēmosynōn*). This may suggest she was a 'woman of means, with the leisure and freedom to do good deeds for others'. Witherington, *Acts*, 331.

- Jesus's rebuke of the Pharisees:
  - 'Be generous to the poor, and everything will be clean for you' (Luke 11:41)
  - 'When you give a banquet, invite the poor, the crippled, the lame, the blind' (Luke 14:13)
- Jesus's instruction to his disciples: 'Sell your possessions and give to the poor' (Luke 12:33)
- Jesus's parable of the great banquet: 'Bring in the poor, the crippled, the blind and the lame (Luke 14:21)
- Jesus's encounter with the rich young ruler: 'Sell everything you have and give to the poor' (Luke 18:22)
- Jesus's encounter with Zacchaeus – 'I give half of my possessions to the poor' (Luke 19:8)
- The summary statements of Acts including the provision for the needy (Acts 2:42–7; 4:32–7)
- The care for the widows seen in Acts 6:1–7.

We need to consider carefully Luke's concern for the poor. Some of the above episodes are designed to reveal idolatry in those with whom Jesus is in dialogue. The term 'poor' can be used to refer to spiritual poverty, not just material poverty. Yet we do see in Luke's Gospel and in Acts a concern with body and soul – a holistic spirituality that recognises the importance of caring for people in every sphere of their being as part of our worship of God and love of neighbour. To see this is not to capitulate to a social gospel or liberation theology. The proclamation of the atoning work of Christ remains ultimate as it meets the deepest and eternal needs of humanity. But we do not need to 'throw the baby out with the bath water' or swing the pendulum so hard the other way that we miss the physical and social aspects of what it means to be a fully devoted follower of Jesus. Luke shows us the integration of word and deed in the body of Christ. Neither the church that is a 'preaching centre' nor the church that is a social project has fully grasped the 'whole of life' call to be the people of God.

Luke's brief portrait of Tabitha is designed to hold her up as an example to the believing community.[22] Her almsgiving sets her apart as

---

[22] Chrysostom says of Tabitha, 'If you want to be remembered and are anxious for true repute, imitate her, and build edifices like that, not going to expense on lifeless matter but displaying great generosity in regard to your fellow human

a virtuous character in Luke's narrative.[23] She is someone who has spread the fragrance of Christ to many through her simple acts of kindness to the needy. Peter's willingness to come to Joppa suggests that Tabitha was known and respected by him.[24]

Luke is not solely interested in the great speeches and the amazing miracles, though they are prominent in driving the narrative forward. Luke wants to stop along the way to notice how God can use 'ordinary' people and their simple acts of kindness to take forward the mission. This is what Chris Wright has termed 'missional ethics' – the idea that there is something missional not just in what we say, but in how we live.[25] We may not all possess the rhetorical gifts of Peter or Paul, but Tabithas are also worth a mention in the story of God's mission.

We should also note Luke's inclusion of women within his narrative. Here is not the place for a full discussion of the topic, but it cannot be denied that women have key roles to play within the believing community and the advance of the gospel.[26]

The second miracle is remarkable in that it was the first time an apostle had raised someone from the dead. This miracle is reminiscent both of Jesus's raising of the little girl (Luke 8:54) and similar miracles performed by Elijah and Elisha (1 Kings 17:19–24; 2 Kings 4:32–5).[27] Having sent everyone out of the room, Peter knelt down and prayed. Then, having commanded her to 'get up', he took her by the hand, helped her to her feet and presented her alive to the believers.

Here we see Peter functioning in the same prophetic line as Elijah and Elisha – the prophets sent to denounce evil and proclaim the rule of God.[28] These prophets, like those who went before and came after, were sent to call people back to relationship with the one true God.

Here is Peter, empowered by the risen Lord. The power of Christ was at work in the apostles as they carry the mission forward at his

---

beings. This is the remembrance that is worth admiring and brings great benefit.' 'Acts', in ACCS 5:116.

[23] Teresa J. Calpino, *Women, Work and Leadership in Acts* (Tübingen: Mohr Siebeck, 2014), 157.

[24] Calpino, *Women, Work and Leadership*, 177.

[25] For more on this theme, see Wright, *The Mission of God,* 357–92.

[26] See Ben Witherington III, *Women in the Earliest Churches* (Cambridge: Cambridge University Press, 1988), 128–57.

[27] A list of the parallels is provided by Tannehill, *Narrative Unity*, 126.

[28] See 1 Kings 17:17–24; 2 Kings 4:18–37.

command.[29] Each and every miracle bears witness to the truth that the same Jesus who performed such things in the Gospels is alive and active by his Spirit in the book of Acts. Given Peter's role in the conversion of Cornelius, it is critical for Luke at this point to establish Peter's authority as an apostle of Christ.[30]

In Luke 7:18–23, John's disciples sent messengers to see if Jesus was truly 'the one who is to come'. Jesus replied, 'Go back and report to John what you have seen and heard: the blind receive sight, the lame walk, those who have leprosy are cleansed, the deaf hear, the dead are raised, and the good news is proclaimed to the poor' (Luke 7:22). The book of Acts shows us that these things were not just confined to Jesus's earthly ministry, but now, by virtue of his resurrection and ascension, his power is at work unto the ends of the earth. The scope of the 'year of the Lord's favour' (Luke 4:19) now extends to all the times and places over which Jesus reigns in his exaltation. This gives us hope and confidence as we seek to live as Christ's ambassadors wherever he has called us.

There are two things worth noting in relation to Peter's second miracle. First, we should have no reason to doubt the veracity of Luke's account. Some have suggested that Tabitha was not really dead, but perhaps in some sort of coma. This is unlikely. The ancient world knew as well as we do when a person had died. Her body had been prepared and she had been laid out in preparation for a burial. There would have been no room for doubt that Tabitha was dead. Given the effect Luke records on the town of Joppa (verse 42), we should accept Luke's version of events. As incredible as it may seem to a post-Enlightenment world view, Peter really did cause someone who had died to come back to life.

The second thing to note is just how remarkable these two miracles were. Many so-called miracle workers today seem to specialise in stiff-backs or arthritic knees. These are not the sorts of healings we see in the Gospels and in Acts. The miracles in Acts are fulfilments of Old Testament prophecies that signify the arrival of the kingdom: the dead are raised, the lame walk, the blind see.[31] While there are claims to these sorts of healings today, we must conclude that many are unsubstantiated.

This is, of course, not to say God cannot perform miracles today. But we need to ask whether we should expect the same sorts and regularity of miracles, performed by a select group of people, in the post-apostolic

---

[29] See Luke 5:17–26; 7:11–17.

[30] Peterson, *Acts*, 320.

[31] See, for example, Isaiah 35; 61; 65–6; Micah 4:6–8; Zephaniah 3:9–20.

era. The apostolic miracles occurred as evidence that the kingdom of God had dawned as foretold in the Old Testament. The signs accredited the apostles and their message. The task of the church in the subsequent generations is to proclaim that message, which has already been accredited. The belief that the apostolic message needs to be accredited afresh with miracles in each new generation cannot be supported by Luke's narrative. The expectation that it should be so often leads to significant hurt, harm and disappointment, as well as a whole raft of charlatans. We would do better today to see what the miracles point to, rather than seek them for their own sake. The miracles testify to the truthfulness of the apostolic message concerning the risen and reigning Lord Jesus Christ. God may heal today, but miracles today lend no new weight to the evidence already seen of the dawning of the kingdom and the preaching of Jesus's appointed eyewitnesses.

As a consequence of Peter's miracle, Luke summarises, 'This became known all over Joppa, and many people believed in the Lord.' The gospel continues to advance through the apostolic witness. Luke informs us Peter stayed in Joppa for some time with a tanner named Simon. Peterson notes, 'Tanners were considered unclean by more scrupulous Jews because of their contact with the hides of dead animals.'[32] For the reader aware of the Jewish background, it sounds strange that Peter should stay with someone many would have considered unclean. This paves the way for the next episode in the narrative. The miracles have served to enhance Peter's authority. This will be significant as he himself is about to be called into Gentile mission. And the mention of Joppa provides the reader with a significant Old Testament echo. As Peter is about to be called to the Gentile Cornelius, the reader wonders, 'Will Peter do a Jonah?'[33] Every indication so far would suggest Peter is more of an Elijah or Elisha – a man who will prove faithful to the call of God.

---

[32] Peterson, *Acts*, 323.
[33] See Jonah 1:3.

9

More Surprising Conversions

ACTS 10:1–11:18

Since the Jerusalem persecution which led to the scattering of the believers (8:1), Luke has recorded several incidents of surprising conversions as the gospel reached unexpected (even 'unclean') places. We have seen the conversion of Samaritans, the Ethiopian eunuch and even Saul. Here, in Acts 10:1–11:18, we see perhaps the climactic moment of the narrative thus far as the gospel reaches a Gentile household. Barrett describes this episode as 'a decisive step, perhaps the decisive step, in the expansion of Christianity into the non-Jewish world'.[1]

The narrative depicts not just the conversion of Cornelius, but also the 'conversion' of Peter – the prophet like Jonah, situated at Joppa, wondering about a call to take God's message of mercy to Gentiles.[2]

This section of Luke's narrative is one of the most important, evidenced by both the amount of space allocated and its repetition (see 11:4–17; 15:7–9).[3] Although we have previously encountered 'outsiders' receiving the grace of God, this is the first account of a Gentile convert, locally placed, who will signal the beginning of Gentile churches and the Gentile mission. The conversion of Cornelius and his family is the event that causes circumcised believers (11:2) to say, 'So then, even to Gentiles God has granted repentance that leads to life' (11:18). This story may have been particularly important for someone like Theophilus who may have been a 'God-fearer' considering his own involvement with this new community of Jesus followers.[4]

The narrative proceeds in four scenes as follows: in scene one, Cornelius has a vision in which he is instructed to send for Peter (10:1–8). In scene two, Peter has a vision instructing him to go to Cornelius (10:9–23a). In scene three, Peter explains the gospel to Cornelius and his family, the Holy

---

[1] Barrett, *Acts 1–14*, 495.
[2] Stott, *Acts*, 186. See Jonah 1:3.
[3] Barrett, *Acts 1–14*, 491.
[4] Bock, *Acts*, 383.

Spirit comes, and Peter baptises the new believers (10:23b–48). In scene four, Peter defends his actions to the believers in Jerusalem (11:1–18).[5] This incident sets the scene for the Gentile mission which will occupy the majority of Luke's narrative moving forward.

1. Cornelius's vision • Acts 10:1–8

Cornelius calls for Peter

10 At Caesarea there was a man named Cornelius, a centurion in what was known as the Italian Regiment. **2**He and all his family were devout and God-fearing; he gave generously to those in need and prayed to God regularly. **3**One day at about three in the afternoon he had a vision. He distinctly saw an angel of God, who came to him and said, 'Cornelius!'

4Cornelius stared at him in fear. 'What is it, Lord?' he asked.

The angel answered, 'Your prayers and gifts to the poor have come up as a memorial offering before God. **5**Now send men to Joppa to bring back a man named Simon who is called Peter. **6**He is staying with Simon the tanner, whose house is by the sea.'

7When the angel who spoke to him had gone, Cornelius called two of his servants and a devout soldier who was one of his attendants. **8**He told them everything that had happened and sent them to Joppa.

Luke introduces the reader to a centurion from the Italian Regiment named Cornelius, who lived in Caesarea – an important military city.[6] Cornelius appears to be a man of means indicated by his servants and attendant mentioned in verse 7. As a centurion he would have been a man of status commanding of a unit of one hundred men.[7]

Last time we heard mention of Caesarea was in Acts 8:40 and 9:30. Caesarea was the place Philip appears to have settled following his meeting with the Ethiopian eunuch (8:40; 21:8). Caesarea was also the place through which Paul travelled on his way to Tarsus (9:30). We might wonder why God couldn't use Philip or Paul to reach Cornelius. Such was the enormity of the events about to happen it required Peter to

---

[5] This is also how Marshall breaks down the section, *Acts*, 183.

[6] See Acts 23:23–35; 25:1–27. Bock notes Caesarea was a 'major administrative and harbor city . . . it had an amphitheater, a hippodrome, and a temple dedicated to Caesar', *Acts*, 385.

[7] Bock, *Acts*, 385.

be the conduit and witness if the credibility of Gentile conversion and mission were to be accepted in Jerusalem.

Luke informs us that Cornelius and 'all his family were devout and God-fearing [*eusebēs kai phoboumenos ton theon*]; he gave generously to those in need and prayed to God regularly.' Cornelius's spiritual status at this point is worth reflecting on. How are we to understand his current status *vis-à-vis* the covenant community?[8] He is on the one hand a God-fearer, who prays, gives to the poor, and is described as righteous and highly respected by the Jewish community (10:2–3, 22). Further he seems to know something of the Jewish story – Peter twice says to him 'you know' (*hymeis oidate*, verses 36–7) followed by an explanation of Israel's history. On the other hand, he is a Gentile and as such considered unclean (10:28) and as yet unsaved (10:43; 11:14, 18).[9]

Cornelius is an intriguing example of a person who is not yet a Christian and yet fears and prays to God (and is heard – verse 4). Cornelius is a reminder that the doctrine of 'total depravity' does not mean people are as bad as they could be. Here is one of the paradoxes embraced by Reformed theology. The noetic effects of the fall leave humans spiritually ignorant, enslaved, blind and dead.[10] And yet by God's common grace, natural revelation and the light of conscience some human beings still reach out to God.[11] Such light is not sufficient for salvation – the work of the Spirit is still necessary to bring regeneration, and this is connected to the preaching of God's word.[12] In terms of the church's mission, we should note that there are people like Cornelius drawn to God through the stories and lives of the covenant community, the beauty of creation and a sense of right and wrong. Being salt and light before others may lead them to give glory to God (Matthew 5:16). The good deeds and reasonable accounts given by individuals and churches are not sufficient to save without the gospel, but neither are they without missional force. These things have missional power, hand

---

[8] Peterson suggests Cornelius may have frequented a local synagogue, without being a full proselyte. *Acts*, 326–37. This would explain his almsgiving, prayers and esteem by the Jewish people (verse 22). See too the discussion in Witherington, *Acts*, 341–4.

[9] *Contra* Calvin who thinks Cornelius must already be regenerate given Luke's description of him, though 10:43 and 11:14, 18 would suggest otherwise. See Calvin, *Acts*, 406–14, 439–40; *Institutes* 3.17.4–5. Tannehill describes him as the most Jewish non-Jew in Acts. *Narrative Unity*, 133.

[10] 1 Corinthians 2:14; John 8:34; 2 Corinthians 4:4; Ephesians 2:1.

[11] Romans 1:18–20; 2:14–15; Acts 17:27.

[12] See Romans 10:9–15.

in hand with gospel proclamation, to attract and convert those who are seeking after truth.

Luke tells us that one day, at three in the afternoon (one of the Jewish hours of prayer), Cornelius received a vision in which he saw an angel of God. Just as Saul and Ananias had received the 'double-vision' in Acts 9, so too here in Acts 10, Cornelius and Peter will both receive a vision. We observed with reference to the double-vision in Acts 9 that it assures the reader that the events are truly from God (see Genesis 41:32). These visions show us beyond doubt that it is God carrying the gospel forward and directing the events – even (especially) the most surprising or controversial.

In the vision, the angel told Cornelius that his prayers and gifts to the poor had come up as a memorial offering to God.[13] Cornelius was instructed by the angel to send to Joppa to bring back Simon Peter. When the angel had left, Cornelius called two of his servants and a devout soldier who was one of his attendants and, having told them everything that happened, he sent them to Joppa.

2. Peter's vision • Acts 10:9–23a

Peter's vision

9 About noon the following day as they were on their journey and approaching the city, Peter went up on the roof to pray. **10** He became hungry and wanted something to eat, and while the meal was being prepared, he fell into a trance. **11** He saw heaven opened and something like a large sheet being let down to earth by its four corners. **12** It contained all kinds of four-footed animals, as well as reptiles and birds. **13** Then a voice told him, 'Get up, Peter. Kill and eat.'

14 'Surely not, Lord!' Peter replied. 'I have never eaten anything impure or unclean.'

15 The voice spoke to him a second time, 'Do not call anything impure that God has made clean.'

16 This happened three times, and immediately the sheet was taken back to heaven.

17 While Peter was wondering about the meaning of the vision, the men sent by Cornelius found out where Simon's house was and stopped at the gate. **18** They called out, asking if Simon who was known as Peter was staying there.

---

[13] The prayers and almsgiving were seen as spiritual sacrifices in lieu of the physical sacrifices Cornelius would have been unable to offer as a Gentile. Witherington, *Acts*, 348.

19While Peter was still thinking about the vision, the Spirit said to him, 'Simon, three^a men are looking for you. 20So get up and go downstairs. Do not hesitate to go with them, for I have sent them.'

21Peter went down and said to the men, 'I'm the one you're looking for. Why have you come?'

22The men replied, 'We have come from Cornelius the centurion. He is a righteous and God-fearing man, who is respected by all the Jewish people. A holy angel told him to ask you to come to his house so that he could hear what you have to say.' 23Then Peter invited the men into the house to be his guests.

_____
a 19 One early manuscript *two*; other manuscripts do not have the number.

The journey from Caesarea to Joppa was around thirty miles.[14] As Cornelius's servants were on their way to the house, Peter had a vision of his own. Luke describes his vision as a 'trance' (*ekstasis*) in which he saw a large sheet being let down to earth containing all the sorts of animals described as unclean in the Old Testament.[15] A voice from heaven commanded Peter to get up, kill and eat, at which point Peter objected, 'I have never eaten anything impure or unclean [*akatharton*]' (verse 14).

It is interesting that Peter protests his concern for purity while staying at the house of a tanner (see note on Acts 9:32–43). It is not necessarily the case that Peter was being deliberately inconsistent. It perhaps was less of a concern for him as he did not have to come into direct contact with Simon's work. Perhaps Peter's own views were softening in some respects through his life with Jesus and involvement in the conversion of the Samaritans (8:14–25). Jesus's own instructions to his apostles had been to take the message to the 'ends of the earth' (Acts 1:8). Had Peter forgotten these instructions? Perhaps more likely Peter, like any Jew of his day, still viewed Gentiles as unclean, and therefore felt unable to freely associate. Peter, like many of us, needed his own subsequent moments of 'conversion' for his life to catch up with his theology. It took this moment to help not just Peter, but also many other Jewish Christians to understand the full implications of Acts 1:8. At this point, on the eating of unclean food he stood resolute. As a Jewish person he was reticent to break God's Law in coming into contact with that which the Law deemed unclean.

As Peter protested his innocence the voice spoke again: 'Do not call anything impure that God has made clean.' Luke tells us this happened three times and immediately the sheet was taken back to heaven.' We can

_____
[14] Barrett, *Acts 1–14*, 504.
[15] See Leviticus 11; Deuteronomy 14.

well imagine why Peter was wondering what the vision meant. The Law was clear. God would not arbitrarily change his mind with regard to the standards of his holiness. In what sense could things unclean suddenly be declared clean?

It is important to recognise at this point that God was not simply setting aside Old Testament Law as no longer relevant or important. The God of the Old Testament is the same as the God of the New Testament. His character and his holiness are unchanged. Unclean things do not simply cease to be unclean – something must happen for unclean things to be made clean.

Jesus, disputing with the Pharisees, said that it is not what enters a person but what comes out of them that defiles (Mark 7:18–23). In this passage Mark tells us that Jesus was declaring all foods clean. So what exactly changed? In the Old Testament, the food laws were given as a sign of God's holiness and the distinctiveness of his people among the nations. The whole system of Temple, priest, sacrifice, clean/unclean was designed to teach the people about the holiness of God and the sinfulness of the people. When Jesus came, he fulfilled the Old Testament types – he was the priest, Temple and sacrifice *par excellence*. He came to make a way for unclean things to be declared clean. As Peterson notes, 'The provisions of the Mosaic law for cleansing and sanctification are fulfilled in Christ.'[16]

As Jesus fulfils all the requirements of the Law, and exhausts all its curses, he is able to impute a new and permanent 'cleanness' to all who are united to him by faith. All the foods previously considered unclean are no longer so since Jesus has fulfilled the Law's demands perfectly. People now relate to God through Jesus. The distinction between clean and unclean no longer applies to external relationships – people, places, foods – but is now considered entirely in relation to Christ. If we are united to him, we are clean; if we are not, we remain unclean. All of this, it appears, was not yet clear to Peter, but as the narrative proceeds these things come into sharper focus.

As Peter was wondering as to the meaning of the vision, the servants of Cornelius arrived at the house and called for Peter. At that moment, the Spirit told Peter about the visitors and instructed him to go with them. The men announced they had come from Cornelius the centurion. They described him as a 'righteous and God-fearing man' [*anēr dikaios kai phoboumenos ton theon*] who is highly respected by all the

---

16 Peterson, *Acts*, 325.

Jewish people.' Peter invited the three men into the house where they spent the night as his guests before setting off on the return journey to Caesarea the next day.

3. The conversion of Cornelius and his household • Acts 10:23b–48

Acts 10:23b–33: Peter at the home of Cornelius

Peter at Cornelius' house

The next day Peter started out with them, and some of the believers from Joppa went along. **24** The following day he arrived in Caesarea. Cornelius was expecting them and had called together his relatives and close friends. **25** As Peter entered the house, Cornelius met him and fell at his feet in reverence. **26** But Peter made him get up. 'Stand up,' he said, 'I am only a man myself.'

27 While talking with him, Peter went inside and found a large gathering of people. **28** He said to them: 'You are well aware that it is against our law for a Jew to associate with or visit a Gentile. But God has shown me that I should not call anyone impure or unclean. **29** So when I was sent for, I came without raising any objection. May I ask why you sent for me?'

30 Cornelius answered: 'Three days ago I was in my house praying at this hour, at three in the afternoon. Suddenly a man in shining clothes stood before me **31** and said, "Cornelius, God has heard your prayer and remembered your gifts to the poor. **32** Send to Joppa for Simon who is called Peter. He is a guest in the home of Simon the tanner, who lives by the sea." **33** So I sent for you immediately, and it was good of you to come. Now we are all here in the presence of God to listen to everything the Lord has commanded you to tell us.'

The next day, Peter, the servants of Cornelius and some believers from Joppa set out for Caesarea, arriving the following day.[17] As they arrived, Cornelius had been expecting them and had invited his own relatives and close friends. One can imagine quite a crowd gathered – Peter and the believers from Joppa, plus Cornelius, his family, friends and servants. There must have been an air of expectancy as Peter arrived. It seems likely the crowd were not entirely unprepared for what they were about to hear. And this wasn't the conversion of just one man,

---

[17] Acts 11:12 informs us that six believers accompanied Peter to Caesarea.

but all present – as Witherington says, 'This was a story of great significance for the Caesarean church, for it was probably a major turning
point in its life.'[18]

It would have been a remarkable sight to see a senior military figure
kneel before Peter the fisherman-cum-apostle. Peter's reply rightly asserted
that the spiritual power and authority was not his but belongs to the
risen Lord. It is a good reminder for us not to place leaders on pedestals
or venerate them as being somehow superhuman or spiritual elites. This
takes different forms in different cultures or denominational traditions,
yet there seems a pervasive tendency in the human heart to venerate
human leaders, rather than God.

It is tempting to wonder what sort of first impression Cornelius
and his friends had of Peter. His opening remark had been to rebuke
Cornelius for his show of reverence. His second statement reminded his
audience that he shouldn't really be there: 'You are well aware that it
is against our law for a Jew to associate with or visit a Gentile' (verse
28). You can imagine an awkward silence at this point as those gathered
wondered where the conversation would turn next. Peter's remarks here
are interesting. There was no law forbidding association with Gentiles *per
se*, though it seems it was frowned upon in Jewish tradition.[19]

Peter relieved the tension in verse 28 by continuing, 'But God has
shown me that I should not call anyone impure or unclean.' The meaning
of the vision seems to have become clear to Peter in the intervening
period. He now recognised the purpose of the vision, as he stood in a
Gentile home. He could visit because God had taught him not to call
Cornelius (or his family and friends) unclean.

In these few verses (10:25–8), Peter repudiated two extremes – one
that would venerate human beings as divine, godlike beings worthy of
worship; and the other that would despise others as unworthy of our
concern. To paraphrase Stott, Cornelius should not view Peter as a god,
and Peter should not view Cornelius as a dog.[20] We live in a world in
which both of these things occur. We view ourselves as little gods with
the authority to determine the purpose, direction and values of our own
lives. The one true God is replaced with the self as the supreme ruler. And

---

[18] Witherington, *Acts*, 354.

[19] Witherington, *Acts*, 353. Jubilees 22:16 says, 'Keep yourself separate from the
nations, and do not eat with them; and do not imitate their rituals, nor associate
with them.'

[20] Stott, *Acts*, 189.

yet we are still capable of horrific acts of violence and injustice towards others. We are so curved in on ourselves that we are at best unconcerned, at worst dismissive, of others and their needs. Luke blows both of those errors out of the water in verses 25–8.

Peter asked Cornelius for the reason why he sent for him (verse 29). Cornelius then recounted his own vision and concluded, 'Now we are all here in the presence of God to listen to everything the Lord has commanded you to tell us' (verse 33). Cornelius demonstrated his faith in the vision he received by affirming his belief that Peter was to bring the word of the Lord.

Acts 10:34–43: Peter's speech

34 Then Peter began to speak: 'I now realise how true it is that God does not show favouritism 35 but accepts from every nation the one who fears him and does what is right. 36 You know the message God sent to the people of Israel, announcing the good news of peace through Jesus Christ, who is Lord of all. 37 You know what has happened throughout the province of Judea, beginning in Galilee after the baptism that John preached – 38 how God anointed Jesus of Nazareth with the Holy Spirit and power, and how he went around doing good and healing all who were under the power of the devil, because God was with him.

39 'We are witnesses of everything he did in the country of the Jews and in Jerusalem. They killed him by hanging him on a cross, 40 but God raised him from the dead on the third day and caused him to be seen. 41 He was not seen by all the people, but by witnesses whom God had already chosen – by us who ate and drank with him after he rose from the dead. 42 He commanded us to preach to the people and to testify that he is the one whom God appointed as judge of the living and the dead. 43 All the prophets testify about him that everyone who believes in him receives forgiveness of sins through his name.'

We can imagine that Peter's speech ran for much longer along the lines Luke outlines. What we have here is another summary of the speech's main contours. It has two main parts. In the first Peter recounts the elements with which it seems Cornelius is already familiar. In the second part Peter elaborates some of the details, including the apostles' own involvement as eyewitnesses. It appears Peter is still talking as the Spirit descends in verse 44.

Peter begins his speech in a conciliatory tone, explaining how he has come to understand that God does not show favouritism but accepts from every nation those who fear him and do right. We ought not think that the 'doing right' is in any sense a meritorious attainment, otherwise how could Jesus accept the thief on the cross? The 'doing right' it would seem is linked to the 'fear of God' – the seeking and the repentance that leads to faith (11:18).[21]

Peter's introduction reminds us of something we regularly need to be reminded of – God does not show favouritism but accepts all. How easy it is for us in churches to look down or avoid people we deem unworthy. Perhaps they've wandered in off the street, or they're covered in tattoos and piercings, or they're known to have a criminal history. Do we welcome such people, or do we slip into patterns of behaviour that communicate we think God would not be interested in them?

More specifically, Peter says God accepts people from every nation. A friend of mine came to the UK as a child from India. She told me about the caste system, how her family were from the second-lowest caste, and there was nothing they could do to escape. They were constantly looked down upon. Another friend told me what it is like to be mixed race and feel rejected by both White and Black people. Racial divide and prejudice are still more prevalent than many of us would like to admit. Every Black friend I have asked has been subject to racist abuse at some point in their life. An Asian friend tells me he's been pulled over by the police more than twenty times, and when he gets on a train people often move to sit elsewhere.

Many of us live with unconscious bias towards people from different ethnic backgrounds. The gospel unites people as citizens of Christ's kingdom and members of his family.[22] The church should be at the forefront of confronting and rooting out racial injustice wherever it may be found. Church leaders must look long and hard at their own leadership and consider whether they are developing and investing in diversity. We need to be vigilant and ruthlessly honest with ourselves if we are to keep fighting to make sure we are not showing the sort of favouritism God rejects.

It is worth noting also that Peter's statement that God 'accepts from

---

[21] We must remember that 'righteousness' (*dikaiosynēn*) has a semantic range and not import Paul's forensic usage into every occurrence. Luke's own use of righteousness language suggests that he does not here mean sinless perfection, but rather the heart that seeks after God (see Luke 1:6, 17, 75; 2:25; 23:50).
[22] The good news of 'peace' is not just vertical, but horizontal. Ephesians 2:11–22.

every nation the one who fears him and does what is right' is not univer-salism, in the sense that all *will* be saved, but that the free offer of the gospel is universal – all *can* be saved if they turn to Christ in repentance and faith.[23] It is not the case that all without exception will be saved, but rather that all without distinction may be saved. Some *from* every nation, not all from every nation.

Further, the story of Cornelius's conversion is not intended to teach religious pluralism – the idea that any 'devout' person from any reli-gion is accepted by God. Cornelius still needed to believe in Christ (10:43), be saved (11:14), and repent (11:18). His devotion is evidence of common grace, not saving grace. Peter had already given his answer to the question of pluralism – 'Salvation is found in no one else, for there is no other name under heaven given to mankind by which we must be saved' (Acts 4:12).

It appears from Peter's speech that Cornelius is already familiar with some elements of the Jewish faith and the stories of Jesus. Peter says Cornelius already knows about the message of good news sent to Israel through Jesus Christ, and about what happened through Judea as Jesus did good and healed many. Peter affirms that these things happened because Christ is 'Lord of all' and 'God was with him' (verses 36, 38). It seems that Cornelius had heard some of the stories about Jesus but had not yet come to see him as Lord and Saviour.

Peter goes on to explain how 'we' (the apostles) were witnesses of everything that happened, how Jesus died and rose again, and how the eyewitnesses were with him post-resurrection until they were appointed to preach Jesus as the one 'appointed as judge of the living and the dead' (verse 42). Peter concludes that Jesus is the one to whom all the prophets testify, and whoever 'believes in him receives forgiveness of sins through his name' (verse 43).

There are a couple of points of interest in Luke's summary of Peter's speech. First, little mention is made of Christ's death as an atoning sacrifice. Peter simply mentions that Jesus was hung on a cross. More emphasis seems to be given to Jesus's miraculous powers and to the resurrection (verses 37–8; 40–42). This has led some to believe that the atonement was a peripheral theme for the apostolic preaching. They were more concerned to demonstrate the Lordship of Jesus seen in his resurrection and exaltation. We must remember that we are dealing with summaries. It is likely Peter said more than what is recorded. Further, there are clues in

---

[23] Green, *The Word of His Grace*, 81.

Luke's summaries of the speeches that suggest the atonement is a central plank of the apostolic gospel. Peter mentions the 'good news of peace' in verse 36. The reference to being hung on a cross has curse-bearing overtones for anyone familiar with the Jewish Scriptures, as Cornelius seems to have been (verse 39; compare Deuteronomy 21:22–3).[24] And Peter claims that forgiveness of sins comes through belief in his name (verse 43). These three things together – peace, his curse-bearing death on the cross and forgiveness of sins – only make sense if we view Jesus's death as a sacrifice of atonement for sin.

Acts 10:44–8: The coming of the Spirit

44 While Peter was still speaking these words, the Holy Spirit came on all who heard the message. **45** The circumcised believers who had come with Peter were astonished that the gift of the Holy Spirit had been poured out even on Gentiles. **46** For they heard them speaking in tongues[b] and praising God.

Then Peter said, **47** 'Surely no one can stand in the way of their being baptised with water. They have received the Holy Spirit just as we have.' **48** So he ordered that they be baptised in the name of Jesus Christ. Then they asked Peter to stay with them for a few days.

_____

b 46 Or *other languages*

As Peter was speaking, the Holy Spirit 'came on all who heard the message'. Luke records the astonishment of those who had accompanied Peter. As evidence that the Holy Spirit had come, the new believers were 'speaking in tongues [*lalountōn glōssais*] and praising God' (verse 46). Some have referred to this event as a Gentile Pentecost.[25] As argued in our examination of Acts 8:14–17 (the Samaritan conversion), I do not think this is a second (or third) Pentecost. Pentecost was a unique, unrepeatable event when the Spirit was given in fulfilment of the prophecy of Joel.[26] What we see in Acts 10:46 is tongues-speech given to accredit a controversial people group. It is perhaps better described as an echo of Pentecost, with all the significance that implies.[27] Luke does

---

[24] In the Greek translation of the Old Testament (LXX), Deuteronomy 21:22–3 uses the same verb ('hang', *kremannumi*) and noun ('tree', *xylon*) to describe those under God's curse. Peter has used the same phrase previously in Acts 5:30.

[25] For example, Tannehill, *Narrative Unity*, 142–3; Venkataraman, 'Acts', in *SABC*, 1479.

[26] Witherington, *Acts*, 360.

[27] Green, *The Word of His Grace*, 79.

not intend us to see tongues-speech as evidence of a second blessing, or something for every believer to pursue as a sign of baptism in the Spirit. Spirit-baptism happens at conversion, not after conversion.[28] The separation of these things is abnormal and best explained in terms of the necessity to accredit those who might otherwise struggle to find full acceptance in the wider church. Tongues-speech here is the necessary evidence to demonstrate that the Gentile believers are truly part of God's church. This event will provide the crucial evidence to convince the circumcised believers (11:2) that God has granted repentance to the Gentiles (11:18).

Since these new believers are so evidently genuine, Peter orders that they be baptised in the name of Jesus Christ. We can imagine how Peter may have hesitated to offer baptism to the uncircumcised, yet the gift of the Spirit is all the proof required that baptism has replaced circumcision as the covenant sign.[29] This passage has sometimes been used as an argument for household baptisms.[30] Just as Cornelius's whole household were baptised, shouldn't we baptise those (infants included) in the households of believers? There are two things to say in reply. First, those arguing for household baptism are really only arguing for infant baptism. They do not argue also for the baptism of an unbelieving spouse, grandparent or lodger. Second, and more importantly, we must note in verse 44 that 'the Holy Spirit came on *all* who heard the message' (my emphasis). There are no 'unbelievers' in this household. Each one received the Spirit and so was baptised. In fact, it was the credible evidence of Spirit-reception that qualified them for baptism.

Peter, it appears, remained for a few days with the new believers. The two parties must have both felt great joy in their respective conversions. Peter (and his friends?) had experienced their own sort of conversion in recognising God's election of Gentiles. Cornelius and his household had experienced a saving conversion in coming to know Jesus Christ as Lord and Saviour.[31] Habits of hospitality are a critical part of developing and fostering gospel unity. All of us could work harder at carving out

---

[28] See John 3:5–8; 1 Corinthians 12:12–13; Titus 3:5–7.

[29] See Augustine in ACCS 5:145–6.

[30] See, for example, Joel R. Beeke and Ray B. Lanning, 'Unto You, And To Your Children', in *The Case for Covenantal Infant Baptism*, ed. Gregg Strawbridge (Philipsburg: P&R, 2003), 51.

[31] Witherington, *Acts*, 361. So too Stott, who goes so far as to claim, 'The principle subject of this chapter is not so much the conversion of Cornelius as the conversion of Peter.' *Acts*, 186.

opportunities for hospitality with people who are different from us, or who are new to the church family. This it seems is one of the most effective strategies employed by the early church in its growth in diversity. It is also a great way to fight the ingrained prejudices or cultural suspicions that exist in every heart.

4. *The conversion of Peter* • *Acts 11:1–18*

Peter explains his actions

11 The apostles and the believers throughout Judea heard that the Gentiles also had received the word of God. **2** So when Peter went up to Jerusalem, the circumcised believers criticised him **3** and said, 'You went into the house of uncircumcised men and ate with them.'

4 Starting from the beginning, Peter told them the whole story: **5** 'I was in the city of Joppa praying, and in a trance I saw a vision. I saw something like a large sheet being let down from heaven by its four corners, and it came down to where I was. **6** I looked into it and saw four-footed animals of the earth, wild beasts, reptiles and birds. **7** Then I heard a voice telling me, "Get up, Peter. Kill and eat."

8 'I replied, "Surely not, Lord! Nothing impure or unclean has ever entered my mouth."

9 'The voice spoke from heaven a second time, "Do not call anything impure that God has made clean." **10** This happened three times, and then it was all pulled up to heaven again.

11 'Right then three men who had been sent to me from Caesarea stopped at the house where I was staying. **12** The Spirit told me to have no hesitation about going with them. These six brothers also went with me, and we entered the man's house. **13** He told us how he had seen an angel appear in his house and say, "Send to Joppa for Simon who is called Peter. **14** He will bring you a message through which you and all your household will be saved."

15 'As I began to speak, the Holy Spirit came on them as he had come on us at the beginning. **16** Then I remembered what the Lord had said: "John baptised with[a] water, but you will be baptised with[a] the Holy Spirit." **17** So if God gave them the same gift he gave us who believed in the Lord Jesus Christ, who was I to think that I could stand in God's way?'

18 When they heard this, they had no further objections and praised God, saying, 'So then, even to Gentiles God has granted repentance that leads to life.'

---

a 16 Or *in*

Word spread quickly to the other apostles and the believers throughout Judea 'that the Gentiles had also received the word of God'. This led to a point of tension and potential division in the early church. We have observed the threat of persecution throughout the early chapters. Here we encounter again the threat of internal division (see Acts 6:1) and its potential to decimate the early church. One of Satan's favourite strategies, it appears, is to pit believers against one another. As Peter went to Jerusalem, he faced criticism from the circumcised believers: 'You went into the house of uncircumcised men and ate with them' (verse 3).[32] This would not be the last time tensions would arise between circumcised and uncircumcised believers.[33] Such divisions always have the potential to destroy the church if not addressed with all the implications of the gospel.

It is one of the ongoing issues we see mentioned throughout the New Testament. Jewish Christians were still committed to certain cultural markers of religious identity – circumcision, food laws and holy days.[34] They did not object to proselytes, but that required a level of commitment that Jewish believers thought ought to extend to all non-Jewish believers. The simple admittance with apparently minimal requirement of Gentile believers was intolerable for those who spent their lives treasuring the Law and the Prophets. The Jewish believers, though no doubt genuine, had not yet fully grasped all the implications of the incarnation and Jesus's fulfilment of the Law's demands and penalties.

We, too, must be wary of requiring more than Jesus himself does of new converts. We sometimes confuse a sort of Christian cultural conformity with biblical obedience and ask people to do things the Bible does not if they are to be fully accepted. We need to be careful to ensure that the requirements we place on others are from Scripture, and not simply the traditions of human beings.[35]

Peter recounts his meeting with Cornelius, including his vision from heaven, the visit from Cornelius's servants, the six brothers who

---

[32] Venkataraman encourages us to imagine the similar feelings that may arise if a high-caste Hindu family were to spend a few days in a Dalit home. 'Acts', in *SABC*, 1480. Chrysostom notes the objection is not, 'Why did you preach to them?' but, 'Why did you eat with them?' The issue at hand is meaningful fellowship with Gentiles. See ACCS 5:142.

[33] We will see this issue surface again when we examine Acts 15.

[34] We can see some of these things in passages such as Romans 14:5–6; 1 Corinthians 10:25–8; Galatians 2:14; 5:2–3; Colossians 2:16–23.

[35] See Mark 7:1–8.

accompanied him and, critically, the gift of the Spirit with accompanying tongues-speech. This last point seems to be what Peter refers to when he says, 'The Holy Spirit came on them as he had come on us at the beginning' (verse 15). Peter concludes, 'If God gave them the same gift he gave us who believed in the Lord Jesus Christ, who was I to think that I could stand in God's way?' (verse 17). As with the speech, it seems appropriate to see this as a summary of the conversation. As Peter concludes, the Jewish believers have no further objections and praise God, saying, 'So then, even to Gentiles God has granted repentance that leads to life' (verse 18).

There are a number of key applications for us from this section. First, we continue to see God working in extraordinary ways to reach unexpected people with the gospel. He is the hero of the story, and we draw great confidence seeing him take forward his mission even to the most unlikely people groups. As Stott notes regarding the conversions of Saul and Cornelius:

> The differences between these two men were considerable . . . Yet both were converted by the gracious initiative of God . . . both were baptized and welcomed into the Christian family on equal terms. This fact is a signal testimony to the power and impartiality of the gospel of Christ.[36]

This gives us great confidence as we serve him in mission.

Second, we see the gospel invitation most clearly opened to all people – even those previously considered 'unclean'. This is an encouragement and a challenge to us. It is an encouragement to take the gospel to all people groups and nations. It is a challenge to make sure we offer acceptance to all people and do not look down on some or consider them too 'unclean' to be reached by God.

Third, this passage reminds us that there are people like Cornelius who are receptive and sensitive to the gospel. Total depravity does not mean that all people are entirely and utterly opposed to God. Cornelius shows us that there are people who, in God's common grace, are receptive to our words, invitations and good deeds. They will see something of God in these things and desire to know more. We should be sensitive to these opportunities to bring the life-giving words of the gospel. Of course, the work of the Spirit is absolutely crucial to bring regeneration, but a

---

[36] Stott, *Acts*, 199.

sensitivity to the seeker is not necessarily an unbiblical capitulation to worldly agendas or methods.

Fourth, this section running from Acts 8–10 shows us the beautiful fulfilment of Isaiah's vision, which should move our hearts to worship:

> Let no foreigner who is bound to the LORD say,
>   'The LORD will surely exclude me from his people.'
> And let no eunuch complain,
>   'I am only a dry tree.'
> For this is what the LORD says:
> 'To the eunuchs who keep my Sabbaths,
>   who choose what pleases me
>   and hold fast to my covenant –
> to them I will give within my temple and its walls
>   a memorial and a name
>   better than sons and daughters;
> I will give them an everlasting name
>   that will endure forever.
> And foreigners who bind themselves to the LORD
>   to minister to him,
> to love the name of the LORD,
>   and to be his servants,
> all who keep the Sabbath without desecrating it
>   and who hold fast to my covenant –
> these I will bring to my holy mountain
>   and give them joy in my house of prayer.
> Their burnt offerings and sacrifices
>   will be accepted on my altar;
> for my house will be called
>   a house of prayer for all nations.'

(Isaiah 56:3–7)

10

The Church at Antioch

ACTS 11:19–30

Since the martyrdom of Stephen and Saul's persecution of the church (7:54–8:3), the narrative has followed the surprising spread of the gospel. We have seen the conversion of various 'unclean' or unexpected groups and persons: the Samaritans (8:9–25); the Ethiopian eunuch (8:26–40); Saul himself (9:1–31); the household of Cornelius (10); and even Peter and the Jerusalem church have their own sort of conversion regarding the gospel welcome to Gentiles (11:1–18). The way has been opened for Gentile mission further afield.

This next section introduces the reader to the Antioch church. This church will play a central role in the remainder of Acts. Each of Paul's three missionary journeys begins from Antioch. This church becomes the 'Jerusalem' of the second half of Acts. It is the sending and planting centre as the narrative expands towards the 'ends of the earth' (Acts 1:8). Luke's depiction in Acts 11:19–30 is of a church that is vibrant and growing, both in number and maturity: 'The Lord's hand was with them, and a great number of people believed and turned to the Lord' (verse 21).

The church in Antioch

19 Now those who had been scattered by the persecution that broke out when Stephen was killed travelled as far as Phoenicia, Cyprus and Antioch, spreading the word only among Jews. 20 Some of them, however, men from Cyprus and Cyrene, went to Antioch and began to speak to Greeks also, telling them the good news about the Lord Jesus. 21 The Lord's hand was with them, and a great number of people believed and turned to the Lord.

22 News of this reached the church in Jerusalem, and they sent Barnabas to Antioch. 23 When he arrived and saw what the grace of God had done, he was glad and encouraged them all to remain true to the Lord with all their hearts. 24 He was a good man, full of the Holy Spirit and faith, and a great number of people were brought to the Lord.

25 Then Barnabas went to Tarsus to look for Saul, 26 and when he found him, he brought him to Antioch. So for a whole year Barnabas and Saul met with the church and taught great

numbers of people. The disciples were called Christians first at Antioch.

27 During this time some prophets came down from Jerusalem to Antioch. 28 One of them, named Agabus, stood up and through the Spirit predicted that a severe famine would spread over the entire Roman world. (This happened during the reign of Claudius.) 29 The disciples, as each one was able, decided to provide help for the brothers and sisters living in Judea. 30 This they did, sending their gift to the elders by Barnabas and Saul.

In Acts 11:19, Luke reports that those scattered in the persecution of Acts 8:1–4 had travelled as far as Phoenicia, Cyprus and Antioch.[1] These scattered believers had spread the word initially only among Jews. We are also told of others who went from Cyprus and Cyrene to Antioch to spread the good news about Jesus to Greeks also. Luke does not name any of these scattered people, but simply records the success God granted. We do well to remember that often God uses ordinary people in the situations he has placed them to grow his church. It is not just the apostles or (insert the name of your favourite celebrity speaker or author or ministry here) that God uses to grow his church, but the ordinary, apparently anonymous, faithfully bearing witness to him. Luke's summary of their success in verse 21 is attributed to the 'Lord's hand' and is another reminder that the risen and exalted Lord Jesus is still very much the central character in Luke's narrative directing and advancing the mission. The church is always utterly dependent on his power and grace as we labour to see the kingdom advance.

News of the success of the Antioch mission reached the church in Jerusalem (verse 22), and they sent Barnabas to encourage them.[2] We have already met Barnabas in Acts 4:36 and 9:27. He was evidently a man who had a reputation for being generous financially and generous in heart. His name means 'son of encouragement' (Acts 4:36).[3] To his generosity

---

[1] Barrett describes Antioch as 'undoubtedly one of the most important cities of antiquity'. *Acts 1–14*, 549. Josephus described it as 'third among the cities of the Roman world' (behind Alexandria and Rome). *Wars* 3.29, cited in Witherington, *Acts*, 366. Witherington notes it was the first 'major cosmopolitan city outside Israel where Christianity clearly established itself', and it 'had an estimated population of a half-million people'. *Acts*, 366. Bock notes there was already a large Jewish population in Antioch, numbering perhaps as many as twenty-five thousand. *Acts*, 413.
[2] Acts 11:22 gives the first instance of the word *ekklesia* ('church') outside Jerusalem, Judea or Samaria. Peterson, *Acts*, 351.
[3] As a Greek-speaking Jew (being from Cyprus), he would also have been an ideal choice to meet the new leaders of the Antioch church. Wall, *Acts*, 175. See Acts 4:36.

Luke adds here his work as a teacher and evangelist. When Barnabas saw 'what the grace of God had done', he rejoiced and encouraged them all to 'remain true to the Lord with all their hearts' (verse 23). This suggests that his work of encouragement would have included some aspect of instruction and teaching.

It is worth pausing to consider Luke's little summary of what Barnabas observed when he met the church at Antioch: he saw, literally, the grace of God (*idōn tēn charin tou theou*). I wonder how many of us look around at our church family on a Sunday and think to ourselves, 'I see the grace of God all around me this morning.' I suspect many of us find it much easier to see the problems or the pain. Yet Barnabas looked at this vibrant local church and said, 'I see the grace of God.' How many of our relational tensions between individuals, groups, even churches, could begin to be resolved by looking at one another and saying, 'I see the grace of God'?

Further, in verse 24 we are told that Barnabas was 'a good man, full of the Holy Spirit and faith'. Only Stephen previously has been described as a man full of faith and the Holy Spirit (6:5).[4] Luke adds that 'a great number of people were brought to the Lord'. Barnabas's character and gifts, anointed by the Spirit's power, made him an effective evangelist also. As Paul would point out to a young Timothy years later, character is more important than gifting when it comes to faithful and fruitful service of the Lord.[5] Any young leader (or old, for that matter) would do well to look at Barnabas and see a man whose life communicated as much as his words.

The impressive picture of Barnabas continues into verse 25 where we can add humility to his list of qualities.[6] It would have been easy for Barnabas to have continued in the work alone, given his apparent success, but instead he draws in others who can help in the work. He travels to Tarsus, a hundred miles north, to find Saul, who we last saw in Acts 9:30.[7] Luke has already noted the power and the passion in Paul's preaching and debating (9:22, 27–9). Barnabas saw it would be beneficial for both Saul and the church for him to join in the work at Antioch.

In these two short verses (verses 25–6), Barnabas shows us some important leadership lessons. First, ministry is not an individual sport,

---

[4] Witherington, *Acts*, 370.
[5] See 1 Timothy 3:1–13.
[6] Stott, *Acts*, 204.
[7] Tarsus was approximately one hundred miles north-west of Antioch. Venkataraman, 'Acts', in *SABC*, 1481

but a team sport. It might be tempting, especially if we are successful, to think we can operate alone without the help of others. Yet finding ways of bringing along others to help us (whether paid or voluntary, full- or part-time) is an excellent way to see both those ministering and those ministered to flourish.

Second, Barnabas demonstrates the humility to seek help. He does not believe he is omni-competent and he is not afraid to draw in others. Barnabas is not a leader with a fragile ego who feels threatened by Saul. He knows that the 'grace of God' is the energising power. But he also sees that seeking help enables the mission to continue and advance.

Third, Barnabas recognises the gifts of others and his own limitations. He presumably has seen something in Saul that would complement his own gifts and abilities. Recognising our weaknesses and limitations is not easy, but it is crucial if we are to maximise the missional potential of the teams we serve in. Barnabas may not have the rhetorical or intellectual gifts of Paul, but he shows himself to be a wise leader in encouraging and promoting the gifts of others for the good of the whole.

In verse 26, Luke reports that Saul and Barnabas spent a year with the church at Antioch teaching great numbers of people. He also adds the detail that it was here that the disciples were first called 'Christians' (*Christianous*). It is unclear whether this was a name they gave to themselves or whether it was perhaps a nickname, possibly derogatory, given by others.[8] If it is the latter, then the name itself demonstrates the faithfulness of their witness to Christ – there was no doubt who they followed. It might be a challenge to us in our own day to consider whether our witness might be conspicuous enough to earn the derogatory name-calling of others. Perhaps our faith is so private that no one in the office, at the school gate or in the marketplace would know we had anything at all to do with the church or Jesus.

In verse 27, Luke tells us, 'During this time some prophets came down from Jerusalem to Antioch.' This is the first mention of New Testament prophets in Acts. All of the previous references to a 'prophet' or 'prophets' have referred to Old Testament prophets or to Jesus.[9] In Acts 2:17–21 the prophecy of Joel foretold that in some sense *all* God's people would receive the Spirit and would 'prophesy'. But here there seems to be a particular group of gifted and recognised 'prophets' in the church, who

---

[8] Marshall thinks it is more likely the latter, given the verb *chrēmatisai* ('be named'). *Acts*, 203.

[9] Acts 2:16; 2:30; 3:22; 7:37, 48, 52; 8:28, 30, 34.

will appear again later in the narrative.[10] This group, it seems, is what Paul refers to when he describes the 'apostles and prophets' as the foundation of the church (Ephesians 2:20; 3:5; 4:11). If this is correct, then these New Testament prophets, like apostles, play a unique role in the foundation of the church, but ought not to be seen as normative (as an office) for subsequent generations. These prophets, like apostles, bring much-needed revelation to the early church at a time when there were no New Testament documents, let alone a closed canon of Scripture.

In verse 28, Luke introduces us to Agabus, who will reappear later in the narrative (Acts 21:10). He predicts that famine that will strike the entire Roman world.[11] It is interesting to observe that there seems to be no need to test this prophecy (see 1 Thessalonians 5:20–21; 1 Corinthians 14:29). The man, Agabus, or the events surrounding the prophecy are indisputable. As a result, the church decides to provide help for the brothers and sisters living in Judea, and they send their gift (diakonian) to the elders by Barnabas and Saul.[12] This is a significant moment in the wider narrative as 'Jerusalem ceases to be the supportive parent and becomes an equal partner'.[13]

Here we see the first mention of elders for the churches (verse 30). Thus far in Acts the term 'elders' has been used of the Jewish leaders.[14] It appears that at some point the same terminology has been applied to leaders of the Christian churches. It is interesting that it is Barnabas and Saul who are sent with the gift. It obviously carries significant responsibility, but this also suggests that Barnabas and Saul have established a leadership mature enough for them to depart without fear that the young church may collapse in their absence.[15]

In some ways this summary of the Antioch church is reminiscent of the earlier summaries of the Jerusalem church. This church enjoys the

---

[10] Acts 13:1; 21:9–10.

[11] Commentators suggest the famine occurred somewhere between AD 45 and 47. Barrett, *Acts 1–14*, 565; Witherington, *Acts*, 368; Peterson, *Acts*, 357–8.

[12] Judea and Jerusalem were around three hundred miles to the south of Antioch. Bock, *Acts*, 418.

[13] Green, *The Word of His Grace*, 82.

[14] Acts 4:5, 8, 23; 5:21; 6:12.

[15] Barrett, *Acts 1–14*, 558–9, suggests this short paragraph (verses 27–30) is key in establishing the self-sufficiency and independency of the Gentile church. That is not to say they are not in fellowship and partnership with others, but they are not dependent on Jerusalem for their survival. They have developed their own leaders and are starting their own mission initiatives.

Lord's hand of grace and favour upon them (see 4:33). They are growing in number (see 2:47). They are devoted to the teaching (see 2:42). And they are committed to generously supporting one another in their material need (see 2:44–5; 4:34–5). The life-transforming grace of God is reaching further and further. This is not just missionary evangelism, but also the planting and establishment of healthy churches, who in turn reach out to bless others. This is a good reminder that healthy churches must be growing in depth as well as in number. The church that sustains itself and its mission, under God's gracious hand, must be raising up new indigenous leaders, growing in depth of knowledge and reaching out to others in word and deed.

We also see here the interdependence of churches. Christians differ on their understanding of church polity and relationships to wider denominational structures and networks. Whatever our ecclesiological convictions, Acts 11:27–30 challenges us to remain always interdependent in our relationships with other gospel churches. This is a normal and healthy part of churches supporting one another in the mission. Bock gives the following challenge:

> Today many churches are interested only in their own ministry or in using their facilities and resources only for their own efforts. It is sad to see large-budget churches that give very little to missions or do very little for other believing communities in need in their own area . . . We must be careful that the desired pursuit of excellence in ministry to our own does not leave us neglecting others whom we could help.[16]

The Antioch church is a striking example of a church growing through discipleship, evangelism and practical care. This church in its maturation will become a significant centre for mission to the ends of the earth. Luke's portrait of this church challenges us to consider whether our own churches are discipling, training and equipping people to 'remain true to the Lord with all their hearts' and live lives that bear powerful witness to Jesus in word and deed.

---

[16] Bock, *Acts*, 419.

11

The Throne of Herod
and the Throne of Heaven

ACTS 12:1–24

In Acts 12 we return to the theme of persecution and martyrdom. These themes have already appeared in Acts 3–7 where the Temple authorities' persecution of the church culminated in the martyrdom of Stephen. In the decade since this event the church had spread, grown and reached new groups, namely Samaritans, an Ethiopian eunuch, one of the leading persecutors of the church (Saul) and the household of Cornelius.[1] As we left the end of Acts 11 we saw a thriving church at Antioch. Perhaps as readers we had been lulled into a false sense of security, seeing the Antioch church as a new dawn, the church going from strength to strength without the sort of opposition previously encountered. Such hopes come crashing down in Acts 12 as we see that it is not just the Temple authorities of Jerusalem who oppose the gospel. Of course, the narrative tension is somewhat heightened when we remember the last person to go after the church was radically converted (Saul, Acts 9). So what might become of Herod, and how should we understand the events that unfold?

This chapter serves to demonstrate that although the persecution in Jerusalem is still a real threat, the protective hand of the Lord has enabled the church to survive and grow (verse 24). And God is still actively protecting his servants from the harm that might befall them. This will be important as the gospel is taken into new territories and the missionaries face new challenges in Acts 13 onwards. Acts 12 provides a bridge from the persecuted but growing church in Jerusalem to the beginnings of the missionary journeys in Acts 13 which will face similar obstacles and require the same confident assurance of God's power to lead, guide and protect.

---

[1] Witherington, *Acts*, 386, suggests ten or eleven years separated the martyrdoms of Stephen and James.

1. The deliverance of Peter • Acts 12:1–19a

Acts 12:1–11: Peter escapes prison

*Peter's miraculous escape
from prison*

12 It was about this time that King Herod arrested some who belonged to the church, intending to persecute them. **2** He had James, the brother of John, put to death with the sword. **3** When he saw that this met with approval among the Jews, he proceeded to seize Peter also. This happened during the Festival of Unleavened Bread. **4** After arresting him, he put him in prison, handing him over to be guarded by four squads of four soldiers each. Herod intended to bring him out for public trial after the Passover.

5 So Peter was kept in prison, but the church was earnestly praying to God for him.

6 The night before Herod was to bring him to trial, Peter was sleeping between two soldiers, bound with two chains, and sentries stood guard at the entrance. **7** Suddenly an angel of the Lord appeared and a light shone in the cell. He struck Peter on the side and woke him up. 'Quick, get up!' he said, and the chains fell off Peter's wrists.

8 Then the angel said to him, 'Put on your clothes and sandals.' And Peter did so. 'Wrap your cloak round you and follow me,' the angel told him. **9** Peter followed him out of the prison, but he had no idea that what the angel was doing was really happening; he thought he was seeing a vision. **10** They passed the first and second guards and came to the iron gate leading to the city. It opened for them by itself, and they went through it. When they had walked the length of one street, suddenly the angel left him.

11 Then Peter came to himself and said, 'Now I know without a doubt that the Lord has sent his angel and rescued me from Herod's clutches and from everything the Jewish people were hoping would happen.'

Luke informs his readers that while the church in Antioch was growing, King Herod was boosting his popularity ratings in Jerusalem by killing apostles.[2] Luke's description of 'Herod, the King' (*Hērōdēs ho basileus*) sets up the narrative as a contest between the throne of Herod and the

---

[2] This Herod is Agrippa I, the grandson of Herod the Great. His reign extended over Judea and Samaria. Barrett says that 'notwithstanding his Roman and Greek interests . . . [he] seems to have been recognized as a good Jew'. Barrett, *Acts 1–14*, 573; Josephus, *Antiquities* 19.292–316.

throne of heaven.[3] The name 'Herod' ought to unnerve the reader. His grandfather had sought to kill Jesus in his infancy (Matthew 2:16). His uncle had had John the Baptist beheaded and conspired to kill Jesus (Luke 9:9; 13:31; 23:6–12).[4] The name 'Herod' sounds an ominous note at this point in Luke's narrative.

This is a significant turning point in the story for two reasons. First, we see persecution arising from those beyond the religious leaders in Jerusalem. From now on the church must deal with opponents from the Gentile realms also. Second, we see that the church must have grown to the point it is attracting attention from other authorities. This is a testament to the power of the gospel to spread and to the distinctiveness of the church in drawing such attention. It must also feel more than a little terrifying to attract this sort of attention.

It is a sobering reminder that historically and globally there have always been state powers ready and willing to persecute the church, or at least look the other way when such persecution happens.[5] The doctrine of sin and the reality of personal evil means we ought not be surprised when opposition to God and his people arises. To some degree it is a mark of faithfulness to attract enmity towards the truth. We of course do not go looking for persecution, but faithful believers should not be surprised when they face opposition for following Christ.

In verse 2 we see that Herod, having imprisoned some of those that belonged to the church, had James, the brother of John, put to death. This James is the son of Zebedee, one of the apostles, mentioned in Mark 1:19–20 and 3:17.[6] Peterson notes, 'Executing one of the apostles was a deliberate attempt to destroy the church by systematically removing its leadership.'[7] As Luke's narrative progresses, we shall see if such a tactic can work. Unlike Stephen, we are not given an account of a trial or a speech from James. Luke simply records his death in an almost matter-of-fact way. Persecution and opposition to the church are no longer headline news, but part of their daily experience. And although James does not occupy as much space in Luke's narrative as Peter or Paul, it

---

[3] Peterson, *Acts*, 361, notes that Caligula had allowed Herod to be called king. Luke will show us in the most dramatic fashion that his claim to be king is almost comical.

[4] Peterson, *Acts*, 361.

[5] Venkataraman, 'Acts', in *SABC*, 1481.

[6] See Witherington, *Acts*, 384. Bock, *Acts*, 425. In Mark 10:39 Jesus predicts that James and John will undergo the same baptism and drink the same cup that Jesus will receive.

[7] Peterson, *Acts*, 361.

is his death that triggers the events that lead up to the death of Herod, and Luke's report of the gospel's spread in verses 23–4. Each of God's faithful witnesses has their own significant part to play in God's mission, however small that may seem from our perspective.[8] Even apparent defeat may turn out to be a victory.

Luke provides a disturbing insight into Herod's character in verse 3, where we see his actions are driven by the people's approval. Encouraged by his surge in approval ratings, he also arrests Peter, presumably with the intention of subjecting him to the same fate as James. Here is a political leader driven not by any higher sense of right and wrong, or good and evil, but simply by what wins the favour of people. Seeing Herod in action reminds us of Paul's instruction to pray for those in authority, 'that we may live peaceful and quiet lives in all godliness and holiness' (1 Timothy 2:2). The potential for power to corrupt is great, and history is littered with examples of leaders like Herod. As much as we pray that God would remove such leaders from office, we should also pray that God might save even the most tyrannical and evil of dictators.

In verse 4, Luke details Peter's guard, which seems rather excessive. There were four squads of four soldiers each. Maybe Herod had heard about what had happened in Acts 5:18–20. Did Herod think a miracle possible? If so, did he think he could thwart God with a bit more security? It is reminiscent of Nebuchadnezzar making the furnace seven times hotter, just to be sure it did the job on Shadrach, Meshach and Abednego (Daniel 3). Even the most powerful cannot stand against the purposes of God.

Luke provides two more details regarding the timing of these events. The arrest of Peter occurred during the Festival of Unleavened Bread, with his trial due to take place after the Passover (verses 3–4). As hearers, we recall Jesus's own trial before Herod's uncle. Will Peter face the same fate? And we also remember that this festival celebrates Israel's liberation from captivity in Egypt. The miracle that follows may remind the reader of more than just Peter's escape from his own captivity.[9]

---

[8] Peterson, *Acts*, 362, notes that the death of James the apostle does not lead to the election of another apostle. Rather the remaining apostles seem to work alongside the emerging leadership of elders, which appear to include James, the Lord's brother (Acts 12:17; 15:2, 4, 6; 21:18).

[9] Tannehill, *Narrative Unity*, 154, notes a host of linguistic connections between Acts 12 and the Exodus narrative. Peter's deliverance is one small echo of the greater liberations in the Exodus and Jesus's own death and resurrection which delivers us from captivity to sin.

As Peter somehow slept in the prison on the eve of his trial, stripped of his clothes and dignity, the church prayed 'earnestly' (verse 5).[10] The adverb translated 'earnestly' (*ektenōs*) is also used of Jesus's prayer in Gethsemane on the night before his own death (Luke 22:44). The church does not possess the weapons of the world – military might or political power – but it does have something greater. It has access to the throne room of the King of kings and Lord of lords. I suspect many of us would have to confess this is not a resource we access enough. Our prayer times (alone or together) are often short and lacking in the sort of 'earnestness' described. It is perhaps worth reflecting on our own practice, as individuals and churches, to consider whether we need to invest more intentionally in coming to the throne room that has infinitely more power than that of Herod.[11]

The night before Peter was due to go on trial, we see a rerun of what had happened in Acts 5, although this account is longer. Again, Luke wants to emphasise the miraculous nature of these events in recording the details. Peter slept between two soldiers, bound with two chains, with two sentries standing guard. An angel appeared and a bright light shone around. The angel woke Peter, striking him on the side. Interestingly the verb 'struck' (*pataxas*) is also used in verse 23 (the angel striking Herod dead) and is commonly used with the striking of the sword.[12] The angelic touch that would put Herod to death had, in a sense, given Peter new life. A new light shone around him. The chains fell from his wrists. Peter was told to get dressed and was led out of the prison by the angel. Peter, it seems, was still half asleep and thought he was seeing a vision (verse 9). Having passed the two guards, the iron gate opened by itself and Peter, led by the angel, escaped. After walking the length of one street the angel left Peter and he came to his senses. Twice Peter had been miraculously delivered from prison.

---

[10] Venkataraman, 'Acts', in *SABC*, 1482, notes stripping someone of their clothes is designed to degrade and humiliate. Bock, *Acts*, 426, points out how remarkable it is that Peter is described as sleeping in verse 6 given what likely lay ahead the following day. It perhaps also suggests those gathered prayed through the night for him.

[11] Calvin, *Acts*, 481, says, 'If we be not inwardly touched with their dangers, we do not only defraud them of the due duty of love, but also treacherously forsake the confession of our faith . . . Unless these provocations sharpen our desire to pray, we be more than blockish; therefore, so soon as any persecution ariseth, let us by and by get ourselves to prayer.'

[12] Matthew 26:51; Luke 22:49; Revelation 19:15. Chance, *Acts*, 198.

It is hard not to see Peter's prison rescue as a picture of salvation. It seems to have inspired at least one famous hymn.[13] He is liberated from the dungeon of darkness. His chains have fallen off. He is given new life. He is raised up. He is led to freedom. Is this a hermeneutical leap too far? It would be difficult to argue that Luke's primary intent was to convey a picture of our salvation. Yet, if we read it in light of the wider testimony of Scripture and its description of our spiritual deliverance, it is perhaps a permissible application as we consider how God offers us miraculous deliverance from our captivity to sin.[14]

Further, Weaver has argued that Luke is 'patterning Peter's escape after Jesus's resurrection . . . the prison-escape recalls and reenacts the decisive victory over the power of death and darkness'.[15] Garrett, appealing to echoes of the Exodus, argues, 'Now the Lord "leads out" a Christian leader from bondage symbolizing the bondage of death.'[16] Peter's escape is therefore a 'typological replay' of Satan's demise.[17]

Acts 12:12–19a: Peter at Mary's house

12 When this had dawned on him, he went to the house of Mary the mother of John, also called Mark, where many people had gathered and were praying. 13 Peter knocked at the outer entrance, and a servant named Rhoda came to answer the door. 14 When she recognised Peter's voice, she was so overjoyed she ran back without opening it and exclaimed, 'Peter is at the door!'

15 'You're out of your mind,' they told her. When she kept insisting that it was so, they said, 'It must be his angel.'

16 But Peter kept on knocking, and when they opened the door and saw

---

[13] See the fourth verse of Charles Wesley's 'And Can It Be' (1738), public domain.

[14] This sort of reading might be termed a 'theological interpretation of Scripture' or a 'canonical' reading. It is interested in the ways in which the individual parts of Scripture and the whole, when read in the light of one another, help us see theological themes. There is, of course, a danger of fanciful and speculative readings. The theological reading must be grounded in the literal sense of the terms. In this case the material rescue prompts the reader to think about that wider theological theme of rescue seen throughout Scripture in different senses. For more on this see J. Todd Billings, *The Word of God for The People of God: An Entryway to the Theological Interpretation of Scripture* (Grand Rapids: Eerdmans, 2010).

[15] John B. Weaver, *Plots of Epiphany: Prison-Escape in the Acts of the Apostles* (Berlin: DeGruyter, 2004), 156–7.

[16] Susan R. Garrett, 'Exodus from Bondage: Luke 9:31 and Acts 12:1–24', in *CBQ* 52 (1990): 675. Cited in Weaver, *Plots of Epiphany*, 157.

[17] Weaver, *Plots of Epiphany*, 157.

him, they were astonished. **17** Peter motioned with his hand for them to be quiet and described how the Lord had brought him out of prison. 'Tell James and the other brothers and sisters about this,' he said, and then he left for another place.

18 In the morning, there was no small commotion among the soldiers as to what had become of Peter. **19** After Herod had a thorough search made for him and did not find him, he cross-examined the guards and ordered that they be executed.

In verses 12–19 we see the almost comical episode of Peter coming to the house of Mary, mother of John.[18] The presence of 'many people' and Rhoda, the servant, would suggest a large house that could accommodate a significant number of people, perhaps regularly used for some house meetings of the church.[19] Peter certainly seems to know where to go. As he arrives, he knocks on the door. Rhoda, the servant, in her sheer excitement at hearing Peter's voice, leaves him outside a little longer while she reports back to those inside. As Witherington observes, Peter has managed to get through the doors manned by soldiers, but he can't get through the door manned by the servant girl.[20]

Rhoda is another of those characters in the narrative that show us the beautiful inclusivity and power of the gospel to use people from all backgrounds. She is the most clear-sighted person in the chapter. Her joy at seeing Peter's deliverance is compelling. From one perspective she might be dismissed as the least important person in the house, but from heaven's perspective she is surely one of the most important. Her simple faith puts the doubters to shame.

Those inside think it simply unbelievable that God might have *actually* answered their prayers in a miraculous way. How often do we pray in a similar fashion, hoping but not really believing God might do more than we ask or imagine? Having spent some time debating with her, they conclude, 'It must be his angel' (verse 15).

---

[18] John Mark himself will play a role in the ensuing narrative (12:25; 13:5, 13; 15:37) and tradition identifies him as the author of Mark's Gospel. Peterson, *Acts*, 365.

[19] We should not assume here a meeting of the entire church, as the message of his delivery needs to be passed on to James and others (verse 17). We do not know how large the entire Jerusalem church was at this point following the persecution and scattering of Acts 8:1–4, but Acts 9:31 suggests a significant recovery. This particular prayer meeting may have been one of the 'house to house' meetings mentioned in Acts 2:46 and 5:42. Bock *Acts*, 428, notes that owning such a premise was obviously not a contradiction of the sharing of possessions described in Acts 4.

[20] Witherington, *Acts*, 376.

This statement raises several further questions. Are there such things as personal guardian angels? If so, why would the angel have turned up at the prayer meeting? Why doesn't somebody just go to the door?! Barrett says, 'Judaism believed in protecting and guiding angels, and these were sometimes thought to resemble the human beings they protected.'[21] In Matthew 18:10 Jesus speaks of the 'little ones' and 'their angels in heaven'. Witherington suggests that identifying the figure with Peter's angel perhaps suggests that they thought Peter was already dead, though the text says his trial was to be the next day (verse 6).[22] The text leaves these teasing questions unanswered. It is enough for us to know there is a spiritual realm that we cannot see, and God may send his angels to work for the provision and protection of his people (for example, 2 Kings 6:17). There is, however, a hermeneutical reminder here to keep the main things the main things and not speculate on those things less clear.[23]

Eventually, those inside decide that perhaps they should go to the door and see for themselves. They open the door and let Peter in, evidently astonished to see him standing there. Peter reports all that has happened and tells them to pass this onto 'James and the other brothers and sisters'.[24] This tells us that this James (the half-brother of Jesus) is already a significant leader in the Jerusalem church, and is presumably about to assume more responsibility in Peter's absence. Peter then, out of necessity, leaves for another place (verse 17).

Meanwhile, Herod gives us another glimpse of his character as he coldly executes his own guards, apparently unwilling to entertain whatever testimony they offer. We do not know what account they may have given. Is Herod ultimately unwilling to believe that perhaps God has miraculously rescued Peter? Is he a leader more concerned with preserving his own status and reputation than seeking after the truth? Though we may not have Herod's power, there is always the danger that we have the same pride that would seek to preserve and protect our own little kingdoms rather than confront the truth that might bring them tumbling down. It

---

[21] Barrett, *Acts 1–14*, 585.

[22] Witherington, *Acts*, 385.

[23] Calvin, *Acts*, 487, says, 'Whether individual angels have been assigned to individual believers for their protection, I dare not affirm with confidence . . . it is not worth-while anxiously to investigate what it does not much concern us to know.' *Institutes* 1.14.7. Or elsewhere, 'Let this be sufficient for us, that the whole host of heaven doth watch for the safety of the Church.'

[24] Many commentators identify this James as the brother of Jesus and a 'pillar of the church' (Galatians 2:9). See Bock, *Acts*, 429; Witherington, *Acts*, 388.

requires great humility to step off our own little thrones and to bow the knee before God's – something we shall see Herod was simply unwilling to do, and for which he would pay the ultimate price.

2. The death of Herod • Acts 12:19b–24

Herod's death

Then Herod went from Judea to Caesarea and stayed there. **20**He had been quarrelling with the people of Tyre and Sidon; they now joined together and sought an audience with him. After securing the support of Blastus, a trusted personal servant of the king, they asked for peace, because they depended on the king's country for their food supply.

21On the appointed day Herod, wearing his royal robes, sat on his throne and delivered a public address to the people. **22**They shouted, 'This is the voice of a god, not of a man.' **23**Immediately, because Herod did not give praise to God, an angel of the Lord struck him down, and he was eaten by worms and died.

24But the word of God continued to spread and flourish.

A third glimpse into the character of Herod comes in verses 20–21. He had been in a dispute with the people of Tyre and Sidon over food provision. They depended upon Herod's country for their food supply. He had an economic power he seems to have been wielding over them. Wall notes in passing how different the sacred and secular are, 'as evidenced by contrasting practices of food distribution'.[25] They sent a servant of the king, Blastus, to seek peace. On an appointed day Herod sat on his throne, wearing his royal robes, and addressed the people. The Jewish historian, Josephus, records this incident and the silver robe he wore and its radiance in the sun.[26] The people cried out, perhaps employing flattery, 'This is the voice of a god, not of a man.' Herod in turn, it seems, accepted their adulation, and consequently 'an angel of the Lord struck him down, and he was eaten by worms and died' (verse 23).[27] In a sobering irony, the

---

[25] Wall, *Acts*, 181. See Acts 2:44–6; 4:32–5; 6:1–6.

[26] Josephus, *Antiquities* 19.344.

[27] Note again the verb 'strike' (*epataxen*) is the same as that used in verse 7 (and in the LXX account of YHWH striking Pharoah – Exodus 12:12, 23, 29). See also Isaiah 51:7–8: 'do not fear the reproach of mere mortals . . . the worm will devour them'. Herod's death probably occurred in AD 44. In the account of Josephus, Herod was seized with severe abdominal pains and died five days later at home. *Antiquities* 19.346–50.

one who would withhold food becomes food! Here we see an angel act both to deliver Peter and to strike down Herod.

Weaver's summary is worth quoting at length:

> The figure of Herod in Acts therefore represents the group of Herodian rulers whose violent and impious hostility would be familiar to Luke's readers. This characterization suggests that Herod's death functions paradigmatically for Luke, exemplifying the fate of others who would resist and oppose as Herod did.[28]

Herod provides an embodied example of sin – the refusal to acknowledge God as God.[29] Luke here includes one of his summary statements that drive the narrative forward: 'the word of God continued to spread and flourish' (verse 24). Similar statements occur in Acts 6:7; 9:31; 19:20. The same words for 'spread' (*ēuxanen*) and 'flourish' (*eplēthyneto*) were used in Acts 6:7, signifying the rapid multiplication of believers. Despite the opposition of a powerful man like Herod, God worked powerfully to overcome the opposition, to rescue his servant and to continue to spread the gospel. There is no force, no matter how powerful and terrifying it may appear, that can stand against the purposes of God. Herod quickly dies. The word continues to grow.[30] The church flourishes 'under its trusty and most victorious defender, Jesus Christ'.[31]

As Stott observes, 'The chapter opens with James dead, Peter in prison, and Herod triumphing; it closes with Herod dead, Peter free, and the word of God triumphing. Such is the power of God to overthrow hostile human plans and to establish his own in their place.'[32] This should give the church comfort and courage to continue in her mission, knowing the power of God, even though it can at times be hugely costly. We must still act with care and wisdom. This is not an encouragement to be reckless. But we can have a quiet confidence in the power of God to take forward his mission through his people, the church.

This episode does raise the question of why Peter was delivered while James was killed. It would be easy to preach a sermon or lead a Bible study from these verses focusing on Peter's experience, noting how God

---

[28] Weaver, *Plots of Epiphany*, 210.
[29] To paraphrase Luther – 'refusing to let God be God' – quoted in Pelikan, *Acts*, 150.
[30] Witherington, *Acts*, 390.
[31] Rudolf Gwalther, *Homily* 85 in *RCS* 6:170.
[32] Stott, *Acts*, 213.

rescues his servants. But James is not rescued. He dies the death of a martyr with nothing by way of explanation. To us it is often a mystery why God miraculously intervenes in some situations but seems absent from others. One friend makes a wonderful recovery from cancer, while another dies. One church experiences revival while another closes its doors. One tyrannical dictator is removed while another seems to grow in power. The doctrine of providence teaches us that God is in control of all things, not just some things. His ways are higher than our ways; his thoughts higher than ours (Isaiah 55:8–9). God has his purposes and works to bring good from evil, even though we may not always be able to see how.[33] Faith trusts that God's providential ordering is ultimately good, even though it is sometimes painful. We walk by faith, not by sight (2 Corinthians 5:7).

Whatever the future holds for the individual Christian and the church, we can be confident in God's good providence, and that his purposes will prevail. His power is able to protect and provide. The ultimate comfort in the face of the martyrdom of James is the assurance that he, like Stephen, saw Jesus once again face to face. Whichever direction our own lives take, we can rest assured that God's providential care will ultimately take us to be with him, where all the pain, all the suffering, all the trials and all the persecutions will be no more. "'He will wipe away every tear from their eyes. There will be no more death" or mourning or crying or pain, for the old order of things has passed away' (Revelation 21:4). This is the ultimate victory that believers await with eager anticipation. The throne of heaven is infinitely more powerful than the throne of Herod.

---

[33] For example, see Genesis 50:20.

12

The Sending of Barnabas and Saul

ACTS 12:25–13:52

Acts 13 marks the beginning of a new section in Luke's narrative. We have noted that Luke charts the fulfilment of Acts 1:8: the disciples were to be witnesses in Jerusalem, Judea and Samaria, and to the ends of the earth. We have seen the gospel make a powerful impact in Jerusalem in Acts 1–7. Persecution caused the scattering of believers throughout Judea and Samaria (Acts 8:1). Those believers 'preached the word wherever they went' (8:4). Luke has recorded a number of important conversion stories, such as the Ethiopian eunuch, Saul and Cornelius. In 12:24 Luke provided another of his summary statements: 'The word of the God continued to spread and flourish.'

Acts 1–8 was based in Jerusalem, and in Acts 8–12 the action spread to Judea and Samaria. Acts 13 begins the journey towards the ends of the earth. This next section of Luke's narrative, which runs from chapters 13 to 21, gives us two new anchor points. The first of those is Saul/Paul, the apostle to the Gentiles (9:15–16). Peter has been the main human character in Acts 1–12. Paul will be the major human character in Acts 13–28.[1] The second anchor point is Antioch. Jerusalem has been the centre of much of the action in the first twelve chapters. The Antioch church will play a key role as the centre of missionary activity over the course of the next eight chapters.

Acts 13 commences the story of Paul's three missionary journeys. The first is described in Acts 13–14, the second in 15:36–18:22 and the third runs from 18:23–21:16. Each journey takes Paul slightly further out in his journey to the ends of the earth. Each of the journeys begins in Antioch, and the first two end in Antioch also. The third journey ends in Jerusalem in 21:16, and there begins Paul's own 'passion narrative' as he journeys through trials, towards imprisonment and an uncertain end.

Of course, the Jerusalem church and its apostles do not disappear

---

[1] Though, as Witherington, *Acts*, 391, notes, '*the* major actor and catalyst of all that happens in this salvation historical drama is God'.

from Luke's narrative, but there is a definite shift towards Paul and the Gentile mission from hereon. Noteworthy in these upcoming chapters are the various ways Paul contextualises his approach and message to reach the different groups he meets. There is much of relevance here for us as we reflect on our own approaches to reaching those around us with the good news.

1. Barnabas and Saul set apart • Acts 12:25–13:12

Acts 13 introduces us to the church at Antioch and the beginnings of Paul's missionary journeys. Paul's first two encounters could not be more different. In Cyprus we meet a proconsul and a sorcerer, and in Pisidian Antioch we find Paul charting Israel's history in the synagogue. In both places we see opposition and challenge, but also God at work. By the end of the chapter, despite opposition, Luke will record that 'the disciples were filled with joy and with the Holy Spirit' (13:52).

Acts 12:25–13:3: The first missionary journey

Barnabas and Saul sent off

25 When Barnabas and Saul had finished their mission, they returned from[a] Jerusalem, taking with them John, also called Mark.

13 1 Now in the church at Antioch there were prophets and teachers: Barnabas, Simeon called Niger, Lucius of Cyrene, Manaen (who had been brought up with Herod the tetrarch) and Saul. 2 While they were worshipping the Lord and fasting, the Holy Spirit said, 'Set apart for me Barnabas and Saul for the work to which I have called them.' 3 So after they had fasted and prayed, they placed their hands on them and sent them off.

_____
a 25 Some manuscripts *to*

In Acts 12:25, Luke picks up the narrative thread from Acts 11:27–30. Agabus, the prophet, had predicted a severe famine and, as a result, the believers had sent aid to the brothers and sisters living in Judea via the hands of Barnabas and Saul. In 12:25 they return to their sending church in Antioch.

Luke has already introduced us to the young church at Antioch in Acts 11:19–26. There Luke described the church as growing, enjoying the grace of God and learning under the teaching of Saul and Barnabas. In 13:1 Luke also tells us that there were prophets and teachers in the church. He names them as 'Barnabas, Simeon called Niger, Lucius of Cyrene, Manaen (who had been brought up with Herod the tetrarch) and Saul'.[2] Here we see gifting and diversity in the leadership of this early church.

Calvin reminds readers of the responsibility that comes with the blessing of having such leaders: 'Even in our time God doth so enrich certain churches more than others, that they be seminaries to spread abroad the doctrine of the gospel.'[3] How tempting it is to keep hold of our best leaders and teachers and fail to consider whether God might be calling us to release our most gifted leaders to places of need.

These 'prophets and teachers' seemed to have exercised a key role in the leadership of the Antioch church.[4] The first explicit mention of elders in the churches appeared in 11:30 (with reference to the church in Jerusalem) and will reappear again in Acts 14:23. It seems that these 'prophets and teachers' were exercising a governing function in the early years of this church, possibly in a way analogous to Paul's description of apostles and prophets as the foundation of the church in Ephesians 2:20; 3:5; 4:11.

Luke describes a time of 'worshipping the Lord and fasting'. It is not immediately clear whether that refers to the group of prophets and teachers or to the whole church. However, the use of the Greek word *leitourgountōn* ('worshipping') would suggest a more formal worship service of the church.[5] As they were worshipping and fasting, the Holy Spirit instructed them, 'Set apart for me Barnabas and Saul for the work to which I have called them' (verse 2). Again, we are not given more detail on *how* the Spirit spoke to them. Whether it was an audible voice, a sign or a shared sense of deep conviction we are not told.

The important thing was that this commission was clearly from God, not human beings. The mission that lay ahead was not simply the private idea or ambition of Barnabas and Saul, but was the command of heaven. This must have been important for them to recall in the trials that lay ahead. In the later pastoral epistles, Paul tells Timothy that the desire to be an overseer is a good thing, but it requires discernment and testing

---

[2] Peterson, *Acts*, 374–5, suggests the most significant thing to note in this list of five is the ethnic and social diversity of the leadership of this church.

[3] Calvin, *Acts*, 498.

[4] It is perhaps best to see one group here – 'prophets and teachers' – rather than two, given that Paul and Barnabas frame the list and are portrayed as both prophets and teachers (see 11:26; 13:9–11). Witherington, *Acts*, 391; Peterson, *Acts*, 374.

[5] Peterson, *Acts*, 375.

on the part of the church.[6] No one should take the call of God towards mission or ministry lightly. The responsibility is a heavy one, and the church should be involved in that process of discernment. This protects the individual and the church and brings assurance to both parties of God's hand over such events.

The church fasted and prayed, placed their hands upon them and sent them out. This again demonstrates the importance of dependence on God and the support of the church in the commission to new ministry endeavours. Time and again in Acts we see the importance of reliance on God in prayer for all that we undertake in his name. How quickly and easily we forget and launch out in our own strength, only to be brought quickly to our knees in prayer. Vision statements and strategy days can be useful, but they should never squeeze out time spent as a church and as leadership teams seeking God in prayer.

One final thing to note here is Paul's strategy in his journeys. Marshall summarises as follows:

> Of all Paul's missionary work this period has the best claim to being called a 'missionary journey', as is customary on Bible maps. The later periods were much more devoted to extended activity in significant key cities of the ancient world, and we gain a false picture of Paul's strategy if we think of him as rushing rapidly on missionary *journeys* from one place to the next, leaving small groups of half-taught converts behind him; it was his general policy to remain in one place until he had established the firm foundation of a Christian community, or until he was forced to move by circumstances beyond his control.[7]

Acts 13:4–12: On Cyprus

On Cyprus

4 The two of them, sent on their way by the Holy Spirit, went down to Seleucia and sailed from there to Cyprus. **5** When they arrived at Salamis, they proclaimed the word of God in the Jewish synagogues. John was with them as their helper.

6 They travelled through the whole island until they came to Paphos. There they met a Jewish sorcerer and false prophet named Bar-Jesus, **7** who

---

[6] See 1 Timothy 3:1–13. Wall, *Acts*, 201.

[7] Marshall, *Acts*, 213–14.

was an attendant of the proconsul, Sergius Paulus. The proconsul, an intelligent man, sent for Barnabas and Saul because he wanted to hear the word of God. **8** But Elymas the sorcerer (for that is what his name means) opposed them and tried to turn the proconsul from the faith. **9** Then Saul, who was also called Paul, filled with the Holy Spirit, looked straight at Elymas and said, **10** 'You are a child of the devil and an enemy of everything that is right! You are full of all kinds of deceit and trickery. Will you never stop perverting the right ways of the Lord? **11** Now the hand of the Lord is against you. You are going to be blind for a time, not even able to see the light of the sun.'

Immediately mist and darkness came over him, and he groped about, seeking someone to lead him by the hand. **12** When the proconsul saw what had happened, he believed, for he was amazed at the teaching about the Lord.

In Acts 13:4, Luke again reiterates that it is divine agency that has sent Paul and Barnabas on their journey.[8] He describes their journey to the city of Salamis on the Island of Cyprus, and how they began their work by seeking out the Jewish synagogues.[9] He also notes the presence of John Mark as their helper.

Here is something we shall see repeatedly in the missionary journeys. Paul almost always sought out the synagogue as his first place of call. This makes good sense. As a Jewish man, he and his colleagues were likely to find a welcome among other Jews. Paul had received a thorough training in the Scriptures under Gamaliel, and so would have felt well equipped to reach fellow Jews. Additionally, there was a natural connection between their message of good news and the Jewish religion. The message of Jesus is the fulfilment of the Jewish story and so it made sense for Paul to go those places where he would receive a welcome and have opportunity to talk about the Messiah. Of course, he would go to the Gentiles also, but Paul saw it as an obvious step to begin his work of witness with people with whom he had a natural contact.

As believers, we can often fall into the trap of thinking that 'mission work' happens thousands of miles away in very different cultures and contexts from our own, all the while forgetting about those we rub shoulders with every day. It is not an 'either-or' situation, and it was not

---

[8] The journey from Antioch to Cyprus was about sixty miles, with the port town of Seleucia around sixteen miles from Antioch. Bock, *Acts*, 442.

[9] Cyprus was a natural place to begin as it was the birthplace of Barnabas and had a large Jewish population (see 4:36; 11:20). Peterson, *Acts*, 378.

so for Paul. Perhaps we need to give a little more thought to how we might be 'strategically social' for the sake of the gospel.[10]

Paul, Barnabas and John travelled throughout the island until they came to Paphos, where they encountered a Jewish sorcerer and false prophet named Bar-Jesus, an attendant of the proconsul, Sergius Paulus (verse 6–7).[11] The name 'Bar-Jesus' means 'son of Jesus', something Paul would challenge shortly.

This account is reminiscent of the encounter Philip, Peter and John had with Simon the Sorcerer in Samaria (Acts 8:9–25). Here again, at the outset of their journey, they were faced with powerful and apparently successful spiritual forces that would seek to oppose them.

The ministry and message of Paul and Barnabas must have had a significant impact on the island as the proconsul, described by Luke as an intelligent man, sent for them 'because he wanted to hear the word of the Lord'. Here was an important local figure who was interested in the message, intelligent, and yet somehow duped by the deceit of Bar-Jesus. It is possible to have a bright mind and a hunger for spiritual things and still listen to the wrong voices. It would take something more than reason and persuasion alone to convert this man.

Elymas did everything he could to dissuade his employer of the truth of Paul's message.[12] Paul did not attempt to engage him in debate but rather rebuked him sharply: 'You are a child of the devil and an enemy of everything that is right! You are full of all kinds of deceit and trickery. Will you never stop perverting the right ways of the Lord?' (verses 9–10). Though his name might mean 'son of Jesus', Paul named him a 'child of the devil'. Paul got to the heart of the opposition – it was not simply an exchange of ideas seeking truth; it was the work of the evil one. Satan, in his attempts to destroy the church, has never been far from the action, whether explicitly or implicitly.[13]

---

[10] I am indebted to my friend and colleague Graham Albans for the phrase 'strategically social'. He uses this term in his course on evangelism, *Building Bridges*, to describe how we can make the most of the relational opportunities that are all around us.

[11] Proconsuls were 'Roman magistrates who headed the government in a senatorial province where no troops were required'. Bock, *Acts*, 444.

[12] At this point Luke begins to refer to Saul by his Roman name, Paul, which perhaps indicates his significance going forward in Gentile mission. Bock, *Acts*, 445.

[13] The word 'Satan' appears in Acts 5:3; 26:18. The word 'devil' appears in Acts 10:38; 13:10.

There is a real spiritual battle in which believers are engaged.[14] Here is another reason why human effort or argument alone cannot carry the day. The Lord is infinitely more powerful than the devil. We need not fear him. But we do need God's power at work to overcome his power and work in our world. Elsewhere he is described as the 'prince of this world' or the 'god of this age'. He is a liar and a schemer. He 'prowls around' looking for someone to destroy.[15] This is why, as we noted above, dependence on God in prayer is so critical to our mission and witness today.

It is also worth noting how the devil was at work in Elymas. Paul described him as being a deceiver and trickster, 'perverting the right ways of the Lord'. Evil is always parasitic on good. There is nothing original or new about the message or methods of the evil one. We can see this most clearly in the Garden of Eden. It is God's good word that the serpent twists to deceive. We can see this in our culture. An evil genius is still in possession of the gift of his intellect. The power of an abuser is dependent on the gift of his strength.[16] Often evil will pick up on something true and good and twist it towards an evil end. The message of God's love can sometimes be used to undermine his holiness. The gift of creativity can be applied in unwholesome ways. The gift of intellect can lead a person to believe in their own autonomy. In a thousand ways the world, the flesh and the devil can pervert the good and true gifts of God towards ungodly, selfish and evil ends.

Having rebuked Elymas, Paul then pronounced a judgment upon him: 'You are going to be blind for a time, not even able to see the light of the sun' (verse 11).[17] As soon as Paul finished speaking the judgment fell. As a result, the proconsul believed, 'amazed at the teaching about the Lord'. It is interesting to note the judgment that came on Saul in his rebellion fell also on Elymas – a temporary blindness. Is there a hint here that Elymas may have been delivered from evil and into the truth?[18] Luke does not tell us. The unbeliever is blind until God himself opens their eyes. This is what Paul says in 2 Corinthians 4:4–6:

---

[14] Ephesians 6:12.

[15] See John 8:44; 16:11; 2 Corinthians 2:11; 4:4; 1 Peter 5:8.

[16] Cornelius Plantinga Jr, *Engaging God's World: A Christian Vision of Faith, Learning, and Living* (Grand Rapids: Eerdmans, 2002), 52.

[17] Garrett suggests that blindness or darkness is a fitting punishment for a son of the devil. See Susan R. Garrett, *The Demise of the Devil: Magic and the Demonic in Luke's Writings* (Minneapolis: Fortress, 1989), 83.

[18] Interestingly, this is the view of a number of the church fathers. See 'Acts', in ACCS 5:161.

The god of this age has blinded the minds of unbelievers, so that they cannot see the light of the gospel that displays the glory of Christ, who is the image of God. [5]For what we preach is not ourselves, but Jesus Christ as Lord, and ourselves as your servants for Jesus' sake. [6]For God, who said, 'Let light shine out of darkness,' made his light shine in our hearts to give us the light of the knowledge of God's glory displayed in the face of Christ.

The call to Jesus's ambassadors is to preach Christ as Lord and trust that God is able, in his sovereign power, to open blind eyes to give us the 'light of the knowledge of God's glory displayed in the face of Christ'.

Our engagement with the spiritual forces of evil may or may not be as dramatic as Paul's. Nonetheless, we must always remember that such things are real. Well-run evangelistic events, engaging speakers, gifted apologists, persuasive books or lives of extraordinary compassion will all have an important place in the church's mission to reach the lost. They are part of what it means to 'live such good lives', to 'make the most of every opportunity' and to 'always be prepared to give an answer'.[19] They are necessary, but not sufficient in and of themselves. This episode reminds us of our need to be courageous in mission and utterly dependent on God's power in all that we attempt.

Perhaps a useful check you could do as a church, or as an individual, is to consider where most of the time, energy and resources are spent in your missionary endeavour. What balance goes to planning events, logistics, talk preparation, web design, printing, social media etc, etc.? And how much time is spent in worship, prayer and fasting, seeking God's blessing on our efforts? None of the things listed is wrong – on the contrary they are good things, so long as we remember where the real power lies.

2. In Pisidian Antioch • Acts 13:13–52

Acts 13:13–41: Paul's speech

In Pisidian Antioch

13 From Paphos, Paul and his companions sailed to Perga in Pamphylia, where John left them to return to Jerusalem. 14 From Perga they went on to Pisidian Antioch. On the Sabbath they entered

---

[19] See 1 Peter 2:12; Colossians 4:5; 1 Peter 3:15.

the synagogue and sat down. **15** After the reading from the Law and the Prophets, the leaders of the synagogue sent word to them, saying, 'Brothers, if you have a word of exhortation for the people, please speak.'

16 Standing up, Paul motioned with his hand and said: 'Fellow Israelites and you Gentiles who worship God, listen to me! **17** The God of the people of Israel chose our ancestors; he made the people prosper during their stay in Egypt; with mighty power he led them out of that country; **18** for about forty years he endured their conduct**a** in the wilderness; **19** and he overthrew seven nations in Canaan, giving their land to his people as their inheritance. **20** All this took about 450 years.

'After this, God gave them judges until the time of Samuel the prophet. **21** Then the people asked for a king, and he gave them Saul son of Kish, of the tribe of Benjamin, who ruled for forty years. **22** After removing Saul, he made David their king. God testified concerning him: "I have found David son of Jesse, a man after my own heart; he will do everything I want him to do."

23 'From this man's descendants God has brought to Israel the Saviour Jesus, as he promised. **24** Before the coming of Jesus, John preached repentance and baptism to all the people of Israel. **25** As John was completing his work, he said: "Who do you suppose I am? I am not the one you are looking for. But there is one coming after me whose sandals I am not worthy to untie."

26 'Fellow children of Abraham and you God-fearing Gentiles, it is to us that this message of salvation has been sent. **27** The people of Jerusalem and their rulers did not recognise Jesus, yet in condemning him they fulfilled the words of the prophets that are read every Sabbath. **28** Though they found no proper ground for a death sentence, they asked Pilate to have him executed. **29** When they had carried out all that was written about him, they took him down from the cross and laid him in a tomb. **30** But God raised him from the dead, **31** and for many days he was seen by those who had travelled with him from Galilee to Jerusalem. They are now his witnesses to our people.

32 'We tell you the good news: what God promised our ancestors **33** he has fulfilled for us, their children, by raising up Jesus. As it is written in the second Psalm:

> ' "You are my son;
>> today I have become your
>>> father."**b**

34 God raised him from the dead so that he will never be subject to decay. As God has said,

> ' "I will give you the holy and
>> sure blessings promised
>>> to David."**c**

35 So it is also stated elsewhere:

' "You will not let your holy one
see decay."[d]

36 'Now when David had served
God's purpose in his own generation,
he fell asleep; he was buried with his
ancestors and his body decayed. **37** But
the one whom God raised from the
dead did not see decay.

38 'Therefore, my friends, I want you
to know that through Jesus the forgiveness of sins is proclaimed to you.
39 Through him everyone who believes
is set free from every sin, a justification
you were not able to obtain under the

law of Moses. **40** Take care that what the
prophets have said does not happen
to you:

41 ' "Look, you scoffers,
wonder and perish,
for I am going to do something in
your days
that you would never believe,
even if someone told you."[e]'

---

a 18 Some manuscripts *he cared for them*
b 33 Psalm 2:7
c 34 Isaiah 55:3
d 35 Psalm 16:10 (see Septuagint)
e 41 Hab. 1:5

If I were preaching a sermon on this passage, I might be inclined to title
it, 'The faithfulness of God with the unfaithfulness of people'. Stott notes
this is Luke's first full summary of one of Paul's speeches.[20] The speech
describes the faithfulness of God throughout Israel's history despite their
frequent failures and rebellions.[21] It climaxes with an appeal: 'Take care
that what the prophets have said does not happen to you' (verse 40).
Luke records the rejection of Paul and Barnabas at the hands of some
of the prominent Jews, which led them to focus their efforts on their
Gentile hearers (verse 44–52).

In verses 13–14 we read of Paul and his companions travelling from
Paphos to Perga, then on to Pisidian Antioch.[22] Luke tells us that John
Mark left Paul and Barnabas at Perga to return to Jerusalem. We are not
told why, but this detail will lead to a significant event later in Luke's
narrative (see Acts 15:36–41). As was their usual practice, Paul and Barnabas
began their ministry in Pisidian Antioch by entering the synagogue on
the Sabbath. They are invited to share a 'word of exhortation', and Luke
provides his summary of Paul's speech.

The speech begins with a brief review of redemptive history, including

---

[20] Stott, *Acts*, 222.
[21] Spangenberg in *RCS* 6:178.
[22] Bock, *Acts*, 450, suggests that the journey from Paphos to Perga was 112 miles,
then from Perga to Pisidian Antioch a further hundred miles. Pisidian Antioch was
a 'civil and military center for the province and so the leading city of the region
and a Roman colony'.

the election of their ancestors, the years in Egypt, the Exodus, the wilderness, the conquest of the land, the period of the judges, and Samuel, Saul and David (verses 17–23). The emphasis of this part of the speech would seem to be on the provision and patience of God:

- God 'chose our ancestors' (verse 17)
- He 'made the people prosper' (verse 17)
- 'With mighty power he led them out' (verse 17)
- 'He overthrew seven nations in Canaan' (verse 19)
- He gave 'their land to his people as their inheritance' (verse 19)
- 'God gave them judges' (verse 20)
- He 'gave them Saul' (verse 21)
- 'He made David their king' (verse 22)

In all these statements it is God who is active and the people who are passive. It is not the people who made themselves prosperous, or who conquered Canaan. God graciously gave them all these things in his kindness and generosity. We can also see statements that describe God's patience with their rebelliousness:

- 'For about forty years he endured their conduct in the wilderness' (verse 18)[23]
- 'God gave them judges' (verse 20)
- 'Then the people asked for a king, and he gave them Saul' (verse 21)
- 'After removing Saul, he made David their king' (verse 22)

Those familiar with Israel's history will know that the period of the judges was not a happy one. The judges were graciously given in response to situations created by Israel's sin, but the downward spiral into greater chaos and evil continued. The request for a king, we read in 1 Samuel 8:7, was in reality a rejection of God as king. Paul, in the first section of his speech, is emphasising the incredible grace, generosity and patience of God with a people that often rebelled and rejected him as king.

It is not unusual today to meet people who have held God at arm's length for much of their lives and perhaps believe, as a consequence, that he could never be interested in them. Perhaps they feel they have drifted too far away. This passage serves as a wonderful description of

---

[23] The Greek has the sense of 'to put up with' or 'endure' (*etropophorēsen autous*). BDAG 1017.

the enduring love of God (note the two time references – forty years and 450 years – in verses 18 and 20) towards those who reject him and rebel against him.

In the second part of the speech, Paul describes how Jesus is the fulfilment of God's redemptive purposes for Israel and the nations. He is the Saviour, come in fulfilment of the promise (verse 23). Although the Jewish authorities failed to recognise Jesus, and in fact sentenced him to death, 'it is to us' (children of Abraham and God-fearing Gentiles – verse 26) he has been sent. All of this demonstrates God's faithfulness in fulfilling his promises:

- He 'brought to Israel the Saviour Jesus, as he promised' (verse 23)
- 'In condemning him they fulfilled the words of the prophets' (verse 27)
- They carried out 'all that was written about him' (verse 29)
- 'What God promised our ancestors he has fulfilled for us' (verses 32–3)

Despite continued rebellion and rejection, God fulfilled his promises. Paul cites a number of passages of Scripture as evidence – Psalm 2, Isaiah 55 and Psalm 16. These Old Testament passages are cited as evidence that Jesus is the anointed Son *par excellence*, who inherits all the Davidic blessings in his resurrection and exaltation. As with many of the other speeches in Acts, the resurrection and exaltation is the climactic event, demonstrating that Jesus is not just Saviour, but also Lord, and is to be worshipped as such.

This must also be a central aspect to our own proclamation of the gospel. In evangelism and discipleship we are calling people to accept Jesus not just as the Saviour, but also as their Lord. It is not enough to simply pray a prayer asking Jesus for forgiveness, receive your 'ticket to the sky when you die' and carry on living life as you please. Jesus is Lord. That means his good rule must encompass every area of our existence. Discipleship means learning more and more of what it means to live every part of our lives in love, obedience and service to him. This is no drudgery, but actually the way we discover how to flourish as human beings (see John 10:10).

We might term the third section of Paul' speech the appeal. In verses 38–9 he says, 'I want you to know that through Jesus the forgiveness of sins is proclaimed to you. Through him everyone who believes is set free from every sin, a justification you were not able to obtain under the law of Moses.'

It is unlikely at this point that we are seeing Paul embody a sort of proto-Lutheran antinomianism, as if the only purpose of the Law was to show us our inability to uphold it. Historically, theologians have recognised a threefold use of the Old Testament Law – the restraint of sin and promotion of righteousness (the 'civil' use); to bring us under the conviction of sin (the 'pedagogical' use); and the rule of life for believer (the 'normative' use).[24] In our interpretation we must always be careful not to make the text bear more weight than its author intended.

Paul is saying that observance of the Law could not lead to justification, a theme he would develop in depth in his letters to the Galatians and Romans. It would also continue to be an issue in disputes that would arise over Jewish laws relating to circumcision, holy days and food laws. This is an issue with which the apostles would wrestle in Acts 15 at the Jerusalem Council.

David Gooding notes that justification is God's instant and permanent declaration of righteousness on the believer, based solely on Christ's life, death and resurrection.[25] It is this that gives freedom from sin's condemnation.[26] Calvin describes justification as involving acquittal, deliverance and the remission of sins.[27] For Calvin and the Reformers this was a critical issue in their debates with the Roman Catholic Church. The issue they repeatedly pursued was whether we are justified by faith alone, or whether our works are somehow part of the basis of our justification.[28]

Paul here helps us see that works are unable to play any part in the grounds of our justification. They are the necessary evidence of our justification, but they play no part in its basis.[29] As John Murray notes, 'Justification is by faith alone, but not by a faith that is alone.'[30]

The good news Paul proclaimed was that Jesus came to live the life of perfect obedience that we could not, and to take on himself the punishment we deserved, in order that he could offer free forgiveness

---

[24] For more on this, see Berkhof, *Systematic Theology*, 614–15.

[25] David Gooding, *True to the Faith* (London: Hodder, 1990), 259.

[26] We can see a forensic background to the language of justification in the LXX of Deuteronomy 25:1, which contrasts justification (acquittal) with condemnation. I am grateful to Dr Lee Gatiss for this insight.

[27] Calvin, *Acts*, 542.

[28] Calvin, *Acts*, 544, speaks against those 'who teach that only original sin and actual sins committed before baptism are clearly and freely forgiven by Christ, and that others are redeemed by satisfactions. But Paul saith plainly that we are justified from sins by Christ through the whole course of our life.'

[29] Grudem, *Systematic Theology*, 731–2.

[30] John Murray, *Redemption Accomplished and Applied* (Grand Rapids: Eerdmans, 1955), 131.

and justification, not because of what we have done, but entirely based on what he has done for us. For Christians we cannot be reminded of this message too many times. This is the basis of our assurance and the motivation for us to live our lives in response to his free grace. A life lived attempting to earn a right standing with God will lead to pride or despair. A life lived in response to God's grace is free and full, and without fear. As Paul would later write, 'Therefore, there is now no condemnation for those who are in Christ Jesus' (Romans 8:1).

As Paul concludes he warns his hearers, 'Take care that what the prophets have said does not happen to you' (verse 40). He warns them against being those who scoff and 'perish' citing Habakkuk 1:5.

Our preaching and teaching must strike that wise balance between invitation and warning. The good news is so good because the bad news is so bad. Of course, in our preaching we need a sensitivity to our context. Paul is here preaching in the synagogue to Jews and God-fearing Gentiles. As we shall see, his speech in Lystra and Derbe (Acts 14) amid a pagan audience is very different. Nevertheless, we must not shy away from difficult themes like judgment. We must handle them with wisdom and sensitivity. We should seek to speak with winsomeness and persuasiveness (see Acts 14:1). Yet warning and invitation must both be spoken of in our own preaching if we are to be faithful to the apostolic message.

Acts 13:42–52: A mixed response

42 As Paul and Barnabas were leaving the synagogue, the people invited them to speak further about these things on the next Sabbath. 43 When the congregation was dismissed, many of the Jews and devout converts to Judaism followed Paul and Barnabas, who talked with them and urged them to continue in the grace of God.

44 On the next Sabbath almost the whole city gathered to hear the word of the Lord. 45 When the Jews saw the crowds, they were filled with jealousy. They began to contradict what Paul was saying and heaped abuse on him. 46 Then Paul and Barnabas answered them boldly: 'We had to speak the word of God to you first. Since you reject it and do not consider yourselves worthy of eternal life, we now turn to the Gentiles. 47 For this is what the Lord has commanded us:

' "I have made you[f] a light for the Gentiles,
that you[f] may bring salvation to the ends of the earth." [g]'

48 When the Gentiles heard this, they were glad and honoured the word of the Lord; and all who were appointed for eternal life believed.

49 The word of the Lord spread through the whole region. **50** But the Jewish leaders incited the God-fearing women of high standing and the leading men of the city. They stirred up persecution against Paul and Barnabas, and expelled them from their region. **51** So they shook the dust off their feet as a warning to them and went to Iconium. **52** And the disciples were filled with joy and with the Holy Spirit.

f 47 The Greek is singular.
g 47 Isaiah 49:6

The reception for Paul and Barnabas was clearly mixed. Many followed, and such was the impact of their message that on the next Sabbath the whole city gathered to hear them (verse 44). Yet others were filled with jealousy, and abused and opposed them (verses 45, 50). We should not be surprised when our own missionary endeavours are met with a mixed reception. Paul elsewhere describes being the aroma of life to some and the stench of death to others (2 Corinthians 2:16). Faithfulness is not measured by success, but perseverance. Ultimately, Paul and Barnabas would increasingly turn their attention to their Gentile hearers, an action that Paul justified on the basis of Isaiah 49:6.[31]

It is worth pausing briefly to note Paul's striking use of Isaiah 49:6. If we were to ask people in our church to whom Isaiah 49:6 refers, I think most of us would naturally answer Jesus. Yet here is Paul applying it to himself and Barnabas. As Marshall says, 'The task of Israel, which she has failed to carry out, has passed to Jesus and then to his people as the new Israel; it is the task of bringing the light of revelation and salvation to all the peoples of the world.'[32] If I dared to quibble I would argue it did not pass to Jesus, as it was always intended to be his task. But what is striking is the way in which Paul incorporates the servants of *the* Servant into this commission.

Luke records that many Gentiles honoured the word of the Lord and 'all who were appointed for eternal life believed' (verse 48).[33] This verse is often appealed to (among others) in defence of the doctrine of predestination, since God's appointment of them occurs prior to their hearing and believing. They are not described as chosen because they believed, but rather they believe because they were appointed for eternal

---

[31] As Bock notes, this turn is not absolute. When Paul visited new places he would often begin in the synagogue, only turning to the Gentiles after being rejected by the Jews. See for example Acts 16:13; 17:1, 10, 17; 18:4, 19; 19:8–9. See Bock, *Acts*, 463.
[32] Marshall, *Acts*, 230.
[33] The verb 'appoint' (*tetagmenoi*) appears also in Luke 7:8; Acts 22:10; Romans 13:1. Here it is in the passive voice emphasising that it is God who does the appointing.

life. God's choice comes before ours. Scripture, in various places, teaches that before the creation of the world God predestined those whom he would call into his family, the church.[34] The doctrine has often been divisive and misunderstood. And we must confess there is an element of mystery. It is worth noting Acts 14:1 – 'they spoke so effectively that a great number of Jews and Greeks believed'. Did they believe because they were appointed or because Paul and Barnabas spoke effectively? The historically orthodox answer is both. We maintain the theological tension. Scripture teaches both God's sovereignty and humanity's responsibility. And so we hold on to both things while confessing we do not fully understand.[35] We do not know who God has appointed and so we continue to preach and witness faithfully, dependent on God, and leaving the results of our efforts in his hands. This is a humbling and liberating place from which we carry out our mission. We need not despair when we don't see great results. And we do not feel proud or self-satisfied when we do. We are his humble servants, labouring in his field, trying to make the most of every opportunity – all the while content to leave the harvest to him.

Luke tells us that the word of the Lord continued to spread through the whole region. The opposition forced Paul and Barnabas to move on, but the disciples were 'filled with joy and with the Holy Spirit' (verse 52).

As we reflect on Paul's speech, we can see the incredible grace, generosity and patience of God with people who are often stubborn and rebellious. Yet our stubbornness does not thwart his plans. The word continues to spread and the Spirit continues to bring new life and new joy. The great faithfulness of God spurs us on in the mission to be witnesses to the nations of the free offer of forgiveness that Jesus has won for us.

---

[34] Romans 8:28–30; Ephesians 1:4–5; 1 Thessalonians 1:4–5; 2 Thessalonians 2:13; Revelation 13:7–8.

[35] Here is Loraine Boettner: 'Whatever God has revealed is undoubtedly true and is to be believed although we may not be able to sound its depths with the line of our reason. In our ignorance of His inter-related purposes, we are not fitted to be His counselors . . . Man knows far too little to justify him in attempting to explain the mysteries of God's rule.' Loraine Boettner, *The Reformed Doctrine of Predestination* (Philipsburg: P&R, 1932), 54–5.

13

The Divine Doorman

ACTS 14

Acts 13–14 chart the story of the first missionary journey of Paul and his companions. Having preached on Cyprus and in the synagogue at Pisidian Antioch, Paul and Barnabas were expelled from the region (13:50). From there they moved on to Iconium, then to the Lycaonian cities of Lystra and Derbe, before returning to their sending church in Antioch (14:26). On their return they reported to the church how God had 'opened a door of faith to the Gentiles' (verse 27). The themes of growth and persecution continue to walk hand in hand as Paul and Barnabas enter new places.

1. At Iconium • Acts 14:1–7

In Iconium

14 At Iconium Paul and Barnabas went as usual into the Jewish synagogue. There they spoke so effectively that a great number of Jews and Greeks believed. ² But the Jews who refused to believe stirred up the other Gentiles and poisoned their minds against the brothers. ³ So Paul and Barnabas spent considerable time there, speaking boldly for the Lord, who confirmed the message of his grace by enabling them to perform signs and wonders. ⁴ The people of the city were divided; some sided with the Jews, others with the apostles. ⁵ There was a plot afoot among both Gentiles and Jews, together with their leaders, to ill-treat them and stone them. ⁶ But they found out about it and fled to the Lycaonian cities of Lystra and Derbe and to the surrounding country, ⁷ where they continued to preach the gospel.

Having been expelled from Pisidian Antioch, Paul and Barnabas arrived in Iconium.[1] According to their usual practice, they went first to the synagogue. Luke records, 'They spoke so effectively that a great number of Jews and Greeks believed.' This verse, taken with Acts 13:48, is a good

---

[1] Iconium is ninety miles south-east of Pisidian Antioch. Peterson, *Acts*, 403.

reminder of the tension to be maintained between God's sovereignty and human responsibility.

In Acts 13:48 we read, 'all who were appointed for eternal life believed'. Here in Acts 14:1 Luke records the effectiveness of Paul's and Barnabas's speech. Of course, it is a great mystery how divine sovereignty and human responsibility intersect, but Scripture affirms the truth of both things, and so we must believe and hold on to both of these truths. We must resist the natural temptation to neatly resolve the mystery in this theological tension.

On the one hand, we must not fall into thinking that since God is sovereign there is really no need for us to think hard about effective communication or outreach. Scripture clearly presents and positively commends Paul and Barnabas who were often strategic in approach and compelling in their speech. The Greek construction, *houtōs hōste* (verse 1), carries the sense of speaking in 'such a way' (ESV) or 'such a manner' (NASB 1995). The sense seems to be that Paul and Barnabas spoke in a way that was convincing and compelling, at least to some hearers. Preachers should give time and attention to their sermons so that they, too, may speak effectively. Preachers should not hide hastily prepared and poorly delivered sermons behind the doctrine of God's sovereignty. Individuals and churches should give time to thinking about how they might 'make the most of every opportunity' (Colossians 4:5), using their gifts and resources in wise ways.

On the other hand, setting Acts 14:1 alongside Acts 13:48 reminds us that the power for conversion rests with God, not humanity. It is liberating and comforting to remember that if someone rejects the message it is not ultimately because we failed to be engaging or persuasive enough. People's eternity does not hang on our ability as speakers. This is good news. It frees us both to work hard at our witness and offer our best and to rest in God's sovereignty to regenerate and illuminate the heart of the unbeliever.

In verse 2, Luke reminds us that not everyone was thrilled with the message. Some of the Jews stirred up other Gentiles and 'poisoned their minds'. It is always a troubling thing when people not only refuse the gospel themselves but also poison the minds of others in the process. Perhaps Paul and Barnabas were slandered or threatened to their faces. Perhaps they were aware of certain ringleaders who were particularly vociferous. I fear I may have fled long before Paul and Barnabas!

It throws the resilience of Paul and Barnabas into even more stark relief: 'So Paul and Barnabas spent considerable time there, speaking boldly for the Lord.' The Greek construction *men oun* ('so then' – verse 3) suggests that the hostility is the very reason they decided to spend more time there.[2] We can perhaps imagine how they must have felt. Some received the message gladly, while others rejected it and stirred up animosity. It would have been easy for Paul and Barnabas to move on and escape the trouble that came upon them. Yet they resolved to stay in a difficult place, for the sake of the gospel and for the sake of the new believers. They chose to endure hardship for the good of their new converts.

God often calls us to places that have their own challenges. It is often tempting to think perhaps the grass is greener elsewhere. Sometimes God calls us to remain in difficult situations, to carry on his work even when it is painful to do so.

The 'boldness' (*parrēsia*) with which they spoke is something spoken of repeatedly in Acts.[3] It seems to be something that is both act and gift. It is 'act' in the sense that it is the human courage of the early Christians in their continued determination to speak of Jesus. It is a gift in the sense that it seems to be something God grants – a certain freedom and liberty to continue speaking in his name. As the apostles step out in courageous faith, God enables them to speak boldly, often confirming their boldness, as here, with signs and wonders. It is a comfort and an encouragement to know that when we speak of Christ we do not do so alone, but his Spirit helps us. When we depend on him, we may experience those times of speaking with a God-given sense of boldness or liberty.

As Paul and Barnabas spoke, the Lord 'confirmed the message of his grace by enabling them to perform signs and wonders' (verse 3). In describing the gospel as 'the message of his grace', Luke is reminding us of something Paul will reiterate in his letters – the gospel is a message of grace, not works. The performance of signs and wonders establishes Paul as an apostle in the same order as the Jerusalem apostles (see 2 Corinthians 12:12). Paul is apostle to the Gentiles, as the miracles demonstrate.

Luke tells us the city was divided between those who supported the apostles and those who opposed.[4] The hostility appeared to increase as the determination to poison minds (verse 2) developed into a plot to ill-treat and stone Paul and Barnabas (verse 5). Having heard of this, Paul and Barnabas fled to Lystra and Derbe where they continued to preach

---

[2] Witherington, *Acts*, 419.
[3] The noun form appears in Acts 2:29; 4:13, 29, 31; 28:31. The verb form appears in Acts 9:27–8; 13:46; 18:26; 19:8; 26:26.
[4] It is only here and in 14:14 that Luke calls Paul and Barnabas apostles.

the gospel.[5] Here we see that God-dependent courage is not without wisdom. Paul and Barnabas were not afraid to endure opposition and hardship. However, when the threat escalated and their lives were in danger, they recognised the need to move on.

Following in the footsteps of our Lord Jesus will entail taking up our cross – Paul will say as much in Acts 14:22. Yet suffering is not to be actively sought, as if it merits special reward. Sometimes Christians encounter suffering and opposition unnecessarily – not because they are being faithful witnesses but because they are being unwise, even reckless, in their engagement with the world. We should not seek to escape suffering for Christ. Some is inevitable and unavoidable if we are to 'contend for the faith' (Jude 3). Yet Paul and Barnabas teach us that sometimes it is wise to remove ourselves from situations of danger so that we might find other opportunities to continue to witness elsewhere.[6] Fellow believers can help us here in some of these difficult situations that often require much wisdom, counsel and discernment.

2. In Lystra and Derbe • Acts 14:8–20

In Lystra and Derbe

8 In Lystra there sat a man who was lame. He had been that way from birth and had never walked. **9** He listened to Paul as he was speaking. Paul looked directly at him, saw that he had faith to be healed **10** and called out, 'Stand up on your feet!' At that, the man jumped up and began to walk.

11 When the crowd saw what Paul had done, they shouted in the Lycaonian language, 'The gods have come down to us in human form!' **12** Barnabas they called Zeus, and Paul they called Hermes because he was the chief speaker. **13** The priest of Zeus, whose temple was just outside the city, brought bulls and wreaths to the city gates because he and the crowd wanted to offer sacrifices to them.

14 But when the apostles Barnabas and Paul heard of this, they tore their clothes and rushed out into the crowd, shouting: **15** 'Friends, why are you doing this? We too are only human, like you. We are bringing you good news, telling you to turn from these worthless things to the living God, who made the heavens and the earth and the sea and everything in them. **16** In the past, he let all nations go their own way. **17** Yet he has not left himself without

---

[5] Lystra is eighteen miles south-west of Iconium, and Derbe a further fifty-five miles. Peterson, *Acts*, 406.

[6] Venkataraman, 'Acts', in *SABC*, 1487.

testimony: he has shown kindness by giving you rain from heaven and crops in their seasons; he provides you with plenty of food and fills your hearts with joy.' **18** Even with these words, they had difficulty keeping the crowd from sacrificing to them.

19 Then some Jews came from Antioch and Iconium and won the crowd over. They stoned Paul and dragged him outside the city, thinking he was dead. **20** But after the disciples had gathered round him, he got up and went back into the city. The next day he and Barnabas left for Derbe.

As Paul and Barnabas were in Lystra they encountered a man who had been lame from birth (verse 8). Paul's healing of the lame man parallels Peter's healing of the lame man in Acts 3:1–10.[7] Luke is demonstrating for his readers that Paul is an apostle just as Peter is, and that the gospel offer of salvation is going in all its power to Gentiles as well as to Jews.[8]

The striking difference between the two miracles lies in the response. Peter and John found themselves in the Temple courts, giving a history of God's dealings with Israel, and would be arrested and imprisoned by the Temple authorities. Paul and Barnabas were at the city gates, worshipped by the people as gods, and giving a quite different speech in response.[9]

Luke informs us that the crowd called Barnabas 'Zeus' and Paul 'Hermes' since he was the chief speaker. The poet, Ovid, records an earlier legend of Zeus and Hermes visiting the region, disguised as humans seeking lodging. Having found 'no room at the inn' at a thousand homes they eventually found an older couple who offered them hospitality. They rewarded the elderly couple who welcomed them and destroyed the houses of all those who did not receive them. It is possible that the crowd's response was linked to this earlier legend that would have no doubt been familiar to the local residents.[10] The priest from the temple of Zeus arrived with bull and wreath ready to sacrifice to Paul and Barnabas.

When Paul and Barnabas understood what was happening, they tore their clothes – a symbol of distress and lament at the blasphemy – and they rushed into the crowd to attempt to persuade the crowd their actions were misdirected. As Peterson notes, 'Unlike Herod in Acts 12:21–23, they

---

[7] Both accounts contain the same opening description (*chōlos ek koilias metros* – 'lame from his mother's womb' – Acts 3:2; 14:8), the same verbs refer to his healing (*allomai* – 'jump up'; *peripateo* – 'walk' – Acts 3:8; 14:10), and the same action of the healer (*atenisas* – 'to look intently' – Acts 3:4; 14:9). Witherington, *Acts*, 422.

[8] Marianne Fournier, *The Episode at Lystra* (New York: Peter Lang, 1997), 202.

[9] Wall, *Acts*, 198–9.

[10] See Ovid, *Metamorphoses* 8.611–724. Witherington, *Acts*, 421–2.

aggressively resisted any implication of divine status and significance!'[11] We may not be tempted to worship gifted Christian leaders as if they were divine, but we must still be wary of the temptation to put people on pedestals and treat them as if they were above all challenge or criticism.[12] The culture of celebrity pastors is all too prevalent in venerating certain individuals as being somehow closer to the divine. Would that some of them would be quicker to tear their designer clothes and humbly point people to the Saviour.

What is particularly noteworthy here is the way in which Paul's speech to a pagan audience was so different from his speech in the synagogue. It reminds us that there is no 'one size fits all' presentation of the gospel. Paul spoke to his audience in terms they could understand.

In verse 15 Paul, began with their commonality: 'We too are only human, like you.' Far from being gods, they were simply messengers bringing 'good news' and telling them to turn from 'worthless things'. Luke does not tell us how the opening statement was received, but we can imagine a degree of consternation at describing the priest, the bulls and the wreaths as 'worthless'. These things would have played an important part in the religious culture of the Lycaonians and Paul in a sentence dismissed them as worthless.

Paul then moved to speak of God as creator. In Jewish contexts, Paul emphasised the work of God as redeemer through Israel's history, from the Patriarchs to the Prophets. Here he spoke instead of the 'living God, who made the heavens and the earth and the sea and everything in them' (verse 15).

Paul continued, 'In the past, he let all nations go their own way' (verse 16). This was not a statement of benign permissiveness that denies culpability.[13] It was rather an act of judgment to give the nations over to their idolatry and its consequences.[14] The gospel is a message of salvation from the emptiness of idolatry and the judgment it brought.[15] 'Yet he has not left himself without testimony' (verse 17). The kindness of God, claimed Paul, is seen in his provision of the rain and the crops. It was the living God, not Zeus or Hermes, who had provided them with food

---

[11] Peterson, *Acts*, 409.

[12] Paul Mumo Kisau, 'Acts', in *ABC*, 1351.

[13] See Daniel Strange, *For Their Rock Is Not as Our Rock: An Evangelical Theology of Religions* (Nottingham: Apollos, 2014), 226–7.

[14] See Romans 1:18–25.

[15] Peterson, *Acts*, 410.

and joy. In theological terms, this is often termed 'general revelation'.[16] This is the truth that in creation God has revealed himself to be existent, powerful and kind.

The first chapter of the Westminster Confession of Faith says the following:

> Although the light of nature, and the works of creation and provi-
> dence, do so far manifest the goodness, wisdom, and power of God,
> as to leave men inexcusable; yet they are not sufficient to give that
> knowledge of God, and of his will, which is necessary unto salvation:
> therefore it pleased the Lord, at sundry times, and in divers manners,
> to reveal himself, and to declare that his will unto his Church; and
> afterwards, for the better preserving and propagating of the truth,
> and for the more sure establishment and comfort of the Church
> against the corruption of the flesh, and the malice of Satan and of
> the world, to commit the same wholly unto writing; which maketh
> the Holy Scripture to be most necessary; those former ways of God's
> revealing his will unto his people being now ceased.

Although human beings suppress this knowledge in their sin, they are without excuse. The image of God, though marred, is not obliterated. God's 'common grace' and the gift of conscience should point human beings to acknowledge there is a Creator.[17] It is the concept of 'general revelation' that enables Paul to make an appeal to a pagan audience. The 'goodness, wisdom, and power of God' are the basis on which he can connect his message to their world.

Missiologists term this process 'contextualisation'.[18] The speaker recognises the commonality that exists by virtue of being made in the image of God and enjoying God's common grace and having access to general revelation. The speaker knows this is not sufficient. Special revelation and

---

[16] See Calvin, *Institutes* 1.5.6–15.

[17] Matthew 5:45; Acts 17:24–7; Romans 1:18–32; 2:14–15.

[18] Keller defines contextualisation as 'giving people *the Bible's answers*, which they may not at all want to hear, *to questions about life* that people in their particular time and place are asking, *in language and forms* they can comprehend, and *through appeals and arguments* with force they can feel, even if they reject them'. Tim Keller, *Center Church* (Grand Rapids: Zondervan, 2012), 89. Italics original. For more on 'contextualisation', see Newbigin, *The Gospel in a Pluralist Society*, 141–54; Strange, *For Their Rock Is Not as Our Rock*, 279–80.

special grace are still required.[19] But common grace and general revelation provide the possibility of an initial connection so that the hearer might listen to the ways in which the good news fills out and completes the error and inadequacy of their own world view.

It is not uncommon to hear some dismiss 'contextualisation' as unnecessary – 'Just preach the gospel!' they argue. Yet Paul here demonstrates the value and necessity of engaging our hearers on their own terms, sensitive to their culture and demonstrating how and why the good news really is the good news.

What is interesting here is that we do not actually see explicit mention of Jesus, his life, his death, his resurrection, ascension and exaltation. These are all critical themes in other speeches, but there is no mention of them here. Of course, what we see here are brief summaries. It seems clear that Paul and Barnabas said more than what we have recorded, and likely had opportunity to explain the message more fully – certainly Acts 14:21–2 suggest this would have been the case.[20]

Having kept the crowd from sacrificing to them, we read of Jews who had followed Paul and Barnabas from Antioch and Iconium who won the crowd over.[21] Not content for them to have left their region, some actively pursued Paul and Barnabas in their fanatical hatred of the gospel. The reception that had been initially positive quickly turned hostile. The adulation of many in the crowd shows itself to have been hollow. Those they had fled in verse 6 had caught up with them. 'They stoned Paul and dragged him outside the city, thinking he was dead' (verse 19). Although Luke does not explicitly tell us Paul's recovery was miraculous, it does seem remarkable that, having been presumed dead, he was able to get up, walk back to the city and be well enough to depart the next day.[22] Here again is a reminder for us all to pray for fellow believers who endure physical violence for their faith. We should be aware and in prayer that God would enable them to endure and remain faithful to him in the midst of enormously challenging circumstances.

---

[19] John 3:3–8; Romans 10:9–15; Titus 3:3–5.
[20] Marshall, *Acts*, 239.
[21] The Jews who had travelled from Antioch in pursuit had travelled more than one hundred miles to persecute Paul, illustrating their zeal.
[22] Bullinger, in *RCS* 6:197.

3. Return to Antioch • Acts 14:21–8

The return to Antioch in Syria

21 They preached the gospel in that city and won a large number of disciples. Then they returned to Lystra, Iconium and Antioch, **22** strengthening the disciples and encouraging them to remain true to the faith. 'We must go through many hardships to enter the kingdom of God,' they said. **23** Paul and Barnabas appointed elders[a] for them in each church and, with prayer and fasting, committed them to the Lord, in whom they had put their trust. **24** After going through Pisidia, they came into Pamphylia, **25** and when they had preached the word in Perga, they went down to Attalia.

26 From Attalia they sailed back to Antioch, where they had been committed to the grace of God for the work they had now completed. **27** On arriving there, they gathered the church together and reported all that God had done through them and how he had opened a door of faith to the Gentiles. **28** And they stayed there a long time with the disciples.

---

[a] 23 Or *Barnabas ordained elders*; or *Barnabas had elders elected*

In verse 21 Luke records the success of Paul and Barnabas in Derbe as they 'won a large number of disciples'. Luke then charts their return journey towards Antioch.

Paul and Barnabas returned to the same places they had previously, with two purposes: strengthening the disciples and establishing elders. This was a critical part of Paul's missionary work. He knew that these groups of believers, in their infancy, would require much encouragement and the stability of structured leadership if they were to survive and grow. It is a reminder of the importance of pastoral work in the strengthening and encouraging of the church. Paul did not simply move on and consider his work done. He often revisited or wrote to the churches he had involvement with. Paul shows us the important way in which the role of missionary and pastor belong together. A pastor must have a missionary heart and a missionary must have a pastor's heart in seeking to play our part in Jesus's Great Commission. We often separate out such roles and gifts, but in Paul we see them working together to serve the churches.

Luke provides a summary of the strengthening and encouraging that Paul and Barnabas sought to bring: 'We must go through many hardships to enter the kingdom of God' (verse 22). At first sight it does not seem to be the most motivational or uplifting of messages. Yet Paul had first-hand experience of the sort of opposition the gospel could bring. It is not hard to find preachers today promising people that if they turn to Christ their problems will be over and their lives will be improved – physically, mentally, relationally, economically. A lady started attending our church who had come from one such church. Her leaders had promised if she gave more of her money to the church her problems would go away, which of course they did not.

Paul was not offering the prosperity gospel. His message to believers is still needed across the world today. Following Christ does not come with a promise of comfort and ease in this life. We need to prepare people in evangelism and discipleship that following Jesus may well mean suffering and hardship this side of eternity. Persecution is not the reserve of far-flung missionaries in unreached places. Paul's words in verse 22 suggest this is the normal experience of any and all who would take up their cross to follow Christ. It will obviously take many different forms, depending on our context, but we should expect opposition if we are seeking to present the reality of human sin and Jesus as Saviour, Lord and the only way to eternal life.

Paul and Barnabas were also keen to appoint elders in every church. We are not told the exact process by which this happened.[23] Were they ordained by Paul and Barnabas? Did the churches appoint their own leaders? Was there a secret vote with a pass mark of 80 per cent? We are simply not told. This perhaps permits churches a degree of freedom in how their leaders are appointed. Different approaches have been employed through the centuries. The whole counsel of Scripture provides healthy principles for discerning and appointing leaders, without ever giving a precise mechanism. Episcopalian, Presbyterian and Congregational churches have taken varying interpretations regarding the different offices and the scope and limits of the power of governance.

Luke is providing description, not prescription, so it is difficult to draw out clear and definite principles that should be binding for the church in every time and place. This is one of those debates where Christians could agree to disagree and still work together in gospel endeavour. It does seem that there was a plurality of elders in each church, and that the churches played some role in the appointment or recognition of their leaders (assuming Luke intends the 'prayer and fasting' to refer to

---

[23] The verb *cheirotonēsantes* ('appointed', verse 23) carries the sense of extending the hands. This could refer to ordination by the apostles, the laying on of hands by the church or a process of voting. The word itself gives no definitive evidence for differing interpretations as to the method of appointment.

the churches, not just Paul and Barnabas).[24] This provides an important protection against the potential for abuse of power if it were invested in just one person.

Luke tracks their movements back through Pamphylia and Perga and finally on to Antioch from where they had been sent in Acts 13:3. Paul and Barnabas gathered the whole church and 'reported all that God had done through them and how he had opened a door of faith to the Gentiles' (verse 27).

Robert Wall, in his commentary on Acts, notes Paul's strategy in his missionary journeys of gravitating towards centres of population density. Paul does not do this because people who live in urban settings are worth more to God than those who live in more rural areas. Paul knows that, strategically speaking, there is value in investing himself in those places where there is a higher concentration of people, who will in turn be able to spread the message further afield.[25]

This seems undeniably part of Paul's missionary strategy. However, we need to be careful in our day and age that we do not fall into the trap of thinking that the best or most important missionary work takes place in cities. There is clearly a strategic significance. However, globalisation and the technological revolution means that physical location is perhaps less important than it would have been even twenty years ago, let alone two thousand years ago. The ease with which many can travel means a church can reach many people across a wide area far more easily than ever before. Often the sheer number of churches in a region means another new church plant may not be the best strategy.

Modern churches will need to reflect carefully on how their own contexts will shape their missional strategy. Churches may need to work together more to consider how best to reach more people in their area with the gospel. The methods of twenty, two hundred or two thousand years ago may not necessarily be the best for the challenges of today. Similarly, the approach that yielded fruit in one particular cultural location may not necessarily translate well to another.[26]

The summary of their missionary report is a heartening reminder of where the power for mission truly rests. Paul and Barnabas were keen to tell of all that *God* had done through them, not all the things *they* had done. They wanted the church at Antioch to draw confidence from

---

[24] On this latter point see Calvin, *Institutes* 4.3.15.

[25] Wall, *Acts*, 202.

[26] For more on this, see Keller, *Center Church*, 154–62.

the fact that *God* had opened the door of faith. We must always resist the temptation to recount the successes that God graciously grants as something *we* have done. All the praise and glory must continually go back to him – it is his power at work within us, and it is the glory of his name that we must seek.

14

Discerning Doctrine in
Debate and Disagreement

Acts 15

Since the conversion of Cornelius and his household in Acts 10, Luke has recorded the spread of the gospel to various regions resulting in newly established local churches that contained both Jews and Gentiles. As a consequence, questions of integration between these two groups naturally arose. Specifically, to what extent were the Jewish believers to continue with Jewish customs and practices? Further, to what extent should Gentile believers observe these customs and practices?

Circumcision, as the sign of the old covenant, was an essential badge of identity for the faithful Jew. It was inevitable that questions around the ongoing observance of such important cultural markers, particularly in relation to new Gentile converts, would need to be addressed. This question had profound theological and practical implications. Peterson says, 'These issues had to be resolved before the work of Paul could continue and new initiatives could be taken with the gospel.'[1] Haenchen describes Acts 15 as a 'centrepiece' providing both the justification for past events and the possibility for further Gentile mission.[2] As we shall see, these questions are not simply of historic interest. There are critical lessons for us to learn today.

1. The Consultation at Jerusalem[3] • Acts 15:1–21

The council at Jerusalem

15 Certain people came down from Judea to Antioch and were teaching the believers: 'Unless you are circumcised, according to the custom taught by Moses, you

---

[1] Peterson, *Acts*, 417.

[2] Ernst Haenchen, *The Acts of the Apostles: A Commentary* (Louisville: Westminster John Knox, 1971), 461.

[3] I am following Bock here in describing this as a consultation rather than a 'council': 'It is not a council in the later technical ecclesiastical sense . . . It includes

cannot be saved.' **2** This brought Paul and Barnabas into sharp dispute and debate with them. So Paul and Barnabas were appointed, along with some other believers, to go up to Jerusalem to see the apostles and elders about this question. **3** The church sent them on their way, and as they travelled through Phoenicia and Samaria, they told how the Gentiles had been converted. This news made all the believers very glad. **4** When they came to Jerusalem, they were welcomed by the church and the apostles and elders, to whom they reported everything God had done through them.

5 Then some of the believers who belonged to the party of the Pharisees stood up and said, 'The Gentiles must be circumcised and required to keep the law of Moses.'

6 The apostles and elders met to consider this question. **7** After much discussion, Peter got up and addressed them: 'Brothers, you know that some time ago God made a choice among you that the Gentiles should hear from my lips the message of the gospel and believe. **8** God, who knows the heart, showed that he accepted them by giving the Holy Spirit to them, just as he did to us. **9** He did not discriminate between us and them, for he purified their hearts by faith. **10** Now then, why do you try to test God by putting on the necks of Gentiles a yoke that neither we nor our ancestors have been able to bear? **11** No! We believe it is through the grace of our Lord Jesus that we are saved, just as they are.'

12 The whole assembly became silent as they listened to Barnabas and Paul telling about the signs and wonders God had done among the Gentiles through them. **13** When they finished, James spoke up. 'Brothers,' he said, 'listen to me. **14** Simon[a] has described to us how God first intervened to choose a people for his name from the Gentiles. **15** The words of the prophets are in agreement with this, as it is written:

16 ' "After this I will return
    and rebuild David's fallen tent.
  Its ruins I will rebuild,
    and I will restore it,
17 that the rest of mankind may seek
    the Lord,
  even all the Gentiles who bear
    my name,
  says the Lord, who does these
    things"[b] –
18   things known from long ago.[c]

19 'It is my judgment, therefore, that we should not make it difficult for the Gentiles who are turning to God. **20** Instead we should write to them, telling them to abstain from food polluted by idols, from sexual immorality, from the meat of strangled animals and from blood. **21** For

---

more than the apostles and engages the Jerusalem congregation in a major way.'
Bock, *Acts*, 486.

the law of Moses has been preached in every city from the earliest times and is read in the synagogues on every Sabbath.'

a 14 Greek *Simeon,* a variant of *Simon;* that is, Peter

b 17 Amos 9:11,12 (see Septuagint)

c 17,18 Some manuscripts *things'* - / *¹⁸the Lord's work is known to him from long ago*

In verse 1 we read of 'certain people' who had travelled from Judea to Antioch and were teaching the believers: 'Unless you are circumcised, according to the custom taught by Moses, you cannot be saved.' Although it might strike modern ears as strange, it would have been a natural question for a first-century Jew to raise. Male converts to Judaism were required to be circumcised. Christianity emerged out of and in the context of Judaism. Jesus and his followers taught in the synagogues and Temple courts, reading from Old Testament texts. Their speeches contained many quotes and allusions to the Old Testament. In the days following Pentecost we see Peter and John going to the Temple to pray (Acts 3:1). Jesus himself viewed the Old Testament Scriptures as unbreakable (John 10:35), authoritative as the word of God. So it is not surprising that the early church wrestled with the question of how to apply Old Testament Scriptures, particularly Jewish customs and practice, to their new life in Christ, which included Gentile believers.

Many of the Jewish believers viewed circumcision as the sign of God's covenant promises to his elect people. It was a sign that identified the recipient with those promises and with God's people. In their eyes, to refuse the sign was to refuse God's word. Yet the apostles knew that Jesus had come in fulfilment of the Old Testament Scriptures (Luke 24:25–7; 44–7) and that in him a new covenant had dawned, bringing with it a new covenant sign – baptism. The question the teachers from Judea brought was not so much whether a Gentile *may* be circumcised (see Acts 16:3), but whether they *must* be circumcised to be saved.

Luke records that Paul and Barnabas entered into 'sharp dispute and debate' with the Judean teachers and so were appointed, along with some others, to take the question to the apostles and elders in Jerusalem (verse 2). As they travelled through Phoenicia and Samaria, they reported how God had saved the Gentiles, a report they shared with the Jerusalem church upon their arrival.

In verse 5, the question for consideration is restated by some believers who belonged to the party of the Pharisees: 'The Gentiles must be circumcised and required to keep the law of Moses.' At this point, Luke tells us the apostles and elders met to consider this question – a question that elicited much discussion before any conclusion was drawn (verses 6–7).

At this point it is worth pausing to note two further discussions that have arisen over the centuries as a result of this debate. First, what is the relationship between the Council of Jerusalem and Paul's epistle to the Galatians? Second, what can be learned from Acts 15 about models of church governance?

First, how are we to understand the relationship between Acts 15 and Galatians 2:1–10?[4] Some see Galatians 2:1–10 as corresponding to Acts 15 – both events happen in Jerusalem, involve the same people and issues, and the chronological fit is good.[5] However, others see Galatians 2:1–10 corresponding to Acts 11:30. The meeting referred to in Galatians 2:2 is private, there is no mention of the conditions set down in Acts 15, and it seems hard to believe that Paul could have written Galatians after the Jerusalem Council. On balance, it seems preferable to see Galatians 2:1–10 as describing Paul's second post-conversion visit to Jerusalem (Acts 11:30), with Acts 15 being his third.[6] Equating Galatians 2:1–10 with Acts 11:30 would explain why there is no mention of the decree in Galatians since it had not yet taken place.[7]

Second, what may we learn here about church governance? This passage has been cited by those in favour of a presbyterian model of church governance.[8] Presbyterian governance has both local and regional elders, the latter being made up from a selection of the former. This model fosters a healthy interdependence between local churches and provides an extra layer of protection, support and wisdom in helping local churches. Historically, Episcopalians have appealed to passages such as Acts 14:23 and Titus 1:5 as justification for the role of bishops. Congregationalists have appealed to passages such as Matthew 18:15–20, 1 Corinthians 5:1–5 and 2 Corinthians 2:5–11 in defence of the autonomy of the local church. Acts 15 would suggest a level of governance beyond a single local church, and a plurality of leaders including those within the local churches. Hence Presbyterians would argue Acts 15 provides scriptural warrant for their approach to church governance.

---

[4] Witherington, Acts, 440–49, has an excellent and detailed discussion of the question.

[5] Witherington, Acts, 440.

[6] Marshall, Acts, 244–5.

[7] Bock, Acts, 490.

[8] A lengthy discussion on Acts 15 can be found in William Cunningham, *Historical Theology, Volume 1* (Edinburgh: T&T Clark, 1870), 43–78. His careful treatment has many helpful insights into the nature, scope and limits of church power, though his contention that the apostles are acting as 'ordinary leaders' rather than 'apostles' is unconvincing.

However, we must be careful to note that Acts 15 arises out of a particular crisis, and there is little in Acts to suggest this is a regular or 'normal' pattern for resolving local church disputes. Further, we should also recognise the unique authority possessed by the apostles of Christ. Acts 15 narrates the wisdom in seeking the counsel of other church leaders and the process of discussion among a plurality of leaders. Yet, given the uniqueness of the historical situation and the uniqueness of the apostolic authority, Acts 15 should not be pressed too hard into providing a clear and prescriptive model for how New Testament churches ought to be governed.[9] The wider testimony of Scripture provides other key principles in deciding how the local church ought to govern itself under Christ's rule.

Acts 15:6–21 describes the progression of the discussion with three main contributions: those of Peter, of Barnabas and Paul and of James. In verse 7, Peter begins by recounting his own experience narrated in Acts 10. He describes how God called him to proclaim the gospel to the Gentiles. He argues that the evidence of their acceptance was seen in the receiving of the Holy Spirit. The gift of the Spirit was part of the promise of the new covenant, symbolising new life and cleansing, something God would only have given if the Gentiles were indeed accepted and cleansed without circumcision.[10] Peter argues that God did not discriminate for 'he purified their hearts by faith'. In other words, it was not by circumcision that the Gentiles found acceptance, but by faith – a theme that is repeated often in Paul's letters. Peter goes on to describe the Law as a 'yoke that neither we nor our ancestors have been able to bear' (verse 10).

The Old Testament Law served in part to show people their sin and need of grace. It was never intended to be the means by which people achieved their justification before a holy God – hence the need for constant sacrifices – with Christ as the culmination and fulfilment. Peter concludes, 'It is through the grace of our Lord Jesus that we are saved, just as they are' (verse 11). This became the cry of the Reformation: we are saved by grace alone through faith alone in Christ alone. The works of the Law could never make the worshipper perfectly righteous before God, so they should not now be imposed on the believer as if they could. Those under the old covenant and those

---

[9] Calvin, *Acts 14–28*, 44, goes too far in saying, 'here is prescribed by God a form and an order in assembling synods'. That this is Luke's purpose seems difficult to justify.

[10] Bock, *Acts*, 500.

under the new covenant both need the blood of the one mediator, Jesus Christ.[11]

The Roman Catholic Church today still teaches that though a person is saved by grace, they maintain, or rather obtain, their justification before God with works.[12] This, it seems, is the sort of theology Peter is countering. Whether Jew or Gentile, salvation is by grace alone through faith alone in Christ alone, to the glory of God alone. It is never faith plus works.

As Bock notes, 'This is the last we see of Peter in Acts.'[13] Peter's final words are in some ways his most important in affirming the basis on which people find acceptance with God: 'It is through the grace of our Lord Jesus that we are saved' (verse 11). This is the message the church is called to proclaim. Whatever a person's past or present, whatever their background, status, class, gender, age or ethnicity, it is the Lord's grace, not our works, that saves. This is the message that the searching and the hurting desperately need to hear.

In the second section of the deliberation, Barnabas and Paul recount 'the signs and wonders God had done among the Gentiles through them' (verse 12). We have noted before that the phrase 'signs and wonders' has a redemptive-historical significance as it occurs most frequently in the account of the Exodus. The logic of the argument would seem to be that God's redemptive activity extended towards the Gentiles before any were circumcised. Paul will employ a similar logic in discussing the calling of

---

[11] Augustine makes this point powerfully: 'You, who are enemies of this grace, reject the idea that we should believe that the people of old were saved by the same grace of Jesus Christ. Rather, you distinguish the different times in the manner of Pelagius in whose books this is found. You say that prior to the law they were saved by nature, then through the law and finally through Christ, as if for the human beings of the two earlier periods, namely, prior to the law and under the law, the blood of Christ was not necessary. In that way, you destroy the statement, "For there is one God and one mediator between God and humankind, the man Christ Jesus."' ACCS 5:184–5.

[12] See Session 6 of The Council of Trent (1564), Canon 9, which says 'If any one saith, that by faith alone the impious is justified; in such wise as to mean, that nothing else is required to co-operate in order to the obtaining the grace of Justification, and that it is not in any way necessary, that he be prepared and disposed by the movement of his own will; let him be anathema.' This suggests the necessity of human cooperation in obtaining the grace of justification, and Protestant teaching is anathematised throughout. Philip Schaff, *The Creeds of Christendom, with a History and Critical Notes: The Greek and Latin Creeds, with Translations* (New York: Harper & Brothers, 1890), 112.

[13] Bock, *Acts*, 501.

Abraham in Romans 4. If God calls people before they are given any sign of the covenant, then any such sign cannot be the basis of the saving gift of grace. Again, it is not that all or any observance of the Law is unimportant, but that observance of the Law cannot be the means of salvation.

The third contribution is given by James. While Peter, Barnabas and Paul have appealed to their own experience, James now demonstrates from Scripture that it was always part of the divine plan to incorporate Gentiles. Strikingly, he refers to a 'people for his name' (*laon tō onomati autou*, verse 14). Stott notes that this language is 'regularly applied in the Old Testament to Israel. James was expressing his belief that Gentile believers now belonged to the true Israel.'[14] He quotes from Amos 9:11–12, which speaks of the rebuilding of David's tent to include the Gentiles.[15] The restoration of the Davidic dynasty is fulfilled in Jesus, who fulfils the promises to David regarding his royal line (2 Samuel 7:11–16) and the promise to Abraham that from his seed would come a blessing for the nations (Genesis 12:3).[16] Amos 9:11–12 is not cited as one proof text, but as an example of the wider teaching of the Old Testament that God would incorporate the nations into his multinational kingdom.[17] James concludes, 'We should not make it difficult for the Gentiles who are turning to God. Instead we should write to them, telling them to abstain from food polluted by idols, from sexual immorality, from the meat of strangled animals and from blood' (verses 19–20).

There has been much discussion regarding the reason for these particular proscriptions. Historically, commentators trace them to a similar list of restrictions given in Leviticus 17–18, or the list given in Genesis 9:3–4.[18]

---

[14] Stott, *Acts*, 247.

[15] Witherington, *Acts*, 459, has a helpful discussion of the differences between the Masoretic Text and the Septuagint (LXX), and concludes that it is possible the LXX offers a more accurate reading of the original Hebrew than that of the Masoretes.

[16] Dirk Phillips describes this event memorably: 'He overcame the young lion, the adversary of Christians, that is, Satan, out of which conquest has come all the sweetness of divine grace, all comfort and refreshing of the soul. With the jawbone of an ass, that is, with his unlearned apostles who were regarded as asses by the world, he overcame the uncircumcised of heart, the worldly-wise and the scribes, the enemies of the gospel. Out of the poor Word of the cross, God gives to all true worshipers the living water of the Holy Spirit through faith, in order to refresh thirsty souls with it.' *RCS* 6:211.

[17] See, for example, Isaiah 2:1–4; Micah 4:1–5; Zechariah 2:10–13.

[18] Marshall, *Acts*, 244. The list in Genesis 9:3–4 says nothing about idolatry or sexual immorality so this is not a good fit. Peterson notes that the legislation of Leviticus 17–18 applied to Jews and resident aliens in the holy land. James would

However, Witherington has written persuasively that the problem is not the menu, but the venue.[19] It is the *place* where these activities routinely tale place that presents the problem.[20] Witherington states, 'The issue is not just where one might find one or another of the four elements of the decree in isolation, but in what social setting one might find them together. Here the answer is again likely to be in a temple, not in a home, and in particular at a temple feast.'[21]

The elders and apostles are encouraging the new Gentile believers to avoid the pagan temples – the places where festivals, food, sexual immorality and idolatry often came together in idolatrous temple feasts. Such places were part of the fabric of densely populated towns and cities. These were the places where food was sold, while people socialised and worshipped the gods. It would, of course, have been a cause of deep offence for Jewish believers to see Gentile believers continuing to frequent such places. This is why James mentions the reading of Moses in the synagogues on every sabbath (verse 21). As Green notes, 'Jewish Christians who have been brought up with the Old Testament laws have certain scruples over food, and the Gentiles would do well to take that into account.'[22] The Gentiles were to abstain from things 'especially offensive to a Jewish sense of cultic purity so that Jewish Christians may remain in the fellowship of the church without being forced to give up their way of life'.[23]

The apostles and elders are in fact addressing both sides. The Jewish believers should not impose customs that would cause the Gentiles to stumble, and the Gentile believers should abstain from customs that would

---

then be applying these laws to Jews and Gentiles living in the Dispersion, which seems unlikely. Peterson, *Acts*, 434–5.

[19] See Witherington, *Acts*, 460–66.

[20] Two items in this list (*alisgēmatōn*, 'pollution'; *pniktou*, 'strangled') do not appear at all in the LXX, which makes it less likely that a particular Old Testament list is being appealed to. The term (*porneias*, 'sexual immorality') seems to be connected here to pagan idolatry. As Bauckham notes 'There is, in fact, no known Jewish parallel to the selection of precisely these four commandments from the Law of Moses.' Cited in Witherington, *Acts*, 465.

[21] Witherington, *Acts*, 461–2. He quotes 2 Maccabees 6:4–5, which describes the defiling of the Temple in Jerusalem by the forces of Antiochus: 'the temple was filled with debauchery and revelling by the Gentiles, who dallied with prostitutes and had intercourse with women within the sacred precincts . . . The altar was covered with abominable offerings that were forbidden by the laws.'

[22] Green, *The Word of His Grace*, 93.

[23] Tannehill, *Narrative Unity*, 191.

cause Jewish believers to stumble. The positive demand for circumcision would be a denial of God's grace received by faith and is thus the more serious issue. On this there can be no compromise. Yet the Gentiles too need to reflect on how their conversion to Christ affects their own cultural norms and practices. There is a cross-cultural sensitivity required to preserve the unity of the church.[24] There is here a significant degree of freedom, yet bound by a concern not to cause unnecessary offence to the conscience of others. James is not an antinomian, as his epistle makes clear. While the Law of God is not able to save, there is a call to take seriously the ethical demands of God's word.[25]

This is an important lesson for us today. Stott notes that the Jerusalem consultation 'secured a double victory – a victory of truth in confirming the gospel of grace, and a victory of love in preserving the fellowship by sensitive concession to conscientious Jewish scruples'.[26] Stott recalls John Newton's instruction to be an iron pillar in essentials and a reed in non-essentials.[27]

Too often, the church has made mistakes in these areas. Gospel fundamentals such as the inerrancy and inspiration of Scripture have been denied, causing much harm, pain and confusion to Christians. At other times, cultural practices have been imposed or insisted upon as if they were some sort of Third Testament. This, too, is an abuse of power, binding the conscience of others without the authority of God's word.

We must work hard to ensure that we are clear, firm and courageous on the things that Scripture is crystal clear on. And we must allow for freedom and flexibility on those things about which Scripture is less clear.[28] In particular, we need to think about how our own actions can cause others to stumble, and perhaps the ways in which we might need to curtail our own freedoms in the service of others.

Christianity is not an abstract set of doctrinal formulas. It is lived out in community, and the way in which we equip and edify one

---

[24] Bock, *Acts*, 507. We see similar issues in Romans 14–15 and 1 Corinthians 10.
[25] Wall, *Acts*, 222. Martin Luther puts this well: 'Works may and ought to be performed, but as long as the conscience does not depend on them and does not place its trust in them. Instead, works are freely performed to honor God and to help our neighbors. The conscience must depend only on faith, on the Word and on the grace of God.' *RCS* 6:204.
[26] Stott, *Acts*, 257.
[27] Stott, *Acts*, 257.
[28] A helpful book on this subject is Gavin Ortlund, *Finding the Right Hills to Die On: The Case for Theological Triage* (Wheaton: Crossway, 2020).

another in God's word is of critical importance. Sensitivity towards one another while seeking to grow in understanding is crucial to maintaining both the unity and the purity of the church. This is a difficult call and requires much grace and patience as we seek to honour God and one another.

Before moving on, it is also worth noting the way James describes idolatry as a polluting force (verse 20). Wall notes, 'The polluting effect of idolatry continues, as witnessed in the unprincipled acquisition of wealth or in triumphal nationalism – and "temples" to these idols are found in our city's marketplaces and town squares.'[29] The called for abstention is not just for the conscience of a fellow believer but is also a necessary act in guarding the church from the pollution that idolatry brings. Idolatry is not a minor thing, concerned only with outward worship. Idolatry pollutes our own hearts, families, friends and churches. If we fail to take idolatry seriously, we are allowing people to poison the well from which others drink. That is why it is such a serious issue throughout Scripture.

2. The verdict is circulated • Acts 15:22–35

The council's letter to Gentile believers

22 Then the apostles and elders, with the whole church, decided to choose some of their own men and send them to Antioch with Paul and Barnabas. They chose Judas (called Barsabbas) and Silas, men who were leaders among the believers. **23** With them they sent the following letter:

The apostles and elders, your brothers,

To the Gentile believers in Antioch, Syria and Cilicia:

Greetings.

24 We have heard that some went out from us without our authorisation and disturbed you, troubling your minds by what they said. **25** So we all agreed to choose some men and send them to you with our dear friends Barnabas and Paul – **26** men who have risked their lives for the name of our Lord Jesus Christ. **27** Therefore we are sending Judas and Silas to confirm by word of mouth what we are writing. **28** It seemed good to the Holy Spirit and to us not to burden

---

[29] Wall, *Acts*, 222.

you with anything beyond the following requirements: 29 You are to abstain from food sacrificed to idols, from blood, from the meat of strangled animals and from sexual immorality. You will do well to avoid these things.

Farewell.

30 So the men were sent off and went down to Antioch, where they gathered the church together and delivered the letter. 31 The people read it and were glad for its encouraging message. 32 Judas and Silas, who themselves were prophets, said much to encourage and strengthen the believers. 33 After spending some time there, they were sent off by the believers with the blessing of peace to return to those who had sent them. [34] d 35 But Paul and Barnabas remained in Antioch, where they and many others taught and preached the word of the Lord.

_____

d 34 Some manuscripts include here *But Silas decided to remain there.*

The apostles and elders in Jerusalem decide to send some of their own men with Paul and Barnabas to deliver the letter to the church at Antioch. The letter is addressed to the wider region of 'Antioch, Syria and Cilicia' – a recognition of the potential for the issue to arise elsewhere. Judas and Silas are elected and are described as both leaders and prophets (verses 22, 32). The content of the letter summarises the narrative of the debate. Those demanding circumcision are not presenting the authorised version of apostolic teaching and have caused distress in their teaching (verse 24). Judas and Silas are sent to confirm by word of mouth the content of the letter (verse 27) – the letter is the authorised teaching of the apostles, and its bearers are the authorised spokespersons of the apostles. In verses 28–9, the same list of requirements is given as listed by James in verse 20.

The content of the letter and the ministry of Judas and Silas greatly encouraged the church, and Paul and Barnabas remained in Antioch, teaching and preaching the word. A situation that could have led to a destructive and disastrous split along ethnic lines was avoided by the wise leadership of the apostles and elders.

It is vital for church leaders to listen carefully to God's word and to consider the cultural needs of those they are appointed to care for if the unity and harmony of the church is to be preserved. This is a high and often difficult calling. Church members must regularly be in prayer for their leaders as they seek to navigate difficult issues and to preserve the purity and unity of the church.

3. Paul and Barnabas separate • Acts 15:36–41

Disagreement between Paul and Barnabas

36 Some time later Paul said to Barnabas, 'Let us go back and visit the believers in all the towns where we preached the word of the Lord and see how they are doing.' **37** Barnabas wanted to take John, also called Mark, with them, **38** but Paul did not think it wise to take him, because he had deserted them in Pamphylia and had not continued with them in the work. **39** They had such a sharp disagreement that they parted company. Barnabas took Mark and sailed for Cyprus, **40** but Paul chose Silas and left, commended by the believers to the grace of the Lord. **41** He went through Syria and Cilicia, strengthening the churches.

Following the Jerusalem consultation and prior to the second missionary journey, Luke records a short but intriguing episode regarding a disagreement between Paul and Barnabas over John Mark. Barnabas suggests that he and Paul revisit the churches they have previously established to 'see how they are doing' (verse 36). Barnabas wants to take his cousin, John Mark, with them.[30] However, Paul has reservations since John Mark left the first missionary journey in Pamphylia (Acts 13:13).

Luke does not give more detail on why John Mark left the first journey. Clifton Black suggests that it was not that he simply 'threw in the towel' but rather withdrew from the mission at the very point at which it was extending itself more and more towards the Gentiles.[31] John Mark may have struggled to come to terms with this development and wrestled with his own hesitancy. Luke records they 'had such a sharp disagreement that they parted company'. Barnabas takes Mark with him to Cyprus, while Paul takes Silas through Syria and Cilicia, strengthening the churches.

What are we to make of this incident? Why has Luke included it in his narrative since it seems to portray Paul and Barnabas in a less-than-flattering light? I think Wall overstates the case when he claims John Mark's defection 'carries the connotation of apostasy'.[32] Luke provides

---

[30] Colossians 4:10.

[31] C. Clifton Black, 'John Mark in the Acts of the Apostles', in *Literary Studies in Luke Acts: Essays in Honor of Joseph B. Tyson* (Macon: Mercer University Press, 1998), 116–17.

[32] Wall, *Acts*, 225. Bede also goes beyond Luke in his assessment: 'When he [John Mark] placed himself in the very front line of the fray, he had been too luke-warm about taking a stand. Therefore Paul rightly rejected him, lest the strength

no such verdict. I do not think this account provides an indictment on John Mark or on Paul and Barnabas. Luke presents the disagreement in a 'matter of fact' kind of way.

Further, the fact that the missionaries are 'commended by the believers to the grace of the Lord' suggests that there is no serious theological or moral failure in the dispute. Some commentators suggest that it is only Paul and Silas who receive the commendation. However, the Greek of verses 39–40 is one sentence and the participial phrase (*paradotheis tē chariti tou kyriou hypo tōn adelphōn* – 'handed over to the grace of the Lord by the brothers') would seem to include both pairings, not just the latter.

In part, I think Luke provides this episode to explain the disappearance of Barnabas from the ensuing narrative. In addition, it demonstrates the reality of missionary endeavour – agreement is not always possible on matters of personnel or strategy, yet this need not lead to permanent divisions. Luke is a realist, not an idealist, and he has no sense of embarrassment in including this episode.

Some issues are not obvious matters of right or wrong. Luke does not leave the impression that either man was in wilful or deliberate sin for their view. Barnabas, it seems, thought it would be good to take John Mark with them. Paul deemed it unwise given his recent defection. Their disagreement was strong enough to cause a temporary separation of the two men. There were now two missionary teams, not one. But the wider testimony of Scripture would suggest that their disagreement fell into the category of wise/unwise, rather than right/wrong. Later in the New Testament we see that the incident did not lead to continuing conflict between Paul and Barnabas or Paul and John Mark.[33]

Cyprus may have even proved to be a place of restoration in service for John Mark. He had apparently been of use there previously (Acts 13:4–12). Perhaps Barnabas thought it would be good for John Mark to return. We often speak negatively of operating within a 'comfort zone'. We are supposed to step out of such things in courageous faith. But perhaps for John Mark this was an avenue of service in which he could remain fruitful.[34] Perhaps our own gifts and temperaments lend us more readily to some ministry contexts and less so to others.

---

of others might be corrupted by the contagious influence, so to speak, of this man.' ACCS 5:193.

[33] See 1 Corinthians 9:6; Colossians 4:10; 2 Timothy 4:11; Philemon 24.

[34] I am indebted for this insight to Dr Alan Wilson, *The Crucible of Leadership* (Rickmansworth: Instant Apostle, 2022), 88–9.

It is hugely helpful to be aware of these distinctions. It can prevent disagreements over strategy decisions developing into full blown divisions within churches. There may be multiple ways to execute ministry plans. People will have differences of opinion on how best to strategise or who the best people might be for the job at hand. Sometimes those differences will mean a variety of approaches and solutions. It is all too easy to demonise those with whom we disagree or to allow division to fester.

Calvin reminds us, 'Be admonished by this example, that unless the servants of Christ take great heed, there be many chinks through which Satan will creep in, to disturb that concord which is among them.'[35] A few pages later he adds, 'We may learn to moderate our desire, even in the best causes, lest it pass measure, and be too fervent.'[36]

It is noteworthy that, despite the disagreement, the men did not divide the church. Both were commended by the church to the grace of the Lord. As Gooding notes:

Nor did Paul and Barnabas commit that grave offence against the name and cause of Christ that has become so widespread in recent centuries. They did not set up distinct groups of churches and label them 'Pauline Churches' and 'Barnabas Churches', each with its own separate headquarters, organization, and distinct set of loyalties, thus making sure that the whole world would take notice of the dispute . . . They simply set up Christian churches . . . and the body of Christ was not divided.[37]

Acts 15 demonstrates the importance of truth and unity. The gospel of free grace by faith alone must be preserved at all costs. And yet unity was of such importance that gospel liberty was not to be used to carelessly cause others to stumble. The sentiment of John Newton at the Eclectic Society in 1799 bears repeating: 'Paul was a reed in non-essentials – an iron pillar in essentials.'[38] May God gives us the wisdom and insight to be likewise.

---

[35] Calvin, *Acts 14–28*, 86.
[36] Calvin, *Acts 14–28*, 89.
[37] Gooding, *True to the Faith*, 283.
[38] Cited in Stott, *Acts*, 257.

15

More Surprising Openings

ACTS 16

Following the separation of Paul and Barnabas, Acts 15:4–18:22 charts Paul's second missionary journey. We see Paul and his companions travel further afield in the second journey. They travel to significant Gentile cultural centres such as Philippi, Thessalonica, Athens and Corinth. The cultures they encounter are still a mix of Jews and Gentiles, and the strategy is still to visit the synagogues first. However, the cities are more predominantly pagan, and Paul and his companions spend less time in synagogues and move more quickly toward Gentile audiences.[1]

Also of interest is that persecution in the second journey comes more from the Gentile opponents, whereas previously it has derived almost exclusively from Jewish opponents. There are a number of trial scenes in the second half of Acts, occurring at Philippi (16:22–4), Thessalonica (17:5–9), Athens (17:19–34), Corinth (18:12–17), Ephesus (19:23–41), then a long ongoing trial running from Jerusalem to Rome (Acts 21–8). We continue to see God overruling for good as persecution and gospel progress walk hand in hand through Luke's narrative.[2]

We also see that Paul spends different lengths of time in various places.[3] In Philippi it is a few days; in Thessalonica a few weeks; in Corinth it is eighteen months. Luke gives no explanation for this. He just describes the reality of Paul's missionary work. Different contexts provide different opportunities and challenges. There is a flexibility in Paul's approach as he takes the gospel to new situations.

---

[1] Wall, *Acts*, 230.

[2] Gooding, *True to the Faith*, 296, notes there is a sense of accusation followed by vindication in the trial scenes that run from Acts 16:16–19:16.

[3] Green, *The Word of His Grace*, 97–8.

1. A new companion and a new opportunity • Acts 16:1–10

Acts 16:1–5: Paul meets Timothy

Timothy joins Paul and Silas

16 Paul came to Derbe and then to Lystra, where a disciple named Timothy lived, whose mother was Jewish and a believer but whose father was a Greek. ²The believers at Lystra and Iconium spoke well of him. ³Paul wanted to take him along on the journey, so he circumcised him because of the Jews who lived in that area, for they all knew that his father was a Greek. ⁴As they travelled from town to town, they delivered the decisions reached by the apostles and elders in Jerusalem for the people to obey. ⁵So the churches were strengthened in the faith and grew daily in numbers.

Paul revisited the churches planted in Lystra and Derbe (Acts 14:8–21). There Paul had healed a lame man (14:8–10), been both idolised as a god and stoned as a heretic (14:12, 19) and won a large number of disciples to the faith (14:21). We can perhaps imagine Paul's trepidation and excitement as he set out to revisit these churches. They too must have been glad to see him. Here we see Paul's pastoral heart for the churches previously established.[4]

Luke tells us of one particular disciple from Lystra, named Timothy – his mother was Jewish, and his father was Greek. He was well spoken of by the other believers (verse 2). Paul already had one travelling companion in Silas but saw the opportunity to take along another in Timothy. Timothy would have a significant part to play within the canon of the New Testament, being a significant leader and co-worker of Paul. This may be the reason for Luke's interest in him at this stage. We may imagine that, at this point, Timothy was far from the finished article, but Paul's actions remind us of the need to train up workers for the harvest field where we have opportunity (see Matthew 9:38). Luke tells us that Paul had him circumcised 'because of the Jews who lived in that area, for they all knew that his father was a Greek' (verse 3).

Paul's decision to have Timothy circumcised is worth reflecting on. The consultation of Acts 15 had rejected the petition of the Christian Pharisees: 'The Gentiles must be circumcised and required to keep the law of Moses' (Acts 15:5). Peter rebutted the claim, noting that God had

---

⁴ Peterson, *Acts*, 449.

'purified their hearts by faith' and that it would be testing God to put 'on the necks of the Gentiles a yoke that neither we nor our ancestors have been able to bear'. His answer to the question was ultimately, 'No! We believe it is through the grace of our Lord Jesus that we are saved, just as they are' (15:9–11).

In Galatians 2:1–5, Paul tells us that Titus, even though he was a Greek, was not compelled to be circumcised. For the apostles, the suggestion that a Gentile had to be circumcised to be saved was contrary to the gospel of salvation by grace through faith, and was to be vehemently opposed.

So why did Paul have Timothy circumcised if he felt so strongly about the issue elsewhere? It appears there is a distinction in Paul's mind between circumcision as a means to salvation and circumcision as a strategic 'missionary accommodation' to minimise any stumbling block in their missional endeavours.[5] Paul was aware that at every new place they would enter synagogues with the aim of sharing the good news. If Timothy were uncircumcised, this may have been a cause of offence to Jewish people who were not yet believers. This would have provided a significant hurdle to overcome before they would be given a hearing for the gospel. It therefore made sense to remove this barrier and make it easier to speak to Jewish audiences about Jesus.[6]

It may be analogous to the observance of food laws discussed in Romans 14–15 and 1 Corinthians 10:23–30.[7] Insistence on such things as necessary for salvation must be resisted as salvation by works of the Law. Yet sensitivity to Jewish scruples was a necessary part of the mission. This in fact was the intent of the advice given by the leaders in Jerusalem in the letter of Acts 15. The Gentile believers should not be compelled to be circumcised for salvation, but they should exercise sensitivity with regard to pagan practices given the presence of Jews in every city (15:21).

Such sensitivity is still important today in different contexts. A western missionary in the Middle East would be wise to cover her head so as not to cause unnecessary offence to those among whom she lives and works. She is not denying the gospel by doing so or expressing her commitment to another religion. She is simply being wise in her attempt to 'make

---

[5] Witherington suggests, 'There is no evidence that Paul objected to Jewish Christians practicing their ancestral religion so long as it was understood that doing so was not *necessary* for salvation.' *Acts*, 474 (italics original). Schnabel describes this event as an example of 'missionary accommodation'. *Acts*, 671.

[6] Eric D. Barreto, *Ethnic Negotiations: The Function of Race and Ethnicity in Acts 16* (Tübingen: Mohr Siebeck, 2010), 116.

[7] Bock, *Acts*, 523.

the most of every opportunity' (Colossians 4:5). This principle of contextualisation has wide-ranging applications as churches think about how they meaningfully engage with the communities they are trying to reach.

The only offence should be the gospel itself. Any other potential for offence ought to be carefully considered and reflected upon. Is it a gospel necessity or a cultural tradition? Are there other ways to do things that might connect well with those who do not yet know Christ? It may be as simple as our style of dress at our Sunday gatherings. It may be the food or drink we serve at an event. It could be the language or images used on our website. For Paul, it seems, if the gospel is not being compromised, he is prepared to go to significant lengths to break down barriers to the good news. I'm not sure Timothy would have been so delighted!

The result of Paul's work is given in verses 4–5. They travelled from town to town, delivering the decisions reached by the apostles and, as they did so, the churches were both 'strengthened' and 'grew daily in numbers'. The ministry of Paul, Silas and Timothy was both edifying and evangelistic. This is yet another useful reminder not to separate these two things. The strengthening leads to outreach and the outreach leads to further strengthening.

Acts 16:6–10: Paul's vision

Paul's vision of the man of Macedonia

6 Paul and his companions travelled throughout the region of Phrygia and Galatia, having been kept by the Holy Spirit from preaching the word in the province of Asia. 7 When they came to the border of Mysia, they tried to enter Bithynia, but the Spirit of Jesus would not allow them to. 8 So they passed by Mysia and went down to Troas. 9 During the night Paul had a vision of a man of Macedonia standing and begging him, 'Come over to Macedonia and help us.' 10 After Paul had seen the vision, we got ready at once to leave for Macedonia, concluding that God had called us to preach the gospel to them.

In verse 6 we see Paul and his companions travelling throughout Phrygia and Galatia, 'having been kept by the Holy Spirit from preaching the word in the province of Asia'. In verse 7 we are told that the 'Spirit of Jesus' would not allow them to enter Bithynia. These intriguing statements are not elaborated on by Luke. How exactly the Spirit had prevented Paul and his companions from going to Asia we are not told. This is one of those places in Scripture where we would love to know more but must be content as interpreters with the silence.

Consequently, they travelled to Troas where, during the night, Paul had a vision of a man from Macedonia who begged him, 'Come over to Macedonia and help us' (verse 9). Paul and his companions got ready to leave at once for Macedonia, concluding, 'God had called us to preach the gospel to them.'[8]

Dreams and visions are one aspect of prophetic ministry and serve to direct key characters forward under divine direction in the mission.[9] Paul is acting in fulfilment of Acts 2:17: 'your young men will see visions, your old men will dream dreams'. Luke is also reminding his readers of the author and director of the mission. It is not simply human effort and agency, but the risen Jesus, by his Spirit, present at every turn to advance his kingdom.

Divine guidance is a complex subject. While God may reveal himself in dreams and visions, it is not always easy to discern the divine from the human. As Christians who live in the post-apostolic era, we have their writings which are our primary and authoritative form of guidance. We also have the community of faith to help us discern the Spirit's leading. We should avoid the two extremes of either dismissing all dreams and visions as merely subjective human desire or the embrace of every vision as from the Lord without careful discernment. Whenever we feel led or prompted by God's Spirit, we should always seek to confirm such leadings by Scripture and the wisdom of fellow believers.

2. The birth of a remarkable church • Acts 16:11–40

The remainder of Acts 16 records three encounters with three very different people – a businesswoman, a slave girl and a jailer. Each is reached in their different circumstances by different means. It is a striking picture of the power and grace of God at work in different and sometimes surprising ways.

---

[8] Acts 16:11 gives us the first of the 'we' passages, suggesting that from this point on Luke himself is one of Paul's companions, at least for some of his travels. We should also note here that the temptation to see this moment as the gospel going to Europe is anachronistic. These new regions were all considered part of the Roman Empire in the first century. Witherington, *Acts*, 485–6.

[9] Salter, *Power of Pentecost*, 49–52.

Acts 16:11–15: Lydia

Lydia's conversion in Philippi

11 From Troas we put out to sea and sailed straight for Samothrace, and the next day we went on to Neapolis. **12** From there we travelled to Philippi, a Roman colony and the leading city of that district^a of Macedonia. And we stayed there several days.

13 On the Sabbath we went outside the city gate to the river, where we expected to find a place of prayer. We sat down and began to speak to the women who had gathered there. **14** One of those listening was a woman from the city of Thyatira named Lydia, a dealer in purple cloth. She was a worshipper of God. The Lord opened her heart to respond to Paul's message. **15** When she and the members of her household were baptised, she invited us to her home. 'If you consider me a believer in the Lord,' she said, 'come and stay at my house.' And she persuaded us.

_____

a 12 The text and meaning of the Greek for _the leading city of that district_ are uncertain.

As Paul and his companions travelled on, they came to the leading city of Macedonia, Philippi.[10] As was his custom, Paul, on the Sabbath, sought out the place where Jewish worshippers assembled. In this case they went outside the city gates, toward the river, where they thought they may find a place of prayer.[11]

Luke reports a gathering of women in that place whom Paul engaged in conversation. One of those listening was a lady called Lydia. She was from the city of Thyatira and a dealer in purple cloth. She was, it seems, a successful businesswoman.[12] However, Beverly Gaventa describes her as in some sense on the margins. She is 'a female, perhaps a freedwoman (i.e., former slave), apparently operating without a male protector, and

_____

[10] Peterson, _Acts_, 458–9, suggests the date for this trip was in the period AD 50–52. The sea voyage from Troas to Neapolis was around 156 miles (a journey of a few days), with Philippi being a further ten miles inland. Philippi was a large and prosperous Roman colony.

[11] The Greek describes it as a _proseuchēn_, which may indicate a meeting or assembly for prayer, rather than a particular place or building. It appears there was no formal synagogue in the city, perhaps because it lacked the ten Jewish men necessary to form a synagogue. Wall, _Acts_, 231. The fact it was outside the city gates perhaps suggests that Judaism was considered a foreign cult and therefore not allowed within the city gates. Witherington, _Acts_, 490.

[12] Purple cloth was generally destined for the wealthy nobility. This suggests Lydia herself moved in such circles and would have been a woman of some means and prominence. Wall, _Acts_, 232.

her story begins outside the margins of the city'.[13] She is the first of the three characters in Philippi, all quite different, yet all reached by the power of the gospel.

As Paul spoke, 'the Lord opened her heart to respond' to his message (verse 14). She and the members of her household were baptised, and Paul and his companions stayed with her.[14] Lydia's generous welcome would play an important part in the life of this church in its infancy (16:40). It reminds us of the importance of hospitality as a means of care and encouragement.[15] In many cultures, relationships are really forged through the fellowship that hospitality and shared meals offer. As Christians, our homes ought to be places where the bonds of fellowship are regularly deepened, and not private castles, seldom open to public viewing!

Lydia is described as a 'worshipper of God' (*sebomenē ton theon*). She is a person who exhibits a sensitivity to and reverence for the things of God but is not yet converted to the gospel of Jesus Christ. Paul shows us the importance of gospel proclamation, though whether his address takes the form of monologue or dialogue here is unclear. It is through his explanation of the gospel that the Lord works to open Lydia's heart to understand the truth of the gospel. The conversion of Lydia reminds us that while deeds of power and compassion play a significant role through Acts, it is ultimately the proclamation of the gospel that is necessary to bring people to a saving knowledge of Christ. This emphasis on a message that needs to be proclaimed should never be lost as the most urgent action of the church this side of Christ's return.

Acts 16:16–23: The slave girl

Paul and Silas in prison

16 Once when we were going to the place of prayer, we were met by a female slave who had a spirit by which she predicted the future. She earned a great deal of money for her owners

---

[13] Beverly Roberts Gaventa, *Acts* (Nashville: Abingdon, 2003), 237.

[14] Peterson, *Acts*, 461, notes that this text 'does not prove the possibility of infant baptism, but it would be remarkable if no babies were included in any of the four household baptisms mentioned by Luke'. Those four household baptisms can be seen in Acts 10:44–8; 16:15, 31–3; 18:7–8. However, we must also note the mention of reception of the Spirit and/or faith in these accounts (10:44; 16:31–2; 18:8). It seems that throughout Acts, baptism is connected to repentance, faith and reception of the Spirit.

[15] Peterson, *Acts*, 426. See also Romans 12:13; 1 Timothy 3:2; Hebrews 13:2; 1 Peter 4:9.

by fortune-telling. [17] She followed Paul and the rest of us, shouting, 'These men are servants of the Most High God, who are telling you the way to be saved.' [18] She kept this up for many days. Finally Paul became so annoyed that he turned round and said to the spirit, 'In the name of Jesus Christ I command you to come out of her!' At that moment the spirit left her.

[19] When her owners realised that their hope of making money was gone, they seized Paul and Silas and dragged them into the market-place to face the authorities. [20] They brought them before the magistrates and said, 'These men are Jews, and are throwing our city into an uproar [21] by advocating customs unlawful for us Romans to accept or practise.'

[22] The crowd joined in the attack against Paul and Silas, and the magistrates ordered them to be stripped and beaten with rods. [23] After they had been severely flogged, they were thrown into prison, and the jailer was commanded to guard them carefully.

In the next scene, Luke records an episode that occurred when they were on their way to the place of prayer mentioned in verse 13. They were met by a female slave who had a spirit that enabled her to predict the future. Luke tells us she made a great deal of money for her owners. We also see encounters with the demonic or magic in Acts 8, 13 and 19. In those instances, too, there are connections to material wealth or status. Luke sees a link between these dark forces and greed.[16] This is a reminder to exercise discernment where we see people amassing huge wealth or influence through their own religious services or ministry.[17] We also see in each case the power of the gospel to conquer such forces. There are a few things here worth noting which readers of English translations may miss.

First, the reference to the 'spirit' uses the same Greek word as is used for the 'Holy Spirit' (*pneuma*) but instead of the adjective 'holy' it is joined to the word *pythōna* ('python'). This is a demonic spirit that has taken possession of the girl.[18] In some ways the 'spirit' has a greater mastery

---

[16] Witherington, *Acts*, 494.

[17] 'The making of money out of religion has been a scandal all down the centuries . . . Nor has Christendom escaped: the exposure of the corruption of certain TV evangelists provides but one more example.' Gooding, *True to the Faith*, 307.

[18] 'It was believed that Apollo was embodied at Delphi in a snake, the Python.' Witherington, *Acts*, 493. The girl is seen, then, as being inspired by Apollo, the Pythian deity. Though this is the belief of those in Philippi, readers of Scripture know the true identity of this evil demonic snake spirit.

over her than her owners. It is a sobering reminder of the presence and power of the demonic in our world.

We need to remember that our battle is 'not against flesh and blood, but against the rulers, against the authorities, against the powers of this dark world and against the spiritual forces of evil in the heavenly realms' (Ephesians 6:12). Sometimes Christians can become overly concerned with the demonic, seeking to diagnose every disorder in these terms. Other Christians are 'functional unbelievers' as far as the 'spiritual forces of evil' are concerned. While we see Jesus and his apostles engage in exorcisms, we should remind ourselves of Paul's remedy – 'put on the full armour of God' (Ephesians 6:11) – which in essence is to clothe ourselves with all that Christ has done for us in the gospel. This is our greatest protection against the devil's schemes.

Second, Luke describes the girl's owners as her *kyriois* ('lords'), using the same word that is applied to Jesus Christ as 'Lord'. What we are about to see is a battle of 'spirits' and 'lords' as we witness where the true authority and power lies.

Third, though the girl is possessed by a demonic spirit, she cannot help but speak the truth. As in the Gospels, it is the demons who see most clearly the identity of Jesus.[19] As the girl follows the men around over the course of several days, she keeps declaring, 'These men are servants of the Most High God, who are telling you the way to be saved' (verse 17). She describes Paul and his companions as servants (*douloi*), a word that can also means slaves. So we have in this episode slaves, lords and spirits apparently competing for the attention of the crowds.

In the end it turns out to be a no-contest. The power of the lords and the spirit associated with the girl are nothing in comparison to the power of the true Lord and the true Spirit. In verse 18, after many days, 'Paul became so annoyed that he turned round and said to the spirit, "In the name of Jesus Christ I command you to come out of her!" At that moment the spirit left her.' With nothing more than a word of command, the spirit must instantly obey the authority of the Lord Jesus and depart.

There are two follow-up questions to this incident. First, why is Paul so 'annoyed'? Second, what becomes of the girl?

First, the description of Paul as 'annoyed' (*diaponētheis*) has perplexed many commentators. It does not seem a particularly good or godly

---

[19] Her words were likely misunderstood by the crowds, given their worship of multiple 'gods'. Yet the evil spirit spoke the truth, even if the crowds did not fully understand.

response to exorcise a demon simply because it's getting on one's nerves. Does Paul just lose his temper or is there perhaps something deeper going on? The word translated 'annoyed' is unusual, only appearing in the New Testament here and in Acts 4:2 with reference to the Jewish authorities being 'disturbed' that the apostles were teaching the people about the resurrection. The sense in Acts 4:2 is more than just irritation; the Jewish leaders are deeply disturbed by the message.

Witherington suggests that Paul is disturbed because her message is misleading, confusing people as to the true identity of the gods.[20] Peterson suggests that Paul's concern is that people might associate the spirit by which she speaks with the Spirit by which they speak.[21] A third possibility is that Luke is describing a sense of deep distress at the evil abuse of this girl by the spirit and her owners. To see the demonic distortion of this girl would have provoked 'revulsion and anger at the malevolent work of the evil spirit'.[22] But, then, why has he not acted sooner? Perhaps he knew the consequences would involve imprisonment or worse and so was reluctant. Maybe it was over the course of those days that his indignation grew. Whatever the motive, Paul's actions are not those of a man who has simply lost his cool, but rather the actions of righteous indignation against evil and its effects – and a willingness to face the consequences of his action.

Second, what becomes of the girl? It seems clear her owners realise there is no money to be made from her any more. Do they release her or retain her for other (worse?!) services? Is this moment a conversion for her and is she perhaps taken in and cared for by someone like Lydia? Stott suggests that placing this narrative between the conversion of Lydia and the jailer implies that she too is saved, not just healed.[23]

Stott's conclusion seems reasonable, though it is always wise to exercise caution when speculating beyond the information Luke provides. Yet the narrative invites us as readers to reflect on our own response. The evil of modern slavery is all around us. People are still trafficked and abused in various heinous ways. Christian churches should reflect on how we would respond if we were to encounter such a girl. If she were released from her slavery, where would she go and who would care? Sometimes the narrative provides more questions than answers, but these are important nonetheless for readers to reflect upon.

---

[20] Witherington, *Acts*, 495.

[21] Peterson, *Acts*, 464–5.

[22] Gooding, *True to the Faith*, 321.

[23] Stott, *Acts*, 265.

Her owners seize Paul and Silas and drag them before the authorities in the marketplace. It is striking that these men, blinded by their greed, have completely missed the significance of the miracle.[24] Previously, Paul has been accused of betraying Jewish customs; now he is accused of betraying Roman customs. Of course, Paul and Silas were not asking the slave owners to 'accept or practise' any such 'unlawful' customs. The motive of the owners is not justice but revenge. As the crowd join in, the magistrates bow to the pressure and have Paul and Silas stripped and beaten with rods and then thrown into prison (verses 22–3). Such punishment would not normally be delivered to Roman citizens, being reserved for trouble-making outsiders.[25] What the authorities do not realise is that their attempts to restore order will cause them more trouble.

Acts 16:24–40: The jailer

24 When he received these orders, he put them in the inner cell and fastened their feet in the stocks.

25 About midnight Paul and Silas were praying and singing hymns to God, and the other prisoners were listening to them. 26 Suddenly there was such a violent earthquake that the foundations of the prison were shaken. At once all the prison doors flew open, and everyone's chains came loose. 27 The jailer woke up, and when he saw the prison doors open, he drew his sword and was about to kill himself because he thought the prisoners had escaped. 28 But Paul shouted, 'Don't harm yourself! We are all here!'

29 The jailer called for lights, rushed in and fell trembling before Paul and Silas. 30 He then brought them out and asked, 'Sirs, what must I do to be saved?'

31 They replied, 'Believe in the Lord Jesus, and you will be saved – you and your household.' 32 Then they spoke the word of the Lord to him and to all the others in his house. 33 At that hour of the night the jailer took them and washed their wounds; then immediately he and all his household were baptised. 34 The jailer brought them into his house and set a meal before them; he was filled with joy because he had come to believe in God – he and his whole household.

35 When it was daylight, the magistrates sent their officers to the jailer with the order: 'Release those men.' 36 The jailer told Paul, 'The magistrates have ordered that you and Silas be released. Now you can leave. Go in peace.'

37 But Paul said to the officers: 'They beat us publicly without a trial, even

---

24 Bock, *Acts*, 538.
25 Peterson, *Acts*, 467.

though we are Roman citizens, and threw us into prison. And now do they want to get rid of us quietly? No! Let them come themselves and escort us out.'

38 The officers reported this to the magistrates, and when they heard that Paul and Silas were Roman citizens, they were alarmed. **39** They came to appease them and escorted them from the prison, requesting them to leave the city. **40** After Paul and Silas came out of the prison, they went to Lydia's house, where they met with the brothers and sisters and encouraged them. Then they left.

The jailer, having been commanded to guard the prisoners carefully, put Paul and Silas in the inner cell and fastened their feet in stocks. It would seem the local authorities had a fear that men who had these supernatural powers might be able to escape without careful guard.

Remarkably, we find Paul and Silas praying and singing hymns to God at midnight, while the other prisoners listened. They would be in great discomfort from their beating, the stocks and sitting on the hard floor, unable to move or sleep in their pain. Yet somehow their spirits are unbroken as they praise God from a prison cell. Erasmus captures the beauty and power of the moment well:

> You see that any time and any place is suitable for evangelical devotion. That prison, so terribly foul, was a temple for the apostles; the dead of night did not stand in the way of their hymns. The gospel is preached in the prison and trophies are taken for Christ; the jail is the magisterial chair of the gospel. [26]

Suddenly a violent earthquake shook the foundations of the prison, causing all the doors to open and all the chains to come loose. The jailer, realising his fate if the prisoners were to escape, was about to take matters into his own hands when Paul shouted, 'Don't harm yourself! We are all here!' (verse 28).

The jailer, having called for lights, came trembling before Paul and Silas and fell at their feet, asking 'Sirs, what must I do to be saved?' (verse 30). The jailer must have seen and heard the praying and singing of Paul and Silas and concluded that the earthquake was an act of God to save his servants. His question was not, 'How can I get myself out of this predicament?' but, 'What must I do to escape the judgement of the God you serve?'[27]

---

[26] Erasmus, *RCS* 6:235.
[27] Bock, *Acts*, 541.

Paul and Silas, understanding the intent of his question, replied, 'Believe in the Lord Jesus, and you will be saved – you and your household.' And they spoke the word to him and to all in his household. The gospel has a beauty and power in its simplicity. It requires nothing more than faith in Jesus, and anyone from any background, with little understanding or experience can find salvation by believing in his name. Sometimes churches require people to clear some high hurdles before they can be accepted for baptism or into membership. There is an understandable desire to protect the purity of the church. Yet we need to be careful that our desire for a credible profession of faith does not in fact set a higher bar than Scripture itself presents.

The jailer cleaned their wounds, then, having washed them, he allowed himself and his household to be washed in baptism. This double washing is a stunning picture of a love for God and love for neighbour. Chrysostom also notes the double 'loosening'. Just as God had loosed the chains and thrown open the doors of the prison, so he had loosed the chains, thrown open the doors and kindled the light in the heart of this jailer.[28] They shared a meal together and rejoiced in their newfound salvation (verses 33–4).[29] Tannehill observes that this was the conversion of not just another Gentile, but also a representative of the Roman system that was seeking to silence them.[30] It is a significant moment in the clash of 'lords' and kingdoms.

The next morning, the magistrate sent word to release the prisoners. However, Paul and Silas knew their rights as Roman citizens and demanded a public escort. They had been mistreated and wanted vindication. Why did Paul and Silas not mention earlier their Roman citizenship? Was it a lack of opportunity or a deliberate strategy? As we will see later in Acts, Paul was not afraid to appeal to the laws of the state where they would offer protection from unjust mistreatment. Paul was showing a concern for 'the fate of the mission before Roman magistrates'.[31] He was seeking to protect the new Christians from further unjust punishment. Christians should know and, where necessary, appeal to their legal rights in seeking to protect themselves and others from unjust treatment. While justice may not always prevail, it should still be sought.

---

[28] Chrysostom, ACCS 5:208.

[29] Spencer notes Paul's words in Philippians 1:12–14 – how his chains had served to advance the gospel – something his Philippian audience would have known very well. *Acts*, 168. See 2 Timothy 2:9.

[30] Tannehill, *Narrative Unity*, 204.

[31] Tannehill, *Narrative Unity*, 201.

Having been released, they visited Lydia's house, where the church met. They encouraged the brothers and sisters and then departed. In Acts we meet a number of locally placed converts who become key figures in the nurture and establishment of new churches via their hospitality.[32] Luke is keen to highlight the contribution that simple hospitality makes to the mission. It is easy to focus on the courage, rhetoric or miracles of figures like Paul and to miss those 'minor' characters and their gifts, which are every bit as important in the growth of the kingdom.[33]

This new church comprised a diverse group of believers. There was Lydia the Jewish businesswoman, perhaps the slave girl was part of them, and a Gentile jailer.

In the ancient world, negative attitudes towards women or those deemed of lesser status were common. Niang cites both Greek and Jewish examples of this.[34] The *Tosefta,* an early compilation of Jewish oral law, calls Jewish men to recite daily a prayer giving thanks for three things: 'Lord, I thank you that I am not a slave, a woman, or a Gentile.'[35] And yet these are the very people the grace and power of Jesus reaches in Acts 16. Tensions between believers from different groups have always dogged the church. Acts 16 gives us an example of a church made up of people from different backgrounds, classes, genders and ethnicities. This is the power of the gospel, to bring together people who, in the world's eyes, have little in common.

In the field of missiology, there is a principle called the homogeneous unit principle (HUP). It is the idea that it is strategically desirable to plant churches that aim to reach a particular people group – people from broadly similar backgrounds, whether that's based on age, class or ethnicity. It is argued that such churches will more easily attract like-minded people and so strategically it is an effective missional approach. Descriptively, it is hard to deny it happens in practice, on the ground. The real question is whether it ought to be a strategy to pursue. Descriptively speaking, the natural tendency towards homogeneity seems to be more an outworking of the fall than the redeeming power of the gospel. We should note that the churches we see in Acts are not homogeneous units. In their diversity they are expressions of the power of the gospel to reconcile on both

---

[32] See also Jason (17:5–9); Aquila and Priscilla (18:2–3); Titius Justus (18:7); Philip (21:8); Mnason (21:16).

[33] Tannehill, *Narrative Unity,* 197.

[34] Aliou Cissé Niang, *Faith and Freedom in Galatia and Senegal* (Leiden: Brill, 2009), 105–6.

[35] Tosefta, *Barakhot* 6.18.

the vertical and the horizontal level. They glorify God in the display of their diversity. The practice of HUP may have a place in some outreach, but if used in the establishment of churches it can undermine the glory and power of the gospel.[36]

Stott notes, 'It would be hard to imagine a more disparate group than the businesswoman, the slave girl and the gaoler.'[37] Acts 16 shows us God using diverse means to bring together diverse people as a manifestation of his glory and power in the church. The 'Gospel is seen to triumph in the midst of the Jewish meeting place (16.14–15), and in the midst of the Roman stronghold (in the city, cf. 16.18–19, and in their prison cf. 16.25–26). It is seen to triumph over natural and supernatural powers, whether it be magistrates and their jails, or demons.'[38] Jesus's mission unstoppable continues to advance, breaking down every barrier in its progress towards the ends of the earth.

---

[36] See Ephesians 2:11–22.
[37] Stott, *Acts*, 268.
[38] Witherington, *Women in the Earliest Churches*, 148.

16

New Contexts and Mixed Responses

ACTS 17

In Acts 17, Luke narrates the continuation of Paul's second missionary journey through the cities of Thessalonica, Berea and Athens. Paul's speech in Athens is one of the best known in Acts for its contextualisation of the gospel message for a pagan audience. Fitzmyer describes this as 'the most important episode' in Paul's second journey.[1] We continue to see opposition and growth walk hand in hand as the gospel reaches new places.

Bock notes in this section some ongoing tensions. Twice Paul faces accusations from Jews and twice from Gentiles.[2] Twice the accusations are upheld and twice dismissed.[3] 'The world's jury is still out on the new faith.'[4]

1. Thessalonica • Acts 17:1–9

In Thessalonica

17 When Paul and his companions had passed through Amphipolis and Apollonia, they came to Thessalonica, where there was a Jewish synagogue. **2** As was his custom, Paul went into the synagogue, and on three Sabbath days he reasoned with them from the Scriptures, **3** explaining and proving that the Messiah had to suffer and rise from the dead. 'This Jesus I am proclaiming to you is the Messiah,' he said. **4** Some of the Jews were persuaded and joined Paul and Silas, as did a large number of God-fearing Greeks and quite a few prominent women.

5 But other Jews were jealous; so they rounded up some bad characters from the market-place, formed a mob and started a riot in the city. They rushed to Jason's house in search of Paul and

---

[1] Fitzmyer, *Acts*, 600. Wall notes, 'The scholarly literature on this passage is voluminous and comes from biblical scholars and theologians ancient and modern – probably more than on any other passage in Acts.' Wall, *Acts*, 243, note 568.

[2] See 16:19–21; 17:5–7; 18:12–13; 19:24–7. Arguably there is a sort of trial scene happening at the Areopagus also.

[3] See 16:22–4; 17:8–9; 18:14–17; 19:35–40.

[4] Bock, *Acts*, 549.

Silas in order to bring them out to the crowd.[a] 6 But when they did not find them, they dragged Jason and some other believers before the city officials, shouting: 'These men who have caused trouble all over the world have now come here, 7 and Jason has welcomed them into his house. They are all defying Caesar's decrees, saying that there is another king, one called Jesus.' 8 When they heard this, the crowd and the city officials were thrown into turmoil. 9 Then they put Jason and the others on bail and let them go.

_____

[a] 5 Or *the assembly of the people*

After Paul and his travelling companions had left Philippi, Luke informs us they travelled through Amphipolis and Apollonia, arriving eventually at Thessalonica.[5] Witherington notes Thessalonica was the capital of the region of Macedonia, an important city that minted its own coins and had its own local government. It still had ties with Rome, and there is evidence of the imperial cult that worshipped Caesar as the universal saviour.[6]

As was Paul's custom, he first visited the synagogue and 'reasoned with them from the Scriptures' on three consecutive Sabbaths (verse 2). Here again Paul was seeking to take the gospel first to the Jew, then to the Gentile (see Romans 1:16). As a Jewish man he knew the synagogue was a strategic place for him to visit. His familiarity with the Scriptures as well as Jewish custom provided a good point of contact from which to engage his hearers.

We also see Paul 'reasoning' with his fellow Jews. Acts 17 shows us the value of apologetic study and debate. In verse 4 we see that some of the Jews were persuaded by Paul's arguments and joined Paul and Silas, along with some God-fearing Greeks and prominent women. Occasionally, the value of apologetics comes under question. Those unsure of its place argue that since the unbeliever is elsewhere described in the New Testament as spiritually dead, blind, enslaved and ignorant, there is little point in attempting to engage the intellect.[7] Instead, what is needed is the simple proclamation of the gospel. This is the means by which God opens the eyes of the unbelievers (2 Corinthians 4:4–6).

However, this is to play one set of Scriptures off against another. We

_____

[5] This was a significant journey. Amphipolis was thirty-three miles south-west of Philippi; Apollonia a further twenty-seven miles, with Thessalonica another thirty-five miles. Peterson suggests that Amphipolis and Apollonia were overnight stopping points on a three-day journey. Peterson, *Acts*, 477.

[6] Witherington, *Acts*, 503.

[7] For example, Ephesians 2:1–3; 2 Corinthians 4:4–6; John 8:34; 1 Corinthians 2:14.

see clearly within Acts the value and efficacy of persuasive reasoning.[8] God uses this in the mystery of his saving purposes to draw people to himself. Therefore, we too should give ourselves to growing in our understanding of good and reasonable arguments for the faith, always being prepared to give an answer, all the while recognising that some will be more gifted in this area than others. Paul knew the people he was most likely to reach and thought about how best to reach them. We, too, should think strategically about our own personal outreach and that of our churches.

The content of Paul's reasoning is given in verse 3: 'explaining and proving that the Messiah had to suffer and rise from the dead. "This Jesus I am proclaiming to you is the Messiah."' We can imagine some of the texts Paul may have appealed to in his attempts to prove that the Messiah had to suffer and rise from the dead.[9] The Messiah was God's anointed king and ruler destined to bring redemption and restoration to God's people. The figure for which the Jewish nation hoped had already come, claimed Paul. Wall notes from this, 'Few passages in Acts so clearly express the importance of Scripture in Christian preaching . . . on successive sabbaths Paul argued and explained and proved the core claims of his gospel from the Scriptures.'[10] We live in a day when preaching is often little more than the sharing of the preacher's own ideas, picking up (and often misusing) the odd proof text here or there. Paul demonstrates the importance of our preaching being rooted in the testimony of Scripture, opening up its meaning and significance to our hearers. It is the living word of God people need to hear, not our own ideas drawn from the latest secular literature on happiness, wealth, success or wellbeing.

As Paul presents his arguments, we see two responses. First, we see a number of people who are persuaded and join Paul and Silas. This includes prominent figures in the community, a fact that may have prompted the response we see in verse 5. We also see other Jews who are described as being 'jealous'. The Greek word translated as jealous (*zēlōsantes*) can also mean zealous. It is hard to know exactly what Luke intends, but it is perhaps a combination of jealousy over Paul's apparent success and a zeal for their own traditions which seemed to them to be under threat. Whatever their motive, the means are clearly not in accordance with Israel's Scriptures. They rounded up some 'bad characters', formed a mob

---

[8] For example, Acts 14:1; 17:2, 4, 17; 18:4, 19; 28:23.

[9] Stott suggests it may have been Scriptures already cited in the speeches of Acts – Psalms 2; 16; 110; 118; Isaiah 52–3. *Acts*, 271.

[10] Wall, *Acts*, 240.

and started a riot in the city. This is not the last riot we shall see in the book of Acts, but it is a sign of the impact and unrest caused by this new message. It is a threat to the traditions and institutions dearly held and is therefore met with forceful opposition. Where the gospel is truly preached, we should not be surprised to see serious opposition. A gospel modified to line up with many of the culture's own values will provide no threat and elicit little in the way of serious opposition. It's a stark warning to the church today. It will take courage to stand firm for the truth, knowing the severity of the persecution it may bring.

The mob rushed to Jason's house in search of Paul and Silas, who were not there. Jason and some other believers were dragged before the city officials. The claim was that the men who had caused trouble 'all over the world' had come to Thessalonica (verse 6).[11] It was quite a claim. Luke does not miss the irony that those who had started a riot were now accusing Paul and his companions of being troublemakers.[12] To be sure, the gospel had made significant inroads, and news had clearly spread, yet it was an overstatement to say it had yet reached all the world. The opponents of Paul had used violence, now they were trying deceit. Their accusation was that Paul and his companions were defying the decrees of Caesar by claiming there was another King called Jesus. Their claim was, in a sense, correct. They perhaps spoke more truth than they realised or intended. There was another King called Jesus, who did in fact have authority even over Caesar. Yet Jesus had never called people to defy Caesar – quite the opposite (Mark 12:17). And the Jews did not care much for Caesar anyhow. The attack was simply an attempt to manipulate the officials into silencing Paul and his friends. Again, we should not be surprised when opponents use worldly means in their opposition to the truth.

It is interesting to note that the city officials did not seem to know quite how to respond. They are described as being in turmoil and so Jason and the others were put on bail and released. This is a pattern we shall see occur again. The city officials do not want the trouble associated with uprising and riots – it is in their interest to keep the peace.

---

[11] Stott suggests that the verb translated as 'caused trouble' (*anastatōsantes*) has revolutionary overtones, and thus the charge is a serious one. *Acts*, 273.

[12] Peterson, *Acts*, 480.

2. Berea • Acts 17:10–15

In Berea

10 As soon as it was night, the believers sent Paul and Silas away to Berea. On arriving there, they went to the Jewish synagogue. **11** Now the Berean Jews were of more noble character than those in Thessalonica, for they received the message with great eagerness and examined the Scriptures every day to see if what Paul said was true. **12** As a result, many of them believed, as did also a number of prominent Greek women and many Greek men.

13 But when the Jews in Thessalonica learned that Paul was preaching the word of God at Berea, some of them went there too, agitating the crowds and stirring them up. **14** The believers immediately sent Paul to the coast, but Silas and Timothy stayed at Berea. **15** Those who escorted Paul brought him to Athens and then left with instructions for Silas and Timothy to join him as soon as possible.

Under the cover of nightfall, the believers sent Paul and Silas away to Berea, a city fifty miles south-west of Thessalonica.[13] We see in Acts both the courage to face persecution and the wisdom to avoid it where possible. Paul does not charge headlong into hostility with the authorities as if that were a badge of being a serious and faithful Christian. When opposition comes, Paul is prepared to face the consequences, but he is also smart enough to realise when it is more strategic to move on to a new place.

As before, Paul begins at the synagogue. Luke describes the Bereans as being 'of more noble character' than the Thessalonians. The reason is because 'they received the message with eagerness and examined the Scriptures every day to see if what Paul said was true' (verse 11). As in Thessalonica, the new believers are made up of Jews, Greeks and prominent women. The difference is that in Thessalonica 'some' were persuaded, while in Berea Luke tells us 'many' believed.

I had the privilege of serving for a number of years in the youth work of a summer conference. Young leaders received training as part of the programme, and they were called 'Bereans'. We wanted them to be people wh searched the Scriptures carefully to make sure that what was being taught was from the Bible, not just the preacher's own ideas. Jesus told his followers to love the Lord with heart, soul, mind and strength (Mark 12:30–31). There is a responsibility for us to grow in our understanding

---

[13] Witherington, *Acts*, 509.

of the Bible's teaching. This is not just the responsibility of the teachers at the front. Each and every individual has this responsibility to dig into the Bible and familiarise themselves with its teaching, so they can see that the things they are being taught are in accord with what the Bible teaches. This is a critical aspect of the growth and maturity of believers and the church. Those of us in leadership should be thinking about how we train others to have this Berean-like quality – eagerly engaging with Scripture in their own growth and development. Stephen Denison, the seventeenth-century English church leader, puts it memorably:

> We ought to be as wary about what we receive into our ears as about what we receive into our mouths; and indeed it is the sin of many, that when they are careful and thoughtful concerning the diet of their bodies and will have a care to eat no food but that which is wholesome and good, in the meantime are careless of the diet of their souls, feeding grossly on the very carrion of human inventions.[14]

Or Johann Spangenberg, a German theologian writing in the sixteenth century:

> If a carpenter or mason is to build something ably, then he must have a plumbline. If a goldsmith is to test gold, then he must have a touchstone. So then, if we Christians are to judge what is God's Word or human teaching, then we too must have a touchstone, and this is holy Scripture.[15]

The Jews from Thessalonica, upon hearing that Paul and Silas had moved to Berea, sent some of their own there to stir up more trouble. This is quite remarkable, given they would have had to travel some forty-five miles in their pursuit of Paul. Timothy and Silas resolved to remain in Berea for some time longer. Paul was escorted to Athens, presumably by means of a three-hundred-mile sea voyage, where he was to await his companions. It seems their persecution was particularly directed at Paul, hence the need to get him away from the situation.

Stott notes the relative brevity with which Luke records the missions to Thessalonica and Berea. One of the chief contrasts he draws is in their

---

[14] Stephen Denison, cited in *RCS* 6:240.
[15] Spangenberg, cited in *RCS* 6:241._

respective attitudes towards the Scriptures.[16] Paul used the Scriptures as his basis for his 'reasoning', 'explaining' and 'proving'. We see the high regard he had for the Old Testament Scriptures as the basis for understanding and truth. The Bereans are also commended by Luke for their serious engagement with Scripture as they examined it carefully to see that what Paul taught could be confirmed. For Paul and his more 'noble' hearers, Scripture was the foundation and authority for faith and mission.

3. The Areopagus • Acts 17:16–34

In Athens

16 While Paul was waiting for them in Athens, he was greatly distressed to see that the city was full of idols. **17** So he reasoned in the synagogue with both Jews and God-fearing Greeks, as well as in the market-place day by day with those who happened to be there. **18** A group of Epicurean and Stoic philosophers began to debate with him. Some of them asked, 'What is this babbler trying to say?' Others remarked, 'He seems to be advocating foreign gods.' They said this because Paul was preaching the good news about Jesus and the resurrection. **19** Then they took him and brought him to a meeting of the Areopagus, where they said to him, 'May we know what this new teaching is that you are presenting? **20** You are bringing some strange ideas to our ears, and we would like to know what they mean.' **21** (All the Athenians and the foreigners who lived there spent their time doing nothing but talking about and listening to the latest ideas.)

22 Paul then stood up in the meeting of the Areopagus and said: 'People of Athens! I see that in every way you are very religious. **23** For as I walked around and looked carefully at your objects of worship, I even found an altar with this inscription: TO AN UNKNOWN GOD. So you are ignorant of the very thing you worship – and this is what I am going to proclaim to you.

24 'The God who made the world and everything in it is the Lord of heaven and earth and does not live in temples built by human hands. **25** And he is not served by human hands, as if he needed anything. Rather, he himself gives everyone life and breath and everything else. **26** From one man he made all the nations, that they should inhabit the whole earth; and he marked out their appointed times in history and the boundaries of their lands. **27** God did this so that they would seek him and perhaps reach out for him and find him, though he is not far from any one of us. **28** 'For in him we live and move and have our

---

[16] Stott, *Acts*, 275.

being."**b** As some of your own poets have said, "We are his offspring."**c**

29'Therefore since we are God's offspring, we should not think that the divine being is like gold or silver or stone – an image made by human design and skill. **30**In the past God overlooked such ignorance, but now he commands all people everywhere to repent. **31**For he has set a day when he will judge the world with justice by the man he has appointed. He has given proof of this to everyone by raising him from the dead.'

32When they heard about the resurrection of the dead, some of them sneered, but others said, 'We want to hear you again on this subject.' **33**At that, Paul left the Council. **34**Some of the people became followers of Paul and believed. Among them was Dionysius, a member of the Areopagus, also a woman named Damaris, and a number of others.

---

b 28 From the Cretan philosopher Epimenides
c 28 From the Cilician Stoic philosopher Aratus

In Athens, we see one of Paul's great speeches as he engages in debate with the philosophers.[17] He skilfully uses their own ideas to show them both the bankruptcy of their own world view as well as its fulfilment in Christ. This is a wonderful example of contextualisation and subversive fulfilment.[18]

Athens was one of the great cities of the ancient world. Its impact and significance had somewhat dwindled under the Roman Empire, yet it remained a centre of learning and its history made it a place of great renown. It had been the home of the greatest philosophers: Socrates, Plato and Aristotle. This was the 'cultural capital of the world' – the ancient equivalent of London, New York, Tokyo or Paris.[19] However, Paul observed that enlightened philosophy was also mixed up with superstitious idolatry.[20] It is interesting to note how often in modern cultures rationalism and superstition coexist.

In verse 16, we see Paul waiting for Silas and Timothy in Athens. As he wandered around the city he was 'greatly distressed' by the idols he saw. Paul saw 'neither the beauty nor the brilliance of the city, but

---

[17] For an excellent analysis of the Areopagus speech, see Strange, *For Their Rock Is Not as Our Rock*, 285–94. Strange picks up on the way in which the speech develops the anti-idol polemic of Isaiah's new Exodus.

[18] Subversive fulfilment is the idea that we can subvert someone's world view by showing how it is inconsistent or unworkable. A person's deepest longings and desires only find fulfilment in the work of Jesus Christ. Thus, we aim to both subvert and fulfil every false world view.

[19] Stott, *Acts*, 276.

[20] Marshall, *Acts*, 281.

its idolatry'.[21] Good missional engagement must begin with these two things – observation and distress. First, we need to see the idols that are all around us. Sometimes they take the crude and obvious form of statues. Sometimes idols are more subtle and take the form of beliefs, values, hopes and dreams. In western cultures, we can easily see materialism, success and relationships as major idols in our society. In other cultures, those idols might be honour, status or the pursuit of transcendent peace.

Calvin once described human beings as 'idol factories'.[22] Humans are constantly looking for that which we believe will fulfil our deepest longings and desires. These things we aim ourselves at are our worship. We serve them in the hope that they will in turn reward us. Part of our cultural engagement is to see what forms the idols around us take.

Second, having observed them, they should cause us distress. As Peter has told us, there is only one name by which we may be saved (Acts 4:12). The idols people put their hope in will ultimately lead to their destruction. The doctrine of hell is something we do not talk or think much about, probably as a sort of self-defence mechanism. It is difficult to think about our friends and family spending eternity under God's wrath. Some theologians have sought to soften this doctrine either by universalism or annihilationism. The Bible is clear. Those who do not put their trust in Christ to be saved will face God's judgment and his wrath, which will cast us away from his loving presence forever. This should distress us. This should motivate our evangelistic efforts. This should cause us to re-evaluate our priorities.

If our churches seek primarily to serve the consumeristic interests of their members, they have not stared long enough at the eternal fate awaiting those around us. At our church, we often talk about being a lifeboat, not a cruise ship. On a cruise ship the customers pay their money for the staff to meet all their wants and needs. If they are unhappy, they may take their custom elsewhere. On a lifeboat, the interests of the crew are secondary. The ride will be bumpy. The work will be hard. But people are drowning and in desperate need of rescue. The idol worship all around us should cause us deep distress when we see where it leads.

As a consequence, we once again see Paul reasoning in the synagogue and in the marketplace day by day with those present. Paul desired to make the most of every opportunity wherever it presented itself. He soon found himself in debate with Epicurean and Stoic philosophers.

---

[21] Stott, *Acts*, 277.
[22] Calvin, *Institutes* 1.11.8.

The Epicureans were materialists who believed life exists by mere chance.[23] The aim of life for an Epicurean is the pursuit of pleasure and the avoidance of pain. They, like Paul, would have been critics of idolatry and the never-ending sacrifice to the gods. They were indifferent to the gods, and it was a waste of time expressing devotion to them. Diogenes summarised their world view: 'Nothing to fear in God; Nothing to feel in death; Good [pleasure] can be attained; Evil can be endured.'[24] Bock likens them to secular agnostics.[25] There are many people today who live with a similar world view.

Stoics, on the other hand, were rationalists, guided by observation, logic and reasoning. They did believe in the divine, but thought the deity was to be found in all things. They were essentially panentheists.[26] Humans were to seek to live in harmony with the cosmos. The deity was not transcendent but immanent, and hardships were to be endured as part of the struggle towards greater harmony with the divine.

These philosophers described Paul as a 'babbler', which was a derisory way of dismissing him and his ideas.[27] Others thought he was advocating 'foreign gods', which of course he was – or, rather, one particular God. They based this on Paul's preaching of Jesus and the resurrection.[28] This second accusation has a more serious note. Socrates was sentenced to death by the Athenians for introducing foreign deities. To accuse Paul of the same thing carries a threatening undertone. We should not be surprised when people dismiss the gospel as something unenlightened, primitive or outdated. For the believer it is the wisdom of God. For the wise of this age, it is abject foolishness (see 1 Corinthians 1:18–31).

They took him along to a meeting of the Areopagus and invited him to share his new and strange teaching (verses 19–20). This is the second of three major speeches in Acts delivered by Paul.[29] Luke comments

---

[23] For a good summary of the beliefs of Epicureans and Stoics, see Gooding, *True to the Faith*, 346–52.

[24] Cited in Bock, *Acts*, 561.

[25] Bock, *Acts*, 561.

[26] Witherington, *Acts*, 514.

[27] The Greek word translated 'babbler' is *spermologos*, which could be literally translated 'seed picker'. In other words, they viewed Paul as just picking up bits of other ideas, rather than developing his own new and sophisticated arguments.

[28] It is possible that Paul's hearer thought he was referring to two gods (they refer to 'gods' in the plural) – Jesus and the feminine counterpart, Anastasis (the Greek word for Resurrection). See Peterson, *Acts*, 491.

[29] See also Acts 13:16–41; 20:18–35.

that the Athenians loved nothing more than debating ideas. There is a difference between intellectual sparring and a genuine seeking after truth. Luke's editorial comment suggests that many of the Athenians were in the former category. He is subtly portraying the Athenians as the 'seed-pickers' they accused Paul of being.[30]

The Areopagus was a large, elevated, open site just west of the Acropolis. The term 'Areopagus' was used to refer to both the council and the place, and here it seems both are in view.[31] It may have been used as a city assembly or council that would hear debates and render verdicts. It seems this was more than just a friendly place to exchange ideas. The scene carries a sense of trial in which the outcome for Paul seems uncertain. His interrogators act as judge and jury as Paul makes his defence.

Paul's speech can be divided into three main sections: the truth about the Creator; the truth about humanity; the truth about the Judge.

The truth about the creator

Paul begins with a somewhat ambiguous statement: 'People of Athens! I see that in every way you are very religious.' Scholars debate Paul's intent here. Is he criticising their bizarre polytheism, commending their interest in spiritual things or simply finding a point of engagement? I suspect the ambiguity of the statement suggests the latter.

Paul is not yet passing judgment on their view, though he will get there. He is simply finding the point of connection by which he can explain the gospel.[32] In our own day, we too could look at our culture and note that in many ways it is very spiritual. This would provide an opening to explain where true spirituality lies. Rather than simply dismissing other views and shutting down any hope of meaningful conversation, we should look for ways in which we can engage others in conversation.

Paul refers to a specific object of worship – an altar to an unknown God. Paul picks up this detail as his opportunity to proclaim to them the identity of the God they do not know. His argument moves from God's creative work to his providential care of creation to the call to return. The altar to the unknown can be seen as the desperate heart yearning for God. There is a deep sense of need and yet utter confusion as to where God

---

[30] Bock, *Acts*, 563.

[31] Peterson, *Acts*, 492.

[32] Stephen G. Wilson, *The Gentiles and Gentile Mission in Luke–Acts* (Cambridge: Cambridge University Press, 1973), 197.

may be found. J. H. Bavinck described this altar as a 'cry of misery, and this made it possible for him [Paul] to sketch boldly the sole way of escape'.[33]

Paul begins by announcing God as the creator and Lord of everything in all creation. His language alludes to passages such as Isaiah 42:5 and Exodus 20:11.[34] He does not live in temples and he is not served by humans.[35] Rather, humans are provided for by God since he is the one who gives life and breath and everything else (verses 24–5). In the first of Isaiah's 'Servant Songs', God is described as the creator of the heaven and the earth, and the one who gives life and breath (Isaiah 42:5). It is the Servant who will be a light for the Gentiles; he who will open blind eyes and release the Gentiles from their groping in darkness. This is the Old Testament context for Paul's theological critique and solution.

The truth about humanity

From this, Paul describes how God is Lord of every nation, since from one man he made every nation. He marked out their appointed times and their boundaries.[36] This would appear to be an allusion to Deuteronomy 32 – the song of Moses. In Deuteronomy 32:8 it is God who 'set up boundaries for the peoples'. And it is God who will ultimately bring healing and restoration to a crooked and corrupt people (Deuteronomy 32:6). God did not just create everything in the world then leave humanity to their own devices. God's creative care extends through time and space. His providence meets each and every need. His care sustains each and every human being throughout history.

Thus, Paul is finding points of connection and correction with both the Epicureans and the Stoics. In agreement with the Epicureans, the God/gods do not need serving by human hands, yet there is a God; the cosmos is not the result of chance natural forces alone. In agreement with the Stoics, the God/gods are involved in the providential care and ordering of the cosmos, and yet the true God is also transcendent – he does not live in temples made by human hands. Paul masterfully demonstrates the

---

[33] J. H. Bavinck, *An Introduction to the Science of Missions* (repr. Phillipsburg: P&R, 1960), 140.

[34] Marshall, *Acts*, 286.

[35] Adjacent to the Areopagus is the huge temple to Athena, which would have made Paul's statement even more striking. I am grateful to Dr Lee Gatiss for this insight.

[36] Old Testament allusions here could include Genesis 1–2; 11; Deuteronomy 32:8. Of course, these verses should not be used to suggest that boundary crossing (migration) is against God's revealed will, as has occasionally been argued in the past.

ways in which the philosophical world views have discovered some truth, but also how they have missed essential parts of it.

Paul claims the reason God did this is so that people would seek after God and find him, though in fact he is not far from each one of us.[37] The knowledge of God that can be understood from the created world should drive human beings to seek after God, though, as Paul makes clear in Romans, humans suppress this knowledge. Daniel Strange notes the crucial distinction between 'God's original positive creational design pre-fall . . . and the current post-fall and more specifically post-Babel polytheistic idolatrous state, which describes in much more negative and pessimistic terms the result of this seeking[38]. For the purposes of this speech, Paul wants his audience to realise that God desires a relationship with humanity. He is not far off and distant but is close and wants humans to know him. The appreciation of God in creation should drive us to seek him in his revelation. Until we reckon with the fulness of God's revelation, we will be groping in the dark.[39]

The Greek poets are cited in support of the argument. Epimenides is supposed to have said, 'In him we live and move and have our being.' Aratus said, 'We are his offspring.' Paul is arguing in familiar terms that the Athenians would have some understanding of. His radical new and strange teaching is not a million miles away from some of the statements in existence. Paul again seeks a point of connection. The Greek philosophers spoke some truth and Paul wants the Athenians to see that the full revelation of that truth is in the one true God. Therefore, says Paul, since we are God's offspring, we should not think of him as a lump of gold or stone – something made by human skill.

The truth about the judge

The climax of Paul's argument is to call his hearers to repentance. God has overlooked such ignorance in the past, but now he calls for repentance, for a day of judgment is coming at the hands of the appointed judge. God's 'overlooking' of ignorance is not meant to imply that they are any less culpable. Romans 1 helps us to see that the darkened mind that leads

---

[37] On this passage, Origen says, 'He is thus, for his part, close, but if we ourselves make no effort, though he be close, to draw near to him, we will not enjoy his nearness. For this reason, sinners are far from God', in ACCS 5:220.
[38] Strange, *For Their Rock is not as Our Rock*, 290.
[39] Bock, *Acts*, 567.

to idolatry is a result of our suppression of the truth we do have access to, revealed through general revelation. God's 'overlooking', then, is his merciful stay of execution.[40] He has borne with patience their idolatry, desiring them to come to a knowledge of truth and repentance. They are not 'off the hook' in claimed ignorance; they are in the last chance saloon of God's patience before final judgment comes (2 Peter 3:9).

The proof of this final judgment is in the raising of this appointed one from the dead. The resurrection is the evidence of Jesus's identity and his mission, which includes salvation and judgment. The only proper response to the resurrection is to worship Jesus as the one true Lord and Judge. And the need is urgent. Jesus has ascended to the right hand of the Father. There is only one 'act' left in the divine drama before the final judgment. That final 'act' is the return of the Lord Jesus. Therefore, the time to repent is 'now', as a matter of urgency, before Jesus returns and all that is left is to face his judgment.

The response is mixed. Some wish to hear more. Some become followers. And others sneer at the idea of the resurrection. For a Greek audience, the notion of a bodily resurrection would be remarkable. It was thought that upon death the soul went to hades with no possibility of return.[41] Paul leaves the council, and two believers in particular are named – Dionysius and Damaris.

Paul's speech to the Areopagus shows us a number of important things. First, the uniqueness of Christ and Christianity. He is not just one among a number of gods. He is the only creator, sustainer, Saviour, Lord and judge. Paul's speech is an anti-idol polemic that highlights the culpability of those who seek to pursue God apart from Christ.[42] Stott notes that many reject the gospel today for different reasons. Some believe it to be untrue; others believe it to be trivial, of little or no real importance.[43] Paul's message shows us how far from the truth this is. Could it be that we, the church, have forgotten just how all-encompassing the gospel is? It is not just a 'ticket to the sky when you die'. It affects all, and the emptiness of idolatry is a truly awful evil. Perhaps today 'we do not speak as Paul spoke because we do not feel as Paul felt. We have never had the paroxysm of indignation which he had. Divine jealousy has not stirred within us.'[44]

---

[40] Stott, *Acts*, 287.

[41] Bock, *Acts*, 558.

[42] Flavien Pardigon, *Paul Against the Idols: A Contextual Reading of the Areopagus Speech* (Eugene: Pickwick, 2019), 224.

[43] Stott, *Acts*, 290.

[44] Stott, *Acts*, 290.

Second, God's providential purposes through history are designed to draw people towards himself. We may not understand how that works. Much of it will be a mystery to us. Yet it is comforting to know that God is at work to fulfil his purposes, even when we struggle to discern his ways and means. There is a healthy humility in this recognition.

Third, Paul shows us the value of carefully argued contextualised preaching. Paul is able to speak persuasively to those in the synagogue, in the market square and to the sophisticated thinkers, adapting his message to suit his audience. As Bock notes, 'Whether in informal conversation or formal settings, the ability to set forth the faith at a level appropriate to the setting is a valuable talent.'[45] The search for the point of contact and the subversive fulfilment are effective ways to communicate with people who are spiritual but ignorant.

Fourth, we see that faithful preaching can have mixed results. In Berea many believed. In Athens just a few believed. This does not mean that Paul failed in his ministry in Athens. We need to resist the urge to assess the supposed success of ministry on numerical results. Our job is to faithfully and wisely proclaim the gospel; the results are with the Lord.

Fifth, we see the importance of not just the message but the motive. Bock speaks powerfully of Paul's 'generous but honest' spirit, and his conclusion is worth citing in full:

> The Paul of Rom. 1 who speaks of the sad state of society is still able to love and connect with that society in Acts 17. This also is an important lesson; sometimes we Christians are so angry at the state of our society that all that comes through is the anger and not the love we are to have for neighbour in need. Those who see this anger and want to represent the faith differently can overreact the other way, almost pretending as if there is no idolatry as long as the religious search is sincerely motivated. Paul avoids both of these extremes. He knows how to confront but does so honestly and graciously. Both message and tone are important in sharing the gospel. Here Paul is an example of both.[46]

---

[45] Bock, *Acts*, 573.
[46] Bock, *Acts*, 573.

17

Highs and Lows in Corinth

ACTS 18:1–22

As Paul enters Corinth, we see a familiar pattern: rejection in the syna-gogue, some success among the Gentiles and accusation before the authorities. We have seen this pattern before in Paul's second missionary journey. We are also introduced to Priscilla and Aquila, figures who play a significant role in supporting and furthering the mission. Paul's letters suggest that Corinth was one of the most challenging churches that he established and supported. Towards the end of Acts 18 we see Paul return to Jerusalem and Antioch. This concludes his second missionary circuit and introduces his third and final journey.

Stott notes that it seems to be Paul's 'deliberate policy to move purposefully from one strategic city-centre to the next. What drew him to the cities was probably that they contained the Jewish synagogues, the larger populations and the influential leaders.'[1] From these cultural centres the gospel would have a greater chance of spreading to the surrounding regions.

Calvin's opening comments on Acts 18 demonstrate the remarkable power of God at work through Paul in Corinth:

> He is a simple man, unknown, having no eloquence or pomp, showing no wealth or power. In that that huge gulf doth not swallow up his confidence and desire which he had to spread abroad the gospel, by this we gather that he was furnished with wonderful power of the Spirit of God; and also that God wrought by his hand after a heavenly manner, and not after any human manner.[2]

We must never lose sight of the unseen main character in the book of Acts – the risen Lord Jesus, working by his Spirit to advance the gospel and protect his people. This is where we draw our confidence as disciples,

---

[1] Stott, *Acts*, 293.
[2] Calvin, *Acts*, 180.

not in our own strength or abilities, but in his grace powerfully at work in us and among us.

1. New colleagues and converts • Acts 18:1–8

In Corinth

18 After this, Paul left Athens and went to Corinth. **2** There he met a Jew named Aquila, a native of Pontus, who had recently come from Italy with his wife Priscilla, because Claudius had ordered all Jews to leave Rome. Paul went to see them, **3** and because he was a tentmaker as they were, he stayed and worked with them. **4** Every Sabbath he reasoned in the synagogue, trying to persuade Jews and Greeks.

5 When Silas and Timothy came from Macedonia, Paul devoted himself exclusively to preaching, testifying to the Jews that Jesus was the Messiah. **6** But when they opposed Paul and became abusive, he shook out his clothes in protest and said to them, 'Your blood be on your own heads! I am innocent of it. From now on I will go to the Gentiles.'

7 Then Paul left the synagogue and went next door to the house of Titius Justus, a worshipper of God. **8** Crispus, the synagogue leader, and his entire household believed in the Lord; and many of the Corinthians who heard Paul believed and were baptised.

Having left Athens, Paul arrived in Corinth.[3] Marshall suggests that Corinth and Ephesus were 'the two most important cities visited by Paul in the course of his missionary work, and he stayed in each for a considerable period in order to establish churches which would then evangelize the surrounding areas'.[4] By the time of Paul's visit in the early AD 50s, Corinth was 'well on the way to becoming the largest, most prosperous city in Greece'.[5] It was a mixture of Hellenistic and Roman influence. It was a significant centre of trade and culture and was religiously pluralistic, combining Hellenistic religion with emperor worship. Corinth had two seaports, it had the temple of Aphrodite, it hosted the biennial Isthmian games and it had a reputation across the ancient world for a hedonistic sexual immorality.[6] Horace describes it

---

[3] Athens to Corinth is an overland journey of around thirty-seven miles. Peterson, *Acts*, 506.
[4] Marshall, *Acts*, 291.
[5] Witherington, *Acts*, 538.
[6] Peterson, *Acts*, 506.

as a town where only the tough survive.[7] It was as influential as it was deceived in its idol worship.

Yet Paul saw this as an opportunity. As Stott notes, 'If trade could radiate from Corinth in all directions, so could the gospel.'[8] Witherington describes Corinth as the 'ideal place for Paul to spend at least eighteen months sharing the gospel'.[9]

In Corinth, Paul met two people who would reappear numerous times in his letters – Priscilla and Aquila.[10] Luke informs us that Aquila was a native of Pontus, and that he and his wife, Priscilla, had recently fled Rome owing to the edict of Claudius.[11] This event is recorded by the historian Suetonius (*Claud.* 25.4): 'Since the Jews constantly made disturbances at the instigation of Chrestus, he expelled them from Rome.'[12] Scholars note it is possible that Chrestus is a misspelling of Christus, and therefore a reference to Christ. However, Chrestus was a relatively common name, so there is no way of being certain who exactly was being referred to here.[13]

Whatever the cause of their departure, God providentially placed Priscilla and Aquila in the way of Paul. They would become a source of great joy in their gospel partnership. It is always worth being sensitive to the ways in which God places certain people in our lives (and us in theirs) to encourage and spur one another on in our life and witness. Such meetings are never coincidences, but gifts from God which we should embrace with thanksgiving.

Paul, having met this couple, worked with them as a tentmaker for some time, until he was reunited with Silas and Timothy.[14] The term *skēnopoioi* (tentmaker) could have a broader sense of leatherworker.[15] It is possible they practised their trade at a shared shop in the marketplace,

---

[7] Horace, *Ep.* 1.17.36, cited in Bock, *Acts*, 577.

[8] Stott, *Acts*, 294.

[9] Witherington, *Acts*, 538.

[10] See Romans 16:3; 1 Corinthians 16:19; 2 Timothy 4:19.

[11] We may wonder how there were Christians in Rome at this point. We must recall Acts 2:10–11: there were at Pentecost 'visitors from Rome (both Jews and converts to Judaism)'.

[12] Trans. J. C. Rolfe, *Suetonius* (Loeb Library), 2:53. Witherington has an extended discussion of the edict in his *Acts*, 539–44.

[13] This event is likely to have happened around AD 49. Peterson, *Acts*, 507.

[14] The trade routes and the biennial Isthmian games made Corinth a centre for travellers, fuelling the tent-making industry.

[15] Wall, *Acts*, 252, has the stimulating suggestion that Paul's tentmaking carries an allusion to Amos's Davidic tent referenced in Acts 15:16 (Amos 9:11–12).

or out of their own home.[16] Peterson notes that in Greek culture manual labour was despised, perhaps one reason for his 'foolishness' in the eyes of some (see 1 Corinthians 1).[17]

Chrysostom notes here in passing the value of Paul's 'ordinary' work and its inherent dignity.[18] For Paul (and Luke), there is no 'second best' in serving God's call and mission through working with his hands. We should remember this when we are tempted to put pastors on pedestals or see their work as somehow more important than the work of others. God can call us and use us in his service in a wide variety of spheres and callings. The people of God may be found serving his call in business, education, healthcare, charities, homes or any number of other places. Let us not despise the particular calling of others or ourselves, so long as we are seeking to serve Christ in the places he puts us.

As was his custom, Paul would visit the synagogue on the Sabbath to share the gospel with the Jews worshipping there. Paul's example shows us how he would do whatever was necessary to continue spreading the message. In this case he worked as a tentmaker. The book of Acts and Paul's writings seem to suggest that Paul, at different points in his ministry, sustained a living in different ways. At times, as here, we see him working as a tentmaker and preaching in his spare time.[19] At other times he seems to have given himself exclusively to preaching, sustaining a living from the support of Christians.[20]

It would appear these decisions were sometimes a necessary part of his work as a pioneer missionary. We ought to be careful we do not use this description as prescription for every minister or missionary in every situation. There is no hint in Acts or Paul's writings that one mode of ministry is more virtuous than the other. It seems that where Paul was able to sustain himself from the gifts of the church, he preferred to give himself full-time to the work, but where that was not possible, he was content to work as a tentmaker.

There may also have been strategic reasons why Paul did not want to be seen as a travelling philosopher, peddling his teaching for money.[21] Churches,

---

[16] Witherington, *Acts*, 545–6.

[17] Peterson, *Acts*, 508.

[18] He states, 'Angels honored him and demons trembled at him, and still he was not ashamed to say, "These same hands served my needs and those who were with me."' 'Acts', in ACCS 5:224.

[19] See Acts 20:33–4; 1 Thessalonians 2:9; 1 Corinthians 9:12.

[20] See Acts 18:5; 1 Corinthians 9:14; Galatians 6:6; 1 Timothy 5:17–18.

[21] Witherington, *Acts*, 547–8.

pastors and missionaries would do well to consider the most strategic approach for their own contexts, whether that is full-time paid ministry or a bivocational 'tentmaker' approach.[22] At the same time they ought to exercise caution in being critical of others who adopt a different approach.

When Paul was reunited with Silas and Timothy, he was able to give himself full-time to preaching. At this point we read that the opposition from the Jews increased.[23] The verb, *antitassomenōn* (oppose – verse 6), suggests organized resistance.[24] We are told that the Jews became abusive. Their 'abuse' (*blasphēmountōn*) could refer to verbal abuse against them or blasphemy against God in the rejection of their message about Christ. Paul shook out his garments against them in a gesture reminiscent of Nehemiah, indicating God's rejection of those who reject him (Nehemiah 5:13). He said, 'Your blood be on your own heads! I am innocent of it. From now on I will go to the Gentiles' (verse 6). Paul was using language from Ezekiel 33:4: 'their blood will be on their own head'. In effect, he is the watchman like Ezekiel, sent to warn Israel of coming judgment and to call them to repentance and faith in Christ. Their rejection tragically seals their fate.

As a result, Paul left the synagogue and began meetings in the home of Titius Justus. One can imagine the ongoing tension between Paul (and his new followers) and the members of the synagogue meeting just next door. That tension must have increased dramatically since Crispus, the leader of the synagogue, and his whole household were converted and meeting next door with Paul and the others.[25] Luke tells us many of the Corinthians believed and were baptised.

This mixed church, containing Jews and Gentiles, sat right next door to the synagogue. Many of its former attendees now worshipped with Paul and the church. They must have felt excited at what God was doing among them, but maybe also afraid at the possible persecution that might come their way. We can perhaps see why the church had some early struggles in the relationships between Jewish and Gentile believers, and also

---

[22] Wall, *Acts*, 256.

[23] 2 Corinthians 11:9 and Philippians 4:14–16 suggest that Silas and Timothy brought with them funds that enabled Paul to devote himself full-time to preaching at this point. This would explain why Paul was able to say he imposed no financial burden on the Corinthians (2 Corinthians 11:9). Marshall, *Acts*, 294.

[24] Bock, *Acts*, 579.

[25] The description of Titius Justus as a 'worshipper of God' (*sebomenou ton theon*) is the last in Acts, perhaps suggesting Paul's direction of travel into ever more hostile territory. Bock, *Acts*, 579.

why there may have been a sense of superiority over the unenlightened worshippers next door![26]

Luke's narrative invites us to reflect on our own hearts towards those from different religious backgrounds. While we maintain there is no other name under heaven by which people may be saved (Acts 4:12), we do not want to slip into the sort of self-satisfied superiority and division that Paul's letters suggest existed within the early life of the Corinthian church.

2. Before God and Gallio • Acts 18:9–17

9 One night the Lord spoke to Paul in a vision: 'Do not be afraid; keep on speaking, do not be silent. **10** For I am with you, and no one is going to attack and harm you, because I have many people in this city.' **11** So Paul stayed in Corinth for a year and a half, teaching them the word of God.

12 While Gallio was proconsul of Achaia, the Jews of Corinth made a united attack on Paul and brought him to the place of judgment. **13** 'This man,' they charged, 'is persuading the people to worship God in ways contrary to the law.'

14 Just as Paul was about to speak, Gallio said to them, 'If you Jews were making a complaint about some misdemeanour or serious crime, it would be reasonable for me to listen to you. **15** But since it involves questions about words and names and your own law – settle the matter yourselves. I will not be a judge of such things.' **16** So he drove them off. **17** Then the crowd there turned on Sosthenes the synagogue leader and beat him in front of the proconsul; and Gallio showed no concern whatever.

As seen in Acts 16:20–24 and 17:5–9 it was not just rejection from the synagogue that Paul and his followers had to contend with. The opposition, sometimes instigated by the Jews, could also come from the local authorities. We will see this a number of times again before we reach the end of Luke's narrative.

In verse 9, Paul is given a vision from the Lord. In Acts 16:9 Paul was given a vision to direct the mission, but here the vision is to give him comfort in the face of opposition. The Lord encourages Paul not to be afraid and to keep on speaking. It is reminiscent of Old Testament visions given to Moses, Joshua and the Prophets.[27] He will be protected from

---

[26] See Paul's letters to the Corinthians. That sense of superiority can be recognised in the opening chapters of 1 Corinthians. See also 1 Corinthians 8–10 for some of issues of tension between Jewish and Gentile believers.

[27] Exodus 3:1–12; Joshua 1:1–19; Isaiah 41:10–14; Jeremiah 1:5–10.

attack and harm because 'I have many people in this city' (verse 10). The vision does not promise that no one will oppose; in fact, opposition is about to arise in verses 12–13. The vision rather promises that Paul will be protected from resultant harm. The vision gives Paul assurance of God's sovereign power and purpose in his circumstances. As Tannehill notes, 'The vision interprets both the mission's success and the escape from danger as manifestations of the Lord's purpose and power. The statement "I am with you" highlights the hidden actor in the narrative.'[28]

It seems this was much needed, given Paul's own words in 1 Corinthians 2:3 about coming to Corinth with much 'fear and trembling'. While we cannot claim this vision as a promise for our own circumstances – indeed, many Christians do suffer attack and harm – the Lord's words do assure us that he is in absolute control of our situations and circumstances, working out his purposes according to his sovereign will. This calls us to continue to be faithful in following Christ, trusting him with the outcomes of our own trials. When we remember that we live our whole lives *coram deo* (before the face of God), it radically reshapes how we conceive of every moment as an opportunity for worship and witness.

In verse 11 we are told Paul stayed in Corinth for eighteen months teaching the church the word of God.[29] This verse is worth reflecting on for three reasons. First, it reminds us that Paul's ministry was more than that of a pioneer planter. Sometimes he would stay in a place for just a few weeks (e.g., Thessalonica). At other times he would stay for a considerable period of time (here and in Ephesus – Acts 19:10). His concern was not just with evangelism, but also with discipleship. Both were an important part of his ministry in establishing and strengthening churches. Both of these things should be important for us also in seeking to establish and strengthen healthy churches. It is all too easy for one or other of these things to become dominant in the life of our churches. Both must be held together, recognising the need of both, and the different gifts given to individuals within the church.

Second, it reminds us of the variety involved in Paul's ministry of evangelism and shepherding. Some will tell us of the value of long pastorates. Others will extol the virtue of pioneer planting. For Paul, it seems the circumstances and context determined whether he stayed a long time or just a short while. Neither should we overly prescribe the shape and nature of individuals' ministries, recognising the variety in Paul's and the situational factors that were determinative.

---

[28] Tannehill, *Narrative Unity*, 226.
[29] This would place his stay at around AD 50–52.

, Third, it is striking that Paul spent a year and a half teaching this church, and it was still one of the most problematic, as his letters would indicate. Surely having the apostle Paul as pastor would mean they would be free of immorality and immaturity! But no, sanctification is a life-long process. There is no short cut. There is no 'silver bullet' discipleship programme that churns out mature believers. Sometimes people mature quickly, while others seem to make little progress in their sanctification over the course of many decades. As John Owen observed:

> The growth of trees and plants is secret and imperceptible . . . The most watchful eye can discern little of its motion . . . It is no otherwise in the progress of holiness. It is not immediately discernible, either by themselves in who it is, or by others that make observation of it. It lies only under the eye of him by whom it is wrought . . . there are trees and plants that have the principle of life and growth in them but yet are so withering and unthrifty that you can only discern them to be alive. And so it is with too many believers . . . some thrive, some decay for a season, but the growth of the best is secret.[30]

All of this can happen under what we might identify as excellent ministry. Our evangelism and discipleship require us to recognise this reality and to endure under the mystery.

The comfort of the vision would be necessary as we read of a united attack made on Paul in verse 12. He was brought before the proconsul, Gallio, at the place of judgment. Gallio was the brother of the famous philosopher and politician, Seneca. Witherington suggests that many Romans of high social status in this period were anti-semitic, and therefore unlikely to give much time to what appeared to be an intra-Jewish dispute.[31] The charge brought against Paul was 'persuading the people to worship God in ways contrary to the law' (verse 13). They were accusing this new faith of being an illicit, unrecognised religion. An edict from Claudius had permitted Jewish worship, but Paul, they claimed, was introducing something new, which would therefore be illegitimate.[32]

---

[30] John Owen, *The Works of John Owen, Volume 3* (repr. London: Banner of Truth, 1965), 396–7 (in his *Discourse Concerning the Holy Spirit*, book 4, chapter 2).
[31] Witherington, *Acts*, 551.
[32] Bock, *Acts*, 581.

Interestingly, Paul was not even given opportunity to defend himself. Just at the moment he was about to speak, Gallio interrupted to dismiss the case.[33] In Gallio's judgment, the dispute was about 'words and names and your own law' and therefore they were to settle it themselves (verses 14–15).

Having had their case thrown out, the crowd turned on Sosthenes, the new leader of the synagogue, and beat him instead. It is unclear whether it was the 'crowd' more broadly that turned on Sosthenes or the Jews in frustration that their leader had failed to prosecute Paul.[34] Intriguingly, the name Sosthenes appears in the opening greeting of Paul's first letter to the Corinthian church. Is it possible that his mistreatment caused him to turn away from Judaism and find faith in Christ? We cannot know for sure, but it remains an intriguing possibility.

Gallio remained unmoved. The Jews and the crowd are portrayed as vengeful and violent in their injustice. Gallio is portrayed as uncaring concerning the violence, which is an injustice of its own. As characters, the mob, the Jews and the authorities all seem incompetent as arbiters of truth and justice.

It is perhaps surprising and unsettling to see God using the incompetent and unjust authority to fulfil the promise of the vision to protect Paul. As Tannehill concludes, 'The human instrument of [God's] protection is no model of just and enlightened policy.'[35] Further, the way God's will is fulfilled is 'often messy and the agents of God's will are sometimes unsavory people'.[36] Peterson also poses the question as to whether Gallio's behaviour lay behind Paul's warning about taking religious matters before unbelieving authorities (1 Corinthians 6:1–18).[37] Many believers in the world today have to struggle on, trusting in God's sovereignty, all the while faced with unjust and uncaring authorities.[38] We must remain informed and remember to pray for brothers and sisters living under regimes that display little compassion or concern for injustice faced by Christians.

---

[33] This should not be taken as some sort of Roman legitimation of Christianity as if Gallio was friendly or sympathetic to the gospel (*pace*; Richard N. Longenecker, *Acts* (Grand Rapids: Zondervan, 1995), 486). More likely here is Gallio's own impatient dismissal based on his own prejudice against the Jews. Witherington, *Acts*, 555.

[34] Witherington, *Acts*, 556.

[35] Tannehill, *Narrative Unity*, 229.

[36] Wall, *Acts*, 256.

[37] Peterson, *Acts*, 518.

[38] Venkataraman, 'Acts', in *SABC*, 1494.

3. Back towards Antioch • Acts 18:18–22

Priscilla, Aquila and Apollos

18 Paul stayed on in Corinth for some time. Then he left the brothers and sisters and sailed for Syria, accompanied by Priscilla and Aquila. Before he sailed, he had his hair cut off at Cenchreae because of a vow he had taken. 19 They arrived at Ephesus, where Paul left Priscilla and Aquila. He himself went into the synagogue and reasoned with the Jews. 20 When they asked him to spend more time with them, he declined. 21 But as he left, he promised, 'I will come back if it is God's will.' Then he set sail from Ephesus. 22 When he landed at Caesarea, he went up to Jerusalem and greeted the church and then went down to Antioch.

Having stayed in Corinth for some time, Paul set sail for Ephesus with Priscilla and Aquila. It seems Paul left of his own volition, rather than being forced away under persecution. It would also appear that Silas and Timothy were left behind to continue to minister in Corinth. Priscilla and Aquila were, for the time being, his travelling companions, an indication of the importance of their role in supporting Paul and the churches planted. Paul would leave them in Ephesus, presumably to support the new Christians until he was able to return.

Before sailing, Paul cut his hair in fulfilment of a vow. This may have been a Nazirite vow or simply a private vow of thanksgiving made in response to the vision of verses 9–10.[39] Marshall suggests the vow was an act of commitment and thankfulness for the promise of protection.[40] This might strike us as a strange thing to do for someone who had been so radically converted away from Judaism to Christianity. Yet we must remember that Paul saw Christianity as in continuity with Judaism, with Christ as the climax and fulfilment of God's covenants with Israel. Thus, he still visited the synagogues, he had Timothy circumcised and he took vows. Many of the cultural practices associated with Judaism were still permissible, even valuable, in Paul's view, so long as they were not seen as a means of justification. As Peterson notes, 'Paul voluntarily continued certain Jewish practices because he did not see them to be inconsistent with his new status in Christ.'[41]

At Ephesus, Paul again entered the synagogue where he appears to

---

[39] See the discussion in Bock, *Acts*, 585–6. See Numbers 6:1–21.
[40] Marshall, *Acts*, 300.
[41] Peterson, *Acts*, 520.

have received a more positive reception. They asked him if he would spend more time with them. Luke does not tell us why Paul declined the request. He simply narrates his departure along with his reply: 'I will come back if it is God's will' (verse 21).[42] Here again was Paul's quiet confidence in God's hand of providence over human affairs. The Heidelberg catechism defines providence as:

> . . . the almighty and ever present power of God by which he upholds, as with his hand, heaven and earth and all creatures and so governs them that leaf and blade, rain and drought, fruitful and barren years, food and drink, health and sickness, riches and poverty, indeed all things come to us not by chance, but by his fatherly hand.[43]

Providence is not a sort of fatalism, but a source of 'consolation and hope, of trust and courage, of humility and resignation'.[44] Herman Bavinck observes, 'Although the riddles are not resolved, faith in God's fatherly hand always again arises from the depths and even enables us to boast in afflictions.'[45] Such was Paul's comfort as he said his first farewell to the Ephesians. The doctrine of providence is an anchor for our anxieties as we trust that the one who is over all things is also the 'Father of compassion and the God of all comfort' (2 Corinthians 1:3).

We are told Paul left Priscilla and Aquila at Ephesus, where they would help the church in its infancy, mentor Apollos, and the church would meet in their home (1 Corinthians 16:19). By the time Paul wrote Romans, Priscilla and Aquila had made their way back there (Romans 16:3–4), but it seems their work in Ephesus made a significant impact, as we shall see, on Apollos and the church.

Paul went on to Caesarea, then to greet the church at Jerusalem, and then returned to the sending church at Antioch. This is the conclusion to Paul's second missionary journey. His return to Antioch reminds us that Paul was not a lone ranger establishing his own ministry but was accountable to a sending church that also provided support and partnership.[46] The book of Acts presents a picture of networks of mutual

---

[42] Some commentators suggest that Paul was keen to get to Jerusalem perhaps in connection with his vow and perhaps to be there for the Passover feast. See Peterson, *Acts*, 521.

[43] Heidelberg Catechism, Lord's Day 10, Q. & A. 27.

[44] Bavinck, *Reformed Dogmatics*, 2:594.

[45] Bavinck, *Reformed Dogmatics*, 595.

[46] Tannehill, *Narrative Unity*, 230.

support and encouragement, critical to the sustainability of the mission. Humans are designed for relationship, and whether we find ourselves as missionaries far from home or as disciples in homes and workplaces, the mutual support and encouragement of other believers is an indispensable part of our Christian life.

Having spent some time with the church at Antioch, Paul would set out once again. Although he did not yet know it, this journey would lead him eventually to imprisonment in Rome, awaiting trial before Caesar. His third journey began with him revisiting the churches in Galatia and Phrygia, strengthening all the disciples. As already noted earlier, here is further evidence of Paul's desire not simply to plant and abandon churches, but to maintain connection and to continue to help and encourage the young churches. The persevering faith of Paul and the providential hand of God enabled the establishment of new churches and the strengthening of old ones.

18

In Ephesus

ACTS 18:23–19:41

23 After spending some time in Antioch, Paul set out from there and travelled from place to place throughout the region of Galatia and Phrygia, strengthening all the disciples.

Acts 14:22 and 18:23 mark the end of the first two missionary circuits with Paul 'strengthening all the disciples' on his way to and from the sending church at Antioch.[1] Paul's time in Ephesus and surrounding regions made up the third journey, which would terminate in his arrest at Jerusalem (21:27).

Most of the narrative of the third journey is taken up with Paul's ministry in Ephesus. This leads Witherington to question whether it is useful to speak of this section as a journey at all.[2] However, other travel is included as part of Paul's work establishing and strengthening churches. This section contains some of the most remarkable and moving scenes in the book of Acts. Luke's description of Paul's Ephesian ministry draws together the key elements of Paul's work: his persuasive preaching, the Spirit's power, the growing opposition and his pastoral concern for the church.

Ephesus was another leading city within the Empire, and the commercial capital of the region. Here we see once more Paul deliberately choosing to reach centres of cultural influence. It was famed for the Temple of Artemis, one of the seven wonders of the ancient world. Religious tourism and the associated trade were important, as many came to see the great temple.[3] It was home to around 250,000 residents, 'making this the largest city of Asia Minor and the third-largest city in the Empire after Rome and Alexandria'.[4] It was a hustling bustling city, and the cult of Artemis was a central part of its communal identity.

---

[1] Peterson, *Acts*, 522.
[2] Witherington, *Acts*, 562.
[3] Witherington, *Acts*, 563.
[4] Witherington, *Acts*, 563.

1. Apollos • Acts 18:24–8

24 Meanwhile a Jew named Apollos, a native of Alexandria, came to Ephesus. He was a learned man, with a thorough knowledge of the Scriptures. 25 He had been instructed in the way of the Lord, and he spoke with great fervour[a] and taught about Jesus accurately, though he knew only the baptism of John. 26 He began to speak boldly in the synagogue. When Priscilla and Aquila heard him, they invited him to their home and explained to him the way of God more adequately.

27 When Apollos wanted to go to Achaia, the brothers and sisters encouraged him and wrote to the disciples there to welcome him. When he arrived, he was a great help to those who by grace had believed. 28 For he vigorously refuted his Jewish opponents in public debate, proving from the Scriptures that Jesus was the Messiah.

_____

a 25 Or *with fervour in the Spirit*

In verse 24 Luke introduces us to Apollos, a Jew from Alexandria who had come to Ephesus.[5] Alexandria was the second largest city of the Roman Empire and the 'leading intellectual and cultural center of the Hellenistic world'.[6] It was the city where seventy Jewish scholars had produced the Greek translation of the Hebrew Scriptures, the *Septuagint*.[7] The great Jewish philosopher, Philo, was also from Alexandria.[8] Apollos is described as a 'learned man, with a thorough knowledge of the Scriptures'. His description as 'learned' (*anēr logios*) could refer to his eloquence or intellectual abilities.[9] He was a man who had been well taught and was a gifted speaker.[10] He is described as someone who spoke with 'great fervour' and with boldness (verses 25–6). Interestingly, Luke tells us that he knew only of the baptism of John, an issue that would reappear in Acts 19:1–7. In contrast to the Baptist's disciples in the following section, Luke intends us to view Apollos as a true believer. He had been 'instructed in the way of the Lord' and 'taught

---

[5] We know from Acts 6:9 that Jews from Alexandria had come into contact with the gospel.

[6] Spencer, *Acts*, 183 cited in Peterson, *Acts*, 525.

[7] Peterson, *Acts*, 525.

[8] Bock, *Acts*, 591.

[9] Keener, *Acts*, 3:2800

[10] Calvin notes that although the gospel does not depend on eloquence (1 Corinthians 2:1–5), neither should it be despised. *Acts*, 199–200.

about Jesus accurately', though he had significant gaps in his learning (verse 25).[11]

When Priscilla and Aquila heard him, they invited him into their home to explain 'the way of God' more adequately. Here we see the importance of sound doctrine for those who would be teachers. A gifted and passionate speaker can easily mislead people without adequate instruction in the word.

Peterson also notes how Priscilla and Aquila helped Apollos in private.[12] They didn't publicly rebuke or denounce his error. Rather, they took him into their home and helped him. There is much wisdom in recognising the benefit of a more personal and edifying approach, particularly when we live in a world in which many seem to delight in rebuking others publicly, often through social media.

Priscilla and Aquila are a wonderful example of hospitality and care as they invite Apollos to their home and explain the gospel to him 'more adequately'. It is a reminder that for figures like Paul we also need individuals or couples like Priscilla and Aquila – people willing to invest their time to disciple others and encourage them in their gifts. We have observed before how these 'minor' characters play such a significant role in the advance of Luke's narrative.

We should also note here the Bible-teaching ministry of Priscilla, alongside Aquila. Christians take a variety of positions on the nature and scope of women's ministry. I myself would hold a complementarian view, believing that the Bible does not permit a woman to be an elder or preach in the public gathering of the church.[13] I recognise not everyone will agree with this position, and this is not the place to defend or critique different views. However, for those of us who take a complementarian position, we need to note here the value and necessity of the teaching ministry of Priscilla, and that it is not confined to other women (see Titus 2:3–5).[14]

The impact they have on Apollos was immediately reported. He departed from Ephesus to Achaia with the blessing of the church. He is described as being a 'great help to those who by grace had believed', for he was able to refute his Jewish opponents in debate, proving from the

---

[11] Significantly, Luke makes no mention of a need for Apollos to be baptised or re-baptised, unlike those in Acts 19:1–7, further highlighting the dissimilarity between the two.

[12] Peterson, *Acts*, 526.

[13] 1 Timothy 2:1–15.

[14] Witherington, *Women in the Earliest Churches*, 153–4.

Scriptures that Jesus was the Messiah (verses 27–8). Here again we see the value in the full variety of gifts God gives to the church, including those who have skill in apologetics and debate.

It is a repeated feature of Acts that the early churches did not seek to keep gifted leaders for themselves, but saw their responsibility and obligation to share them, sending them to new places to equip, reach and encourage others. Luke illustrates the 'interconnection and interdependence of churches in the apostolic period' – something we could learn from today.[15] Sometimes there are good reasons for keeping gifted leaders in our churches, but we must also consider the needs elsewhere and prayerfully reflect on whether we are called to raise up and send out godly and gifted people for service elsewhere.

2. The disciples of John the Baptist • Acts 19:1–7

Paul in Ephesus

19 While Apollos was at Corinth, Paul took the road through the interior and arrived at Ephesus. There he found some disciples ²and asked them, 'Did you receive the Holy Spirit when[a] you believed?'

They answered, 'No, we have not even heard that there is a Holy Spirit.'

³So Paul asked, 'Then what baptism did you receive?'

'John's baptism,' they replied.

⁴Paul said, 'John's baptism was a baptism of repentance. He told the people to believe in the one coming after him, that is, in Jesus.' ⁵On hearing this, they were baptised in the name of the Lord Jesus. ⁶When Paul placed his hands on them, the Holy Spirit came on them, and they spoke in tongues[b] and prophesied. ⁷There were about twelve men in all.

_____
a 2 Or *after*
b 6 Or *other languages*

Here is one of the more curious episodes in the book of Acts. As Paul returned to Ephesus, he met some disciples (*mathētas*) who had not yet received the Holy Spirit; more than that, they had not even heard of the Holy Spirit (verse 2). Paul enquired as to what baptism they had received, to which they replied they had received 'John's baptism' (verse 3). Having explained to them that John's baptism was a baptism of repentance pointing towards Jesus, the disciples were baptised in the name of Jesus. When Paul placed his hands on them, they received the Holy Spirit,

_____
15 Peterson, *Acts*, 523.

spoke in tongues and prophesied. Luke tells us there were about twelve men in all (verse 7). This passage raises a number of questions which we shall attempt to answer in turn.

First, how are we to understand this group of disciples who had neither heard of nor received the Holy Spirit? The other twenty-five occurrences of the word *mathētēs* (disciple) in Acts refer to Christian believers within the church.[16] And the reception of the Spirit seems to be *the* distinguishing mark of the true believer post-Pentecost.[17] Further, if we date Paul's meeting with Pricilla and Aquila (Acts 18:2) to be around AD 52–3, following the edict of Claudius, Paul's encounter with these men is some twenty years after the day of Pentecost. So how are we meant to understand a group of twelve men called disciples but who have not yet received the Spirit or even heard of the Holy Spirit?[18]

It would appear that they are perhaps second- or third-generation disciples of John the Baptist and should not be understood as Christian disciples (yet). The fact that they have not even heard of the Holy Spirit suggests they have picked up parts of John's teaching second-hand.[19] It would seem they are poorly taught followers of the Baptist's teaching. Their knowledge is deficient, and it is this lack that Paul needs to correct in order that they might receive Jesus as their Lord and Saviour.

Second, what does it mean that they have received 'John's baptism'? Again, it is worth remembering that John the Baptist had been dead more than twenty years. In what sense did they receive John's baptism? Were they baptised by John himself? This would seem unlikely unless the twelve had been with John in Galilee, relocated together to Ephesus and neither heard of nor met another Christian.

Is it possible that John's disciples continued his mission of preaching and teaching concerning the Messiah to come and the need of repentance beyond the borders of Israel? It seems we do have an extremely unusual case of a group of John's disciples who have somehow entirely missed all that Pentecost has ushered in. Somehow, they have not yet met another Christian, and it is Paul who shares with them the good news

---

[16] However, as Witherington notes, this is the only time in Acts the word *mathētēs* ('disciples') occurs without the definite article. *Acts*, 570.

[17] Witherington, *Acts*, 570.

[18] The Greek reads *oud' ei pneuma hagion estin ēkousamen* ('we have not even heard that there is a Holy Spirit'). It is possible this means they have not yet heard that the Spirit has come. Witherington, *Acts*, 571.

[19] See, for example, John's teaching on the coming Spirit in Luke 3:16.

of the gospel. The Messiah John spoke of has already come. He has been crucified, he has been raised from the dead, he has ascended into heaven to sit at the right hand of the Father and he has poured out his Holy Spirit. It is in his name that they are now to be baptised.

John's baptism was a preparatory rite that pointed to the need for repentance in light of the coming Messiah. It was he who would baptise in the Holy Spirit. It was baptism in Jesus's name that signified the reception of all the blessings that came with repentance and faith in his name.[20]

Third, how are we to understand the tongues-speech and prophecy? Some have seen in this episode justification for the view that there is a second blessing subsequent to conversion, a baptism in the Spirit, evidenced by speaking in tongues. It would be better to see this episode as the evidence that these disciples of John have received the fullness of all that John spoke about. It is in some ways a parallel to the Samaritan incident in Acts 8:15–17. Luke is not 'indicating that the gift of the Spirit is normally a supplement to baptism'.[21] It is not so much the case that they experience their own 'mini-Pentecost', more that 'Pentecost caught up on them'.[22] They were, in a sense, Old Testament believers living in the New Testament age.[23] The manifestations of tongues-speech and prophecy are 'not to be regarded as normative for ongoing Christian experience . . . they were a transitional group, whose full incorporation into the church needed to be openly demonstrated'.[24]

Fourth, why does Luke include this story here? Tannehill suggests the references to the ongoing influence of John the Baptist's ministry in Acts 18:24–19:7 are important in clarifying the relationship and differences between Christianity and the ongoing existence of followers of John the Baptist.[25] Witherington notes, 'The Baptist movement seems to have continued well into the fourth century A. D.'[26] Luke intends his readers to see clearly that the followers of John the Baptist had missed the Messiah to which he pointed. These were not just two different Jewish sects,

---

[20] Bede says, 'repentant people received this washing as a singular mark of their devotion. Nevertheless, it also figuratively pointed to Christ's baptism, by which remission of sins would be given.' See 'Acts', in ACCS 5:233.

[21] Peterson, *Acts*, 532.

[22] Stott, *Acts*, 305.

[23] Stott, *Acts*, 304.

[24] Peterson, *Acts*, 533.

[25] Tannehill, *Narrative Unity*, 233–4.

[26] Witherington, *Acts*, 569.

much as we might view differences between modern Christian denominations. The disciples of the Baptist had missed the Saviour. Luke is no universalist, applauding the sincerity of various groups and their views. Doctrinal truth matters, and it is critical that the fundamental tenets of the gospel are not missed or minimised.

3. The seven sons of Sceva • Acts 19:8–22

Acts 19:8–12: Paul in the synagogue and lecture hall

8 Paul entered the synagogue and spoke boldly there for three months, arguing persuasively about the kingdom of God. **9** But some of them became obstinate; they refused to believe and publicly maligned the Way. So Paul left them. He took the disciples with him and had discussions daily in the lecture hall of Tyrannus. **10** This went on for two years, so that all the Jews and Greeks who lived in the province of Asia heard the word of the Lord.

11 God did extraordinary miracles through Paul, **12** so that even handkerchiefs and aprons that had touched him were taken to those who were ill, and their illnesses were cured and the evil spirits left them.

Previously, Paul had been well received at Ephesus, and those present requested he spend more time with them (18:20). We see this positive reception born out, at least initially, as Paul spent three months debating and reasoning in the synagogue (19:8).

As seen previously, some of those in the synagogue began to oppose Paul. Luke describes them as becoming hardened (*esklērynonto*), and in their unbelief they spoke evil of the Way (*tēn hodon*) before the crowd (verse 9). As a result, Paul left the synagogue and held daily discussions in the lecture hall of Tyrannus.[27] Luke tells us, 'This went on for two years, so that all the Jews and Greeks who lived in the province of Asia heard the word of the Lord' (verse 10). Witherington's comments on the religious culture of Ephesus are worth noting:

---

[27] This is likely the name of the person who owned the building, or the name of a local philosopher who held classes there. The name means 'tyrant', which was perhaps the name given to him by his students. Bock suggests Paul would have taught during the middle or 'siesta' hours of the day when the hall would have been more readily available. Bock, *Acts*, 601.

> The Jewish community in Ephesus was a large one, the largest in the areas, and had been there since the third century B.C. (see Josephus, *Ant.* 12.3.2) . . . More to the point the syncretism that characterized much religion in the region had affected Judaism in that locale, with the result that both Jews and then Christians dabbled in the magical arts while still practicing their traditional religions.[28]

I suspect many of us wonder what these daily discussions in the lecture hall would have been like, and how we would love to have been there to hear them. One of the striking things about Paul's ministry was his flexibility to make the most of every opportunity. Whether Paul was in the synagogue, marketplace or lecture hall, he continuously looked for new opportunities to share the gospel with others.

Our own circumstances and situations will all be different, but it is challenging to ask ourselves whether there might be new opportunities for us to share the good news with others. It might be a mid-morning Bible study group in a home; it could be a lunchtime course at a workplace; it could be a one-to-one Bible study, or an evening meeting in a café answering difficult questions; it could be open-air conversations. We don't all have the same gifts or opportunities, but we need to lean in to those the Lord has given to us. It is striking that though this change was to some degree forced on Paul through opposition, the result was that all the Jews and Greeks heard the word of the Lord. Sometimes the Lord can use opposition and hostility to open a new door of opportunity for his word.

Through Paul, God did extraordinary miracles reminiscent of those done through Jesus (Luke 6:18–19) and Peter (Acts 5:15). Paul, like Peter, is being authenticated, as the same power at work in Jesus is at work in him. Jesus's power at work through Paul demonstrates him to be a true apostle, even though he was not one of the original twelve. Luke is keen to show that God is still powerfully at work through his appointed messengers as the gospel travels further afield. Unlike the fraudulent attempt Luke is about to describe, the power at work through Paul is the real deal.

---

[28] Witherington, *Acts*, 574.

Acts 19:13–22: True power

13 Some Jews who went around driving out evil spirits tried to invoke the name of the Lord Jesus over those who were demon-possessed. They would say, 'In the name of the Jesus whom Paul preaches, I command you to come out.' **14** Seven sons of Sceva, a Jewish chief priest, were doing this. **15** One day the evil spirit answered them, 'Jesus I know, and Paul I know about, but who are you?' **16** Then the man who had the evil spirit jumped on them and overpowered them all. He gave them such a beating that they ran out of the house naked and bleeding.

17 When this became known to the Jews and Greeks living in Ephesus, they were all seized with fear, and the name of the Lord Jesus was held in high honour. **18** Many of those who believed now came and openly confessed what they had done. **19** A number who had practised sorcery brought their scrolls together and burned them publicly. When they calculated the value of the scrolls, the total came to fifty thousand drachmas.^c **20** In this way the word of the Lord spread widely and grew in power.

21 After all this had happened, Paul decided^d to go to Jerusalem, passing through Macedonia and Achaia. 'After I have been there,' he said, 'I must visit Rome also.' **22** He sent two of his helpers, Timothy and Erastus, to Macedonia, while he stayed in the province of Asia a little longer.

---

c 19 A drachma was a silver coin worth about a day's wages.
d 21 Or *decided in the Spirit*

In verses 13–20 we encounter another striking episode in Luke's narrative. Here we are introduced to the seven sons of Sceva, a Jewish priest, who seemed to have a reputation locally for their ability to exorcise demons. This in itself is worth pausing to consider. Here we have those who were not Christians yet seemed to have some sort of authority over evil spirits (verse 13).

We recall Jesus's words in John 8:31–47, indicating that all those who reject him are still under slavery to sin and children of the devil. And Jesus also taught that a kingdom divided against itself would fall (Matthew 12:22–37). Perhaps we are meant to view these seven sons of Sceva as charlatans – those who would make a name for themselves by claiming to cast out demons. Yet in reality they had no real spiritual power or authority. The unfolding events would bear this out. As they attempted to invoke the name of Jesus in an encounter with a real demonic force, they found themselves utterly overpowered as the man

ACTS

with the evil spirit assaulted them, and all seven fled the house, naked and bleeding.[29]

Peterson notes the contrast between this story and Jesus's encounter with the Gerasene demoniac. In Luke 8:26–39 Jesus was alone while the demons were many; here there are seven sons and only one demon. The humiliation and nakedness are inflicted on the exorcists rather than the exorcised. The result in Luke 8 is total victory and restoration; here total defeat and humiliation.[30] The tragedy of the story is that 'those who claim to be able to harness the powers of the spirit world are themselves in fact not its masters but its victims'.[31] This is something worth reflecting on today when we see others who claim to have spiritual power or insight.

Luke's narrative here is not a manual for spiritual warfare. It is a real example of the awfully destructive power of evil and of the unique power of Jesus over evil, which cannot be imitated or compared. It is the unique power and authority of Jesus alone that can overthrow the forces of evil in our world. Those who 'play' with spiritual forces risk great harm to themselves and others.[32]

It is noteworthy in the apostolic correspondence with the churches that there is never an instruction to attempt the exorcism of evil spirits. The weapons with which we fight are prayer and the full armour of God (Ephesians 6:10–18). The instruction to the followers of Jesus is to shelter and fight in what he has already done in conquering evil on the cross. That is how we fight against the devil's schemes. It is the proclamation of this victory that has the greatest power to liberate from Satan's blinding, deceiving and enslaving work. Green also notes Paul's reticence here: 'Neither the miracle of the handkerchiefs nor the opposition of Satan is something Paul courted, and apparently it was enough for him to preach the message.'[33]

When this incident became known to those living in Ephesus, the Jews and the Greeks 'were all seized with fear, and the name of the Lord Jesus was held in high honour' (verse 17). The power of the word of God was

---

[29] Witherington notes the reversal of the normal procedure 'where the demon is asked to name itself before it is driven out . . . These exorcists are not known by name and so are themselves exorcised.' *Acts*, 581, note 93.

[30] Peterson, *Acts*, 540; Todd Klutz, *The Exorcism Stories in Luke–Acts: A Sociostylistic Reading* (Cambridge: Cambridge University Press, 2004), 235.

[31] Gooding, *True to the Faith*, 390.

[32] Rick Strelan, *Strange Acts: Studies in the Cultural World of the Acts of the Apostles* (Berlin: Walter de Gruyter, 2004), 112.

[33] Green, *The Word of His Grace*, 106.

seen to be infinitely greater than the power of the spells and incantations. We need to ensure our confidence remains in this all-powerful word. The temptation to see real spiritual power in new experiences, movements or programmes is real. As Gooding says, 'The desire for instant spiritual experience can make both individuals and congregations impatient of serious Bible study and Bible-based preaching.'[34] Yet here is the place 'where the real spiritual battle is to be won'.[35]

It seems many who were previously converted had continued to practise magic and sorcery, hence they came to confess what they had done and to publicly burn their scrolls (verses 18–19).[36] Peterson notes:

> In many cultures today, those who profess to be believers hold on to animistic or magical beliefs and practices. In some situations, this syncretism or folk religion is overlooked and disregarded by church leaders. However, as in ancient Ephesus, there can be no spiritual advance of the church unless such ties are broken and supernatural forces of evil are renounced.[37]

We see magic in the book of Acts in 8:9–24; 13:6–12 and here in 19:13–20. It appears to always have an evil or demonic origin and is a real power of evil confronting the apostles as they seek to spread the good news of the gospel. Such instances force us to consider our own understandings and experience. Magic in Scripture is not the same as miracle. The latter is done by the hand of God; the former is the attempted manipulation of the spirit world by human beings. The magician claims himself to be great. The miracles attest the message that God alone is great.

We should also note that the magic we see in the Bible is not what we might call 'illusion' today. Sleight of hand illusion should not be placed in the same category as the magic seen in Scripture. There is a real spiritual force of evil at work in our world, seen in occult activities, more prominent in some cultures than others. Its efficacy is demonic in origin and therefore to be treated with utmost seriousness.

We also ought to be careful how we view the magical with our children.

---

[34] Gooding, *True to the Faith*, 391.

[35] Gooding, *True to the Faith*, 391.

[36] Witherington notes that the public burning of scrolls was a subversive and radical act. A drachma was equivalent to a day's wages. We might equate fifty-thousand drachmas to a year's salary for a hundred workers. This would have been a remarkable event. See Witherington, *Acts*, 582.

[37] Peterson, *Acts*, 552.

It is easy to trivialise 'magic' as something pretend or fantastic. Equally, we can sometimes stray too far in attempting to ban any books or films that contain the magical as if they might corrupt children's minds. We need wise and careful discernment. In a sense, depictions of spiritual or magical realms are *more* real than a lot of other secular media we consume. Worlds containing lions, dragons, angels and demons furnish our literary imagination, enabling us to be better readers of Scripture. We ought not be overly prescriptive with how other believers engage with such material, but we all need to carefully reflect on how we receive and interpret their stories.

After this, Paul left Ephesus to visit Jerusalem, passing through Macedonia and Achaia.[38] Paul's pattern of revisiting previously established churches is something already seen in Acts 15:36–16:5; 18:23. Paul also sent two of his helpers, Timothy and Erastus, to Macedonia. His intent was to visit Rome, and this he would do, though not under the circumstances for which he was hoping.

4. The riot in Ephesus • Acts 19:23–41

The riot in Ephesus

23 About that time there arose a great disturbance about the Way. 24 A silversmith named Demetrius, who made silver shrines of Artemis, brought in a lot of business for the craftsmen there. 25 He called them together, along with the workers in related trades, and said: 'You know, my friends, that we receive a good income from this business. 26 And you see and hear how this fellow Paul has convinced and led astray large numbers of people here in Ephesus and in practically the whole province of Asia. He says that gods made by human hands are no gods at all. 27 There is danger not only that our trade will lose its good name, but also that the temple of the great goddess Artemis will be discredited; and the goddess herself, who is worshipped throughout the province of Asia and the world, will be robbed of her divine majesty.'

28 When they heard this, they were furious and began shouting: 'Great is Artemis of the Ephesians!' 29 Soon the whole city was in an uproar. The people seized Gaius and Aristarchus, Paul's travelling companions from Macedonia, and all of them rushed into the theatre together. 30 Paul wanted to appear before the crowd, but the disciples would not let him. 31 Even some of the officials of the province, friends of

---

[38] Paul's own account of this trip is in Romans 15:23–6, 'where taking the collection for Jerusalem is a major motive for the trip (1 Corinthians 16:1–4; 2 Corinthians 8–9)'. Bock, *Acts*, 605.

Paul, sent him a message begging him not to venture into the theatre.

32 The assembly was in confusion: some were shouting one thing, some another. Most of the people did not even know why they were there. **33** The Jews in the crowd pushed Alexander to the front, and they shouted instructions to him. He motioned for silence in order to make a defence before the people. **34** But when they realised he was a Jew, they all shouted in unison for about two hours: 'Great is Artemis of the Ephesians!'

35 The city clerk quietened the crowd and said: 'Fellow Ephesians, doesn't all the world know that the city of Ephesus is the guardian of the temple of the great Artemis and of her image, which fell from heaven? **36** Therefore, since these facts are undeniable, you ought to calm down and not do anything rash. **37** You have brought these men here, though they have neither robbed temples nor blasphemed our goddess. **38** If, then, Demetrius and his fellow craftsmen have a grievance against anybody, the courts are open and there are proconsuls. They can press charges. **39** If there is anything further you want to bring up, it must be settled in a legal assembly. **40** As it is, we are in danger of being charged with rioting because of what happened today. In that case we would not be able to account for this commotion, since there is no reason for it.' **41** After he had said this, he dismissed the assembly.

In verse 20, Luke reported that 'the word of the Lord spread widely and grew in power'.[39] As a consequence, we read of another incident that happened as the church began to grow in number and reputation.

One of the silversmiths, Demetrius, brought together his fellow craftsman, since they were concerned about the growing influence and impact of Paul's message. They made silver shrines which would have been miniature replicas of the temple of Diana.[40] Artemis ('Diana' in Latin) was the daughter of Zeus and seen as a provider of help and health. She was a fertility goddess, a 'huntress with a bow and arrow, and the goddess of death'.[41] The Temple of Artemis was four times larger than the Parthenon at Athens and one of the seven wonders of the world.[42] The cult of Artemis was one of the largest in the ancient world, and a festival in her honour was held each spring.[43] The cult of Artemis was

---

[39] This is one of Luke's summary statements. See 6:7; 12:24.

[40] Peterson, *Acts*, 545.

[41] Bock, *Acts*, 607.

[42] Witherington, *Acts*, 587. Bock also notes the temple was larger than a football field – the largest building in the Greek world. It was the central site, though there were thirty-three shines to her in other locales. Bock, *Acts*, 607–8.

[43] Bock, *Acts*, 608.

at the heart of all aspects of life in Ephesus.[44] We can see how Paul's message that such 'gods' were really no gods at all was a bold challenge to one of the most significant 'gods' of the day.

The message was spreading and obviously threatening to the trade and income of Demetrius and his fellow tradesmen. Demetrius claimed that he had a concern for the reputation of Artemis (verse 27), but Luke's report leaves the reader in little doubt that the main concern of Demetrius was his income (verses 25, 27). One of Luke's repeated themes is the evil of the greedy pursuit of wealth, particularly where people are mistreated in the pursuit of economic gain.[45] It is also likely that in a shame–honour culture the threat to the honour of the tradesmen was a threat to their income also.[46]

As is often the case with such events, there are those who are incensed and those who seem to simply enjoy the spectacle. Luke tells us soon the whole city was in uproar (verse 29), though many seem to have had no idea what was going on (verse 32).

The mob took hold of Gaius and Aristarchus and dragged them into the open-air theatre. Bruce suggests this open-air theatre, often used for festivals and performances, may have been able to hold as many as 25,000 people.[47] The very real danger of the situation is seen as companions and friends of Paul begged him not to appear in front of the crowd, even though that was his desire (verses 30–31).

In the confusion of the assembly, a Jewish man, Alexander, was pushed forward to make a defence. It is unclear as to why he was put forward, though it is possible the Jews wanted their representative to dissociate them from the Christians.[48] Yet when they realised he was a Jew, they drowned him out with chants of 'Great is Artemis'. Luke reports that this continued for two hours. One can only imagine the fear Gaius and

---

[44] Rick Strelan, *Paul, Artemis, and the Jews in Ephesus* (Berlin: Walter de Gruyter, 1996), 24.

[45] For example, see Luke 16:1–14; 19:1–10; Acts 5:1–11; 8:20–22; 16:16–18. Calvin says, 'Demetrius doth in this place filthily betray his malice . . . He doth not inquire whether this be true or no; but being blinded with a desire to get gain, he is carried headlong to oppress . . . every one of us ought more to suspect himself, when the question is touching our own gain and profit, lest the same covetous desire which made these men so mad take away all difference of justice and injustice.' *Acts*, 225–6.

[46] Witherington, *Acts*, 592.

[47] Bruce, *Acts*, 418.

[48] Peterson, *Acts*, 549.

Aristarchus experienced as they endured that two hours, wondering what might happen to them.

Luke's reporting suggests that eventually the city clerk arrived to deal with the situation. He pacified the crowd by speaking of the undoubted greatness of Artemis and imploring them to do nothing rash (verses 35–6). He sounds almost like a preacher encouraging his congregation to trust in their great goddess. Gamaliel had spoken with a similar pragmatism in Acts 5:33–9. The clerk's defence of Paul and his companions was that they had not robbed temples or blasphemed the name of Artemis (verse 37).

In fact, the message of the gospel *was* a direct threat to Artemis, but the clerk was either unaware or unwilling to acknowledge this. If Demetrius and his colleagues had a grievance, they were to take it through the courts and settle in a legal manner. The clerk's fear was that the people of Ephesus might be charged with rioting, since there was no reason for the assembly. Having said this, he dismissed the crowd.

Though this is not a formal trial scene, it is another example of the way in which the early Christian movement encountered and had an impact on societies and cultures. As the gospel gained a foothold, so public opposition and hostility grew. The authorities, it seems, did not quite know how to deal with this movement. It did not appear at first glance to be an illegal movement, but neither was it a recognised religious group, as, for example, was Judaism. From this point on in the narrative Paul will be caught up in further arrests, hearings and trials as growth and opposition continue.

In the midst of the chaos and confusion, we can observe the hand of God. The word of the Lord continued to spread and grow in power. Paul's three-year ministry in Ephesus had seen significant results that had affected the wider culture and society. He would describe this to the Corinthians as a 'great door for effective work' (1 Corinthians 16:8–9).

God is at work to advance the gospel, grow the church and protect his servants. The opposing powers, whether human or demonic, are really powerless to stop the ongoing work of the risen and exalted Lord Jesus by the power of his Spirit. This truth, seen repeatedly through Acts, gives believers today great confidence to continue living as faithful servants, confident in God's power and purposes, however chaotic and difficult our circumstances appear.

There is one more challenge to consider from Paul's ministry in Ephesus. Revelation 2:1–7 shows us it is possible to have the apostle Paul as your pastor for three years and yet still, over the course of time, to lose your first love. The church had endured hardship, it had rejected evil, it had worked hard, yet somehow, in a few short years, it had lost its love for the Saviour in its activism and even in its pursuit of sound doctrine. Reading Acts 19 in the wider context of Scripture reminds us of our need to keep close to Jesus, to rejoice often in our salvation, lest our right doing and right believing actually cool our hearts to our beautiful Saviour.

19

Farewell to the Ephesian Elders

ACTS 20

Following the riot at Ephesus, the narrative resumes with Paul's desire to travel to Jerusalem and Rome (Acts 19:21; Acts 20:16). He wants to reach Jerusalem with the collection by Pentecost.[1] He hopes then to continue his missionary travels on to Rome. He will indeed reach both destinations, but his reception will not be that for which he may hope.

Wall notes a sort of parallelism here between Paul and Jesus in their journeys towards Jerusalem and the reception that awaits. Here is Paul in solidarity with Jesus, whose humiliation and suffering in Jerusalem is for the benefit of the nations.[2]

The chapter is bookended by two farewells – first to the disciples in Ephesus (verse 1) and then to the elders of Ephesus (verses 36–8). It sounds a sombre note in the narrative as Paul's journey leads him towards an unknown and unpleasant fate.

The brief description of the churches scattered around the Aegean, in the opening half of the chapter, resembles that of the early church in Jerusalem – devoted to the apostles teaching, fellowship, the breaking of bread and prayer. They care for the needy and are strengthened by the word of grace.

Paul's farewell to the Ephesian elders, in the second half of the chapter, is the most moving of his three major speeches.[3] It summarises Paul's ministry and his heart, leaving the church instruction and example to follow.

---

[1] More information about the collection can be seen in Acts 24:17; Romans 15:26–7; 1 Corinthians 16:3–4; 2 Corinthians 8–9.

[2] Wall, *Acts*, 275–6.

[3] See Acts 13:16–41; 17:22–31 and here in 20:18–38.

1. Travels and travelling companions • Acts 20:1–6

Through Macedonia and Greece

20 When the uproar had ended, Paul sent for the disciples and, after encouraging them, said goodbye and set out for Macedonia. ²He travelled through that area, speaking many words of encouragement to the people, and finally arrived in Greece, ³where he stayed three months. Because some Jews had plotted against him just as he was about to sail for Syria, he decided to go back through Macedonia. ⁴He was accompanied by Sopater son of Pyrrhus from Berea, Aristarchus and Secundus from Thessalonica, Gaius from Derbe, Timothy also, and Tychicus and Trophimus from the province of Asia. ⁵These men went on ahead and waited for us at Troas. ⁶But we sailed from Philippi after the Festival of Unleavened Bread, and five days later joined the others at Troas, where we stayed seven days.

After the disturbance of the riot in Ephesus, Paul said goodbye to the disciples at Ephesus and set sail for Macedonia. This section of Luke's narrative contains details of Paul's movements, presumably because Luke was a travelling companion, as evidenced by the repeated 'we' statements.[4]

Paul travelled through the region – his purpose stated in verse 2 – 'speaking many words of encouragement to the people'. He likely used the opportunity to strengthen those churches previously established in Philippi, Thessalonica and Berea.[5] Here again we see the pastoral heart of the apostle in seeking to encourage the believers in the churches he had previously planted. The word 'encourage' (*parakalesas*) has also occurred in Acts 14:22; 15:32; 16:40.

Luke tells us Paul finally arrived in Greece, where he stayed for three months. Peterson suggests this would have been in Corinth, from where he wrote his epistle to the Romans in the winter of AD 56–7.[6]

It is noteworthy that Paul's travel plans often seem to change. In this case opposition arises which forces him to travel through Macedonia rather than sail for Syria. While Paul is not afraid to face opposition, even persecution, he is also wise enough to avoid it where possible.

In verses 4–6 we meet a number of Paul's other travelling companions:

---

[4] For example, Acts 20:6, 7, 13, 14, 15. These travels probably occurred between AD 55 and 57. Bock, *Acts*, 617.

[5] Stott, *Acts*, 316.

[6] Peterson, *Acts*, 555. See Romans 16:1, 23.

Sopater from Berea; Aristarchus and Secundus from Thessalonica; Gaius from Derbe; Timothy also, and Tychicus and Trophimus from the province of Asia.

We have already met Gaius and Aristarchus. They were the men seized and rushed into the theatre in Ephesus in Paul's absence (Acts 19:29). Aristarchus is also mentioned in Paul's list of imprisoned co-workers in Colossians 4:10 and Philemon 24. Gaius appears again in Romans 16:23 as the person in whose home the church meets. Tychicus, too, seems to play a significant role in Paul's ministry. He appears to be the person who bears the letter to the Ephesians and Colossians (Ephesians 6:21; Colossians 4:7). He is also sent to Crete to relieve Titus (Titus 3:12). Trophimus only appears outside Acts in 2 Timothy 4:20 where we are told he was left sick in Miletus. These travelling companions would appear to be representatives of the churches, accompanying Paul in taking the collection to Jerusalem.[7]

Stott suggests three things we can learn from this list of fellow travellers: first, the sense of unity among the early churches; second, the fruitfulness of Paul's missionary work in establishing such healthy churches; third, the servant-hearted missionary mindset of the early churches. They are glad to help Paul in his work of spreading the gospel and carrying the collection to the needy believers in Jerusalem.[8]

There is a tantalising detail in verse 6 as we see Paul (and Luke) celebrate the Passover in Philippi. Is this a further indication that a neat break between Judaism and Christianity had not yet fully occurred? Jewish believers still celebrated their ancestral festivals while seeing Jesus as the fulfilment of all that Passover pointed towards. Is it possible the previously pagan Gentiles, who had now been converted, joined in with this festival? Or could it be they were celebrating the Christian fulfilment of Passover – Easter – together as believers?[9] This is one of those places in Acts where we find ourselves wanting more information than Luke provides. As interpreters we need to be careful we do not read more into Scripture than is actually there.

2. A soporific Bible study • Acts 20:7–16

Eutychus raised from the dead at Troas

7 On the first day of the week we came together to break bread. Paul spoke to the people and, because he intended to leave the next day, kept on talking until

---

7 Witherington, *Acts*, 602–3.
8 Stott, *Acts*, 318.
9 Marshall, *Acts*, 325.

midnight. **8** There were many lamps in the upstairs room where we were meeting. **9** Seated in a window was a young man named Eutychus, who was sinking into a deep sleep as Paul talked on and on. When he was sound asleep, he fell to the ground from the third storey and was picked up dead. **10** Paul went down, threw himself on the young man and put his arms round him. 'Don't be alarmed,' he said. 'He's alive!' **11** Then he went upstairs again and broke bread and ate. After talking until daylight, he left. **12** The people took the young man home alive and were greatly comforted.

Paul's farewell to the Ephesian elders

13 We went on ahead to the ship and sailed for Assos, where we were going to take Paul aboard. He had made this arrangement because he was going there on foot. **14** When he met us at Assos, we took him aboard and went on to Mitylene. **15** The next day we set sail from there and arrived off Chios. The day after that we crossed over to Samos, and on the following day arrived at Miletus. **16** Paul had decided to sail past Ephesus to avoid spending time in the province of Asia, for he was in a hurry to reach Jerusalem, if possible, by the day of Pentecost.

This is one of the more unusual, even humorous, episodes in the book of Acts. The travelling companions, having been separated briefly, were reunited at Troas, where, Luke tells us, 'On the first day of the week we came together to break bread' (verse 7). This is perhaps an indication that the early church viewed the first day of the week as the Christian Sabbath, or, as it is elsewhere termed, the Lord's Day – a 'continual memorial to the Lord's resurrection'.[10] Christians have debated the extent to which the commandment regarding Sabbath continues into the new covenant era, but what seems undeniable is that the early church did celebrate the first day of the week and held it as a special 'Lord's Day'.

The meeting to break bread possibly suggests that some sort of Lord's supper was a feature of their weekly meeting.[11] This would likely have been part of a meal. If this were the case, it would challenge the view that the Lord's supper is something that can be practised very infrequently. We must exercise due caution as Luke's narrative is descriptive, not

---

[10] 1 Corinthians 16:2; Revelation 1:10; Wall, *Acts*, 277.

[11] Wall, *Acts*, 277, suggests this 'refers to a common meal rather than to the Lord's supper and is symbolic of their social and spiritual solidarity'. However, Witherington, *Acts*, 606, thinks it is possible that the Lord's Supper was shared in the context of a Graeco-Roman meal.

prescriptive. Yet we do get a sense of the importance of regular meetings to share fellowship and food (physical and spiritual).

Since Paul intended to depart from Troas the next day, he felt it necessary to make the most of this last opportunity to speak with the believers. This was most likely an extended discussion based on the Jewish Scriptures and Jesus's life and death in fulfilment. Luke tells us Paul spoke with them late into the night. A young man named Eutychus, whose name means lucky(!), was seated in the window. As Paul talked 'on and on', Eutychus drifted into a deep sleep. As a result, he fell out of the third-storey window and was picked up dead on the ground outside (verse 9).[12]

Paul, in an act reminiscent of Jesus, Peter, Elijah and Elisha, threw himself on the young man and brought him back to life.[13] They all went back upstairs and continued to eat and talk until daybreak. Luke adds, with some understatement, 'The people took the young man home alive and were greatly comforted' (verse 12).

Why does Luke include this story here? It is a remarkable miracle, without doubt. It would seem the intent is to link Paul once again with Peter who had performed a similar miracle with Dorcas in Acts 9. Further, it would link both miracles to Jesus and to the Old Testament prophets Elijah and Elisha. Such miracles attest the divine authentication of these messengers. They are in the same line and they have the same power working in them as the great prophets and even Jesus himself. Throughout the book of Acts, the risen and exalted Jesus continues to work and act, by the power of his Spirit, through his chosen servants. This miracle is one more piece of evidence demonstrating the divine appointment of Paul as apostle to the Gentiles.

It is possible it may also serve to remind the reader of the need to remain spiritually alert and awake. Before dismissing such a reading too quickly, it is worth recalling how such imagery is used elsewhere in Luke–Acts. Peter, John and James almost missed the transfiguration because they were 'very sleepy' (Luke 9:32). In the garden of Gethsemane Jesus rebuked his disciples for sleeping when they should have been praying (Luke 22:45–6). Elsewhere Jesus instructed his followers to be watchful and ready at any hour (Luke 12:35–40; 21:34–6). We must be cautious about fanciful spiritualising in our interpretation of narrative. However,

---

[12] Some scholars debate whether he was really dead, as Paul says, 'He's alive.' However, Luke seems clear the boy was dead (verse 9), and it makes little sense to record the narrative if he merely knocked himself unconscious.

[13] See Mark 5:40; Acts 9:40–41; 1 Kings 17:21–2; 2 Kings 4:34–5.

it seems there is here at least the possibility of observing the intertextual connections, reflecting on the dangers of spiritual drowsiness and the importance of vigilance.[14] This interpretation was not uncommon among the church fathers.

Perhaps also in this brief episode we see the gospel in miniature. We see the community gathered on the Lord's Day around the table and the word. The gospel word and the gospel meal speak of the life-giving power of grace, something enacted in the raising of Eutychus.[15] Paul's farewell meal is reminiscent of Jesus's final meal with his disciples.[16] As Paul follows in the footsteps of the Master, we know that the triumph and tribulation must walk hand in hand.

Verses 13–16 describe Paul's travels to Assos, Mitylene, Chios, Samos and Miletus.[17] Paul's desire was to reach Jerusalem by Pentecost. He wished to celebrate the festival and deliver the Macedonian collection to the believers in Jerusalem.[18]

Bock notes the sense this unit provides of Paul's concern for the churches: 'to ensure that he leaves behind not a monument to himself, but Christians who are a monument to God in their faithfulness'.[19]

3. A final farewell • Acts 20:17–38

17 From Miletus, Paul sent to Ephesus for the elders of the church. **18** When they arrived, he said to them: 'You know how I lived the whole time I was with you, from the first day I came into the province of Asia. **19** I served the Lord with great humility and with tears and in the midst of severe testing by the plots of my Jewish opponents. **20** You know that I have not hesitated to preach anything that would be helpful to you but have taught you publicly and from house to house. **21** I have declared to both

---

[14] Andrew Arterbury, 'The Downfall of Eutychus: How Ancient Understandings of Sleep Illuminate Acts 20:7–12', in *Contemporary Studies in Acts*, ed. Thomas E. Phillips (Mercer: MUP, 2009), 201–21.

[15] Wall, *Acts*, 278.

[16] Tannehill, *Narrative Unity*, 251.

[17] It was at Miletus that Paul met the Ephesian elders. This would have been a journey of around thirty miles each way for these elders. Peterson, *Acts*, 562.

[18] The distance from Miletus to Jerusalem is around 610 miles and Paul had, by this point, around five weeks to get there (20:6–16). Bock, *Acts*, 621.

[19] Bock, *Acts*, 622.

Jews and Greeks that they must turn to God in repentance and have faith in our Lord Jesus.

22 'And now, compelled by the Spirit, I am going to Jerusalem, not knowing what will happen to me there. 23 I only know that in every city the Holy Spirit warns me that prison and hardships are facing me. 24 However, I consider my life worth nothing to me; my only aim is to finish the race and complete the task the Lord Jesus has given me – the task of testifying to the good news of God's grace.

25 'Now I know that none of you among whom I have gone about preaching the kingdom will ever see me again. 26 Therefore, I declare to you today that I am innocent of the blood of any of you. 27 For I have not hesitated to proclaim to you the whole will of God. 28 Keep watch over yourselves and all the flock of which the Holy Spirit has made you overseers. Be shepherds of the church of God, a which he bought with his own blood. b 29 I know that after I leave, savage wolves will come in among you and will not spare the flock. 30 Even from your own number men will arise and distort the truth in order to draw away disciples after them. 31 So be on your guard! Remember that for three years I never stopped warning each of you night and day with tears.

32 'Now I commit you to God and to the word of his grace, which can build you up and give you an inheritance among all those who are sanctified. 33 I have not coveted anyone's silver or gold or clothing. 34 You yourselves know that these hands of mine have supplied my own needs and the needs of my companions. 35 In everything I did, I showed you that by this kind of hard work we must help the weak, remembering the words the Lord Jesus himself said: "It is more blessed to give than to receive." '

36 When Paul had finished speaking, he knelt down with all of them and prayed. 37 They all wept as they embraced him and kissed him. 38 What grieved them most was his statement that they would never see his face again. Then they accompanied him to the ship.

---

a 28 Many manuscripts *of the Lord*

b 28 Or *with the blood of his own Son*

Paul's farewell to the Ephesian elders is surely the most moving of all of the speeches in the book of Acts. It is also the only speech in the book that is addressed to Christians. We can almost feel Paul's heartbeat for the church and imagine the tearful embrace as he said his final farewell and boarded the ship. It is a crucial speech as it provided critical instruction for the elders in seeking to care for the church in the post-apostolic era. Wall suggests it is analogous to Jesus's commissioning speech to his apostles in Acts 1:4–8. Here we have the departure of the leader and the succession of new leaders.[20]

The speech gives us the twin foundations of godly leaders: godly character and sound doctrine. Whatever other gifts leaders may have, these two are foundational. The speech contains repeated words or phrases suggesting the following structure:[21]

- 'You know' (verse 18)
  o 'with great humility and with tears' (verse 19)
    ▪ 'I have not hesitated' (*hypesteilamēn* – verse 20)
      • 'I have declared' (*diamartyromenos* – verse 21)
        o 'The Holy Spirit warns me' (*diamartyretai* – verse 23)
      • 'testifying' (*diamartyrasthai* – verse 24)
    ▪ 'I have not hesitated' (*hypesteilamēn* – verse 27)
  o 'night and day with tears' (verse 31)
- 'You know' (verse 34)

If this analysis has merit, we can see Paul's emphasis on the importance of the witness provided by the Spirit to him and by him to the church. The 'witness' is that central energising 'word of grace' that drives him on, although he knows trouble awaits, but desires only to finish the race.

Paul begins his speech with a moving account of his own ministry: 'You know how I lived the whole time I was with you' (verse 18). He describes his three-year ministry as being one of humility and tears, and 'in the midst of severe testing by the plots of my Jewish opponents' (verse 19). The humility spoken of is perhaps not so much of manner, but rather of circumstances. He ministered under difficult conditions, often facing threats from different quarters. His humility (*tapeinophrosynēs*) speaks of a sense of weakness and vulnerability.

Paul did not claim to be any kind of super-apostle. His hardships made him weep. His circumstances were difficult. He was not ashamed to confess his weakness and his tears. How many leaders, out of a sense of pride, are unable to show weakness or confess their struggles? Do churches provide safe environments for pastors to be vulnerable? Do we expect them to be omnicompetent beings? If so, we are, perhaps, setting them up for a fall.

Further, Paul's description of his own humility reminds us that ministers

---

[20] Wall, *Acts*, 281.
[21] Broadly following Tannehill, though my suggestion offers a centre and notes the 'humility and tears'. See *Narrative Unity*, 253.

should never be overbearing or domineering.[22] Sadly, there have been many cases of ministers having to resign their positions because they abused their positions of power to intimidate, manipulate and coerce others. Humble servants, who serve with tears, should never mistreat the sheep as if they were somehow an end to their own vanity projects. It is seldom quite this obvious, but the temptation is subtle, and Paul's example reminds us of its utter inappropriateness for the under-shepherd.

In such an environment, Paul reminded the Ephesian elders that he had 'not hesitated to preach anything that would be helpful to you' (verse 20). He had taught them in public and house to house. Here we see the variety of Paul's approach. Paul was not just the 'big name' preacher wheeled out onto the platform before the masses each week, then not seen again until the following Sunday. He was in people's homes, he was in the marketplace, the synagogue, the lecture hall. He was involved in the lives of those he served in a way that seems quite different from those caught up in the modern cult of the celebrity pastor.

The main thrust of his message had been on the necessity of repentance and faith (verse 21). This is the essence of the apostolic message. The gospel is a message that calls for repentance – a recognition and confession of sin, and a turning away from it. It is also a call to faith – to put all our trust in Christ and his work on the cross, bearing the penalty we deserve in our place. Sadly, in some churches today, the message of repentance and faith has been lost. It has been exchanged for a message that emphasises love and acceptance, and plays down any need for repentance before a holy God. The Scripture 'God is love' (1 John 4:8) is quoted, while 'God is light' (1 John 1:5) is neglected.

Of course, we should always want to make much of God's love, mercy and grace. Yet if we fail to talk about the seriousness of sin and the need for repentance, we cheapen mercy and grace and make them paradoxically much smaller and less significant. On 31 October 1517, Martin Luther nailed his Ninety-five Theses to the cathedral door in Wittenberg. They were his protest against abuses in the Catholic Church of his day. The very first thesis reads, 'When our Lord and Master, Jesus Christ, said, "Repent" (Matthew 4:17), he willed the entire life of believers to be one of repentance.'[23] A gospel that requires no repentance is really no gospel at all.

---

[22] Kisau, 'Acts', in *ABC*, 1360.

[23] Martin Luther, *Luther's Works, Volume 31: Career of the Reformer I*, ed. Jaroslav Jan Pelikan, Hilton C. Oswald, and Helmut T. Lehmann (Philadelphia: Fortress Press, 1999), 25.

Paul knew his own future to be uncertain. He claimed his only certainty was that prison and hardship faced him in every place (verse 23). His only aim was to 'finish the race and complete the task the Lord Jesus has given me – the task of testifying to the good news of God's grace' (verse 24). It is a remarkable statement of Paul's willingness to face any hardship in being faithful to God's call on his life. He knew things would be difficult. He knew his life would likely be cut short. Yet he considered his life as being worth nothing, as long as he can faithfully finish the work entrusted to him. The Damascus Road experience had completely transformed him from a man who would kill those who love Jesus to a man willing to be killed for his love for Jesus.

His mission was to testify to the good news of God's grace (verse 24). It was this grace of God that had transformed his life and given him his new perspective – a willingness to die for the gospel. The good news of grace is good news to those who will come in repentance and faith. It is God's undeserved riches given at Christ's expense. It was Luther's discovery of grace that kickstarted the Reformation. He understood that it wasn't 'grace plus works' that saved a person, but grace alone – all of God's work for us, gifted to us, by the work of the Son. This gospel of grace was spreading through the Empire, transforming individual lives, having a huge impact on societies and cultures. This was what Paul was absolutely committed to and willing to die for.

Paul's awareness of his fate led him to give his pastoral charge to the Ephesian elders. He considered himself innocent of their blood, for he had declared to them the whole counsel of God. The counsel (boulēn) refers to God's sovereign purposes through the work of Christ, and then, by his Spirit, in the mission of the church.[24]

Their duty was to, 'Keep watch over yourselves and all the flock of which the Holy Spirit has made you overseers. Be shepherds of the church of God, which he bought with his own blood (verse 28). Peterson notes, 'This Trinitarian reference makes it clear that the church belongs to God and is fundamentally in his care.'[25]

It is noteworthy that their first duty is to keep watch over themselves. Before they are able to take care of the flock, they need to tend their own souls.[26] The pastor's first duty is to feed himself and watch his own

---

[24] Acts 2:22–3; 4:28; 5:38; 13:36. Wall, *Acts*, 283.

[25] Peterson, *Acts*, 568.

[26] Stott, *Acts*, 326.

life and doctrine carefully, for a sick or malnourished shepherd is in no position to give care to the sheep.

Here, too, is a reminder of the one to whom the church belongs. The flock belongs to God – he has purchased them with 'the blood of his Own'.[27] All pastors are under-shepherds. A pastor should not refer to his local situation as 'my church'. The church does not belong to the pastor. It belongs to Jesus. He rules it, by the power of his Holy Spirit, through his word, and at the hands of his appointed under-shepherds.

If pastor are to remain humble and faithful, they must remember to whom the church really belongs. The reference to the 'blood of his Own' reminds us of the atoning work of Christ. His death on the cross is the foundation of the church in establishing its existence and maintaining it as the 'eschatological people of God'.[28] As Stott reminds us, pastors will be helped to persevere in their work when they see the immense value and worth of the sheep to the Great Shepherd.[29]

Richard Baxter, a minister from Kidderminster, wrote *The Reformed Pastor* in 1656. It is, in essence, an exposition of Acts 20:28. As he concludes his chapter on 'the oversight of the flock', he says the following:

> Oh then, let us hear these arguments of Christ, whenever we feel ourselves grow dull and careless: 'Did I die for them, and will not thou look after them? Were they worth my blood and are they not worth thy labour? Did I come down from heaven to earth to seek and to save that which was lost; and will thou not go to the next door or street or village to seek them . . . was I willing to make thee a co-worker with me, and wilt thou refuse that little that lieth upon thy hands? Every time we look upon our congregations, let us believingly remember that they are the purchase of Christ's blood, and therefore should be regarded by us with the deepest interest and the most tender affection.'[30]

---

[27] Witherington suggests this translation makes sense of the phrase 'his own blood' (*tou haimatos tou idiou*) and is therefore a reference to the Son. *Acts*, 623. Although the early church did not have a problem with the idea of God shedding his blood. Here is Bede: 'He did not hesitate to say "the blood of God," because of the oneness of person in two natures of the same Jesus Christ.' Bede, 'Acts', in ACCS 5:254.

[28] Peterson, *Acts*, 570.

[29] Stott, *Acts*, 329.

[30] Richard Baxter, *The Reformed Pastor* (repr. Edinburgh: Banner of Truth, 1974), 131–2.

It is also worth noting the three different words used of leaders here. The terms are *presbyterous* ('elders', verse 17); *episkopous* ('overseers', verse 28); *poimainein* ('shepherd', verse 28). This would indicate that these terms are used synonymously of the same group, rather than describing different types or tiers of leaders.[31] There are only two offices in the New Testament: elders and deacons. Further, there is a plurality of elders responsible for shepherding the flock, rather than a single individual (see Acts 14:23).

Significantly, the infinitive verb, *poimainein* ('shepherd'), amplifies the imperative 'keep watch' (*prosechete*) and the noun 'overseers' (*episkopous*). In other words, the overseers shepherd by keeping watch, particularly in the light of the threat expounded in verses 29–31.

The necessity of faithful shepherding is seen in verses 29–31, where Paul warns the church that after his departure, 'savage wolves will come in among you and will not spare the flock. Even from your own number men will arise and distort the truth in order to draw away disciples after them.' This is a sobering warning, not least because the wolves will arise even from within the church. As Peterson notes:

> History shows that in every generation it has been all too easy for Christian leaders to attract others to their own way of thinking . . . Pastors need to be realistic about the way sin can manifest itself in distortions of the truth and create destructive divisions among Christians.[32]

Doctrinal purity is an important part of the pastor's work in guarding the sheep. Calvin says, 'The corruption of doctrine is a most deadly plague to the sheep . . . the fountain and beginning of this evil is noted, because they will draw disciples after them. Therefore, ambition is the mother of all heresies.'[33]

Paul is here showing us what it means to be a shepherd. It means to teach truth and protect against error. Sometimes today the work of the shepherd is described in softer, more therapeutic terms, as if the primary call of the shepherd were something more akin to a chaplain or counsellor. While this care and compassion for the flock is surely a part of the call, we should note the primary emphasis of Paul's description of 'pastoral care' falls on the doctrinal – teaching truth and protecting against error.[34]

---

[31] 'According to the use of Scripture bishops differ nothing from elders.' Calvin, *Acts*, 255.

[32] Peterson, *Acts*, 571.

[33] Calvin, *Acts*, 258.

[34] Stott, *Acts*, 323.

We should note here that when it comes to the pursuit of doctrinal purity, there is a careful balance to be struck. On the one hand, some pastors (and church members) seem obsessed with finding every whiff of error and rooting it out as if they were part of the Spanish Inquisition. They will die on almost any doctrinal hill. The boundaries of doctrinal soundness are drawn in ever smaller circles. There is little charity or grace given to those who disagree. Brothers and sisters are too quickly dismissed as wolves. On the other hand, there are those who seem to care little about doctrinal purity. Any and every person who claims to be a follower of Jesus is accepted and partnered with, regardless of their theological and moral convictions. Wise pastors must work hard to understand the issues around which we can unite with others and those on which we must separate.[35]

As Paul closes his speech, he commits them to 'God and to the word of his grace, which can build you up and give you an inheritance among all those who are sanctified' (verse 32). Here again is Paul's confidence in the word of grace. It is this word that enables the church to grow and persevere to the end. We must never tire of the word of grace. Sometimes Christians seem to think these things somehow basic or dull. They desire to move on to more controversial theological debates, or new strategies for successful ministry.

The truth the believer needs to hear every week is the word of grace. Whether we are speaking to ourselves, to fellow elders, to believers or to non-believers, we all still need to hear the same message of grace. It punctures our desire to make ourselves righteous through our own efforts and points us continually back to all that Jesus has done. This gives us the comfort and encouragement to live for Jesus wherever he has placed us. As soon as we forget grace, we find ourselves again in the pit of guilt, deeply aware of our failures and limitations. The 'word of his grace' picks us up and tells us the basis on which we are loved and accepted. This is the message that builds up the church and assures her of her future inheritance.

Paul concludes by reminding the Ephesian elders of his own character – that he never took advantage of them financially. He provided for his own needs and demonstrated his concern for the weak.[36] I recently heard the story of a disgraced pastor who had to resign his post following

---

[35] For more on this, see Ortlund, *Finding the Right Hills to Die On*.

[36] This may have been especially necessary as Paul was carrying with him the collection for Jerusalem. Witherington, *Acts*, 625.

revelations of abuse and bullying. As he resigned, his church gave him a severance package of one year's salary. His salary for the previous year had been US$650,000 . It is hard to fathom how any church could have thought this was an appropriate sum to support the man and his family in the work of the gospel. It is hard not to draw the conclusion that this man had, to use Paul's words, coveted the flock's silver and gold. As Paul notes elsewhere, it is appropriate, where possible, to support a pastor's needs so he can devote himself to the work full-time.[37] Yet such support should be coupled with a concern (shown by the pastor and the church) for the needs of the weak. Paul is warning against the temptation to be drawn towards positions or opportunities solely because they may offer significant financial reward. Leaders would benefit from seeking external accountability in this area.

Paul concludes by quoting Jesus: 'It is more blessed to give than to receive.' While this saying cannot be found word for word in the Gospels, it summarises many of Jesus's teachings on wealth and possessions, and there were of course many things Jesus said and did that went unrecorded.

After this, Paul prayed with the leaders. They wept, embraced and kissed, knowing this would be the last time they would see one another.

Paul's instructions to the Ephesian elders highlight the main dangers that threaten the church and her leaders: 'purity, possessions, and power'.[38] There is to be a purity in terms of both exemplary character and doctrine (20:18, 27). Resisting the desire for undue power lies in recognising that the church does not belong to us, but to God, who purchased it with nothing less than the blood of Christ (20:28). And the temptation towards wealth and possessions is to be resisted, lest the flock be used and abused because of covetousness and greed (20:33–5).

Paul placed a high calling on the Ephesian elders. Yet he could be confident, since he knew that the power to live out that calling did not depend on their own resolve, but on the power of God, the presence of his Spirit, the interceding work of Christ and the 'word of his grace' – this was able to build them up and give them a future inheritance.

---

[37] See 1 Corinthians 9:14; 1 Timothy 5:18.
[38] Wall, *Acts*, 285.

20

The Beginning of the End

ACTS 21:1–36

In Acts 21, we see Luke narrate Paul's journey towards, and arrival at, Jerusalem. Along the way he stopped at a number of locations to spend time with existing groups of disciples. In two cases they urged him not to go on to Jerusalem, with Agabus prophesying his arrest. Upon arrival, Paul met with the elders and undertook purificatory rites. Having been identified in the crowd, he was seized and only rescued from death by the intervention of the Roman soldiers.

This chapter demonstrates Paul's fearless pursuit of God's call on his life. He travels to Jerusalem knowing the danger that awaits. His faith in God triumphs over his fear of humanity. We also note God's strange providence, as Paul's arrest in Jerusalem will prove to be the catalyst that will see him take the gospel to more influential and significant figures within the Empire. God often moves in mysterious ways, but his unstoppable mission keeps moving forward.

1. The journey to Jerusalem • Acts 21:1–16

On to Jerusalem

21 After we had torn ourselves away from them, we put out to sea and sailed straight to Kos. The next day we went to Rhodes and from there to Patara. **2** We found a ship crossing over to Phoenicia, went on board and set sail. **3** After sighting Cyprus and passing to the south of it, we sailed on to Syria. We landed at Tyre, where our ship was to unload its cargo. **4** We sought out the disciples there and stayed with them seven days. Through the Spirit they urged Paul not to go on to Jerusalem. **5** When it was time to leave, we left and continued on our way. All of them, including wives and children, accompanied us out of the city, and there on the beach we knelt to pray. **6** After saying goodbye to each other, we went aboard the ship, and they returned home.

7 We continued our voyage from Tyre and landed at Ptolemais, where we greeted the brothers and sisters and stayed with them for a day. **8** Leaving the next day, we reached Caesarea and stayed at the house of Philip the evangelist, one of the Seven. **9**He had four unmarried daughters who prophesied.

10After we had been there a number of days, a prophet named Agabus came down from Judea. **11**Coming over to us, he took Paul's belt, tied his own hands and feet with it and said, 'The Holy Spirit says, "In this way the Jewish leaders in Jerusalem will bind the owner of this belt and will hand him over to the Gentiles."'

12When we heard this, we and the people there pleaded with Paul not to go up to Jerusalem. **13**Then Paul answered, 'Why are you weeping and breaking my heart? I am ready not only to be bound, but also to die in Jerusalem for the name of the Lord Jesus.' **14**When he would not be dissuaded, we gave up and said, 'The Lord's will be done.'

15After this, we started on our way up to Jerusalem. **16**Some of the disciples from Caesarea accompanied us and brought us to the home of Mnason, where we were to stay. He was a man from Cyprus and one of the early disciples.

As Paul arrives in Jerusalem, we see the end of his third missionary journey. In fact, it will be the end of all journeys undertaken of Paul's own volition. His arrest in Jerusalem marks the beginning of the end of Luke's story. The remaining chapters will be taken up with Paul's various trials before officials, culminating in his house arrest in Rome. Luke will use the remaining eight chapters of his narrative to chart the four years of Paul's detention. And while the apostle is chained, we shall see the word is not.

Commentators note the parallels between Paul and Jesus here in their final journeys to Jerusalem: there is a prediction of suffering, a plot to kill, the involvement of Roman authorities and a resolved resignation to God's will.[1] The point of these parallels is perhaps to show that Paul, like Jesus, is obedient to God's call on his life, even ready to die in his service to the Lord. The opposition to God's Messiah is now centred on God's apostle to the Gentiles, Paul, and he is prepared to follow in the footsteps of his Saviour and Lord. He is obedient in denying himself and taking up his cross. How many of us could say we would be willing to lose everything in our dedication to Christ?

The opening sixteen verses of Acts 21 chart Paul's journey from Miletus, where he had bid an emotional farewell to the Ephesian elders, to Jerusalem. His voyage began by sailing to Kos, then sailing along the coastline via Rhodes and Patara, before taking another ship to Phoenicia

---

[1] Witherington, *Acts*, 628.

(verses 1–2).[2] The detail of the narrative and the repeated 'we' statements suggest Luke's presence on the journey and add historical credibility to the account.

Paul and his travelling companions sailed on to Syria, landing at Tyre, where Luke informs us Paul spent seven days with the disciples there (verses 3–4). Although Paul was keen to get to Jerusalem, here, once again, we see his heart for his fellow believers in his desire to spend time with them. Paul was not just planting churches and leaving them to it. Repeatedly we see him revisiting churches and believers to strengthen and encourage them. It is another reminder that church leaders should not use people as a sort of 'means' towards their own 'ends', as if they were just there to serve the leader's own mission. Church leaders must have a heart for the people they reach and serve. We see this time and again in Paul's letters as we have here in Luke's narrative.

Having spent time in Tyre, Luke tells us the church urged Paul not to continue his journey towards Jerusalem. Luke says this happened 'through the Spirit' (*dia tou pneumatos*). Given the ensuing narrative, and the prophetic figures of Philip's daughters and Agabus, it seems likely that this warning also came via a prophetic word. However, as we shall see, Paul was determined to carry on his journey to Jerusalem. Paul was not acting in disobedience to the voice of the Spirit. In both prophecies the Spirit revealed what would happen, but there was no prohibition on Paul's resolve to go to Jerusalem. God's guidance was here preparing Paul to complete his calling to Jerusalem (see Acts 19:21; 20:22), not to avoid the pain and suffering that accompanied God's leading.[3] How easy it is to follow God's leading when the path is pleasant and to resist when it appears painful.

When the time came to leave, the believers, including their wives and children, accompanied them to the ship. Luke provides a moving description of the group kneeling to pray together on the beach before Paul's departure (verses 5–6). There is a touching 'everyday' quality about the spirituality of Paul and his friends. Their religious activity was not confined to formal gatherings to worship on the Lord's Day. It was much more in the mould of Deuteronomy 6:7: 'when you sit at home and when you walk along the

---

[2] This journey, hugging the coastline of various islands, was common for small ships. The journey to Kos was around forty miles, Rhodes another ninety miles, then Patara another sixty miles. Patara to Phoenicia would have required a larger ship, being a journey of around four hundred miles and taking three days. See Bock, *Acts*, 636; Peterson, *Acts*, 577.

[3] Gooding, *True to the Faith*, 430–31.

road, when you lie down and when you get up'. It is perhaps a challenge to us to consider how we can be more 'prayerfully present' in the moment, stopping to pray with others at life's various crossroads. Paul must have been anxious about what lay ahead and eager to get moving, but he was still present enough in the moment to take the time to pray with others before he embarked on the next leg of his journey.

From Tyre, Paul sailed to Ptolemais, where he stayed for a day with the believers there (verse 7). The next day the travelling group arrived at Caesarea, where they stayed with Philip the evangelist – a key figure from Acts 6–8. Philip, we are told, had four unmarried daughters who prophesied. This would suggest a period of around twenty years between Philip settling in Caesarea (8:40) and Paul's arrival here in Acts 21:8.[4] Prophets or prophesying are mentioned at numerous points in the book of Acts.[5] Philip's daughters are an example of the fulfilment of Joel 2, cited in Acts 2:18.[6]

After a few days, they were joined by another prophet from Judea, named Agabus. Just as the disciples in Tyre had warned Paul through the Spirit not to continue to Jerusalem, so too Agabus gave a similar warning. He took Paul's belt, tied his hands and feet and said, 'The Holy Spirit says, "In this way the Jewish leaders in Jerusalem will bind the owner of this belt and will hand him over to the Gentiles"' (verse 11).

There are two questions to consider from Agabus's message. First, to what extent does he get it right? Second, how are we to understand such prophetic messages today?

First, to what extent does Agabus's message correctly predict future events? As far as the specific details go, it does not seem that he correctly predicted what would happen to Paul. He was not bound by the Jewish leaders in Jerusalem, but rather by the Romans. So what are we to make of Agabus's claim to speak by the Holy Spirit? Surely Bock is correct to note, 'The reference to Jewish involvement in the binding here is "causative" in force: the Jews will not physically bind Paul but will be responsible for his being arrested . . . The prophecy is accurate in this sense and is not to be pressed too literally.'[7]

Second, what does this teach us about similar prophetic messages today?

---

[4] Stott, *Acts*, 331. Stott suggests this meeting may have been the occasion for Luke to gather material about Philip's earlier ministry.

[5] See Acts 2:17–18; 11:27–8; 13:1; 15:32.

[6] We ought to remember that 'prophecy' carries a range of meaning, and we should not use this verse to justify an egalitarian approach to office-bearing, *contra* Kisau, 'Acts', in *ABC*, 1363.

[7] Bock, *Acts*, 638; Keener, *Acts*, 3:3106.

There are many believers around the world who value prophetic ministry as an invaluable part of discerning the Lord's leading for individuals or churches. However, we need to exercise caution here for a number of reasons. First, as noted before, Luke is providing description, not prescription. Agabus's ministry is not intended to provide a blueprint for every Christian or church in the post-apostolic era. Second, key moments in Luke's narrative are taken forward under the direction of the Spirit.[8] This, for Luke, demonstrates the divine authentication of the early Christian movement and provides for the church in its infancy. The repeated instruction for those in the post-apostolic age is to hold on to the apostolic teaching. There is a unique moment here in redemptive history that should caution us against viewing every action or incident as normative for the post-apostolic church. Third, the church of Acts was living in an era when there was no accepted canon of the New Testament. At this point the church in Caesarea probably did not have access to any of the writings we would now include in our New Testament. Inevitably in this era the prophetic had a crucial role and authority in the life of the early church.

We need to exercise an enormous amount of discernment whenever we encounter 'prophetic words'. Often they can be so vague as to be practically meaningless. At other times people predict things that do not come to pass. At still other times people will bring to mind certain Scriptures or promises which can, if properly applied, be edifying. For the church today, living in the post-apostolic period, our sure and infallible foundation is Scripture, by which all else must be tested. If we set ourselves on the foundation of the apostolic teaching, we can be sure that we too are being led by the words of the Spirit.[9]

Paul's response to the prophetic word of Agabus is resolute: 'I am ready not only to be bound, but also to die in Jerusalem for the name of the Lord Jesus' (verse 13). When the people saw that Paul could not be dissuaded, they said, 'The Lord's will be done.' This simple phrase is an expression of faith in God's power and sovereign purpose. Erasmus said it is an expression 'that ought always to be in everyone's heart, even if it is not on the lips, no matter what is imminent, whether joy or sorrow: The Lord's will be done'.[10]

---

[8] For example, Acts 1:8; 2:4; 8:29, 39; 10:44–5; 11:28; 13:2; 16:6–7; 20:22.

[9] For more on this subject, see Stott, *Baptism and Fullness*, 100–102; Richard B. Gaffin, *Perspectives on Pentecost* (Philipsburg: P&R, 1979), 55–72; O. Palmer Robertson, *The Final Word* (Edinburgh: Banner of Truth, 1993), 1–21.

[10] Erasmus, in *RCS* 6:295.

The believers understood that God was on his throne and that nothing would thwart his purposes, and so they were able to trust him with whatever the future might bring. This is clearly not a licence for believers to be reckless with their lives. But it does encourage us to persevere in faith, knowing that God is working out his purposes through the varied circumstances and pressures in which we find ourselves.

Paul continued his journey towards Jerusalem, accompanied by some of those from Caesarea.[11] Luke tells us he stayed in the house of Mnason, one of the early disciples. Whether Mnason was on the way to Jerusalem or in Jerusalem is unclear.[12] The stage was set for Paul's entry into Jerusalem, which he must have known carried a degree of risk, given his past history.

2. Paul's visit to the Temple • Acts 21:17–26

Paul's arrival at Jerusalem

17 When we arrived at Jerusalem, the brothers and sisters received us warmly. **18** The next day Paul and the rest of us went to see James, and all the elders were present. **19** Paul greeted them and reported in detail what God had done among the Gentiles through his ministry.

20 When they heard this, they praised God. Then they said to Paul: 'You see, brother, how many thousands of Jews have believed, and all of them are zealous for the law. **21** They have been informed that you teach all the Jews who live among the Gentiles to turn away from Moses, telling them not to circumcise their children or live according to our customs. **22** What shall we do? They will certainly hear that you have come, **23** so do what we tell you. There are four men with us who have made a vow. **24** Take these men, join in their purification rites and pay their expenses, so that they can have their heads shaved. Then everyone will know there is no truth in these reports about you, but that you yourself are living in obedience to the law. **25** As for the Gentile believers, we have written to them our decision that they should abstain from food sacrificed to idols, from blood, from the meat of strangled animals and from sexual immorality.'

26 The next day Paul took the men and purified himself along with them. Then he went to the temple to give notice of the date when the days of purification would end and the offering would be made for each of them.

---

[11] The journey from Caesarea to Jerusalem would have been around sixty miles and taken three days on foot. Peterson, *Acts*, 582.

[12] See Bock, *Acts*, 639.

The beginnings of Paul's time in Jerusalem are reported very positively: they are received warmly, they spend time with James and the elders and they report all that the Lord has done, resulting in praise to God (verses 17–20).[13] One interesting detail here is the absence of Peter. By this point it seems the 'apostles and elders' of Acts 15:6 has become 'James, and all the elders'. As the apostles begin to depart the narrative, the leadership of the church is entrusted to the elders, as we have seen in Acts 20:13–38.

As the church praises God for all he has done through Paul, there is also a controversy simmering that they are keen to address. The leaders of the church in Jerusalem rejoice with Paul that many thousands of Jews have converted to Christianity, and these Jews are very zealous for the Law. The confusion or controversy arises because many of these new Jewish believers understand Paul to be teaching them to turn away from the Law of Moses, and not to circumcise their children or to live according to the Jewish customs.

This controversy is interesting because it raises the question of Paul's relationship to such things. Did he or did he not teach Jewish Christians to turn away from Moses and the customs? The answer to that question is a sort of 'yes' *and* 'no'. Negatively, it is clear from Acts that Paul did not necessarily always encourage Jewish believers to turn away from Moses or Jewish customs. Paul himself had taken a Nazirite vow (Acts 18:18), and he had Timothy circumcised (Acts 16:3). We will see later in Acts Paul teaching from the Law of Moses (see Acts 26:22; 28:23). We could also go to Paul's letters to find numerous examples of him upholding the Law of Moses.[14]

However, Paul has taught repeatedly that the Jewish Law and customs are unable to save or justify a person – that is done by grace alone, through faith alone in the atoning sacrifice of Christ alone. We have seen Paul fight this battle in Acts 13:38–9 and Acts 15:1–11. Again, Paul's letters repeatedly show us that Paul does not see himself as 'under the Law' if the Law is seen as a means of salvation – in this case it rather leads to condemnation.[15]

Paul's teaching has not been a command to turn away from Jewish Law and custom *per se*, but to stop seeing the Law of Moses and Jewish customs

---

[13] Paul's arrival in Jerusalem can be dated to around AD 57. Bock, *Acts*, 643.

[14] See, for example, 1 Corinthians 9:8–10; Ephesians 6:1–3.

[15] See, for example, Romans 6:14; 1 Corinthians 9:20–21; Galatians 4:4–5; 5:18.

as a way to gain (or maintain) acceptance and justification before God.[16] Provided this understanding of the customs is in place, Paul is content for Jewish Christians to continue in them.

Over time, such customs would fade for Jewish Christians, particularly after the catastrophic events of AD 70 when the Temple in Jerusalem was destroyed. Gooding suggests that the early decades of the church provided a gracious period of transition to help Jewish converts move into their freedom in Christ.[17] Augustine comments similarly:

> Gradually, therefore, and by degrees, through the fervent preaching of the grace of Christ, by which alone believers were to know that they were justified and saved . . . all that activity of the shadows was to be ended. This was to be enough praise for it, that it was not to be avoided and despised as idolatry was, but was to have no further development and was not to be thought necessary.[18]

Without wishing to push the analogy too far, there may be contemporary parallels in reaching our own cultures. Customs that do not transgress Scripture perhaps do not need to be strictly prohibited. There may be a strategic missional and pastoral accommodation that aids converts in transitioning away from their old life and into their new life in Christ. The gospel must be fought for, but cultural accommodation is possible, at least for a time, so long as the gospel is not threatened.

This would seem to be supported by the solution to the controversy that the leaders proposed and Paul accepted. Paul was to join with four other men in their purification rites at the Temple, so that 'everyone will know there is no truth in these reports about you, but that you yourself are living in obedience to the law' (verse 24). For Paul, the Law needed

---

[16] Interestingly, this would perhaps suggest that for Jewish believers the dual practice of circumcision and baptism had been occurring for some time. This would be an argument against the view that baptism is a like-for-like replacement of circumcision as the covenant sign. It would be more accurate to say, following Paul in Colossians 2:11–12, that baptism corresponds to the circumcision of the heart. That which circumcision anticipated, baptism celebrated. See Martin Salter, 'Does Baptism Replace Circumcision? An Examination of the Relationship between Circumcision and Baptism in Colossians 2:11–12', in *Themelios* 35.1 (2010): 15–29; Martin Salter, 'The Abrahamic Covenant in Reformed Baptist Perspective', in *Themelios* 40:1 (2015): 35–49.

[17] Gooding, *True to the Faith*, 441–3.

[18] Augustine, 'Acts', in ACCS 5:264.

to be properly interpreted and applied within the redemptive historical context, but, given that caveat, the customs of the Law could still be followed.[19]

There is much contemporary debate around how Christians are to appropriate the Old Testament Law.[20] Some would see aspects of the Law as a continuing guide and authority for moral and civic life (the moral law), while other aspects have ceased to have authority for the believer (the ceremonial law). Others would see the 'law of Christ' as a new dispensation, with the Law of Moses having no authority for the Christian. There is no shortage of literature and opinion. This is not the place to attempt to resolve that debate. Whichever position one adopts, we need to preserve the apostolic gospel – that no one is justified by observing the Law – while also noting that the Law is not completely abolished in the apostolic understanding. The way in which it is appropriated and applied today will require careful thought and reflection on the totality of the scriptural witness.

We should note that for Paul there seemed to be a critical difference between an appropriate 'obedience to the law' (verse 24) and the idea of being 'under the law' (see Romans 6:14; 1 Corinthians 9:20–21; Galatians 4:4–5). This distinction, it seems, is helpful for us today as we seek to navigate our own relationship to the Old Testament Law. Appropriately interpreted and applied, we could say we are to be 'obedient to the Law' of Moses, recognising its fulfilment in Christ. But we are not 'under the Law' of Moses, as if its observance had (or was ever intended to have) any power to justify us before a holy God.

In verse 25, the Jerusalem consultation is recalled, with its judgment for Gentile Christians and the need for sensitivity towards Jewish custom. Paul, accepting the recommendation of the Jerusalem church leaders, went to the Temple the next day to 'give notice of the date when the days of purification would end and the offering would be made for each of them' (verse 26).

Paul here is displaying cultural sensitivity to his Jewish fellow believers. As he had written to the Corinthians, 'To the Jews I became like a Jew, to win the Jews' (1 Corinthians 9:20). Sometimes we must recognise that

---

[19] Marshall suggests this was a Nazirite vow as they were to shave their heads. *Acts*, 345.

[20] For more on this see Stanley N. Gundry (ed.), *Five Views on Law and Gospel* (Grand Rapids: Zondervan, 1996); Vern Poythress, *The Shadow of Christ in the Law of Moses* (Brentwood: Wolgemuth & Hyatt, 1991); Frame, *The Doctrine of the Christian Life* (Phillipsburg: P&R, 2008), 176–99.

cultural practices, while not binding in and of themselves, can have value in removing the 'static' that can get in the way of sharing the gospel.[21]

3. Paul arrested at the Temple • Acts 21:27–36

Paul arrested

27 When the seven days were nearly over, some Jews from the province of Asia saw Paul at the temple. They stirred up the whole crowd and seized him, **28** shouting, 'Fellow Israelites, help us! This is the man who teaches everyone everywhere against our people and our law and this place. And besides, he has brought Greeks into the temple and defiled this holy place.' **29** (They had previously seen Trophimus the Ephesian in the city with Paul and assumed that Paul had brought him into the temple.) **30** The whole city was aroused, and the people came running from all directions. Seizing Paul, they dragged him from the temple, and immediately the gates were shut. **31** While they were trying to kill him, news reached the commander of the Roman troops that the whole city of Jerusalem was in an uproar. **32** He at once took some officers and soldiers and ran down to the crowd. When the rioters saw the commander and his soldiers, they stopped beating Paul.

33 The commander came up and arrested him and ordered him to be bound with two chains. Then he asked who he was and what he had done. **34** Some in the crowd shouted one thing and some another, and since the commander could not get at the truth because of the uproar, he ordered that Paul be taken into the barracks. **35** When Paul reached the steps, the violence of the mob was so great he had to be carried by the soldiers. **36** The crowd that followed kept shouting, 'Get rid of him!'

As the seven days of Paul's purification were drawing to a close, Luke tells us that some Jews from the province of Asia recognised Paul and stirred up the whole crowd against him (verse 27). They seized him and incited the crowd by shouting the accusation that Paul was teaching 'everyone everywhere against our people and our law and this place' (verse 28). In addition, they accused him of defiling the Temple by bringing Gentiles into it.[22] Luke notes this charge is misplaced based on a sighting of Paul

---

[21] Bock, *Acts*, 648.

[22] The charge relates to bringing a Gentile into the 'inner court of the Israelites'. Bock cites Josephus to demonstrate that Gentiles were not permitted into the main Temple area. See Josephus, *Antiquities* 15.11.5; Bock, *Acts*, 651.

with Trophimus the Ephesian in the city and the assumption that he had brought him into the holy place (verse 29). There is an irony here as Paul is accused of causing defilement even while undertaking the rites of purification. The real defilement is about to be seen in the violence that ensues.

Witherington notes how volatile Jerusalem was during this period – a volatility that would culminate in the revolt against Rome and the destruction of the Temple in AD 70. He says, 'Anything that was perceived to threaten the purity of the national shrine . . . would be reacted to with great emotion.'[23] The situation was extremely dangerous for Paul.

It is noteworthy that both accusations were, in fact, untrue. Paul, we infer from Luke's comment, had not defiled the holy place. And, as discussed above, he had not taught everyone everywhere against the Law and Temple. The opponents had deliberately twisted Paul's teaching and jumped to the wrong conclusion regarding Trophimus.

Opponents of the gospel may sometimes misrepresent Christians and their teaching in their opposition. It can be one of the most painful things to endure as a believer. It is hard to be opposed because of what we believe; it feels somehow harder to be opposed for things we do not actually believe. Such opposition often feels like it bears the fingerprints of the evil one. It requires much patience and endurance to persevere in such circumstances. We are not to engage opposition using the weapons of the world, but we are to entrust ourselves to the one who judges justly, trusting him with the outcome in our trials (1 Peter 2:23).

The crowd grew, and they seized Paul, dragged him outside the Temple and shut the gates. It is worth pausing here to note the tragedy and sadness of this moment. It is the final scene in the Temple courts in the book of Acts. There is injustice, lies and violence. There is the rejection of God's messenger of salvation. The doors to the Temple are shut.[24] As the Jewish leaders attempt to pass their verdict on the gospel, God, via means of Luke's narrative, is passing his verdict on them in their rejection of him.

News of the uproar reached the Roman commander, and he took some soldiers with him and ran down to the crowd. Stott notes that the Roman barracks were 'in the fortress of Antonia, which Herod the Great had built at the north-west corner of the temple area'.[25] From there they could intervene if and when trouble erupted.

---

[23] Witherington, *Acts*, 643.

[24] Bock, *Acts*, 652.

[25] Stott, *Acts*, 344.

When the rioters saw the soldiers, they stopped beating Paul. The commander arrested Paul – a further injustice given his innocence as the victim. The commander questioned the crowd as to the nature of Paul's crimes. Luke notes the commander was unable to get at the truth because of the uproar – some shouting one thing, others another. Luke's description reinforces the sense of chaotic injustice in the scene. Any hope of getting to the truth is nullified by the noise of the crowd. We are probably justified in concluding they were not in fact interested in the truth. They just wanted rid of this apparent enemy.

The violence was so great that the commander had to carry Paul out and into the barracks as the mob chanted 'Get rid of him!' (*aire auton*). This exact phrase had been used almost thirty years earlier by the mob towards Jesus in Luke 23:18, indicating the seriousness of the situation in which Paul found himself.[26] Tannehill notes that there was to be no miraculous prison escape like those seen previously in Acts 5, 12 and 16.[27] The remainder of Luke's narrative would follow Paul's four-year period of detention, with his fate ultimately unresolved.[28] It is a sobering reminder that faithfulness to God's call does not always come with a happy ending, at least in this life.

Although the circumstances of persecution vary greatly, the human heart of opposition seems to remain the same. Here we see opposition take the form of twisting the truth, jumping to bad assumptions, shouting down any pursuit of truth, and the desire to be rid of the one opposed. Modern societies talk of tolerance and acceptance, yet the truth is that all societies will find things they simply will not tolerate. The biblical doctrine of the sinfulness of humanity reminds us that we should not be surprised when unbelievers reject God's word and God's people. Believers will be angrily shouted down, they will be misrepresented, they will be driven out, and mechanisms of enforcement will be used. This is a difficult reality to face, but, as Paul said to the church in Antioch, 'We must go through many hardships to enter the kingdom of God' (Acts 14:22).

---

[26] Witherington, *Acts*, 658.

[27] Tannehill, *Narrative Unity*, 271.

[28] See Acts 24:27; 28:30 for reference to the two years Felix left Paul in prison, and then the two years under house arrest in Rome.

21

Paul's Defence Begins

ACTS 21:37–22:29

Acts 22–26 presents a lengthy series of trials and defence speeches that Paul delivers to both Jewish and Roman audiences. The obvious question to ask as readers is why Luke devotes so much of his narrative to these various trial scenes. There would appear to be two main concerns that Luke is keen to address in the final section of his narrative.

First, some of these speeches appear to defend 'the Way' against the charge that it is a threat to Rome. As Witherington notes, 'The stress is placed on the judgment that there is nothing about Paul and his preaching that should concern Roman jurisprudence, much less cause a guilty verdict to be rendered against Paul.'[1] This may have been something that a reader like Theophilus (Luke 1:1–4) needed to hear. Christianity is not a movement of revolt seeking to threaten or disrupt the state.

Second, some of the speeches in Acts 22–26 appear to defend 'the Way' against the charge that it is anti-Jewish. Questions are addressed around the identity of the Messiah, God's plans for his people, who is included and by what means.[2] Christianity is not seeking to destroy the religion of Israel, but rather to demonstrate how God's covenants with Israel have reached their climax in Jesus, the Messiah. Debates around the observance of the Law recognise cultural sensitivities and address the basis of justification.

As Bock notes, Paul is not just a preacher of the faith, but also a defender of the faith in the public square.[3] This final quarter of Luke's narrative is an *apologia* for the legitimacy of 'the Way' within the cultural settings it inhabits.

Additionally, the narrative 'progress' holds together the tension between hardship and gospel progress (Acts 14:22). Although Paul is imprisoned, the gospel continues to advance through the Empire. This tension of

---

[1] Witherington, *Acts*, 660.
[2] Witherington, *Acts*, 660.
[3] Bock, *Acts*, 655.

suffering and advance is characteristic of Luke's narrative and serves to remind subsequent readers of the nature of discipleship. Paul is a paradigm of faithful endurance through significant hardship.

1. Paul's Jewish defence • Acts 21:37–22:21

Paul speaks to the crowd

37 As the soldiers were about to take Paul into the barracks, he asked the commander, 'May I say something to you?'

'Do you speak Greek?' he replied. 38 'Aren't you the Egyptian who started a revolt and led four thousand terrorists out into the wilderness some time ago?'

39 Paul answered, 'I am a Jew, from Tarsus in Cilicia, a citizen of no ordinary city. Please let me speak to the people.'

40 After receiving the commander's permission, Paul stood on the steps and motioned to the crowd. When they were all silent, he said to them in Aramaic[a]:

22 1 'Brothers and fathers, listen now to my defence.'

2 When they heard him speak to them in Aramaic, they became very quiet.

Then Paul said: 3 'I am a Jew, born in Tarsus of Cilicia, but brought up in this city. I studied under Gamaliel and was thoroughly trained in the law of our ancestors. I was just as zealous for God as any of you are today. 4 I persecuted the followers of this Way to their death, arresting both men and women and throwing them into prison, 5 as the high priest and all the Council can themselves testify. I even obtained letters from them to their associates in Damascus, and went there to bring these people as prisoners to Jerusalem to be punished.

6 'About noon as I came near Damascus, suddenly a bright light from heaven flashed around me. 7 I fell to the ground and heard a voice say to me, "Saul! Saul! Why do you persecute me?"

8 ' "Who are you, Lord?" I asked.

' "I am Jesus of Nazareth, whom you are persecuting," he replied. 9 My companions saw the light, but they did not understand the voice of him who was speaking to me.

10 ' "What shall I do, Lord?" I asked.

' "Get up," the Lord said, "and go into Damascus. There you will be told all that you have been assigned to do." 11 My companions led me by the hand into Damascus, because the brilliance of the light had blinded me.

12 'A man named Ananias came to see me. He was a devout observer of the law and highly respected by all the Jews living there. 13 He stood beside me and said, "Brother Saul, receive your sight!" And at that very moment I was able to see him.

14 'Then he said: "The God of our ancestors has chosen you to know his will and to see the Righteous One and

to hear words from his mouth. **15** You will be his witness to all people of what you have seen and heard. **16** And now what are you waiting for? Get up, be baptised and wash your sins away, calling on his name."

17 'When I returned to Jerusalem and was praying at the temple, I fell into a trance **18** and saw the Lord speaking to me. "Quick!" he said. "Leave Jerusalem immediately, because the people here will not accept your testimony about me."

19 ' "Lord," I replied, "these people know that I went from one synagogue to another to imprison and beat those who believe in you. **20** And when the blood of your martyr[a] Stephen was shed, I stood there giving my approval and guarding the clothes of those who were killing him."

21 'Then the Lord said to me, "Go; I will send you far away to the Gentiles." '

a 40 Or possibly *Hebrew*; also in 22:2
a 20 Or *witness*

As Paul was about to be taken into the barracks, he requested to speak with the commander, a man named Claudius Lysias (Acts 23:26), who asked Paul if he spoke Greek (verse 37).

The commander was apparently confused by this situation. He supposed Paul may have been an Egyptian man, who had started a rebellion, leading four thousand terrorists into the wilderness (verse 38). We find a similar account in the work of the Jewish historian, Josephus.[4] The Egyptian considered himself to be a new Moses, who would lead his people in defeating their Roman overlords and bringing down the walls of Jerusalem. The Governor, Felix, had killed four hundred of the rebels and captured another two hundred, but the Egyptian had escaped, never to be seen again.[5] It would have been quite a coup for the commander to have captured this Egyptian revolutionary leader.[6]

Paul replied that he was a Jew and a citizen of Tarsus in Cilicia – no ordinary city. Tarsus had half a million inhabitants and was a centre of Hellenistic culture and philosophy. It had a vibrant textile industry and was a centre for trade and literature.[7] 'With Ephesus and Smyrna, it was one of the three great cities on the southern coast of Asia Minor.'[8] In

[4] Josephus, *War* 2:254–7; *Antiquities* 20:162–5; 185–7.
[5] Peterson, *Acts*, 592, notes the 'terrorists' (*sikariōn*) were known as the 'dagger men'; they were 'the most fanatical of Jewish nationalists . . . bitter enemies of pro-Roman Jews'. Bruce, *Acts*, 452, suggests these events occurred around three years prior to this current scene.
[6] Wall, *Acts*, 298.
[7] Bock, *Acts*, 658.
[8] Bock, *Acts*, 658.

antiquity, a person's honour or status was bound up with the place of their birth.[9] Paul was keen to establish before Lysias that he was not a troublemaker.

Paul requested permission to speak to the people. The commander granted this request and Paul motioned to the crowd to listen to him. Having quietened the crowd he began to address them in Aramaic, their native language.

Gooding asks an important question at this point: why did Paul bother trying to persuade the mob, who had just beaten him and who clearly wanted to kill him? The answer, Gooding suggests, is simply his love for his fellow Jews: 'He had done what he had done in the temple to help the believing Jews; for he loved them.'[10] He understood them. He had been like many of the Jewish people who opposed Christianity, blinded by his zeal for the Law and traditions. And his life had been transformed by the mercy and grace of Christ. He loved his fellow Israelites and longed for them to come to know the love of Jesus for themselves (see Romans 9:1–5). Paul's example challenges us, as readers, to consider whether we too have this sort of love for those around us, even those who would oppose and mistreat us. Does the love of Christ constrain us to witness for him, that others may hear and come to know of that same love for themselves?

The main aim of Paul's defence was to demonstrate that he too was a loyal Jew, equally zealous and concerned for the honour of God's name. His defence began with the address, 'Brothers and fathers', a notably respectful opening towards those who moments earlier were intent on beating him to death.

Paul's defence began with an account of his upbringing and training. Having been born in Tarsus he had grown up in Jerusalem. He had been under the tutelage of Gamaliel and described himself as 'thoroughly trained in the law of our ancestors' (verse 3). This was the same Gamaliel who was part of the Sanhedrin in Acts 5:34.

Paul's upbringing and former training demonstrated his zeal and his orthodoxy. He would have likely begun an apprenticeship under Gamaliel as young as thirteen years old. His training would have involved memorising significant portions of the Old Testament under the tutelage of his rabbi.[11] As Johannes Brenz , the sixteenth-century German pastor,

---

[9] Peterson, *Acts*, 592.

[10] Gooding, *True to the Faith*, 446.

[11] Craig L. Blomberg, *Making Sense of the New Testament* (Grand Rapids: Baker Academic, 2004), 34.

theologian and Reformer observed, 'It is not because of lack of know-ledge or simplicity that he now follows the gospel he once persecuted.'[12]

Paul claimed to be every bit as zealous for the Law as his persecutors. In fact, he himself had persecuted the church, imprisoning both men and women, and travelled beyond Jerusalem in his effort to persecute believers (verses 4–5). His devotion and abilities had meant he had carried letters of reference from Jerusalem, giving him authority to arrest and extradite Christians as he travelled to other places.[13]

This account of Paul's previous life suggests he was a significant figure in Jerusalem. He was trained by a member of the Sanhedrin, acquainted with officials, possibly a member of the Sanhedrin himself.[14] Paul was an unimpeachable devotee of the Torah. His persecutors should not have thought of him as an apostate. Instead, they should have considered what it would have taken to convert such a zealous Jew to become a follower of Jesus Christ.

Paul's brief pre-conversion autobiography is a reminder of the power of God to change the hearts of even those most opposed to the gospel. It encourages us to keep bearing witness to him, confident that he can draw anyone, however hostile, to himself. We often lose heart when we try to share our faith with others and they seem to quickly dismiss us or distance themselves from anything to do with the gospel. This can be disheartening and discouraging. We may tend to give up on people quickly and think maybe they are beyond reach, or at least beyond our reach. In a sense that's true – but they are not beyond God's reach. If God can change Saul into Paul, he can transform those close to us who seem so far from him. We may doubt our own powers of persuasion, but we must not doubt the divine power to change even the hardest heart.

Having described his previous life and zeal for Judaism against Christianity, Paul then moved to describe his conversion experience. The account of this event occurs three times in Acts (9:1–18; 22:5–16; 26:12–18), demonstrating its significance for Luke's narrative. The differences between this account and the earlier one given in Acts 9 are as follows:[15]

---

[12] Brenz, in *RCS* 6:305.
[13] Witherington, *Acts*, 670.
[14] Peterson, *Acts*, 598.
[15] See Witherington, *Acts*, 670; Peterson, *Acts*, 598; Wall, *Acts*, 306–7.

- The story is told from Paul's point of view, rather than the narrator's.
- There are two questions addressed to Jesus, rather than one.
- Only in this account is Jesus described as being 'of Nazareth'.
- The experience of Paul's travelling companions is described in slightly different (though not contradictory) terms.
- The speech of Ananias in Paul's commissioning is expanded.

Paul described his journey towards Damascus and his encounter with the risen Christ (as Luke narrated in Acts 9). About noon one day a bright light from heaven flashed around him. He fell to the ground and heard a voice saying, 'Saul! Saul! Why do you persecute me?' (verse 7). Such is the union between Christ and his church, that to persecute believers is to persecute Jesus himself. This union and 'communion of saints' is just one of the reasons we are called to 'rejoice with those who rejoice; mourn with those who mourn' (Romans 12:15).

Paul replied, 'Who are you, Lord?' to which the answer came, 'I am Jesus of Nazareth, whom you are persecuting' (verse 8). This is a significant turning point, not just for Paul, but also in the speech. The very figure whose followers he had been zealous to pursue was not a fraud, but was in fact God's Messiah, risen and alive, reigning at the right hand of the Father. Paul, zealous for God, had been doing the very opposite of God's will and had now come to a stunning realisation of that fact.

While the travelling companions of Paul did not understand the voice, they too saw the bright flash of light.[16] Paul recounts his next question, 'What shall I do, Lord?' to which the reply was given, 'Get up . . . and go into Damascus. There you will be told all that you have been assigned to do' (verse 10).

Paul, having been blinded by the light, was led by his companions into Damascus and to the house of Judas, where he met Ananias. Paul was keen to point out at this point in his defence that Ananias too was a 'devout observer of the law and highly respected by all the Jews living there' (verse 12). Ananias is another orthodox Jewish figure in Paul's story, further bolstering his defence. Ananias demonstrates that being a follower of 'the Way' was not in contradiction to his Jewish orthodoxy. Ananias stood beside Paul and said, 'Brother Saul, receive your sight!' at which point Paul's sight was restored (verse 13).

After this, Ananias said to Paul:

---

[16] Acts 9:7 suggests the companions did hear the sound, but here Paul suggests they did not comprehend the sound they heard.

The God of our ancestors has chosen you to know his will and to see the Righteous One and to hear words from his mouth. You will be his witness to all people of what you have seen and heard. And now what are you waiting for? Get up, be baptised and wash your sins away, calling on his name. (Acts 22:14–16)

The mention of 'the God of our ancestors' and 'the Righteous One' employs Jewish concepts to demonstrate that Paul is standing in continuity with historic Judaism. The title of 'Righteous One' (*ton dikaion*) has been used previously in Luke 23:47; Acts 3:14; 7:52 (see 1 John 2:1). Paul is not starting a new religious cult but is working in accordance with the historic plan of God to reach the nations.

In Ananias's words we see the hint of Paul's mission beyond the Jewish people. He is to be a 'witness to all people'. The 'all people' (*pantas anthrōpous*) on the lips of Ananias is different from the mention of Gentiles (*ethnōn*) by Jesus (Acts 9:15). Again, this is most likely a deliberate attempt to minimise the offence to Paul's hostile audience.[17] Ultimately, such offence will be unavoidable, as we shall see below, but Paul is working hard to keep his listeners on side for as long as possible. This is simply worth noting in passing with reference to our own apologetics. There is wisdom in minimising offence for our hearers in order to win a hearing, as far as this is possible.

We also see in Ananias's words an aspect of that which baptism signifies – the washing away of sins, calling on his name. Elsewhere in the New Testament we see in baptism the symbolism of death and resurrection (Romans 6:3–4), a spiritual circumcision (Colossians 2:11–12) and a pledge/appeal to God (1 Peter 3:21). Here we see the symbolism of baptism as a washing away, or a cleansing from sins, as the person baptised calls on Jesus's name.[18] It is the outward sign of an inward change. This washing is made effective, we see elsewhere, by the shed blood of Christ (Revelation 7:14). We are not cleansed by our own moral effort or determination, but wholly by that which Christ has done for us in shedding his blood on the cross. Baptism speaks of our trust and faith in him.[19]

Paul, having returned to Jerusalem, recalls an experience in the Temple. This would seem to have been during Paul's first visit to Jerusalem,

---

[17] Witherington, *Acts*, 672.

[18] The idea of 'washing' can also be seen in 1 Corinthians 6:11; Ephesians 5:26; Titus 3:5; Hebrews 10:22. Peterson, *Acts*, 603.

[19] For more on the New Testament imagery of baptism, see Schreiner and Wright (eds), *Believer's Baptism* (Nashville: B&H, 2006).

which happened three years after his Damascus Road conversion (Acts 9:26–30; see Galatians 1:17–19).[20] He describes falling into a trance and seeing the Lord Jesus speaking to him. The risen Lord warned him of impending danger, that 'the people here will not accept your testimony about me' (verse 18). Paul omits his departure from Damascus because of conflict with the Jews (Acts 9:23–5) and emphasises his commitment to the Temple as a place of prayer and worship.

His vision in the Temple aligns him with other prophets such as Isaiah (Isaiah 6:1–13) or Samuel (1 Samuel 3:1–18), and recalls other Temple scenes in Luke's two-volume work that speak of the message of salvation as being for all nations (Luke 2:30–32; Acts 3:25).[21] Implied in Paul's account is the claim that the risen Lord Jesus is also Lord of the Temple – the very place where Jesus had been condemned, and the site of Paul's attempted murder.[22] It is holier ground than Paul's opponents realise.

Paul replied, 'Lord . . . these people know that I went from one synagogue to another to imprison and beat those who believe in you' (verse 19). The greatest evidence of Paul's prior zeal for Judaism was his hand in the martyrdom of Stephen. He claimed to have been standing there giving his approval and guarding the clothes of those who were killing him (see Acts 7:57–60). However, his reference to Stephen as a 'witness' (*martyros*) implies Paul's recognition that Stephen was in fact a true witness to God's Messiah.

Paul's reply did nothing to change the command of the Lord: 'Go; I will send you far away to the Gentiles' (verse 21). As Peterson notes, 'God's purpose cannot be denied or ignored, no matter what the implications for the existing structures of religion, culture, and society, or for the individuals who proclaim God's will.'[23]

Acts 22:22–4a: The crowd oppose Paul

Paul the Roman citizen

22 The crowd listened to Paul until he said this. Then they raised their voices and shouted, 'Rid the earth of him! He's not fit to live!' 23 As they were shouting and throwing off their cloaks and flinging dust into the air, 24 the commander ordered that Paul be taken into the barracks.

---

[20] Peterson, *Acts*, 604.
[21] Witherington, *Acts*, 674.
[22] Peterson, *Acts*, 604.
[23] Peterson, *Acts*, 606.

Luke records that the crowd listened to Paul up until this point. At the mention of his mission to the Gentiles (*ethnē*), they raised their voices and shouted, 'Rid the earth of him! He's not fit to live!' (verse 22). At this point we can see Paul's attempt at a defence has failed. The verdict and the sentence are returned with speed and vehemence.

There is deep tragedy in the response of the crowd. The teachings and traditions of the Jewish leaders had forgotten the call upon the people to be a blessing to the nations.[24] It is a sobering reminder of how easy it is for our own established traditions to distort or deny the foundation upon which they are built.[25] I was talking to a friend recently who had come from a church tradition that insisted that men wore suits and women wore hats to church on a Sunday. He noted a man sitting at the back of our own church meeting who wore ripped jeans and a beanie hat, and had a large tattoo on his face. He observed that such a man would not find a welcome in his previous church. It is a tragic thing when human traditions obscure our calling to reach the least and the lost.

The crowd were shouting, throwing off their cloaks and flinging dust into the air. It is possible that what is intended is something similar to the 'shaking out' of the dust from garments – a gesture of rejection, as mentioned in Acts 13:51. It is also possible that the removal of coats symbolises a desire or intent to stone Paul, just as they had stoned Stephen (see Acts 7:58).[26]

It was around 450 years ago that the Reformer Rudolf Gwalther (1519–86) made the following observation:

> This is a miserable blindness and perverseness of the world, that while in profane and worldly matters everyone prays and holds advised deliberation, in matters of religion and the common case of eternal salvation, many think the matter should be handled and dispatched with unreasonable noise, furious braids, uproars and rebellion.[27]

We may observe that people can become just as vexed about 'worldly' matters today. It is a caution to us to consider the way in which we

---

[24] For example, Genesis 12:1–3; Deuteronomy 4:5–8; Psalm 67; Isaiah 49:1–6.
[25] Bock, *Acts*, 665.
[26] Wall, *Acts*, 308.
[27] Gwalther, in *RCS* 6:309.

engage with those with whom we disagree. The mob are unable to listen and consider, since they are so blinded by their rage and so persuaded they are right. We always ought to be careful to act with restraint and respect, even when we disagree with others. As Paul says in his letter to the Philippians, 'Let your gentleness be evident to all' (Philippians 4:5).

We also need to note here that the gospel 'makes particular and absolute claims about who God is, what God does, and to whom God belongs'.[28] Sometimes these claims will prove deeply unpopular in our own cultures. It requires a tremendous amount of faith and courage to contend for the faith when our lives could be much easier if we were to give the baying mob the words their itching ears want to hear. Courage to contend for the issues of first importance is a necessary mark of the true church, even when it is costly and painful.

2. Paul's Roman defence • Acts 22:24b–9

He directed that he be flogged and interrogated in order to find out why the people were shouting at him like this. 25 As they stretched him out to flog him, Paul said to the centurion standing there, 'Is it legal for you to flog a Roman citizen who hasn't even been found guilty?'

26 When the centurion heard this, he went to the commander and reported it. 'What are you going to do?' he asked. 'This man is a Roman citizen.'

27 The commander went to Paul and asked, 'Tell me, are you a Roman citizen?'

'Yes, I am,' he answered.

28 Then the commander said, 'I had to pay a lot of money for my citizenship.'

'But I was born a citizen,' Paul replied.

29 Those who were about to interrogate him withdrew immediately. The commander himself was alarmed when he realised that he had put Paul, a Roman citizen, in chains.

If we suppose that the commander did not understand the speech, owing to it being in Aramaic, we can only imagine how he must have felt as the crowd erupted with fury.

The commander ordered that Paul be taken into the barracks and there he directed that Paul be flogged and interrogated to find out why the crowd were so incensed. This was a common practice in the ancient world, used to elicit information under torture. Witherington observes,

---

[28] Wall, *Acts*, 315.

'This was a regular and legal, though brutal, Roman means of extracting testimony from someone, often used against either slaves or aliens.'[29] The scourge would have consisted of multiple thongs of leather, strung with pieces of lead or bone. It could tear flesh, maim and even kill if used repeatedly.[30]

As they prepared to administer the flogging, Paul spoke up: 'Is it legal for you to flog a Roman citizen who hasn't even been found guilty?' (verse 25). Paul was aware of the Roman law that it was not permitted to administer such a punishment upon a Roman citizen.[31] We may wonder why Paul waited until this moment to reveal his Roman citizenship. Perhaps it was not advantageous to his defence before the Jews to do so earlier.[32]

At this point, the centurion reported Paul's words to his commander, asking what they should do, since it was not legal to flog a Roman citizen. The commander returned and asked Paul if he was a Roman citizen, to which Paul replied that he was (verses 26–7).

The commander was clearly bewildered, since he had been required to pay a significant sum of money for his Roman citizenship. Paul's answer was that he was born a Roman citizen. This placed the commander in an awkward position since he had mistreated someone who was technically in a place of greater social status than the commander himself. Bock suggests that the commander had been required to pay an illegal bribe to obtain his citizenship, a common practice under the reign of Claudius, whereas Paul was a *bona fide* citizen, having inherited his citizenship from his father or grandfather.[33].

The soldiers withdrew, and the commander was alarmed that he had put a Roman citizen in chains. This was a severe breach of Roman custom, and the commander certainly did not want to put himself in the position of having broken the law. Witherington concludes, 'From henceforth, Paul's Roman citizenship and Roman law will dictate how

---

[29] Witherington, *Acts*, 677.

[30] Witherington, *Acts*, 677.

[31] 'The Lex Valeria and the Lex Porcia were ancient laws that prohibited the beating, and even fettering, of Roman citizens, and this right was confirmed by the Lex Julia which gave citizens in the provinces the right of appeal to Rome.' Marshall, *Acts*, 358–9.

[32] Cicero records an instance where a claim to citizenship actually provoked a harsher punishment from an unjust and unsympathetic governor. Cited in Keener, *Acts*, 3:3250, note 1086.

[33] Bock, *Acts*, 665.

the narrative will proceed, determining not only who will try Paul's case, but ultimately where it will be tried.'[34]

Here we see Paul making use of the state law to his own advantage. Robert Wall notes the caution required in interpretation at this point.[35] Many people idealise the interaction between Paul and Lysias as a model for the relationship between church and state. Lysias represents the state – disinterested and unconcerned about religious dispute yet acting to preserve the freedom to practise one's religion against violence and persecution. There may be some truth in this. Paul used the advantages that the secular state offered him to further the cause of the gospel. Elsewhere Paul would describe the state as appointed by God to uphold civic justice (Romans 13:1–7).

However, we must also remember the state is not always positively characterised in Scripture. It can be a force for real evil, even against God's people (Revelation 12–13). It is perhaps better to recognise that Christians are permitted, where possible, to appeal to the state for their freedom and protection, all the while recognising that sometimes such freedoms will not be upheld. Christians can and should campaign for such protection, all the while hoping the state will be a good model of God-appointed rule.

Abraham Kuyper understood the value of sphere sovereignty.[36] God gives different persons differing spheres of authority – in the home, the workplace, the state and the church. When these boundaries are recognised and adhered to, everyone may flourish. Sadly, this is often not the case. State authorities can easily become corrupt and fall short of their God-given calling. Christians will need to pray, campaign, wait and even be willing to suffer in faithful obedience to God's call. This is never an easy thing to do, but faithfulness brings its own reward, although there is no guarantee that the reward will come in this life. Our hope must be in the Lord first and foremost, not in the power of the state.

What we can see here is that in the lengthy narrative of Paul's various imprisonments, Paul demonstrates 'endurance and resourcefulness in using the opportunities that may come' to one who is relatively powerless.[37] Christians throughout history, and throughout the world today, often suffer as marginalised and oppressed groups without the worldly levers of

---

[34] Witherington, *Acts*, 684.
[35] Wall, *Acts*, 299.
[36] Abraham Kuyper, *Lectures on Calvinism* (repr. Peabody: Hendrickson, 2008), 65–95.
[37] Tannehill, *Narrative Unity*, 284.

power. Yet God protects his people, and the gospel continues to flourish. Christians are called to patience, wisdom and faithful endurance in seeking to 'make the most of every opportunity' (Colossians 4:5). This will seldom be easy, but we 'press on to take hold of that for which Christ Jesus took hold of me' (Philippians 3:12).

22

From Jerusalem to Caesarea

ACTS 22:30–23:35

Having escaped the violence of the mob and a flogging by the Roman authorities, Paul now faces the next in a series of trials before Jewish and Roman authorities. The commander still wants to get to the bottom of the trouble, hence the need to set Paul before the Sanhedrin. Their failure to secure charges against him results in a vigilante group plotting his assassination. When news of this reaches the Roman commander he delivers Paul under the cover of night to Felix, the governor in Caesarea.

Within the wider section (Acts 21–8), we can see that this is the second defence speech before the Jews, which will be followed by a dangerous journey. Then we shall see three more defence speeches before Roman authorities (Felix, Festus and Agrippa) before another dangerous journey (Acts 27–8). At every step we sense Paul's peril, but also the way in which God is protecting him and preparing him to testify in Rome.[1]

We continue to see through this narrative God's mysterious providence in protecting Paul, the confusion of the local authorities as they struggle to understand what to make of this man and his message, and the gospel spreading into new places as Paul gets the opportunity to speak to significant authority figures.

As we have already noted, Luke is keen to demonstrate that Christianity is not a threat to either Jerusalem or Rome. He is innocent before them both, and he is innocent before God. The integrity of the man and his message is the point Luke continues to stress.

1. The trial before the Sanhedrin • Acts 22:30–23:11

Paul before the Sanhedrin

30 The commander wanted to find out exactly why Paul was being accused by the Jews. So the next day he released him and ordered the chief priests and all the members of the Sanhedrin to

---

[1] Peterson, *Acts*, 611.

assemble. Then he brought Paul and set him before them.

23 Paul looked straight at the Sanhedrin and said, 'My brothers, I have fulfilled my duty to God in all good conscience to this day.' **2**At this the high priest Ananias ordered those standing near Paul to strike him on the mouth. **3**Then Paul said to him, 'God will strike you, you whitewashed wall! You sit there to judge me according to the law, yet you yourself violate the law by commanding that I be struck!'

4Those who were standing near Paul said, 'How dare you insult God's high priest!'

5Paul replied, 'Brothers, I did not realise that he was the high priest; for it is written: "Do not speak evil about the ruler of your people."**a**'

6Then Paul, knowing that some of them were Sadducees and the others Pharisees, called out in the Sanhedrin, 'My brothers, I am a Pharisee, descended from Pharisees. I stand on trial because of the hope of the resurrection of the dead.' **7**When he said this, a dispute broke out between the Pharisees and the Sadducees, and the assembly was divided. **8**(The Sadducees say that there is no resurrection, and that there are neither angels nor spirits, but the Pharisees believe all these things.)

9There was a great uproar, and some of the teachers of the law who were Pharisees stood up and argued vigorously. 'We find nothing wrong with this man,' they said. 'What if a spirit or an angel has spoken to him?' **10**The dispute became so violent that the commander was afraid Paul would be torn to pieces by them. He ordered the troops to go down and take him away from them by force and bring him into the barracks.

11The following night the Lord stood near Paul and said, 'Take courage! As you have testified about me in Jerusalem, so you must also testify in Rome.'

_____

a 5 Exodus 22:28

In 22:30 we learn that the commander was still unsure as to the nature of the accusations against Paul. In his desire to learn more, he delivered Paul back before the Sanhedrin. Peterson suggests that the 'abrupt introduction to proceedings here suggests that the Sanhedrin had met for a pre-trial hearing rather than for a formal trial'.[2] It would seem that the Sanhedrin were still trying to establish how they could bring a charge that would render Paul guilty under Roman law.[3] It was not enough to bring charges based on Jewish law; they would need a charge that would see him condemned by Rome.

_____

[2] Peterson, _Acts_, 612.
[3] Witherington, _Acts_, 684.

The first reported words come from the mouth of Paul, who began his defence as follows: 'My brothers' (*andres adelphoi*). This may have been an attempt to ingratiate himself to his hearers, or perhaps more likely a statement that he saw them as his equals, not his superiors, and certainly not his judges.[4] As Peter had already made clear to the Sanhedrin back in Acts 4:19, it is God's voice that is our ultimate authority, not that of any human court.

Next, he said, 'I have fulfilled my duty to God in all good conscience to this day' (23:1). The language of fulfilling duty (*pepoliteumai tō theō*) in good conscience (*pasē syneidēsei agathē*) was Paul's way of saying his life had been lived in a way that was obedient and pleasing to God. His conversion to Christianity was in no way a rejection of the God of the Jews – in fact, it was the only way to please him. This claim to have been serving God in his actions was evidently considered blasphemous by the high priest, Ananias. He ordered those standing near Paul to strike him on the mouth.[5] Ananias revealed himself to be man of temper and violence, enraged by any supposed opposition to his authority. He was a man more concerned with his power and reputation than with the truth. If this was the character of the high priest, it raises questions about the moral state of the whole Sanhedrin, a point reinforced as the narrative progresses. Their actions revealed their own spiritual condition, and who was really representing God's truth.

Paul responded by rebuking Ananias, calling him a 'whitewashed wall' and one who had violated God's Law in commanding he be struck. Jesus had similarly described the teachers of the law and Pharisees as 'whitewashed tombs, which look beautiful on the outside but on the inside are full of the bones of the dead and everything unclean' (Matthew 23:27).

It seems that Paul was perhaps appealing to the prophetic tradition and Ezekiel who rebuked the false prophets for misleading the people: 'They lead my people astray, saying, "Peace", when there is no peace, and because, when a flimsy wall is built, they cover it with whitewash, therefore tell those who cover it with whitewash that it is going to fall' (Ezekiel 13:10–11). Paul, in making this allusion, was accusing the Jewish

---

[4] Witherington, *Acts*, 687.

[5] Ananias served as high priest between AD 47 and 59. 'After that he continued to wield great authority until he was murdered in AD 66 by revolutionaries, because of his collaboration with Rome.' Peterson, *Acts*, 613. Josephus described Ananias as a 'great hoarder up of money'. *Antiquities* 20.9.2.

leaders of being false prophets, who stood condemned before the God they claimed to represent. They were like flimsy walls, a thin coat of plaster covering deep cracks, or, as Augustine graphically described, 'an inner slimy filthiness'.[6]

The leaders had failed to properly investigate the claims against Paul and condemned him without any evidence or proof. In this way they had violated the very commandments they sought to uphold (see Leviticus 19:15). We can see why Paul was so concerned in his correspondence with younger leaders to emphasise the importance of character.[7] Without godly character, leaders bring harm not only to themselves, but also to their followers. Character trumps competence as the primary qualification for any Christian leader. While we are often drawn to charisma, ability, background or gifting, we need to ensure that the leaders we appoint have the Christlike character necessary to be under-shepherds of his flock.

The text suggests that Paul did not realise he was addressing the high priest at this moment, though how this was possible is a valid question (verses 4–5). Having been informed, Paul offered something of a retraction without quite apologising for his words. He simply claimed not to have known that he was addressing the high priest, quoting words from Exodus 22:28, 'Do not speak evil about the ruler of your people.' He can respect the office, if not the man.

It is possible that Paul was speaking somewhat ironically here. He would not speak evil of the ruler, but in Ananias he did not recognise a legitimate ruler of the people.[8] German theologian Johann Spangenberg (1484–1550) offered the following striking paraphrase of Paul's intent:

> The high priest should be kind and merciful to those who cry out to him, listening, protecting and sheltering poor, innocent people. But now he allows me, a poor man, to be hit in the face, here in public council on account of a truthful word that I said, namely, that I have walked in all good conscience before God up to this day. Thus, I do not consider him the high priest. He is not so before God but is a true tyrant, a whitewashed wall, an external mask, a

---

[6] Augustine, 'Acts', in ACCS 5:276.
[7] See 1 Timothy 3:1–13; Titus 1:5–9.
[8] Marshall, *Acts*, 364; Wall, *Acts*, 310; Calvin, *Acts*, 318. Witherington, *Acts*, 688, notes that Ananias was known for his acts of bribery, theft and violence.

hypocrite, who should be sitting sooner in a pigsty among pigs than here in the priestly chair among rational people.[9]

At this point Paul changed tack, realising there was a significant theological issue that would create disagreement among the Sanhedrin and therefore acquit him of their charges. Paul knew that the Pharisees believed in a bodily resurrection of the dead at the eschaton, whereas the Sadducees did not.[10] Nor did they believe in angels or spirits, whereas the Pharisees did (verse 8).[11] Knowing this, Paul used it to his advantage. The resurrection was of course a centrepiece of Christian faith, but it was also a point of contention among his hearers. This truth would serve to divide his hearers and rescue him from their murderous intent.

He called out, 'My brothers, I am a Pharisee, descended from Pharisees. I stand on trial because of the hope of the resurrection of the dead' (verse 6). Paul knew this was the equivalent of lighting the fuse on a firework. A dispute arose between the Pharisees and the Sadducees. Luke describes the disagreement as vigorous, ultimately becoming violent (verses 9–10). The Jewish leaders, it seems, were more concerned to fight for their own party line than to consider the claims of truth. They would rather fight each other at this point than pursue Paul. Sadly, churches can sometimes look more like the Sanhedrin than the united body of Christ.[12] As Marshall notes, 'Theologians will argue on ticklish points whenever they get the chance.'[13] We could add that some Christians have a similarly unpleasant predisposition.

The Pharisees, having been opposed to Paul, now find themselves defending him, suggesting that an angel or a spirit had spoken to him. The scene feels almost comical and the leaders ridiculous. Whether or not they really believed this or whether they were simply scoring points in the argument is unclear. As the argument intensified, the commander was afraid Paul would be torn to pieces and so ordered his troops to remove him and escort him back to the barracks.

Jesus said to his disciples that they were to be 'as shrewd as snakes and as innocent as doves' (Matthew 10:16). Here was Paul employing

---

[9] Spangenberg, in *RCS* 6:314.

[10] See Luke 20:27–40; Josephus, *War* 2.163–5; *Antiquities* 18.14–16.

[11] Bock and others suggest that the denial of angels and spirits refers to the idea of the intermediate state, as it would be hard to conceive that the Sadducees denied something so clearly mentioned in the Pentateuch. See Bock, *Acts*, 671–2.

[12] Venkataraman, 'Acts', in *SABC*, 1500.

[13] Marshall, *Acts*, 365.

his own shrewdness to turn the situation to his favour. He did not lie, deceive or manipulate. He simply stated the facts he knew in such a way as to work them to his own advantage. Such action is sometimes necessary in seeking to protect ourselves, others or the gospel. It is not sinful to make legitimate use of the tools at our disposal in the interests of the kingdom. Sometimes that will mean Christians use the laws of the land to protect freedoms or campaign for justice. This should be done respectfully and in good conscience, but it is not somehow less spiritual than the surrendering passivity of 'let go and let God'. Such thinking owes more to fatalism than responsible Christianity that seeks to exercise godly wisdom in every situation.

The following night, the Lord appeared to Paul to reassure him: 'Take courage! As you have testified about me in Jerusalem, so you must also testify in Rome' (verse 11). The use of the word 'must' (*dei*) speaks not of vague hope, but of certain necessity.[14] The Lord was directing events towards his appointed ends, and no human authority would thwart his purposes. The command most often repeated in the Bible is, 'Do not be afraid.' This command occurs seventy-seven times through Scripture. The command to 'be strong and courageous' appears eleven times. The Lord had already said to Paul, 'Do not be afraid,' in Acts 18:9, and this would be repeated in Acts 27:24.

If even the great apostle needed the Lord's encouragement, how much more do we need to hear that same word of encouragement? There is much around us to discourage and dishearten. Yet we need to recall the Lord's command to be strong and courageous. Courage is not the absence of fear, but the determination that something else is of greater importance.

Aristotle said courage is the middle way between cowardice and being foolhardy.[15] Biblical courage does not call us to abandon all thought and wisdom. But it does call us to courage, recognising that we can only be courageous because we know the power of him who said he would never leave nor forsake us. I know of one church that has 'courage' as one of its values, using the following statement to explain:

> We are only courageous because we are utterly dependent on God's power at work in us. We are courageous because of his promise to never leave us nor forsake us. We are courageous because we know

---

[14] Tannehill, *Narrative Unity*, 292.
[15] Aristotle, *Nicomachean Ethics* III.vi.

he is able to do immeasurably more than we ask or imagine. We want to be a people who discern God's leading and step out in courageous faith.

This statement recognises both the power of God and our responsibility to live out courageous faith. For Paul, he knew his journey was not yet done. He would testify to the gospel in what was, at the time, the capital of the world – we might even say, in some sense, the ends of the earth (see Acts 1:8). This would be equivalent to an audience with any of today's major global leaders. Paul would testify on the greatest stage, and God would make it happen. As unlikely as it must have seemed at this stage, God would do more than Paul could ask or imagine. His faith in God enabled him, as it enables us, to take courage in the power of God to work through the toughest of circumstances.

2. The plot to kill Paul • Acts 23:12–24

The plot to kill Paul

12 The next morning some Jews formed a conspiracy and bound themselves with an oath not to eat or drink until they had killed Paul. 13 More than forty men were involved in this plot. 14 They went to the chief priests and the elders and said, 'We have taken a solemn oath not to eat anything until we have killed Paul. 15 Now then, you and the Sanhedrin petition the commander to bring him before you on the pretext of wanting more accurate information about his case. We are ready to kill him before he gets here.'

16 But when the son of Paul's sister heard of this plot, he went into the barracks and told Paul.

17 Then Paul called one of the centurions and said, 'Take this young man to the commander; he has something to tell him.' 18 So he took him to the commander.

The centurion said, 'Paul, the prisoner, sent for me and asked me to bring this young man to you because he has something to tell you.'

19 The commander took the young man by the hand, drew him aside and asked, 'What is it you want to tell me?'

20 He said: 'Some Jews have agreed to ask you to bring Paul before the Sanhedrin tomorrow on the pretext of wanting more accurate information about him. 21 Don't give in to them, because more than forty of them are waiting in ambush for him. They have taken an oath not to eat or drink until they have killed him. They are ready now, waiting for your consent to their request.'

22 The commander dismissed the

young man with this warning: 'Don't tell anyone that you have reported this to me.'

Paul transferred to Caesarea

23 Then he called two of his centurions and ordered them, 'Get ready a detachment of two hundred soldiers, seventy horsemen and two hundred spearmen^b to go to Caesarea at nine tonight. 24 Provide horses for Paul so that he may be taken safely to Governor Felix.'

_____

b 23 The meaning of the Greek for this word is uncertain.

The debacle at the Sanhedrin was a frustrating failure for Paul's opponents, who had hoped to secure some charge against him that would lead to his death. Instead, they had descended into infighting that had led to Paul being removed back to the care of the Roman authorities. As a consequence, we read of some forty Jews who formed a plot to assassinate Paul. This sort of behaviour further highlights the political unrest and tensions that existed in Jerusalem at this time.[16]

These men took an oath, refusing to eat or drink until Paul was a dead man (verse 12). Peterson notes the perversity of their religious zeal – taking an oath, refusing to eat and drink, until they had broken the sixth commandment.[17] Given the ensuing narrative and the failure of the plot, one wonders what happened to these forty men – did they in fact die of thirst, or did they renege on their vow?

The official means of securing a guilty verdict had failed, so we find some who will ignore justice and take matters into their own hands. We should never be surprised that people who do not get their way through legal means will resort to illegal means to obtain their goal. This is not an option for followers of 'the Way'. Whatever our frustrations, we must be prepared to suffer injustice, and not resort to underhand, illegal or unethical means to secure hoped-for outcomes. We may be shrewd as snakes within the law, but we must also remain innocent as doves. As the apostle Peter wrote elsewhere, Christians are to entrust themselves to the one who judges justly (1 Peter 2:23).

What is striking in this scene is that the actions of the forty are not contained to themselves. In verse 14 we read that they informed the chief priests and the elders of their plot and asked them to join their cause. They asked the Sanhedrin to petition the commander to bring Paul back before the Sanhedrin 'on the pretext of wanting more accurate

_____

[16] We noted this in commenting on Acts 21:38.
[17] Peterson, _Acts_, 620.

information about his case' (verse 15). The very people who accuse Paul of violating the law are conspiring in the plot to murder him.[18]

This is not just the injustice of the mob; it is now also the injustice of the authorities. They become complicit in conspiring against Paul, knowing full well the plan is to murder him. Their guilt is in helping these forty men exercise their wickedness.

Sadly, many Christians in the world today suffer under unjust regimes. It is not just the illegal actions of individuals or vigilante groups, but the state-sponsored persecution, or sometimes the turning a blind eye to the crimes committed by others. This is a grievous evil. Those of us who do not suffer in this way ought to do everything we can to support, campaign and pray for brothers and sisters facing such situations. We may wonder why God allows such suffering to go on, but then we often read of the church growing fastest in such places.

In verse 16 we read about Paul's nephew who, having discovered the plot, reported it to Paul, who in turn passed it on to the commander. As Stott notes:

> It is tantalizing to read these references to Paul's sister and her son, and to have no further information . . . Were they believers? Did they have some association with Jewish leaders which made it natural for Paul's nephew to learn of the plot . . . Luke does not satisfy our curiosity.[19]

The commander hatched his own plan. He would escort Paul away from Jerusalem under the cover of night. We can see how seriously he took the threat. He sent Paul along with two hundred soldiers, seventy horsemen and two hundred spearmen (verse 23). By outnumbering Paul's opponents by ten to one, Lysias was keen to discourage any potential ambush from attempting to get to Paul.[20]

Lysias's plan to deliver Paul to safety does not necessarily indicate that he was particularly sympathetic to Paul. He was rather concerned to make sure a prisoner, and perhaps some of his own men, were not killed on his watch by an ambush. As Wall notes, 'This is not to claim that Rome's

---

[18] Peterson, *Acts*, 620.

[19] Stott, *Acts*, 355.

[20] Antipatris was about thirty-fives miles away, with Caesarea another twenty-five miles further on. While thirty-five miles in one night would have been a strenuous effort, Witherington provides good evidence to support the historicity of Luke's narrative. See Witherington, *Acts*, 697.

perspective on Paul and his mission is favourable; rather, it is simply to assert that the Rome of Acts is more obedient to its constitutional law than unrepentant Israel of Acts is to its biblical law.'[21]

This is the final time we see Paul in Jerusalem. There is a sense in Luke's narrative in which Paul's departure signals the gospel's departure. Their rejection of him is a rejection of his message. The hope of the resurrection that Paul had held out was not welcomed, but rather dismissed. It is a sad reminder of the urgency and need of the gospel hope to be taken to the ends of the earth.

Bock notes God's hand of providence at work:

> It is unlikely that if Paul had journeyed as part of a missionary outreach to Rome on his own, such a high-level audience would be possible. It is one of the mysteries of God and his providence that many times we cannot see why things are happening as they are. Yet God is surely at work in ways we could not have planned for ourselves.[22]

Sometimes in Acts, God works through the miraculous – think of the prison escapes we see in Acts 5, 12 and 16. Here there is no miraculous escape from the threat, yet that does not mean God is not at work. Here we see God working through the ordinary human actions of Paul's nephew and the commander, Lysias. We ought not to think that God is only at work in the obvious miracle. He is working every bit as much through the ordinary actions of human actors to bring his purposes to fruition.

3. Paul's escape • Acts 23:25–35

25 He wrote a letter as follows:

26 Claudius Lysias,

To His Excellency, Governor Felix:

Greetings.

27 This man was seized by the Jews and they were about to kill him, but I came with my troops and rescued him, for I had learned that he is a Roman citizen. **28** I wanted to know why they were accusing him, so I brought him to their Sanhedrin. **29** I found that the

---

[21] Wall, *Acts*, 313.
[22] Bock, *Acts*, 679.

accusation had to do with questions about their law, but there was no charge against him that deserved death or imprisonment. **30** When I was informed of a plot to be carried out against the man, I sent him to you at once. I also ordered his accusers to present to you their case against him.

31 So the soldiers, carrying out their orders, took Paul with them during the night and brought him as far as Antipatris. **32** The next day they let the cavalry go on with him, while they returned to the barracks. **33** When the cavalry arrived in Caesarea, they delivered the letter to the governor and handed Paul over to him. **34** The governor read the letter and asked what province he was from. Learning that he was from Cilicia, **35** he said, 'I will hear your case when your accusers get here.' Then he ordered that Paul be kept under guard in Herod's palace.

Having made plans for Paul's escape, Claudius Lysias wrote a letter to the governor Felix, explaining the situation and his understanding.[23]

The letter begins by outlining the facts of the case. Paul was seized by the Jews who wanted to kill him, but Lysias and his troops rescued him, having learned he was a Roman citizen. This is, of course, not quite the whole truth. Lysias omits the part where he was about to have Paul flogged. It was only at this point that he learned of his Roman citizenship. This reminds us that while the Roman authorities are not hostile to Christianity in the same way the Jewish authorities are, they are also not exactly friends of 'the Way'. What motivates Lysias ultimately is his own self-interest and self-preservation.[24]

Lysias then outlines his own attempt to understand the reason why the Jews were accusing Paul. His own conclusion is that the matter 'had to do with questions about their law, but there was no charge against him that deserved death or imprisonment' (verse 29). This is similar to the conclusion drawn by Gallio in Acts 18:14–15. Similar statements of Paul's innocence will appear in Acts 25:25, 26:31 and 28:18.[25]

As we have noted before, Luke is keen to show that Christianity is not a threat to Rome and is promoting nothing that would contravene Roman law. It is a legitimate religion operating within Roman law

---

[23] Some question how Luke would have obtained access to the letter. Bock suggests Luke is summarising the contents of a document that would have been made public at Paul's hearing. *Acts*, 682.

[24] Peterson, *Acts*, 619.

[25] Bock, *Acts*, 683.

and should be given the same permissions and freedoms as other religions.

It is also worth noting that Lysias's conclusion is similar to that delivered by Pilate concerning Jesus – 'no basis for your charges against him . . . he has done nothing to deserve death' (Luke 23:14–15). Paul is following in the footsteps of his Lord, which casts a shadow over any potential outcome. And yet, as we have seen, new life can come from death. Sometimes God moves in mysterious ways to advance the cause of the kingdom.

The letter ends with an explanation for sending Paul. Lysias has uncovered a plot to assassinate Paul, and he is therefore sending him to Felix for his own protection, until such a time as his accusers can present their case before Felix.

The soldiers do as instructed, escorting Paul to Caesarea. There they deliver Paul and the letter to the governor, Felix. Having read the letter and inquired as to where Paul was from, he orders that Paul be kept under guard at Herod's palace until his accusers arrived and he could hear their case (verse 35).[26] Felix could have sent Paul on to his home province, Syria, for pretrial, but the inconvenience caused would probably bring more hassle to Felix, hence his decision to keep Paul for trial in Caesarea.[27]

This section portrays two different responses to the gospel. On the one hand, we see the hostility and rejection of Paul's Jewish opponents. On the other hand, we see the functional apathy towards Paul's message. The Roman authorities will protect Paul, but there is little evidence at this stage that Lysias is interested in what Paul has to say. Sometimes we encounter outright opposition. More often we encounter a sort of unconcerned apathy towards the message. Many people are happy to advocate for freedom of religion so long as it does not interfere with their own daily affairs. Both groups have equal need for the gospel.

And we see God's overruling hand carrying Paul onwards to Rome, where he will testify before a higher authority still. Trials and imprisonments do not look like fertile ground for the gospel, yet God is able to work in the most unpromising of circumstances. As Stott describes, 'Between these two powers, religious and civil . . . Paul found himself

---

[26] 'Paul was placed under guard at the Praetorium, or governor's residence, which was originally built by Herod the Great.' Witherington, *Acts*, 702.

[27] Bock, *Acts*, 684.

trapped.'[28] Yet his confidence in his Saviour and in the truth of the gospel enabled him to 'take courage' and persevere. He knew he was ultimately innocent before the charges of Jerusalem and Rome, and before God himself. And so he was able to trust himself to the promise of God, whatever came his way.

---

[28] Stott, *Acts*, 357.

23

Paul Before Felix

ACTS 24

Paul had been accosted in the Temple courts in Jerusalem and nearly killed by his opponents (21:27–36). He had narrowly avoided being flogged by the Roman authorities (22:22–9). He had been delivered from a plot to assassinate him following his appearance before the Sanhedrin (23:12–35). Now we find Paul before the governor, Felix, making a further defence in the presence of his accusers. This would happen again in front of Festus and Agrippa before Paul would finally be transferred to Rome.

At this point we must ask why Luke devotes so much space in his narrative to the various trial scenes. What is it that Luke intends to communicate to his readers? As we have previously noted, in part Luke is concerned to demonstrate that 'the Way' is no threat to Rome. It is not an illegal sect bent on causing trouble. Christianity is to be recognised as a legitimate religion and individuals should be free to commit themselves to 'the Way'. This may have been a much-needed message for Theophilus (Luke 1:1–4).

We have also noted Luke's desire to demonstrate that 'the Way' is no contradiction to Judaism, in the sense that Jesus is their long-awaited Messiah – the fulfilment and climax of God's redemptive plan revealed through the covenants of the Old Testament. Jesus Christ was not starting a breakaway cult in contradiction to Judaism. He was the fulfilment to which the entire story of the Old Testament pointed. Luke wants his Jewish readers to behold and receive their Messiah.

We must also at this point note a third motive for Luke in devoting so much space in his narrative to Paul's various trials. Luke is concerned to demonstrate what it means to be a follower of Jesus Christ. This is no triumphal procession to glory. Christianity is not a conquest over the rulers of Rome. As Paul has previously said, 'We must go through many hardships to enter the kingdom of God' (Acts 14:22). Luke wants to show that the normal Christian life is one of trial, tribulation and hardship. Seeking first the kingdom means denying self and taking up the cross. Opposition and persecution are the narrow road every believer must walk.

As Paul stands before Felix, we once again see him give a defence of his actions and his faith. He is an innocent man who has broken no laws, and there is no proof or evidence that he had done anything illegal. Paul's speech not only demonstrates his innocence but also serves to intrigue Felix, who desires to hear more about 'the Way'.

1. The accusation • Acts 24:1–9

Paul's trial before Felix

24 Five days later the high priest Ananias went down to Caesarea with some of the elders and a lawyer named Tertullus, and they brought their charges against Paul before the governor. **2** When Paul was called in, Tertullus presented his case before Felix: 'We have enjoyed a long period of peace under you, and your foresight has brought about reforms in this nation. **3** Everywhere and in every way, most excellent Felix, we acknowledge this with profound gratitude. **4** But in order not to weary you further, I would request that you be kind enough to hear us briefly.

5 'We have found this man to be a troublemaker, stirring up riots among the Jews all over the world. He is a ringleader of the Nazarene sect **6** and even tried to desecrate the temple; so we seized him. **[7]ᵃ 8** By examining him yourself you will be able to learn the truth about all these charges we are bringing against him.'

9 The other Jews joined in the accusation, asserting that these things were true.

---

a 6-8 Some manuscripts include here *him, and we would have judged him in accordance with our law. 7But the commander Lysias came and took him from us with much violence, 8ordering his accusers to come before you.*

Paul had been kept under guard by Felix for five days before his accusers arrived from Jerusalem. Luke tells us that the travelling party included the high priest Ananias, some of the other elders and a lawyer named Tertullus (verse 1). The term 'lawyer' (*rhētoros*) only occurs here in the New Testament. This is not another teacher or scribe but seems to have been especially employed for the purpose of presenting the most rhetorically persuasive case against Paul.[1] We may liken him to a skilful barrister. Paul's Jewish opponents seem to have stooped to new lows, such was their contempt of him and desire to kill him. How often we see the opponents of Christianity today employ whatever means available to them in their attempt to discredit or punish the followers of Christ.

---

[1] Witherington, *Acts*, 703–4.

In verse 2 we see that it is Tertullus who presented the case, beginning with some well-aimed flattery of Felix: 'We have enjoyed a long period of peace under you, and your foresight has brought about reforms in this nation. Everywhere and in every way, most excellent Felix, we acknowledge this with profound gratitude' (verses 2–3).[2] Historically, this was simply not true. Felix's reputation was that of a brutal ruler who did as much as any before him to exacerbate tensions between Jerusalem and Rome.[3] It is said that flattery will get you everywhere, and this view would seem to have beeen shared by the loquacious Tertullus.

Having concluded the opening praise of Felix, the charge is finally presented. Paul has been found to be a 'troublemaker, stirring up riots among the Jews all over the world. He is a ringleader of the Nazarene sect and even tried to desecrate the temple' (verses 5–6). The term 'troublemaker' (loimon) can be translated more literally as 'plague', as in Luke 21:11.[4] Paul is seen as being like a disease that needs to be eradicated. In the Temple, Paul was accused of speaking against the Law and the Temple. Here the direction of attack is changed and Paul is accused of being a disrupter of the peace.[5] This is a serious charge, if true. Stott observes, 'There were many Jewish agitators at that time, Messianic pretenders who threatened the very "peace" which Tertullus had attributed to Felix.'[6]

As we recall Luke's narrative, we can see that the charges are far from true. The trouble that Paul has encountered has not been initiated by him, but rather by his Jewish opponents. Further, as Paul will argue, 'the Way' is not a sect, but rather stands in continuity with the Law and the Prophets of Judaism. Finally, Paul was in no way desecrating the Temple, but rather went through purificatory rites to ensure such an accusation could not be brought.

The final flourish of Tertullus is to suggest that a man as intelligent as Felix will certainly discover the truth of these things for himself in examining Paul (verse 8).[7]

---

[2] Marshall, Acts, 374. This sort of introduction to a speech was common. It was termed the captatio benevolentiae. The complimentary nature of the opening comments was designed to win the favour of the hearer. Calvin calls it what it really is – 'a filthy and flattering exordium'. Calvin, Acts, 339.

[3] Venkataramen, 'Acts', in SABC, 1501.

[4] Bock, Acts, 690.

[5] Tannehill, Narrative Unity, 297.

[6] Stott, Acts, 360.

[7] 'Thus do false accusers boldly boast that their matter is plain, that they may blind the eyes of the judges.' Calvin, Acts, 342.

Tertullus's speech employed all the devices of the ancient rhetorician in attempting to persuade Felix of Paul's guilt. No doubt it delighted Ananias and the Jewish elders. At this point they are no longer interested in truth – they simply want Paul convicted and condemned. Their hostility towards Paul is a hostility towards God's Messiah. In their actions they do not realise that it is in fact they themselves who stand on trial before the judge of all the earth. With every word and deed, they further condemn themselves. The real tragedy is their own guilt, not Paul's.

It is a reminder for us to view the opponents of Christianity not as enemies we wish to conquer, but rather as people made in God's image facing his eternal judgment. Our hearts should be moved with the tragedy of what lies before them if they will not repent and believe. Jesus reminded his followers to pray for our enemies and bless those who persecute us. This is easier said than done.

Yet as we look at Ananias (or whoever our own equivalent may be), we should not see a pantomime villain who will get what's coming to them, but a sinner far from God, lost and facing judgment. We do not see as the world sees. We do not seek revenge. We love and pray for even those most bitterly opposed to us. We pray that God would so move not just to acquit his persecuted saints, but also to change the hearts of their accusers. This is the counter-cultural action of 'the Way'.

2. The defence • Acts 24:10–21

10 When the governor motioned for him to speak, Paul replied: 'I know that for a number of years you have been a judge over this nation; so I gladly make my defence. 11 You can easily verify that no more than twelve days ago I went up to Jerusalem to worship. 12 My accusers did not find me arguing with anyone at the temple, or stirring up a crowd in the synagogues or anywhere else in the city. 13 And they cannot prove to you the charges they are now making against me. 14 However, I admit that I worship the God of our ancestors as a follower of the Way, which they call a sect. I believe everything that is in accordance with the Law and that is written in the Prophets, 15 and I have the same hope in God as these men themselves have, that there will be a resurrection of both the righteous and the wicked. 16 So I strive always to keep my conscience clear before God and man.

17 'After an absence of several years, I came to Jerusalem to bring my people gifts for the poor and to present offerings. 18 I was ceremonially clean when they found me in the temple courts doing this. There was no crowd with

me, nor was I involved in any distur- | crime they found in me when I stood
bance. **19** But there are some Jews from | before the Sanhedrin – **21** unless it was
the province of Asia, who ought to be | this one thing I shouted as I stood in
here before you and bring charges if | their presence: "It is concerning the
they have anything against me. **20** Or | resurrection of the dead that I am on
these who are here should state what | trial before you today." '

Paul's own defence speech, in contrast to the prosecution, begins with
no empty flattery. Paul simply states that he is glad to make his defence
before Felix since he has been judge over the nation for a number of
years. The essence of Paul's defence is to assert that there is no proof or
evidence of the charges. He states, 'My accusers did not find me arguing
with anyone at the temple, or stirring up a crowd in the synagogues or
anywhere else in the city. And they cannot prove to you the charge they
are now making against me' (verses 12–13). Essentially, the charges they
bring are false, and they can produce no evidence or proof of the things
of which they accuse Paul. Felix will be able to easily verify all of this
when Lysias arrives.

Paul's actions and character have been above reproach. He has not behaved
in the way he stands accused. Whatever the opponents of Christianity may
wish to assert, Christians should be able to say with a clear conscience
that they have not broken any laws or behaved in ways that would be
considered immoral. People may dislike the message, but we should give
no grounds to substantiate false allegations. As Peter said, we should be able
to live such good lives that even though others accuse us of doing wrong,
opponents will be ashamed of their slander on the day of his visitation (1
Peter 2:12–13). We should never stoop to the world's tactics. We should
conduct ourselves in ways that are upright and holy. When people oppose
or accuse us, there should be nothing in our conduct that would condemn
us, other than our faithfulness to the Lord Jesus.

While Paul denies the charges, he is readily prepared to admit:

> I worship the God of our ancestors as a follower of the Way, which
> they call a sect. I believe everything that is in accordance with
> the Law and that is written in the Prophets, and I have the same
> hope in God as these men themselves have, that there will be a
> resurrection of both the righteous and the wicked. (Acts 24:14–15)

Here we see Paul affirming his continuity with Judaism. He worships the
same God as their ancestors. He denies that the followers of Christ are a

new sect. He believes everything written in the Law and Prophets, and claims the same hope in God of the resurrection of the dead.

All of these things, apart from him being a follower of 'the Way', put him in association with his opponents. Paul is not a follower of a newly invented religion. His assertion is that Jesus is the fulfilment of everything written in the Law and Prophets. He believes the same fundamental tenets of Judaism; he has just come to see that Jesus was and is the long-awaited Messiah.

In effect, Paul is saying to Felix, 'I believe everything they do; it's just that I also have come to believe Jesus is our Messiah.' Of course, to Paul's Jewish opponents this was blasphemy worthy of the death penalty, but before a Roman judge this would have appeared to be an obscure theological squabble, and not something warranting further action. Yet Paul's defence is not yet finished.

In verses 17–21 Paul goes on to make clear he has not done anything that would constitute a crime worthy of punishment. He outlines his movements in Jerusalem. He brought gifts for the poor and undertook ceremonial cleansing.[8] He was not with any crowd in the Temple, nor causing any disturbance. Those who think differently ought to be present to make their case if they can demonstrate wrongdoing. Similarly, the Sanhedrin found no guilt or crime. Paul has not disturbed the *pax Romana* or done anything for which he should be punished. Once again, he alludes to the theological disagreement that does exist: 'It is concerning the resurrection of the dead that I am on trial before you today' (verse 21). As we saw in Acts 23, the Sanhedrin themselves could not agree on this theological debate, yet they were not putting one another on trial and seeking the death penalty – so how could they do such a thing to Paul? The apostle here acts with both integrity and wisdom. He has committed no crime punishable by Rome, and his theological disagreement with his Jewish opponents is not a matter of state interest.

In many parts of the world, Christians enjoy a high degree of religious freedom, but in other places they do not. Luke intends to show that Christianity is no threat to the laws of the land, and that followers of Jesus act with integrity and respect. As such, they should be given the freedom to worship according to conscience. The state should recognise

---

[8] Paul's letters describe more fully this significant sum of money brought as a gift to the poor saints in Jerusalem from their Gentile brothers and sisters across the Empire. See 1 Corinthians 16:1–4; 2 Corinthians 8–9; Romans 15:25–33. Marshall, *Acts*, 378.

this, and Christians will sometimes need to campaign for such freedoms to be upheld and recognised.

In some places, such freedoms are not enjoyed. Christianity is outlawed and the punishments are severe. This is an incredibly difficult situation. We need to pray for our brothers and sisters in such places that they will be empowered by God's Spirit to be faithful witnesses and people of integrity. Luke shows us that God can often move in such difficult circumstances to advance his kingdom.

3. The verdict and aftermath • Acts 24:22–7

22 Then Felix, who was well acquainted with the Way, adjourned the proceedings. 'When Lysias the commander comes,' he said, 'I will decide your case.' **23** He ordered the centurion to keep Paul under guard but to give him some freedom and permit his friends to take care of his needs.

24 Several days later Felix came with his wife Drusilla, who was Jewish. He sent for Paul and listened to him as he spoke about faith in Christ Jesus.

25 As Paul talked about righteousness, self-control and the judgment to come, Felix was afraid and said, 'That's enough for now! You may leave. When I find it convenient, I will send for you.' **26** At the same time he was hoping that Paul would offer him a bribe, so he sent for him frequently and talked with him.

27 When two years had passed, Felix was succeeded by Porcius Festus, but because Felix wanted to grant a favour to the Jews, he left Paul in prison.

Having heard the case, Felix adjourns until Lysias arrives. He will be able to verify whether or not Paul has in fact incited a disturbance. Until he arrives Paul is kept under guard, though permitted to have care and visitation from his friends.[9] The sentence seems fair. Paul is treated well and not condemned without proper evidence. He is given some freedoms. And yet we see that Paul is kept under such a condition for more than two years (verse 27). He has not been found guilty of anything at this point and yet his freedom has still been significantly curtailed. Felix is clearly trying to appease both parties.

---

[9] Witherington, *Acts*, 714–15, suggests Paul remained in the governor's palace while his needs were provided for by his friends. Peterson, *Acts*, 639, suggests that this two-year period may have been when Paul wrote the letters to the Colossians, Ephesians, Philippians, Philemon and 2 Timothy.

He does not want to simply release Paul and upset his Jewish accusers, but neither does he want to condemn Paul without proper proof. He opts for a pragmatic punt into the long grass. There is no indication of when Lysias might arrive, if at all, and after two years what might he be expected to remember of the incident? Felix perhaps hopes things will die down and he will be able to quietly let Paul go without too much trouble.

Sometimes human authorities operate more under self-interested pragmatism than a real desire for justice. In fact, such an approach is really an injustice, as Paul is kept under guard without any verdict given. Christians need much patience and trust in God's sovereign purposes to endure such injustices, all the while maintaining their integrity.

Intriguingly, Luke informs us that Felix was well acquainted with 'the Way'. Where had he found out about Christianity? What had he heard and what did he know? What was his own opinion? Luke does not give us much more information, other than he had a Jewish wife named Drusilla. Perhaps she knew something of 'the Way' also? Calvin recalls that Drusilla was the daughter of Herod Agrippa who had met a gory end in Acts 12.[10] Perhaps Drusilla had become acquainted with 'the Way' in the aftermath. Felix clearly had some interest in what Paul had to say as he held frequent audience, along with his wife, with the apostle (verses 24–6).

As Paul had opportunity to speak to Felix, he spoke of faith in Christ Jesus, righteousness, self-control and the judgment to come. In essence, provided with an opportunity, Paul shared the gospel with this official and his wife. Here is a fulfilment of Jesus's words in Luke 21:12–15: the apostle is given words to say when brought before kings and governors.[11] He spoke about sin, judgment and faith. It is striking that, given an opportunity to speak for Christ, Paul shared the gospel. He didn't speak of his own cause or case. He simply pointed them to Jesus, knowing where their greatest need lay. There was a powerful courage and boldness here in Paul as he was empowered by God's Spirit. How often do we fail to take an opportunity out of fear of what others may think of us? Yet Paul found a way to share something of his faith in a way that had an obvious impact.

Also noteworthy here is that Paul did not shy away from difficult topics in his gospel presentation. As he spoke of righteousness and self-control,

---

[10] Calvin, *Acts*, 353.
[11] Tannehill, *Narrative Unity*, 301.

he presumably struck a nerve, given Felix's situation with Drusilla.[12] Like John the Baptist before Herod, Paul challenged the ruler's own sexual immorality. Paul did not water down the holiness of God to win the ear of Felix. He also did not hesitate to speak about the judgment of God. Increasingly today, this is a topic that many preachers shy away from. We are told instead to tell people simply that God loves them. Of course, it is true that God loves all whom he has made. But we must also speak of God's holy and righteous judgment. If people are not convicted of the 'bad news', they will not know why they need the 'good news' of Jesus, the Saviour.

Clearly, we need to find winsome, sensitive and persuasive ways to speak on such difficult and emotive subjects, but speak of them we must. We cannot shy away from them because they might be seen as unpopular, unattractive or intolerant. We must not be afraid to cause offence, where the offence is that of the gospel message itself. People need to know they are 'destined to die once, and after that to face judgment' (Hebrews 9:27). Without this they will see no need for Jesus's atoning sacrificial death as the only payment for sins and their only hope of forgiveness, salvation and eternal life. Paul shows us the critical importance of these themes in our witness.

Felix was unusual in that he was a former slave and not part of the aristocracy. The historian Tacitus describes Felix as having 'practiced every kind of cruelty and lust, wielding the power of a king with all the instincts of a slave'.[13] Witherington notes that Felix was recalled to Rome around AD 59 following the 'violent and unsuccessful way he dealt with riots between Jews and Gentiles in Caesarea'.[14] Witherington continues, 'Despite all of this, he somehow managed to marry three women of royal birth . . . the first being the granddaughter of Antony and Cleopatra and the last being Drusilla the daughter of Herod Agrippa I.'[15]

Given this information, we can see why Paul's speech concerning righteousness and self-control would have made for uncomfortable listening for Felix.

Luke also alludes to a mixed motive in Felix's repeated invitations

---

[12] Witherington says of Drusilla that Felix had 'lusted after [her] while she was still the teenage bride of Azizus the king of Emesa'. *Acts*, 715. Bock notes that Drusilla was the third wife of Felix, he having persuaded her to leave her first husband. *Acts*, 695.

[13] Cited in Peterson, *Acts*, 626.

[14] Witherington, *Acts*, 699.

[15] Witherington, *Acts*, 699–700.

to hear Paul. He was 'hoping that Paul would offer him a bribe' (verse 26).[16] While Felix had some interest in hearing Paul speak of 'the Way', he again revealed something of his true colours here. His real desire was that Paul might line his pocket and that he might financially benefit from granting Paul freedom. After all, Paul had proven himself adept at collecting funds when he needed them.[17]

Once again, the one responsible for administering justice proves himself inadequate for such a task. We perhaps wonder if Paul were ever tempted to gain his freedom in this way. It would have enabled him to travel, to start new missionary journeys, to reach more people, to plant new churches. Was he tempted? Did others persuade him that this was what everyone else did? Perhaps the end could justify the means. 'Not so,' is the answer implied by Luke's narrative. Paul would not do something he knew to be wrong, whatever his own personal benefit or the potential 'greater good'.

Utilitarianism was the ethical philosophy popularised by Jeremy Bentham (1748–1832). The 'right' was determined by the greatest good for the greatest number. The end could justify the means. On the contrary, the Bible says the means matter. We should not attempt to obtain some higher good via immoral means. In parts of the world today, rulers are accustomed to using positions of power to obtain bribes. Paul shows us that we ought to do right and trust God with the outcomes. Paul models integrity in both speech and action that should characterise every believer.

The two years of imprisonment must have felt, as Jennings describes, an absurd waste to Paul.[18] Many of us may wonder how our own circumstances can be part of God's purposes – an absurd waste of our time and talents. Our prisons may not be physical, but they may constrain us every bit as much as Paul's. We must continue to trust that God has purposes, for us and for others, in those times when we feel sidelined and unfruitful in his service. We might see broken pieces; God sees the mosaic.

After two years, Festus succeeded Felix as governor.[19] As Felix wanted

---

[16] 'The taking of bribes was of course forbidden by Roman law, but it was hard to bring a governor to account for such a misdemeanour, and the custom was far from uncommon.' Marshall, *Acts*, 382.

[17] Gooding, *True to the Faith*, 465.

[18] Jennings, *Acts*, chapter 15, paragraph 4.

[19] Felix likely left for Rome in AD 58, with Festus succeeding him in AD 59. Witherington asks what Luke may have been doing during these two years and suggests that this may have been the period he 'carefully investigated everything from the beginning' (Luke 1:3). See Witherington, *Acts*, 716–17.

to grant the Jews a favour, he left Paul in prison (verse 27). It was one final unjust act from the supposed arbiter of justice. He had the status and position – a façade of dignity and respectability.[20] But Felix was a man seduced by power, sex and money: three gods he would rather serve than bow the knee before the one true Lord.

Believers should not expect an easy life as they choose to take up their cross; it will be suffering now, glory later. Paul learned to entrust himself to the one who judges justly. This is still a critical message for our world today. Following Jesus is not offered as an easy or a happy life. Faithfulness will mean hardship, but with it a deeper joy of knowing life in all its fullness. Faithfulness for the disciple will mean the need to face many trials of our own as we seek to spread the gospel and be faithful witnesses to the risen Christ. This we must embrace as a natural part of our own discipleship. The prosperity gospel is a deceit. There is no promise of health, wealth and happiness this side of heaven. Being a follower of the Lord Jesus calls us to take up our cross as we seek to bring glory and honour to his name.

---

[20] Venkataraman, 'Acts', in *SABC*, 1502.

24

Paul Before Festus

ACTS 25:1–22

Previously Paul found himself on trial before the Sanhedrin and before Felix. In both cases his opponents failed to prove their charges against him. Now, having been kept under guard for two years, Paul must again face his accusers, this time before Festus. At every point in the narrative, Luke is keen to demonstrate that the charges against Paul are spurious. Paul has done nothing that would make him a threat to either Jerusalem or Rome. God is at work throughout to protect his servant and continues to open the doors towards an audience with Caesar in Rome.

There are some parallels between Jesus and Paul in their trial scenes before Jewish and Roman authorities.[1] The innocence of both is stressed, as are the unjust actions of their accusers. Though the ultimate outcome of Paul's trials is not provided, we can see in both men that the way of obedience and faithfulness is often the way of unjust suffering and opposition. Yet God finds surprising ways to bring new life from the bleakest situations.

1. The trial before Festus • Acts 25:1–12

Paul's trial before Festus

25 Three days after arriving in the province, Festus went up from Caesarea to Jerusalem, ²where the chief priests and the Jewish leaders appeared before him and presented the charges against Paul. ³They requested Festus, as a favour to them, to have Paul transferred to Jerusalem, for they were preparing an ambush to kill him

along the way. ⁴Festus answered, 'Paul is being held at Caesarea, and I myself am going there soon. ⁵Let some of your leaders come with me, and if the man has done anything wrong, they can press charges against him there.'

⁶After spending eight or ten days with them, Festus went down to Caesarea. The next day he convened the court and ordered that Paul be brought

---

[1] Peterson, *Acts*, 644.

before him. **7** When Paul came in, the Jews who had come down from Jerusalem stood round him. They brought many serious charges against him, but they could not prove them.

8 Then Paul made his defence: 'I have done nothing wrong against the Jewish law or against the temple or against Caesar.'

9 Festus, wishing to do the Jews a favour, said to Paul, 'Are you willing to go up to Jerusalem and stand trial before me there on these charges?'

10 Paul answered: 'I am now standing before Caesar's court, where I ought to be tried. I have not done any wrong to the Jews, as you yourself know very well. **11** If, however, I am guilty of doing anything deserving death, I do not refuse to die. But if the charges brought against me by these Jews are not true, no one has the right to hand me over to them. I appeal to Caesar!'

12 After Festus had conferred with his council, he declared: 'You have appealed to Caesar. To Caesar you will go!'

In Acts 24:27, Luke informed us that Felix, as a favour to the Jews, left Paul in prison for two years. The idea of political favour will appear repeatedly throughout Acts 25 as leaders demonstrate a greater concern for power than for truth and justice.

After Felix left, he was succeeded by Festus. The limited information available about Festus suggests his tenure in Judea was brief – perhaps just two to three years – before he died in office around AD 61 or 62.[2] From the brief accounts of Josephus, it appears that Festus may have been viewed as more of an ally to Jewish interests than his predecessor.[3] He certainly appears on the face of things to be more moderate, yet as the narrative progresses we see that he was just as seduced by the 'channels of influence' as his predecessor.

Just three days into his new post, Festus decided to travel to Jerusalem, 'where the chief priests and the Jewish leaders appeared before him and presented the charges against Paul' (verse 2).[4]

Jerusalem was the second largest city under his jurisdiction, so it was prudent to make a good first impression with a group possessing significant influence. Two years had passed since the Jewish leaders had attempted to have Paul convicted and put to death. They obviously had long memories and their desire to be rid of Paul had clearly not cooled in the intervening period. This may suggest that the followers of 'the

---

[2] Witherington, *Acts*, 717.

[3] Witherington, *Acts*, 717–18. See too Josephus, *Antiquities* 20:182–97; *War* 2:271.

[4] The Greek word for leaders is *prōtoi* ('leaders') not *presbyterous* ('elders'), perhaps signifying a more coordinated attack against Paul. Wall, *Acts*, 325.

Way' in Jerusalem had continued to go from strength to strength, much to the annoyance of the Jewish elites.[5]

We may recall, from Acts 23:12–22, the plot hatched by the Jewish conspirators. Their plan had been to ask the commander, Lysias, to transfer Paul from the barracks to the Sanhedrin for further questioning. Their plan had been to ambush him and kill him on the way. In Acts 25:3 we see the same plan being attempted for a second time: 'They requested Festus, as a favour to them, to have Paul transferred to Jerusalem, for they were preparing an ambush to kill him along the way.' The term 'favour' (*charis*) is repeated in verse 9, casting a shadow over Festus's impartiality as a judge.

Once again, we see the leaders of the Jewish people – the supposed pillars and exemplars of the community – fuelled by a demonic hatred of Paul and his message. Their hearts had not softened one bit during the intervening two years. If anything, they seem more determined than ever to silence him. Sometimes the seasons of opposition are brief; sometimes they are protracted, yet Luke is demonstrating that even in weakness God is still advancing his purposes.

Whether Festus was aware of the previous attempt is unclear, but he answered the Jewish leaders by inviting them to accompany him to Caesarea and present their charges there (verse 4–5). This was probably an attempt to keep the Jewish leaders on side by granting the trial, but also an assertion of his own authority by requiring them to travel to him.

Having spent eight or ten days in Jerusalem, Festus returned to Caesarea, presumably accompanied by some of the Jewish leaders, as the next day he convened the court and ordered that Paul be brought before him (verse 6). As before, the Jews brought many serious charges against Paul and, as before, they were unable to prove any of them (verse 7). Paul was innocent. He had done nothing to warrant a guilty verdict or the accompanying penalty. Repeatedly in this latter section of Acts, Luke is at pains to demonstrate this point.

One wonders whether Paul's opponents believed the accusations themselves. Were they aware that many of the charges were fabricated but, blinded by their hatred, were spurred on to do whatever necessary in their attempt to win a conviction? Perhaps they had convinced themselves over time that the charges really were true. Psychologists speak of 'confirmation bias' – the idea that if you want to believe something enough you will interpret the evidence in such a way as it confirms that which you have already come to believe.

---

[5] Wall, *Acts*, 324.

The Jewish leaders were so hardened against Paul and his message that they were no longer interested in evidence or truth. Their minds were made up. Nothing could change them. The battle against opposition, Paul reminds us in his letters, is not just against 'flesh and blood'. There is a spiritual element involved: 'the powers of this dark world and the spiritual forces of evil in the heavenly realms' (Ephesians 6:12). It is for this reason that we must respond with love and prayer for our enemies (Matthew 5:44). We love them because we see the awful reality of Satan's blinding and bewitching work. We pray because we recognise that human persuasion alone will not open blind eyes. We must pray that God himself, by the power of his Spirit, would bring illumination and regeneration to those dead in their trespasses and sins (Ephesians 2:1).

In the absence of evidence, Paul makes his own defence. We must presume, as elsewhere in Acts, that Luke is presenting a summary of the sorts of things Paul said in his defence speech. In essence, Paul makes three important claims in verse 8: he has not done anything against the Jewish Law, against the Temple or against Caesar. There is no proof of wrongdoing that would convict him in a Jewish court or a Roman court. Paul is innocent of wrongdoing before Caesar and the laws of Rome. He is also innocent before the Jewish Law, and therefore, by implication, the God of Judaism. Paul is keen to demonstrate that he stands in line with the Jewish Law and tradition as it points towards its Messiah. It is the Jewish leaders who are guilty before God since they have rejected his Son, their Messiah.

Festus, eager to ingratiate himself with the Jewish leaders, asks Paul whether he would be prepared to be transferred to Jerusalem to stand trial there (verse 9).[6] At this point, as Tannehill observes, 'Roman justice is being undermined by political calculations . . . [Festus] needs to placate a powerful pressure group.'[7] Paul has already survived one ambush attempt and therefore probably has his own suspicions regarding the reason why the Jewish leaders may want to see him transferred.

Paul's reply is polite but firm: 'I am now standing before Caesar's court, where I ought to be tried' (verse 10). There is no reason for a transfer. He is standing in the place where justice ought to be administered. Festus has taken his seat in the judge's chair. It is his responsibility to judge the case on the evidence presented. And yet he seems reluctant, and justice does not seem to be forthcoming.

---

[6] Here is the second use of the word 'favour' (*charis*, see verse 3).
[7] Tannehill, *Narrative Unity*, 306.

Paul reiterates his defence: 'I have not done any wrong to the Jews, as you yourself know very well' (verse 10). There is an implied critique of Festus here. The evidence is clear – or rather it is clear that there is no evidence! A judge of any competence would see this. The charges are unsubstantiated. The case ought to be thrown out, not drawn out. If Festus were to follow the principles of his own law, Paul ought to be found 'not guilty'. There is no case for a transfer or retrial.

Paul exhibits his willingness to submit to the legal system. If he has done anything deserving death he is unafraid to die. Yet if the charges are unproven, then 'no one has the right to hand me over to them' (verse 11). As Christians we ought to be prepared to submit to the laws of the land as far as it is possible. If we break a just law, we should expect to face the consequences. In extreme circumstances we may even have to face the ultimate penalty if the requirement of gospel faithfulness is obedience to God not people (see Acts 4:19).

In this case, Paul has done nothing deserving death. He is innocent, as Festus well knows. The motive behind Festus's request is therefore highly questionable. He seems more interested in making friends than upholding justice.[8] As Witherington says, 'Justice ceases to be blind when Festus succumbs to the desire to placate the Jewish elite and do them a favour in the Paul matter.'[9] Sadly, this is often where injustice begins – turning a blind eye or ingratiating oneself with others by granting favours. Such acts of injustice are often subtle rather than blatant. But one small injustice often begets another larger injustice. Sometimes rules are gently bent rather than broken outright. How should Christians respond in such circumstances? The answer to that will vary from situation to situation. At the very least, the Christian must pray and entrust themselves to the one who judges justly (1 Peter 2:23). But Paul goes further.

At this point, Paul may perhaps sense that Festus is little better than Felix. Faced with the prospect of transfer and ambush, he plays his trump card as a Roman citizen – he appeals to Caesar (verse 11).[10] This appeal is known as the *provocatio*: 'an appeal of a citizen for Caesar's judgement'.[11] A Roman citizen has the right to such an appeal in extraordinary cases

---

[8] The word translated as 'hand over' (*charisasthai*) is a cognate of the word *charis* ('favour') used in verses 3 and 9. Paul can see the motivation behind Festus's suggestion. Peterson, *Acts*, 649.

[9] Witherington, *Acts*, 720.

[10] Witherington has a detailed excursus on the origin and process of appeal for Roman citizens in the provinces. *Acts*, 724–6.

[11] Bock, *Acts*, 702.

(those outside the legal code) and where the seriousness of the charges may result in the death penalty.[12] It also highlights Paul's lack of confidence in Festus's ability to fairly judge his case.

It is right for Christians to make proper use of good laws to protect themselves. It is not worldly, nor is it a failure to trust God. It is being 'shrewd as snakes' (Matthew 10:16) and making appropriate use of the protection offered. Good laws are set up to protect people from injustice, and by making use of them justice is further promoted and upheld. It is therefore a service to others, not just an act of self-interest. Paul also knew that he had been given a divine appointment in Rome, and so he was unafraid to place himself in the hands of Caesar (Acts 23:11).

Festus, clearly taken aback by Paul's appeal, conferred with his council. He knew his hands were tied to some degree at this juncture. He did not want to upset the Jewish leaders, but he did not dare to act in a manner contrary to Roman law – he was stuck between a rock and a hard place.[13] His own failure to act justly had brought him more problems, not fewer. Due process required him to honour Paul's request, so he declared (much to the frustration of the Jewish opponents, one imagines): 'You have appealed to Caesar. To Caesar you will go!' (verse 12).[14]

The Caesar in question at this time was Nero. It may seem strange, given Nero's later reputation for persecuting Christians, for Paul to want to appear before such a man. However, this period was part of the early years of Nero's reign when he appears to have been more temperate.[15] In addition, Paul is not afraid to die so long as he can complete the task the risen Lord had given him (Acts 20:24).

2. Festus consults King Agrippa • Acts 25:13–22

Festus consults King Agrippa

13 A few days later King Agrippa and Bernice arrived at Caesarea to pay their respects to Festus. 14 Since they were spending many days there, Festus discussed Paul's case with the king. He said: 'There is a man here whom Felix left as a prisoner. 15 When I went to

---

[12] Bock, *Acts*, 702–3.

[13] Stott, *Acts*, 367.

[14] Festus was not at liberty to deny the request. His decision to take counsel perhaps suggests his own uncertainty and inexperience – a further Lucan question mark over his competence to judge. 'It would not look good to have such a case poorly handled in the province and then referred to the emperor.' Peterson, *Acts*, 650.

[15] Bock, *Acts*, 703.

Jerusalem, the chief priests and the elders of the Jews brought charges against him and asked that he be condemned.

16 'I told them that it is not the Roman custom to hand over anyone before they have faced their accusers and have had an opportunity to defend themselves against the charges. 17 When they came here with me, I did not delay the case, but convened the court the next day and ordered the man to be brought in. 18 When his accusers got up to speak, they did not charge him with any of the crimes I had expected. 19 Instead, they had some points of dispute with him about their own religion and about a dead man named Jesus whom Paul claimed was alive. 20 I was at a loss how to investigate such matters; so I asked if he would be willing to go to Jerusalem and stand trial there on these charges. 21 But when Paul made his appeal to be held over for the Emperor's decision, I ordered him to be held until I could send him to Caesar.'

22 Then Agrippa said to Festus, 'I would like to hear this man myself.'

He replied, 'Tomorrow you will hear him.'

Having appealed to Caesar, it appears Paul is retained in custody until the time comes for him to sail for Italy (Acts 27:1). Meanwhile, Luke introduces one more significant figure into the trial scenes. He tells us, 'A few days later King Agrippa and Bernice arrived at Caesarea to pay their respects to Festus' (verse 13).

The Agrippa in question is Herod Agrippa II, the last in the Herodian line. His great-grandfather had been Herod the Great, the ruler who had attempted to kill the infant Jesus. His father, Agrippa I, had beheaded James and imprisoned Peter. His death is recorded in Acts 12:23. Neither of these names and associations fills the reader with much hope regarding Paul's predicament. The Herodian dynasty could hardly be seen as friendly towards Jesus and his followers! Yet Agrippa would have had a familiarity with Jewish Law and customs which would explain Festus's desire to consult with him over this case. Bernice was Agrippa's sister (as was Drusilla, wife of Felix – see 24:24), though there were rumours of an incestuous relationship between them.[16] Bock notes the irony in having this pair sit in judgment on Paul who, as Luke makes clear, is innocent: 'this is a world turned upside down'.[17]

Since they were there for some time, Paul's case came up in conversation between them. Festus recounted the events of the trial and confessed his own bewilderment at the charges and how to investigate them.

---

[16] Witherington, *Acts*, 728; Josephus, *Antiquities* 20.145–7.
[17] Bock, *Acts*, 710.

He recalled how the Jewish leaders had spoken with him on his visit to Jerusalem – they brought charges against Paul and asked that he be condemned. Festus informed them of the Roman custom – a man should have a chance to defend himself. Of course, Paul had already done that on more than one occasion – a detail Festus left out. Luke's portrayal of Festus here is that he is 'not only self-serving but also a novice'.[18] As Agrippa's conclusion demonstrates, 'This man could have been set free if he had not appealed to Caesar' (Acts 26:32). This is an implicit criticism directed at Festus's inability to render the obvious verdict.

Festus confessed his surprise that the Jewish leaders did not bring any of the charges he expected them to bring. Rather, they had 'some points of dispute with him about their own religion and about a dead man named Jesus whom Paul claimed was alive' (verse 18–19). These may have been similar charges to those brought previously by Tertullus (24:5–8). Once again, Luke is stressing Paul's innocence. Gallio had come to the same conclusion in Corinth (18:12–17), as had the commander, Lysias, in his letter to Felix (23:29). Before the court of Rome this was deemed a petty theological dispute, and not something worthy of their attention. In one sense they were correct. As far as Rome was concerned, this was a minor and insignificant issue.

Of course, on the other hand, this is the most important issue in all of human history: 'a dead man named Jesus whom Paul claimed was alive'. At the heart of all Paul's defence speeches is the resurrection.[19] This is the turning point of history. It is the vindication of Jesus as God's Messiah. It is the beginning of the last days. It is a deeply political announcement concerning the King of kings and Lord of lords. Nothing could be more significant or more of a threat to the authority claims of Caesar.

This is the message committed to the followers of Jesus. While it has become fashionable in some theological circles to deny the actual bodily resurrection of Jesus, it is the critical plank in a biblical Christology that connects his work on the cross to our eternal future. As Paul said to the Corinthians, 'if Christ has not been raised, your faith is futile; you are still in your sins' (1 Corinthians 15:17). Our world needs to know that Jesus is Lord, not just Saviour. In fact, he cannot be the Saviour without also being the Lord of all.

Jesus is not just a good moral example, though he is that. The resurrection tells us that what Jesus did on the cross was accepted by the

---

[18] Witherington, *Acts*, 729.
[19] Acts 22:6–8; 23:6; 24:21; 26:8.

Father. It tells us that he can get us through death because he got himself through death. It tells us that he now lives and intercedes before the Father on our behalf. It tells us that he is sovereign over human history. The resurrection is the gospel announcement that changes everything.

The sixteenth-century Copernican Revolution discovered that the sun does not revolve around us, but rather we revolve around the sun. The gospel revolution tells all humankind that life does not revolve around us; rather everything, my life included, revolves around the Son, with him at the centre of all. This transforms not just individual lives, but the whole course of human history. It is this we are to proclaim until he returns.

Festus confessed that he was 'at a loss how to investigate such matters; so I asked if he would be willing to go to Jerusalem and stand trial there on these charges' (verse 20). As readers, we suspect that there is a combination here of Festus's own incompetence and his desire to ingratiate himself with the Jewish authorities. He then recalled Paul's appeal to Caesar and his decision to hold him until such a time as he could send him to Caesar.

At this point, Agrippa said to Festus, 'I would like to hear this man myself,' to which Festus replied, 'Tomorrow you will hear him.' Again, we see God moving in mysterious ways to provide Paul with opportunities to speak of Jesus before significant figures in authority.[20] It is not quite witness to 'the ends of the earth' (see 1:8), but it feels like it is getting close.

Through Paul's trials and difficulties, God is at work, spreading the message through him across the Empire. Though Paul looks like a 'passive pawn' being passed around in events beyond his control, God is moving every piece in accordance with his master plan.[21] How often in Scripture do we see God move in unexpected ways, often in people's struggles and weakness, to advance his cause? This gives great comfort to believers everywhere feeling their own inadequacy or trial. God is not limited by our limitations. He can still work in surprising ways through us, if we are prepared to remain faithful and are open to being used as witnesses for him.

---

[20] As noted above, this is in fulfilment of Luke 21:12–15 and Acts 9:15.
[21] Johnson, *Acts*, 422.

25

Paul Before King Agrippa

ACTS 25:23–26:32

Witherington describes this scene as a 'theatre of the absurd'.[1] Paul finds himself in a sort of 'show trial' for the intrigue or entertainment of King Agrippa and his esteemed friends. That is not to say that Agrippa has no genuine interest, but there would be less-public means for Agrippa to speak with Paul. It is worth noting that Paul is not making a legal defence at this point. Agrippa will merely give his opinion to Festus. Paul is using this opportunity to bear witness to the risen Lord Jesus.

Festus continues to look weak and incompetent as Paul's appeal has left him with a real difficulty. How can he send Paul on to Rome without any substantial charges against him? Of course, all of this was propagated by Festus's own attempt to despatch Paul to almost certain death in Jerusalem.[2]

Paul takes the opportunity to give one of the fullest and clearest explanations of his own story and the gospel message. Agrippa may not have any serious interest in becoming a Christian, but Paul makes the most of the opportunity to speak boldly (*parrēsiazomenos*) before this audience of influential persons.

Once again, Luke demonstrates the clear innocence of Paul – a conclusion drawn by all those present (26:31–2). And once again we see God fulfilling his purposes, just as he foretold: Paul would bear witness before 'Gentiles and their kings and to the people of Israel' (Acts 9:15).

For the reader, there is an important question running through the narrative. Festus does not know how to give an account to 'His Majesty' ('Lord'). Agrippa the King seems perplexed by the case. Paul knows who the true Lord and King is and calls those listening to make the same confession.

---

[1] Witherington, *Acts*, 734.
[2] Peterson, *Acts*, 654.

1. A royal audience • Acts 25:23–7

Paul before Agrippa

23 The next day Agrippa and Bernice came with great pomp and entered the audience room with the high-ranking military officers and the prominent men of the city. At the command of Festus, Paul was brought in. **24** Festus said: 'King Agrippa, and all who are present with us, you see this man! The whole Jewish community has petitioned me about him in Jerusalem and here in Caesarea, shouting that he ought not to live any longer. **25** I found he had done nothing deserving of death, but because he made his appeal to the Emperor I decided to send him to Rome. **26** But I have nothing definite to write to His Majesty about him. Therefore I have brought him before all of you, and especially before you, King Agrippa, so that as a result of this investigation I may have something to write. **27** For I think it is unreasonable to send a prisoner on to Rome without specifying the charges against him.'

The scene begins with the 'great pomp' (*phantasia*) of Agrippa and Bernice entering the audience room with 'high-ranking military officers and the prominent men of the city' (25:23). Paul's defence hearing has become the occasion for 'royal entertainment and theatre'.[3] As Peterson notes, 'The contrast between the prisoner's clothes and condition and the ostentation of those gathered to hear him must have been stark.'[4] Yet here is a reminder that there is also a heavenly court watching on and giving a quite different verdict on who is worthy of honour. As Stott says, 'Wearing neither crown nor gown, but only handcuffs and perhaps a plain prisoner's tunic, he nevertheless dominated the court with his quiet, Christ-like dignity and confidence.'[5]

With the audience assembled, Festus presents the case under investigation. He outlines the facts of the case, though as readers we are left to wonder about the competence and integrity of Festus. As Tannehill notes, 'He attempts to make his own handling of Paul's case look better than it was.'[6]

He begins with the claim that 'the whole Jewish community has petitioned me about him in Jerusalem and here in Caesarea' (25:24).

---

[3] Witherington, *Acts*, 732.
[4] Peterson, *Acts*, 655.
[5] Stott, *Acts*, 369.
[6] Tannehill, *Narrative Unity*, 311.

Luke has informed us of the opposition of a significant portion of the Jewish community (21:27–32), and the opposition of the leaders in particular (24:1–8; 25:6–7). However, given the significant Christian community that existed in Jerusalem, it seems an exaggeration to say that 'the whole Jewish community' wanted Paul dead. That said, the phrase 'whole Jewish community' (*plēthos tōn Ioudaiōn*) may simply refer to a multitude, or more specifically the Jewish leaders as representatives of the community.[7]

Festus goes on to confess that he has not been able to find Paul guilty of anything deserving death. Just as Jesus was declared innocent of any crime deserving death, so too now Paul.[8] The Jews have presented their charge, but the evidence is wanting. Since Paul has appealed to Caesar, Festus has no choice but to send him on to Rome (verse 25). Festus's problem is that he does not know what to write concerning Paul to 'His Majesty' (*tō kyriō*, verse 26). Therefore, Festus is seeking the help of Agrippa to determine which charges he should specify in sending Paul on to Rome (verses 26–7).

The reader gets a sense of Festus's predicament. He is eager to ingratiate himself with the Jews and assuage their anger. Yet he cannot find evidence of any guilt on Paul's part that would warrant his death. Paul has appealed to Rome, and Festus does not even know the charge against which Paul is appealing. The situation is farcical and entirely of Festus's own making.[9] Paul appealed to Rome because Festus was about to send him to almost certain death at Jerusalem. Festus is now seeking to be reasonable (verse 27), but it is too late; reason should have stopped things long before now. Festus is more concerned for himself: 'It could prove fatal to one's career to send a person to the emperor on appeal with few or no charges to report.'[10]

In all of this we sense the malice of Paul's Jewish opponents, the incompetence of the Roman official and Paul's total innocence before people and before God. As we have seen repeatedly, Christianity is no threat to Jerusalem or Rome. And God is working out his purposes in spreading the good news of Jesus to ever more influential figures.

---

[7] See Witherington, *Acts*, 732–3.
[8] See Luke 23:4, 15, 22; Acts 23:29; 25:25; 26:31. Witherington, *Acts*, 733.
[9] Marshall, *Acts*, 390.
[10] Witherington, *Acts*, 734.

2. Paul's defence • Acts 26:1–32

26 Then Agrippa said to Paul, 'You have permission to speak for yourself.'

So Paul motioned with his hand and began his defence: **2** 'King Agrippa, I consider myself fortunate to stand before you today as I make my defence against all the accusations of the Jews, **3** and especially so because you are well acquainted with all the Jewish customs and controversies. Therefore, I beg you to listen to me patiently.

4 'The Jewish people all know the way I have lived ever since I was a child, from the beginning of my life in my own country, and also in Jerusalem. **5** They have known me for a long time and can testify, if they are willing, that I conformed to the strictest sect of our religion, living as a Pharisee. **6** And now it is because of my hope in what God has promised our ancestors that I am on trial today. **7** This is the promise our twelve tribes are hoping to see fulfilled as they earnestly serve God day and night. King Agrippa, it is because of this hope that these Jews are accusing me. **8** Why should any of you consider it incredible that God raises the dead?

9 'I too was convinced that I ought to do all that was possible to oppose the name of Jesus of Nazareth. **10** And that is just what I did in Jerusalem. On the authority of the chief priests I put many of the Lord's people in prison, and when they were put to death, I cast my vote against them. **11** Many a time I went from one synagogue to another to have them punished, and I tried to force them to blaspheme. I was so obsessed with persecuting them that I even hunted them down in foreign cities.

12 'On one of these journeys I was going to Damascus with the authority and commission of the chief priests. **13** About noon, King Agrippa, as I was on the road, I saw a light from heaven, brighter than the sun, blazing around me and my companions. **14** We all fell to the ground, and I heard a voice saying to me in Aramaic,[a] "Saul, Saul, why do you persecute me? It is hard for you to kick against the goads."

15 'Then I asked, "Who are you, Lord?"

'"I am Jesus, whom you are persecuting," the Lord replied. **16** "Now get up and stand on your feet. I have appeared to you to appoint you as a servant and as a witness of what you have seen and will see of me. **17** I will rescue you from your own people and from the Gentiles. I am sending you to them **18** to open their eyes and turn them from darkness to light, and from the power of Satan to God, so that they may receive forgiveness of sins and a place among those who are sanctified by faith in me."

19 'So then, King Agrippa, I was not disobedient to the vision from heaven. **20** First to those in Damascus, then to those in Jerusalem and in all Judea, and then to the Gentiles, I preached that they should repent and turn to God and demonstrate their repentance by their deeds. **21** That is why some Jews seized me in the temple courts and tried to kill me. **22** But God has helped me to this very day; so I stand here and testify to small and great alike. I am saying nothing beyond what the prophets and Moses said would happen – **23** that the Messiah would suffer and, as the first to rise from the dead, would bring the message of light to his own people and to the Gentiles.'

24 At this point Festus interrupted Paul's defence. 'You are out of your mind, Paul!' he shouted. 'Your great learning is driving you insane.'

25 'I am not insane, most excellent Festus,' Paul replied. 'What I am saying is true and reasonable. **26** The king is familiar with these things, and I can speak freely to him. I am convinced

that none of this has escaped his notice, because it was not done in a corner. **27** King Agrippa, do you believe the prophets? I know you do.'

28 Then Agrippa said to Paul, 'Do you think that in such a short time you can persuade me to be a Christian?'

29 Paul replied, 'Short time or long – I pray to God that not only you but all who are listening to me today may become what I am, except for these chains.'

30 The king rose, and with him the governor and Bernice and those sitting with them. **31** After they left the room, they began saying to one another, 'This man is not doing anything that deserves death or imprisonment.'

32 Agrippa said to Festus, 'This man could have been set free if he had not appealed to Caesar.'

_____

a 14 Or _Hebrew_

Commentators note that this speech is the last given in Acts and therefore serves as a climactic summary of the Christological preaching seen throughout Luke's second volume.[11] Given that the context is an 'audience' rather than a trial _per se_, Paul's speech is more than just a defence; it is an act of testimony or witness and ends with Agrippa, rather than Paul, on the defensive.[12]

Paul's defence begins with an acknowledgment of Agrippa's familiarity with Jewish Law and customs. It is this common ground that will enable Paul to present his case that he stands in continuity with the Jewish traditions.

Paul recounts his Jewish childhood and training. He was well known in Jerusalem, a member of the 'strictest sect' – a Pharisee (verse 5). Paul continues, 'It is because of my hope in what God has promised our

_____

[11] Witherington, _Acts_, 735.
[12] Witherington, _Acts_, 736.

ancestors that I am on trial today' (verse 6). The hope to which Paul alludes is surely the hope of the Messiah – this will become more explicit in verse 9.[13]

Paul appeals to the Jewish belief in the resurrection and asks, 'Why should any of you consider it incredible that God raises the dead?' (verse 8). As seen previously, the resurrection, though denied by the Sadducees, was commonly held and believed in Jewish tradition. The concept of resurrection should not have been controversial. The question had really become whether God had raised *this* man, Jesus, from the dead as the firstfruits of the final end-time resurrection of all. Once again, as in other speeches, Paul focuses on the resurrection as the evidence that Jesus of Nazareth is the long-awaited Jewish Messiah.

Paul recalls his own opposition to such an idea. He did 'all that was possible to oppose the name of Jesus of Nazareth' (verse 9). On the orders of the chief priests, he put many Christians in prison and cast his vote against them when they were put to death.[14] He went from synagogue to synagogue to have the followers of Jesus arrested, convicted and condemned. He recounts his obsession as he would even travel to foreign cities to hunt and persecute the Christians (verses 10–11).

Paul is keen to show he is not a gullible fanatic swept up in this new Christian movement. He once opposed it strongly and actively. Paul is begging the question for his audience, what must have happened for Paul to have completely changed his mind about Jesus?

Repeatedly in Acts we see Paul share not only the facts of the gospel but also his personal experience. Our own personal testimony and experience of God's grace is a powerful witness to the work of God in our lives. Many of us feel anxious about answering difficult questions or explaining some aspect of theology. We fear being put on the spot by such questions and so we are often hesitant to start conversations about faith. But each of us can speak of the very personal way Jesus has met us and is changing us. We should never underestimate the power of our own personal story in sharing our faith.

Here we have the third account of Paul's conversion on the Damascus

---

[13] This is the hope outlined in key Old Testament passages already referred to in Acts, such as Psalms 2, 16, 110; Isaiah 53. Peterson, *Acts*, 661.

[14] There is debate around this verse as Paul would have to have been a member of the Sanhedrin to cast a vote, which is possible, but unlikely given his age and lack of any other mention. It is more likely that he is expressing his full support of their decision. See Witherington, *Acts*, 741–2; Bock, *Acts*, 715; Peterson, *Acts*, 663.

Road.[15] It follows a similar pattern to the others. We have the account of the bright light and the voice: 'Saul, Saul, why do you persecute me? (verses 12–14). And again, we hear of Paul's commission to be a witness to the Gentiles, to 'open their eyes and turn them from darkness to light' (verses 16–18).

The voice said to Paul, 'It is hard for you to kick against the goads' (verse 14). The 'goad' was a pointed stick used as a cattle prod. This proverbial image was not uncommon in the ancient world.[16] There is an implicit challenge in Paul's account as those who resist his message will also be kicking against the risen Lord.[17]

The difference in this account of Paul's conversion is in the lengthier commission given to him by the risen Jesus. In Acts 9:6 and 22:10 Jesus told Paul to go into the city; there he would be told what to do. Here in chapter 26 we do not have any mention of Paul's blindness or the role of Ananias, but we do have a much fuller account of the words of Jesus.

There are four parts to Paul's commission. First, he was appointed to be 'a witness of what you have seen and will see of me' (verse 16).[18] Second, he would be rescued from persecution and would be a witness primarily among the Gentiles (verse 17). Third, in so doing he would 'open their eyes and turn them from darkness to light, and from the power of Satan to God' (verse 18). Fourth, the result is that they would 'receive forgiveness of sins and a place among those who are sanctified by faith in me' (verse 18).

Each of these elements is significant in the context of Paul's current situation. He is claiming to be an eyewitness of the risen Christ. He is claiming that his rescue from his persecutors is of God and not of humanity. He is claiming that his message is from the 'light' and therefore those who oppose are in 'darkness' and under the power of Satan.[19] He is claiming that the 'sanctified' (*hēgiasmenois*) are those who have faith in Jesus, including Gentiles.

---

[15] The other two accounts of Paul's conversion can be seen in Acts 9:1–19 and 22:6–16.

[16] See Stott, *Acts*, 372.

[17] Wall, *Acts*, 337.

[18] This probably refers to the ongoing visions Paul receives as an apostle and eyewitness of the resurrected Jesus (see Acts 16:7; 18:9; 22:17; 23:11). Witherington, *Acts*, 744.

[19] Themes of light, darkness and cosmic conflict can be seen in numerous places in the Pauline literature: Romans 2:19; 13:12; 2 Corinthians 4:4–6; 6:14; 11:14; Ephesians 5:8–9; Colossians 1:12–13; 1 Thessalonians 1:9–10.

The language and imagery used has multiple Old Testament echoes and places Paul in a long line of faithful prophets sent with a message to turn Israel back from darkness to light.[20] All of these were ill-treated, but history proved the truth of their words. There is an implicit appeal here, which will become explicit, to turn from Satan and darkness back to the light of God's revelation.

The theme of 'light and darkness' has been significant in Luke's two-volume work. In the opening chapters of Luke's Gospel, Zechariah spoke of the one who would 'shine on those living in darkness' (Luke 1:79), and Simeon spoke of the 'light for revelation to the Gentiles, and the glory of your people Israel' (Luke 2:32). In the conclusion to Paul's first speech in Pisidian Antioch, he cited Isaiah 49:6: 'I have made you a light for the Gentiles, that you may bring salvation to the ends of the earth' (Acts 13:47). And here in Paul's final speech he recalls his divine commission to 'turn them from darkness to light' (Acts 26:18). We could see this as a summary of Luke's overall message: the Davidic Messiah, through his death and resurrection, is bringing light to the darkness. This is not just a personal invitation to salvation, but also an international plan for the establishment of God's rule on earth.

These things together present a strong case for serious consideration. Paul is expressing the sentiment of Gamaliel in Acts 5:39: 'If it is from God, you will not be able to stop these men; you will only find yourselves fighting against God.'

Paul here knows he is speaking with someone who is aware of Jewish Law and custom and is therefore speaking with greater boldness about the spiritual realities at stake. It is another example of a sensitive contextualisation, framing the message in terms that the hearer can understand and appreciate.

Paul continues his defence by claiming obedience to the divine instruction (verse 19). His message has been one of repentance, made evident by deeds. Here we have an echo of John the Baptist, another figure rejected and scorned by Jews and the Herodian dynasty. He rebuked the Jewish leaders for their hypocrisy: 'Produce fruit in keeping with repentance' (Luke 3:8).

Paul was no antinomian. 'He did not believe that someone who had faith could do whatever one wished without concern for God's moral standards . . . he exhorts his audience to live, in response to grace, in a

---

[20] Isaiah 42:6–7; 49:6; 51:4; 58:8–10; 60:1–3; Jeremiah 13:16; Amos 5:18–20; Micah 7:8–9.

way that produces fruit reflecting the change of direction called for by forgiveness.'[21] As stated in the Westminster Standards, repentance is:

> . . . a saving grace, wrought in the heart of a sinner by the Spirit and word of God, whereby . . . he so grieves for and hates his sins, as that he turns from them all to God, purposing and endeavouring constantly to walk with him in all the ways of new obedience.[22]

This is important in a day when holiness can be seen as unimportant. We can so emphasise the free offer of grace that we play down the importance of demonstrating true repentance through deeds.[23] These deeds in no way justify, but they are the necessary evidence of the Spirit's work in a believer's life.

Once again Paul claims his message is 'nothing beyond what the prophets and Moses said would happen – that the Messiah would suffer and, as the first to rise from the dead, would bring the message of light to his own people and to the Gentiles' (verses 22–3). This message can indeed be seen in Old Testament Scriptures. For example:

- That the Messiah would suffer: Psalm 22; 118; Isaiah 53
- That the Messiah would be raised: Psalm 16; 110
- Light would be proclaimed among the nations: Isaiah 42; 49; 60

Just as Jesus instructed his first followers, so too Paul is reading the Old Testament Christologically, 'with special attention to the death and resurrection of Jesus and the world mission to Jews and Gentiles'.[24] The Old Testament is not merely a collection of laws, stories, poems and prophecies. It is a united witness pointing forward to Christ as the fulfilment of all these things.

Verse 23 contains a wonderfully brief, yet rich, summary of the apostle's preaching. It includes Jesus's death, resurrection and commission. There are two conditionals here (*ei*) smoothed out by the NIV translation. More literally it might read, 'If the Messiah would suffer, if he was first to rise from the dead, a light he would proclaim . . .' The word *ei* may be translated with the sense of 'that' as in the NIV or it could be taken

---

[21] Bock, *Acts*, 719.
[22] Westminster Larger Catechism Q. 76.
[23] See James 2:14–26.
[24] See Luke 24:25–7, 44. Tannehill, *Narrative Unity*, 327.

as the more indefinite 'if'. In the latter case it would be for rhetorical effect. Since these things have in fact happened, then we can be certain that the light has dawned for Jew and Gentile alike.[25]

We can sense that Paul has moved from outlining the facts of his case to making his implicit appeal. At this juncture Festus interrupts Paul, clearly thinking he has gone too far: 'You are out of your mind Paul! . . . Your great learning is driving you insane [*mania*]' (verse 24). It is interesting to consider why Festus responds this way. He does not appear to be a man personally acquainted with the Jewish religion. Perhaps it was mention of the resurrection that led him to his conclusion. It is interesting to note that the charge of insanity uses the same verb (*mainomai*) Paul used to describe his former life persecuting 'the Way' (see verses 11, 24–5).[26] He was out of his mind before, but not now. By implication, the person siding with his Jewish persecutors would be the person who is out of their mind.

Our world considers the gospel to be foolishness. Paul said this would be the case in 1 Corinthians 1:18: 'For the message of the cross is foolishness to those who are perishing, but to us who are being saved it is the power of God.' However, we see in this passage that it is actually opposition to Christ and his people which is folly. Recognising and responding to him puts us back into our right minds. This can only happen by the miraculous supernatural regenerative work of God's Spirit – to open blind eyes and make the light of the gospel shine into the darkness (see 2 Corinthians 4:4–6). Persuasive rhetoric will not cure the insanity of unbelief. We must pray that God would work in the hearts of those around us to bring them to saving faith. To quote again E. M. Bounds, 'Talking to men for God is a great thing, but talking to God for men is greater still.'[27]

Paul replies, describing Festus as 'most excellent' – a restrained word of commendation aimed at proving he is in full control of his faculties. The apostle Peter reminded his readers to answer people with 'gentleness and respect' (1 Peter 3:15). There is no excuse for communicating with others in ways that are rude or disrespectful. Sadly, the behaviour of many Christians today, especially on social media, seems to have forgotten Peter's instruction and Paul's example.

Paul claims his message is true and reasonable. He goes further,

---

[25] See the discussion in Witherington, *Acts*, 747–8.

[26] Peterson, *Acts*, 664, note 33.

[27] E. M. Bounds, *E. M. Bounds on Prayer*, 115.

suggesting that the things of which he speaks are familiar already to Agrippa. He asserts that 'none of this has escaped his notice, because it was not done in a corner' (verse 26). Given Luke's own statements regarding the number of believers, the spread of the gospel and the very public events around the trials of Jesus and some of the apostles, we should agree with Marshall: 'The Christian movement must have been well known in Palestine.'[28]

Paul's closing statement appeals personally to King Agrippa, 'Do you believe the prophets? I know you do' (verse 27). Witherington notes that Paul puts Agrippa in a difficult position here. If he believes the prophets, then he must believe what they say about the Messiah. If he does not believe them, he cannot be seen as a good Jewish ruler.[29] Paul is unafraid to speak to a man familiar with the Jewish religion and appeal to him directly, that he might respond to the message. The tables are turned. Agrippa finds himself on trial, with Paul asking the probing questions.

Agrippa is not going to be so easily persuaded in front of esteemed company. He replies, 'Do you think that in such a short time you can persuade me to be a Christian?' (verse 28). Paul is unperturbed: 'Short time or long – I pray to God that not only you but all who are listening to me today may become what I am, except for these chains' (verse 29). While the NIV may be right to translate *en oligō* as 'short time', it could also carry the sense of 'short argument/few words'.[30] Either way, the overall sense is clear. There is a refreshing boldness in Paul's answer. He does not think conversion needs to be a matter of drawn-out discussion. He is inviting Agrippa to bow the knee in the here and now before the King of kings.

Recall Witherington's description, already cited, of this whole scene as a 'theatre of the absurd . . . another hearing that resolved nothing'.[31] How often does sharing the gospel feel like this? We can speak in ways we think winsome, careful and persuasive, and we can often feel like our words cut no ice. Paul is undeterred and content to leave the results with God. As he said to the Corinthians, 'I planted the seed, Apollos watered it, but God has been making it grow' (1 Corinthians 3:6).

Having left Paul, Agrippa, Bernice and those with them begin saying to one another, 'This man is not doing anything that deserves death or

---

[28] Marshall, *Acts*, 399.

[29] Witherington, *Acts*, 750.

[30] Bock, *Acts*, 723.

[31] Witherington, *Acts*, 734.

imprisonment' – a verdict with which Agrippa himself concurs: 'This man could have been set free if he had not appealed to Caesar' (verse 32). This seems to be the verdict of all those present. Although Agrippa and the prominent persons present do not convert, they recognise that Paul is innocent of anything deserving death. As we have observed before, this may be an important message for Theophilus to hear. Prominent persons give Christianity a serious hearing, and it is no crime to be a follower of 'the Way'.

While Paul's chains limit his freedom, whenever he has opportunity he seizes it to speak of his hope in Christ. As Tannehill notes, 'Paul is not just a helpless victim. As opportunity comes, he continues to bear witness to his Lord. Although Paul continues to be denied justice and freedom, the saving purpose of God still has use for this resourceful and faithful prisoner.'[32]

Skinner uses the language of 'providential failure': Paul's detention, 'instead of putting an end to his mission, provides the occasions for him to explain the gospel to powerful figures . . . an obstacle such as imprisonment, persecution, or execution paradoxically becomes the means for God to multiply the success of expansion of the mission'.[33]

We may feel like our opportunities are limited, for all sorts of reasons. Yet we should, with Paul, put our hope in Christ and have the boldness to say something when and where we can. This does not mean we should be clumsy or insensitive. We see Paul exercising real thoughtfulness and sensitivity towards his audience. We will still need courage to wisely take the opportunities God presents to us, however unlikely our surroundings may be. As Skinner says, 'What appear to be places of obstacle can be used by God's agents for other purposes.'[34]

The trial scenes occupy a significant space in Luke's narrative. Luke is showing Paul to be a man who exercised 'a long obedience in the same direction'.[35] Paul endured significant hardship. He had been kept under guard unjustly for more than two years. At each point he demonstrated his innocence. At his three trials he showed his loyalty – 'to Moses and the prophets, to Caesar, and above all to Jesus Christ . . . He was a faithful

[32] Tannehill, *Narrative Unity*, 314–15.

[33] Matthew L. Skinner, *Locating Paul: Places of Custody as Narrative Settings in Acts 21–28* (Leiden: Brill, 2003), 138.

[34] Skinner, *Locating Paul*, 200.

[35] This is the title of a book by Eugene Peterson (Downers Grove: InterVarsity Press, first edition 1980).

Jew, a faithful Roman and a faithful Christian.'[36] Here is a model of a faithful witness, patiently enduring in his obedience before God and people, entrusting himself to the one who judges justly.[37]

In addition, Luke is perhaps showing something of the 'normal' Christian life. Paul and Barnabas had previously stated, 'We must go through many hardships to enter the kingdom of God' (Acts 14:22). If we only had the first six chapters of Acts, we might be tempted to think the Christian life is filled with astonishing miracles and explosive church growth. The life of Paul shows us that proclamation is often met with persecution. Faith in the sovereign purposes of God is crucial in making sense of hardship and apparent failure. If we 'zoom out' of Luke's narrative, we can clearly see God at work, fulfilling his purposes to take the gospel to the 'ends of the earth' (Acts 1:8). But often, when we are 'zoomed in', we can feel like frustrated failures, bewildered by circumstances. Paul models the three great Christian virtues in the midst of real hardship: faith, hope and love.

---

[36] Stott, *Acts*, 378.
[37] 1 Peter 2:23.

26

Paul Sails for Rome

ACTS 27:1–28:16

In Acts 20–21 Paul had visited Jerusalem and been seized by his Jewish opponents. Having narrowly escaped death, he had been kept in Roman custody. Over the course of more than two years Paul had been held under guard and faced a number of trials before the Sanhedrin, Felix, Festus and, most recently, King Agrippa (Acts 26). In the course of these trials, Paul had appealed to Caesar, according to his right as a Roman citizen. This had happened because the Roman authorities had failed to deal justly and had sought to appease the Jewish leaders. Paul knew this would have led to his death. As we arrive at Acts 27, the scene is set for Paul's journey towards Rome and his audience before Caesar.

One common question surrounding Acts 27–8 is why Luke gives so much space to the sea-voyage and shipwreck. What purpose does it serve? One answer is that Luke was part of the travelling party so was naturally inclined to provide more detail. However, there is also an increasing consensus that Luke's ending is a skilful and deliberate piece of narrative theology with a rhetorical purpose.[1]

The account of Paul's journey illustrates in various (and some surprising) ways Paul's innocence and God's protection over his apostle. It serves to vindicate the messenger *and* his message. All the way to the end we see it is the risen Lord Jesus who is directing events in accordance with his promise and purpose. The political actors of the Empire are 'the public instruments of God's sovereign purpose'.[2] As Witherington says, 'God's plan and providence were such that even severe obstacles were overcome in getting Paul to Rome and his appearance before the emperor.'[3] This gives great assurance to believers struggling to make sense of their circumstances today.

---

[1] See the summary of recent scholarship in Charles B. Puskas, *The Conclusion of Luke–Acts: The Significance of Acts 28:16–31* (Eugene: Pickwick, 2009), 13–14.

[2] Wall, *Acts*, 345.

[3] Witherington, *Acts*, 758.

Additionally, the narrative points to 'God as Creator and Saviour, and to Paul as his prophet or representative'.[4] God is at work, displaying his Lordship over sea and souls, vindicating message and messenger.

1. *Paul sets sail* • *Acts 27:1–12*

Paul sails for Rome

27 When it was decided that we would sail for Italy, Paul and some other prisoners were handed over to a centurion named Julius, who belonged to the Imperial Regiment. **2** We boarded a ship from Adramyttium about to sail for ports along the coast of the province of Asia, and we put out to sea. Aristarchus, a Macedonian from Thessalonica, was with us.

3 The next day we landed at Sidon; and Julius, in kindness to Paul, allowed him to go to his friends so they might provide for his needs. **4** From there we put out to sea again and passed to the lee of Cyprus because the winds were against us. **5** When we had sailed across the open sea off the coast of Cilicia and Pamphylia, we landed at Myra in Lycia. **6** There the centurion found an Alexandrian ship sailing for Italy and put us on board. **7** We made slow headway for many days and had difficulty arriving off Cnidus. When the wind did not allow us to hold our course, we sailed to the lee of Crete, opposite Salmone. **8** We moved along the coast with difficulty and came to a place called Fair Havens, near the town of Lasea.

9 Much time had been lost, and sailing had already become dangerous because by now it was after the Day of Atonement.[a] So Paul warned them, **10** 'Men, I can see that our voyage is going to be disastrous and bring great loss to ship and cargo, and to our own lives also.' **11** But the centurion, instead of listening to what Paul said, followed the advice of the pilot and of the owner of the ship. **12** Since the harbour was unsuitable to winter in, the majority decided that we should sail on, hoping to reach Phoenix and winter there. This was a harbour in Crete, facing both south-west and north-west.

_____

a 9 That is, Yom Kippur

In verses 1–2 we read that Paul travelled with a number of other prisoners under the guard of a centurion named Julius. We know nothing of the other prisoners; perhaps some were destined to die in the arena at the gladiatorial games, but we are simply not told why the others were also being taken to Rome.

_____

[4] Peterson, *Acts*, 696.

Luke provides some details of the route and would appear to include himself in the travelling party (see the 'we' at the start of verse 2). Under good conditions the journey would take around five weeks; this particular journey would take much longer.[5] There was no state fleet for transporting prisoners of the Empire. The soldiers and prisoners would have had to board various cargo ships, sailing along the coastline and stopping in various ports.[6]

Also mentioned is a man named Aristarchus, a Macedonian from Thessalonica. Aristarchus has already been mentioned as a travelling companion of Paul in Acts 19:29; 20:4. He is also described as a co-worker and fellow prisoner in Colossians 4:10 and Philemon 24.

In verse 3, Luke includes a very human detail, which demonstrates not all Roman officials were incompetent or corrupt: 'Julius, in kindness to Paul, allowed him to go to his friends so they might provide for his needs.' Paul, it would seem, had visited the city of Sidon previously, perhaps on one of his trips to or from Jerusalem.[7] Although he would have been accompanied by a guard, he was clearly seen as no great threat – a further indication of his innocence.

Having sailed from Sidon to Lycia, the travelling party boarded a larger Alexandrian grain ship sailing for Italy. Luke describes the slow and difficult journey making 'slow headway' (verse 7–8). Luke informs his readers that much time had been lost and, as a consequence, 'sailing had already become dangerous because by now it was after the Day of Atonement' (verse 9).[8]

Given the late date and prior struggles, Paul warned his companions, 'Men, I can see that our voyage is going to be disastrous and bring great loss to ship and cargo, and to our own lives also' (verse 10). Given that no lives were actually lost, we should see this not as prophetic insight or prediction, but rather as the common sense of a seasoned traveller.[9] This is no lack of faith on Paul's part; it is simply the application of wisdom to circumstances. There is nothing righteous in reckless risk. Paul had undertaken a number of sea voyages between Acts 9 and 28 and in 2

---

[5] Bock, *Acts*, 731. Bock dates the journey as commencing in the autumn of AD 59.

[6] Bock, *Acts*, 732.

[7] Witherington, *Acts*, 761.

[8] This day fell on or around 5 October. After this point, conditions became more treacherous and most sailing ceased until after the winter storms had passed. Sea travel was normally avoided after mid-September because of the more dangerous conditions. Peterson, *Acts*, 685.

[9] Witherington, *Acts*, 763; Wall, *Acts*, 346.

Corinthians 11:25 he says that he had been shipwrecked three times, and even spent a day and night in the open sea. Paul was an experienced traveller by sea, and so his advice was more than merely intuition.[10]

The centurion had been portrayed in a positive light, as a man of kindness in verse 3. Yet here he decides to listen to the advice of the owner and pilot of the ship. Perhaps the economic interest of the owner won the day, over Paul's more cautious and sensible approach. Since they were unable to winter in the harbour at Fair Havens, the majority decided it would be best to sail on, hoping to winter in Phoenix. This was just fifty miles further up the coast – a journey that could be done in fair conditions in a day.[11] The plan seems reasonable, but Luke, being a skilful narrator, is setting us up as readers for the trouble that is to come.

Previous generations of Christian commentators have noted that Paul's difficult journey reminds us that life here is a pilgrimage. The Christian should not expect to avoid hardship and suffering. Trials are no indication of particular guilt, and their avoidance is no sign of virtue or innocence. The journey of faith in this life will involve struggle, for all manner of reasons, in God's providential purposes.[12]

2. The storm • Acts 27:13–26

The storm

13 When a gentle south wind began to blow, they saw their opportunity; so they weighed anchor and sailed along the shore of Crete. **14** Before very long, a wind of hurricane force, called the 'North-Easter', swept down from the island. **15** The ship was caught by the storm and could not head into the wind; so we gave way to it and were driven along. **16** As we passed to the lee of a small island called Cauda, we were hardly able to make the lifeboat secure, **17** so the men hoisted it aboard.

Then they passed ropes under the ship itself to hold it together. Because they were afraid they would run aground on the sand-bars of Syrtis, they lowered the sea anchor[b] and let the ship be driven along. **18** We took such a violent battering from the storm that the next day they began to throw the cargo overboard. **19** On the third day, they threw the ship's tackle overboard with their own hands. **20** When neither sun nor stars appeared for many days and the storm continued raging, we finally gave up all hope of being saved.

---

[10] Witherington, *Acts*, 754.

[11] Bock, *Acts*, 734–5.

[12] See the comments of Spangenberg, Gwalther and Calvin in *RCS* 6:348–350.

21 After they had gone a long time without food, Paul stood up before them and said: 'Men, you should have taken my advice not to sail from Crete; then you would have spared yourselves this damage and loss. **22** But now I urge you to keep up your courage, because not one of you will be lost; only the ship will be destroyed. **23** Last night an angel of the God to whom I belong and whom I serve stood beside me **24** and said, "Do not be afraid, Paul. You must stand trial before Caesar; and God has graciously given you the lives of all who sail with you." **25** So keep up your courage, men, for I have faith in God that it will happen just as he told me. **26** Nevertheless, we must run aground on some island.'

_____
b 17 Or *the sails*

When a convenient opportunity presented itself, the group set sail again, but we read that almost immediately conditions worsened and a wind of 'hurricane force' (*typhōnikos*) drove them along (verses 14–15). The men had to bring the lifeboat aboard and passed ropes under the ship to prevent it from breaking apart in the force of the storm (verses 16–17).[13] Luke describes such a 'violent battering' from the storm that they resorted to throwing some of the cargo overboard (verse 18–19).[14] The inability to see sun or stars (verse 20) meant that they were not only battered but also lost at sea.

This perilous and terrifying state of affairs continued for many days, with the storm continuing to rage, such that Luke says, 'We finally gave up all hope of being saved' (verse 20). The verb *sōzō* ('to save') will appear repeatedly, raising deeper questions of where salvation may ultimately be found.

Storm and shipwreck occur frequently in ancient Graeco–Roman literature. To encounter and battle the storm is to encounter and battle the gods. They are almost always seen as a sign of divine displeasure.[15] However, to come through and survive a storm or shipwreck was a sign

---

[13] Passing the ropes under the ship to hold it together was a technique called 'frapping'. They may have also tied ropes 'around the hull or transversely across the deck'. Peterson, *Acts*, 687–8.

[14] Verse 38 shows they did not throw all of the cargo overboard at this point.

[15] See, for example, Herodotus, *Histories*, 187–92; Homer, *Odyssey* 5:290–470; 9:61–81; 12:201–303. See also Gary B. Miles and Gary Trompf, 'Luke and Antiphon: The Theology of Acts 27–28 in the Light of Pagan Beliefs about Divine Retribution, Pollution and Shipwreck', *HTR* 69 (1976): 259–67; Susan M. Praeder, 'Acts 27:1–28:16: Sea Voyages in Ancient Literature and the Theology of Luke–Acts', *CBQ* 46 (1984): 683–706.

of divine favour. Luke is tapping into these motifs of classical antiquity to establish the innocence of his central character.

As the situation worsened, Paul stood before them and gave them a message of hope and encouragement. He began by rebuking them for not listening to him earlier when he advised them not to sail from Crete. As the context will show, this was not Paul delivering an irritating 'I told you so' with the benefit of hindsight. He was a man who spoke from God, and so they should have listened carefully to him. He exhorted them, 'Keep up your courage, because not one of you will be lost' (verse 22). This was quite a claim given their circumstances. I suspect more than a few of them wondered on what authority he could make such an outlandish promise.

Paul continued, 'Last night an angel of the God to whom I belong and whom I serve stood beside me and said, "Do not be afraid Paul. You must stand trial before Caesar; and God has graciously given you the lives of all who sail with you"' (verses 23–4). Paul was unashamed to speak of the God whom he served and of the promise delivered by the angel. He was inviting his hearers to put their trust in him and, by implication, in his God. The promise from the angel was a reiteration of that previously given to Paul in Acts 23:11 that he must testify in Rome.

Angels have appeared a number of times in Luke's two-volume work to bring a message of God's saving work.[16] The function of angels in Luke's narrative is to emphasise the divine presence, initiative and vindication of God's servants.[17] As such, their ministry is particularly connected to Christ and his apostles, and should not be viewed as something to be expected today, when we have the collected canon of apostolic witness.

We should not miss the remarkable nature of this promise. Paul was in the midst of a severe storm, and all had given up hope. Yet even in the place of death and chaos, the angel of God was with him. God saw his situation and was at work to protect and preserve his life and the lives of those with him. Paul was living out the prayer of David in Psalm 139:7: 'Where can I flee from your presence?' Paul encouraged those with him to have faith in God. Nevertheless, divine intervention is not opposed to human wisdom, and so the ship needed to find a place to run aground (verse 26).

It is striking that Paul here was occupying the role of 'captain' of the ship. He had moved from being a prisoner under guard to directing the

---

[16] See Luke 1:26; 2:9–13; 22:43; Acts 5:19; 7:26; 10:3; 12:7. Wall, *Acts*, 349.

[17] Hermie C. van Zyl, 'Vehicles of Divine Initiative: The Function of Angels in Acts', *Journal of Early Christian History* 1.1 (2011): 205–20.

events and calling the shots, all the while pointing those around him to the God who can save.[18]

3. The shipwreck • Acts 27:27–44

The shipwreck

27 On the fourteenth night we were still being driven across the Adriatic[c] Sea, when about midnight the sailors sensed they were approaching land. **28** They took soundings and found that the water was forty metres deep. A short time later they took soundings again and found it was thirty metres deep. **29** Fearing that we would be dashed against the rocks, they dropped four anchors from the stern and prayed for daylight. **30** In an attempt to escape from the ship, the sailors let the lifeboat down into the sea, pretending they were going to lower some anchors from the bow. **31** Then Paul said to the centurion and the soldiers, 'Unless these men stay with the ship, you cannot be saved.' **32** So the soldiers cut the ropes that held the lifeboat and let it drift away.

33 Just before dawn Paul urged them all to eat. 'For the last fourteen days,' he said, 'you have been in constant suspense and have gone without food – you haven't eaten anything. **34** Now I urge you to take some food. You need it to survive. Not one of you will lose a single hair from his head.' **35** After he said this, he took some bread and gave thanks to God in front of them all. Then he broke it and began to eat. **36** They were all encouraged and ate some food themselves. **37** Altogether there were 276 of us on board. **38** When they had eaten as much as they wanted, they lightened the ship by throwing the grain into the sea.

39 When daylight came, they did not recognise the land, but they saw a bay with a sandy beach, where they decided to run the ship aground if they could. **40** Cutting loose the anchors, they left them in the sea and at the same time untied the ropes that held the rudders. Then they hoisted the foresail to the wind and made for the beach. **41** But the ship struck a sand-bar and ran aground. The bow stuck fast and would not move, and the stern was broken to pieces by the pounding of the surf.

42 The soldiers planned to kill the prisoners to prevent any of them from swimming away and escaping. **43** But the centurion wanted to spare Paul's life and kept them from carrying out their plan. He ordered those who could swim to jump overboard first and get to land. **44** The rest were to get there on planks or on other pieces of the ship. In this way everyone reached land safely.

c 27 In ancient times the name referred to an area extending well south of Italy.

---

[18] Peterson, *Acts*, 680.

After two weeks, one can only imagine the mental and physical state of all those aboard. Exhausted, the sailors sensed that they were approaching land (verse 27). Having taken multiple soundings, they dropped the anchors and prayed for daylight (verses 28–9).

Some of the sailors, it seems, preferred to take their chances rather than trust in Paul's message from God. Luke tells us they 'let the lifeboat down into the sea, pretending they were going to lower some anchors from the bow' (verse 30). Paul warned the centurion and the soldiers, 'Unless these men stay with the ship, you cannot be saved' (verse 31). So the soldiers went and cut the ropes holding the lifeboat so that it drifted away from the ship. Remarkably, the soldiers trusted Paul's word at this moment of dark uncertainty. These hardened Roman soldiers had seen and heard enough from Paul in the previous two weeks that they were willing to do as he said and put their trust in him over a lifeboat. In effect, they were making the God of Paul their lifeboat.

As dawn approached, Paul encouraged all on board to eat. He conducted something that feels akin to a 'last supper', though he had already assured them of survival. While it would be wrong to read too much into this scene, as if it were a 'Lord's Supper', it still carried something of the sacred as they sat and ate under the promise of God's deliverance. The meal was led by Paul as a moment to thank God and trust him. He had become their leader. As the apostle to the Gentiles, here was a moment where Paul gathered the people around himself and encouraged them to put their trust in his message and his God. Luke tells us there were 276 on board. Before them all, Paul took bread, gave thanks to God, broke it and began to eat (verse 35). Luke reports they were all encouraged and ate as much as they wanted before throwing the grain into the sea (verses 36–8).

As daylight came, the sailors sighted a bay with a sandy beach and drove the ship towards it. Having cut loose the anchors and hoisted the foresail, they made for the beach. Before they could get there, they struck a sandbar and became stuck fast (verse 41). The waves began to break up the stern of the ship.

At this point, Luke's narrative takes a sombre turn. We read the soldiers decided their only option was to kill the prisoners to prevent their escape. The punishment for a soldier who had allowed a prisoner to escape was death, so we can sense something of their desperation in the face of what lay before them.[19] Thankfully, the centurion intervened

---

[19] Witherington, *Acts*, 774.

again as he wanted to spare Paul's life. God can work through all kinds of circumstances and people to fulfil his plans and purposes. Those who could swim were ordered to jump; others were to get to shore on planks or pieces of the ship. Luke tells us that in this way everyone reached land safely (verse 44).

When we recall the ancient beliefs around storms and shipwrecks, we can see that Luke is portraying Paul as innocent and favoured by the deity. To survive a storm or shipwreck was considered to be a sign of divine favour. Whatever became of Paul in Rome is, in many ways, irrelevant for Luke. Paul had been 'acquitted by a tribunal no less formidable than the divinely controlled ocean itself'.[20]

The verb, $s\bar{o}z\bar{o}$ ('to save') and its cognates appears seven times in relation to the storm and shipwreck.[21] Daniel Marguerat has argued that the storm and shipwreck become a kind of 'metaphor of salvation'.[22] Paul is a sort of Jonah, but in reverse. Just as Jonah's guilt threatened the safety of all on board, so Paul's innocence becomes a means of salvation for all on board.[23] It is only because Paul is innocent and favoured that this 'salvation' can come. Salvation through the waters of judgment may even point to the salvation offered to Gentiles through the gospel.[24] Those on board (and the reader also) are invited to ponder the nature and source of the ultimate salvation from death and destruction.

---

[20] Miles and Trompf, 'Luke and Antiphon', 267. A similar conclusion is drawn by C. J. Hemer, 'First Person Travel Narrative in Acts 27–28', *TynBul* 36 (1985): 80.

[21] The verb $s\bar{o}z\bar{o}$ appears in 27:20, 31; $dias\bar{o}z\bar{o}$ is used in 27:43, 44; 28:1, 4; the noun, $s\bar{o}t\bar{e}ria$, is used in 27:34.

[22] Daniel Marguerat, 'The Enigma of the Silent Closing of Acts', in *Jesus and the Heritage of Israel*, ed. David P. Moessner (Harrisburg: Trinity, 1999), 292.

[23] Praeder, 'Acts 27:1–28:16', 704. Paul's innocence has already been stressed in 16:38–9; 18:14–15; 20:26; 23:3, 9; 24:12–13; 25:28, 25; 26:31–2. Marguerat, 'The Enigma of the Silent Closing', 292.

[24] Tannehill, *Narrative Unity*, 336; Peterson, *Acts*, 680; *pace* Witherington, *Acts*, 772. Tannehill posits a double reading of this thematic emphasis – salvation from the sea, and God's eternal salvation offered in the gospel. Salvation through water is clearly a scriptural theme – think of Noah and his family being delivered through the waters of judgment (Genesis 6–8); the Israelites as they cross the Red Sea (Exodus 14); Jonah saved from the depths; the conquering of the sea monsters (Revelation 13) or even that which baptism signifies (1 Peter 3:20–21).

4. Ashore on Malta • Acts 28:1–10

Paul ashore on Malta

28 Once safely on shore, we found out that the island was called Malta. **2** The islanders showed us unusual kindness. They built a fire and welcomed us all because it was raining and cold. **3** Paul gathered a pile of brushwood and, as he put it on the fire, a viper, driven out by the heat, fastened itself on his hand. **4** When the islanders saw the snake hanging from his hand, they said to each other, 'This man must be a murderer; for though he escaped from the sea, the goddess Justice has not allowed him to live.' **5** But Paul shook the snake off into the fire and suffered no ill effects. **6** The people expected him to swell up or suddenly fall dead; but after waiting a long time and seeing nothing unusual happen to him, they changed their minds and said he was a god.

7 There was an estate near by that belonged to Publius, the chief official of the island. He welcomed us to his home and showed us generous hospitality for three days. **8** His father was ill in bed, suffering from fever and dysentery. Paul went in to see him and, after prayer, placed his hands on him and healed him. **9** When this had happened, the rest of those on the island who were ill came and were cured. **10** They honoured us in many ways; and when we were ready to sail, they furnished us with the supplies we needed.

Having made land, Luke tells us something of the winter spent on Malta. He notes the 'unusual kindness' of the islanders, who built a fire and welcomed them all (verses 1–2). While the portrayal of the Jews and Romans had been less than positive, these *barbaroi* (islanders) in contrast displayed the ancient ideals of kindness and hospitality. God's common grace finds its way into unexpected places.

Here Luke recounts the incident of Paul being bitten by a snake. As he gathered wood, a viper fastened itself to his hand. The islanders concluded that Paul must be a guilty man – a murderer even – because the goddess Justice had finally got her man. He may have escaped the sea, but the snake had got him. Paul, however, simply shook the snake off into the fire and suffered no ill effects.[25] He snatched victory from

---

[25] The Church Father, Arator, offers a stimulating reading at this point: 'You wickedly hurtful serpent . . . O lover of death, whose very parent you are, why do you renew your warfare upon the redeemed? You come as a plunderer, but you lie there as plunder, and, bringing death [from a tree] you are destroyed by the

the jaws of defeat, quite literally in this case. Since Paul did not swell up and drop dead, the people reversed their opinion of him and concluded he must be a god.

The brevity with which Luke gives this account makes it almost humorous. For the islanders, Paul is either a murderer or a god – nothing in between. Yet the reader knows what the islanders will come to learn: Paul is not a god, but he does have the one true God looking after him. Paul has survived storm, shipwreck and now snakebite. As Marguerat concludes, 'Paul's innocence crystallizes in a chain of signs adapted to the pagan world.'[26]

Luke also records the generous hospitality offered by the chief official of the island – a man named Publius. He stands in sharp contrast to so many of the other officials encountered in the recent chapters of Acts. Here is a man who is generous, hospitable and open to Paul's message. Is this one more glimpse of the gospel reaching towards the 'ends of the earth' (see Acts 1:8)? Is this another snapshot of the message reaching the most unlikely sorts of people? As Paul wrote to the Corinthians, that which is wise or foolish in the world's eyes is so often the inverse of God's wisdom (see 1 Corinthians 1–2).

Publius's father was gravely ill, suffering from fever and dysentery.[27] Paul visited him 'and, after prayer, placed his hands on him and healed him' (verse 8). After this, many others who were ill came to see Paul and they too were cured.

Luke concludes his account of the time on Malta by noting, 'They honoured us in many ways; and when we were ready to sail, they furnished us with the supplies we needed' (verse 10).

5. Paul sails to Rome • Acts 28:11–16

Paul's arrival at Rome

11 After three months we put out to sea in a ship that had wintered in the island - it was an Alexandrian ship with the figurehead of the twin gods Castor and Pollux. 12 We put in at Syracuse and stayed there three days. 13 From there we set sail and arrived at Rhegium. The next day the south wind came up, and on the following

---

branches of a second tree, O evil one, and since the cross of Christ, death is your portion of the wood.' 'Acts', in ACCS 5:311–12.

26 Marguerat, 'The Enigma of the Silent Closing', 293.

27 Bock suggests such a condition can be caused by a microbe in goat's milk and can cause sickness lasting months or even years. Bock, *Acts*, 744.

day we reached Puteoli. **14**There we found some brothers and sisters who invited us to spend a week with them. And so we came to Rome. **15**The brothers and sisters there had heard that we were coming, and they travelled as far as the Forum of Appius and the Three Taverns to meet us. At the sight of these people Paul thanked God and was encouraged. **16**When we got to Rome, Paul was allowed to live by himself, with a soldier to guard him.

Following a three-month winter on Malta, the travelling party set sail again for Rome. It is now most likely mid-February in AD 60.[28] Luke includes the detail that they sailed in an Alexandrian ship with the twin figure heads of Castor and Pollux. These Roman gods were said to watch over sailors and protect them. Luke has shown that there is indeed divine favour over this party, but it has not come from Castor and Pollux. Although it is only the Lord who providentially directs the course of Paul's travels, in a sense there is no better sign for Paul to sail under.[29]

Luke provides the essential geographical details of the trip – they sailed from Syracuse to Rhegium to Puteoli.[30] Here they found some of the brothers and sisters and spent a week with them.

In verse 14 Luke finally reports, 'And so we came to Rome.' The trip from Malta has taken three weeks; in total the journey has taken more than four months.[31] As Bock notes, 'God's word has come to pass: Paul has made it to Rome.'[32] It has not been easy or straightforward. A journey that could have taken five weeks has taken more than four months and involved storm, shipwreck and snakebite. While God's purposes cannot be frustrated, often the journey he leads us on is far from smooth.

Some believers had heard of their imminent arrival and came to meet them. They travelled some distance – the Forum of Appius (forty miles

---

[28] Bock, *Acts*, 744.

[29] Spencer and Peterson see Luke here making a negative judgment about the impotence of pagan deities. See F. Scott Spencer, *Journeying Through Acts* (Peabody: Hendrickson, 2004), 236; Peterson, *Acts*, 703. Witherington, however, sees Luke making a more positive comment about divine ordering. *Acts*, 781. There is perhaps some truth in both points of view. Luke has made it clear that God is directing Paul's movement, yet it is also God who has providentially ordained for Paul to sail under the ensign of the Dioscuri – a fitting banner to publicly proclaim Paul's innocence.

[30] The distances between them are as follows: Malta to Syracus: ninety miles; Syracuse to Rhegium: seventy miles; Rhegium to Puteoli: 175 miles. Witherington, *Acts*, 784.

[31] Bock, *Acts*, 746.

[32] Bock, *Acts*, 746.

away) and Three Taverns (thirty miles away). Their presence was a great encouragement to Paul, and he himself was allowed to live by himself under Roman guard (verses 15–16). Here is another touching human element in the story. The beauty of encouragement from one believer to another should not be glossed over. Luke does not waste a word in his narrative. He intends us to notice the power of encouragement that exists in simple Christian fellowship.

Here we see Paul living under the least restrictive and most lenient form of Roman custody.[33] This may in small part be owing to his Roman citizenship. However, Rapske seems to be correct in stating that 'the only other rationale for such a light custody must be found in the weakness of the case against Paul'.[34] Here is a detail Luke provides that further suggests both his innocence and the favourable providence of God upon him.

As Peterson says, 'This lengthy narrative was included, not simply for dramatic effect, but to teach something further about divine providence and Paul's role within God's plan for the nations.'[35] Paul is God's ambassador to the Gentiles. He is innocent of the spurious charges the Jews tried to level against him. He is a faithful servant, and we see God's 'mission unstoppable' marching forward, even in strange or challenging circumstances. The challenge for the reader is in considering who we look to for our ultimate deliverance and salvation.

Paul is a model of faithfulness and patience in difficult circumstances. God works to protect him, and Paul continues to discharge his ministry.

How often we look at our own circumstances and wonder how God is at work. Or perhaps we look at news stories from around the world, or read prayer letters from the persecuted church. Is God really in control over the seemingly unending tempests of our lives and world?

We are not apostles like Paul, and therefore we need to exercise extreme caution in claiming God will deliver us as he delivered Paul. Sometimes the miraculous rescue does not present itself. However, we can still be assured about two important realities.

First, God is always working out his purposes for good and for the glory of his name. Whatever befalls us is part of his providential plan to glorify his name in his world. We may not understand how God can use evil and hardship for good. But we can trust he is doing just that, even when it's far from clear to us.

---

[33] Witherington, *Acts*, 790.

[34] B. Rapske, *Paul in Roman Custody* (Grand Rapids: Eerdmans, 1994), 181.

[35] Peterson, *Acts*, 679.

Second, we can trust in God's ultimate salvation. Even if we aren't delivered from persecution, sickness or trial in this life, we know that on the other side waits the perfect peace of being absent from the body but present with the Lord (2 Corinthians 5:8). For all who trust in him, our ultimate salvation into paradise is never in doubt. This gives us hope to live faithful lives in his service in the present, knowing that our future is utterly secure.

Paul knew this comfort, and it enabled him to continue to witness to Christ, whatever his circumstances. Paul was more concerned with faithfully completing the task entrusted to him than his own comfort and security in this life. This is a challenging word and example to us.

27

The End of the Beginning

Acts 28:17–31

Paul has finally reached Rome. The story that began in Jerusalem has reached a symbolic 'ends of the earth' (Acts 1:8). Stott notes that Rome was the 'largest and most splendid of ancient cities . . . the capital and symbol of the Roman Empire . . . Rome presided magisterially over the whole known world.'[1] The message of the kingdom has gone beyond the borders of Jerusalem and Samaria and is reaching an ever-wider Gentile audience. But what of Paul's fate?

As we get to the end of Luke's narrative, things appear to be unresolved. Paul has finally reached Rome, and as readers we may expect to hear of Paul's exoneration or execution, but neither is recorded. The outcome of Paul's appeal to Caesar is not provided. Paul himself remains under house arrest. As Wall notes, 'Only passing mention of Paul's appeal to Caesar is made (28:19a); he is not here as a citizen of Rome with legal problems to settle but as a prophet-like-Jesus with a gospel to proclaim.'[2]

Many have wondered at the reason for such an ending. Is this as much source material as was available to Luke at the time of writing? Was Luke composing a third volume? Did he die before he could write any more? Or was there a deliberate purpose in Luke's open ending? The third option is the one that will be contended for here. Luke intends the reader to continue the mission to 'the ends of the earth'. While Paul is chained, the gospel is not.

Luke's ending serves to vindicate both Paul and the Gentile mission by means of one final 'reverse-trial' and an 'unchained word'. Wall argues, 'Luke is disinterested in Rome's verdict on Paul and so concludes Acts without legal closure.'[3] This is overstating the case. Luke clearly is interested in Paul's defence before Jewish and Roman authorities and has devoted significant space to this. It is perhaps better to say Luke is not

---

[1] Stott, *Acts*, 383.

[2] Wall, *Acts*, 359.

[3] Wall, *Acts*, 304.

ultimately interested in the human verdicts. It is the ongoing work of the divine that is his primary interest.

1. *A reverse trial* • *Acts 28:17–28*

Paul preaches at Rome under guard

17 Three days later he called together the local Jewish leaders. When they had assembled, Paul said to them: 'My brothers, although I have done nothing against our people or against the customs of our ancestors, I was arrested in Jerusalem and handed over to the Romans. **18** They examined me and wanted to release me, because I was not guilty of any crime deserving death. **19** The Jews objected, so I was compelled to make an appeal to Caesar. I certainly did not intend to bring any charge against my own people. **20** For this reason I have asked to see you and talk with you. It is because of the hope of Israel that I am bound with this chain.'

21 They replied, 'We have not received any letters from Judea concerning you, and none of our people who have come from there has reported or said anything bad about you. **22** But we want to hear what your views are, for we know that people everywhere are talking against this sect.'

23 They arranged to meet Paul on a certain day, and came in even larger numbers to the place where he was staying. He witnessed to them from morning till evening, explaining about the kingdom of God, and from the Law

of Moses and from the Prophets he tried to persuade them about Jesus. **24** Some were convinced by what he said, but others would not believe. **25** They disagreed among themselves and began to leave after Paul had made this final statement: 'The Holy Spirit spoke the truth to your ancestors when he said through Isaiah the prophet:

26 ' "Go to this people and say,
'You will be ever hearing but never
understanding;
you will be ever seeing but never
perceiving.'
27 For this people's heart has
become calloused;
they hardly hear with their ears,
and they have closed their eyes.
Otherwise they might see with their
eyes,
hear with their ears,
understand with their hearts
and turn, and I would heal them." ' [a]

28 'Therefore I want you to know that God's salvation has been sent to the Gentiles, and they will listen!' [29] [b]

---

a 27 Isaiah 6:9,10 (see Septuagint)
b 29 Some manuscripts include here *After he said this, the Jews left, arguing vigorously among themselves.*

In 28:17–28, the expectant reader finally observes a trial, but not quite as expected. Here is a trial in which the roles are, to some degree, reversed. In verse 17 Paul summons the local leaders of the Jewish people to come to him, and then *he* initiates proceedings. Jewish communities in Rome at this time were substantial, and we should recall that wherever Paul travelled he sought the Jews first, then the Gentiles.[4]

He begins by offering his own account and the reason he is under house arrest in Rome. He claims to have done 'nothing against our people or against the customs of our ancestors' (verse 17). In fact, although he was arrested, he was found 'not guilty of any crime deserving death' (verse 18). It was because the Jews objected to his release that he was compelled to appeal to Caesar (verse 19).[5] Witherington notes that this last claim contains an 'ominous overtone'.[6] Judaism was not a proscribed religion by Roman law, so if Paul was chained for Jewish beliefs this should be a cause of great concern to his Jewish audience. Paul is attempting to demonstrate that his predicament has been caused by the Jewish leaders in Jerusalem. He has no problem with these Jewish leaders he is meeting in Rome. Paul is only teaching as a faithful Jew in accordance with the Scriptures. He is innocent. His accusers in Jerusalem are in the wrong.

He concludes his initial address with his desire to speak with the Jewish leaders: 'It is because of the hope of Israel that I am bound with this chain' (verse 20). The 'hope of Israel' most likely refers to Paul's previous message about Jesus Christ – Israel's long-awaited Messiah who bore our sin and was raised from the dead to bring forgiveness for sin and freedom from its penalty and power. This has been Paul's message throughout his ministry. It is this 'hope' that he wishes to share with the Jews in Rome.

In verse 21 they begin their reply somewhat surprisingly. They claim to have received no letters from Judea concerning Paul. Neither has anyone come from Judea with a bad report about Paul. Given the force of opposition against Paul seen previously, one might expect that they would have sent letters or messengers to the Jewish leaders in Rome concerning Paul. Letters taken by land could have plausibly reached Rome

---

[4] Commentators suggest that there was a population of anywhere between twenty to fifty thousand Jews in Rome by AD 60. Rome was estimated at this point to have a total population of around one million. Estimates also reckon there may have been a dozen or more synagogues. See Witherington, *Acts*, 794–5; Bock, *Acts*, 751; Wall, *Acts*, 360.

[5] Although we are not told that either Festus or Felix wanted to release Paul, this is the implication of Agrippa's statement in Acts 26:32. Witherington, *Acts*, 797.

[6] Witherington, *Acts*, 799.

ahead of Paul. However, it is equally plausible that the Jewish leaders in Jerusalem decided not to pursue their case, for a number of reasons. It would have incurred greater expense to continue their pursuit of Paul; they perhaps considered themselves unlikely to win given that Paul was a Roman citizen and they were not; and Paul was now out of sight and out of mind – unlikely to return to Judea any time soon, if ever. The Jewish leaders had no need to go to any further effort or expense, and their case had already been demonstrated to be weak.[7]

Verse 22, however, suggests that news of 'this sect' has spread widely and so, although they have not had direct news about Paul, they are keen to hear his views. Earlier in Acts we have seen mention of this 'sect' of Judaism and the way in which it was spoken against.[8] The Jewish leaders in Rome may be concerned not just about theology, but also about the potential social and political implications of this 'sect'.[9]

Having arranged to meet Paul at a later date, Luke tells us that they came in even greater numbers to hear Paul at the place where he was staying (verse 23). This suggests that his rented quarters were spacious enough to accommodate a sizeable number of guests. He witnessed to them from morning till evening.[10] The verb 'witness' (*diamartyromenos*) is used elsewhere to carry a sense of solemn testimony, even charge or warning.[11] Paul is not simply providing legal defence or conducting a debate about aspects of Jewish law. He is urging his hearers to take seriously his message. It is a reminder to all those who preach or teach that our aim is not simply intellectual stimulation but also changed lives. Our subject matter is not just another part of a religious education curriculum; it is concerned with nothing less than eternal life and death. Capturing interest is not our aim. Entertaining people with rhetorical skill is not the aim. Making people feel better about themselves is not the aim. We must 'witness' with a solemn urgency, praying that God himself would change people's lives.

Paul's subject matter is laid out in verse 23: 'explaining about the kingdom of God, and from the Law of Moses and from the Prophets he tried to persuade them about Jesus'. These have been repeated themes

---

[7] Witherington, *Acts*, 799.

[8] See Acts 24:5, 14.

[9] Peterson, *Acts*, 713.

[10] Here is the fulfilment of Acts 23:11. Peterson, *Acts*, 714.

[11] See Luke 16:28; Acts 8:25; 20:21, 24; 1 Thessalonians 4:6; 1 Timothy 5:21; 2 Timothy 2:14; 4:1; Hebrews 2:6.

throughout Luke–Acts.[12] Jesus himself explained to his disciples that the Law and Prophets had all been pointing towards him (Luke 24:25–7, 44–9).

The response to Paul's message was mixed. Luke tells us, 'Some were convinced by what he said, but others would not believe' (verse 24). While Paul received a friendly reception from the Gentiles on Malta, this is set in contrast to the persistent rejection of the Jews, as seen again here in Rome.[13] As they leave, disagreeing among themselves, Paul delivers his own final judgment on his hearers. He has turned the tables. He is no longer on trial. It is rather his hearers who are on trial before the judge of all the earth. Those who have failed to accept Paul's message about Jesus are now subject to his verdict.

Paul cites Isaiah 6:9–10, applying it to those who have come to hear him. Paul introduces his quotation with 'The Holy Spirit spoke . . .' The Scriptures are not simply the record of human opinion or experience. They are the living and active word of God. Polhill notes, 'In every instance in Acts where a scriptural quote is introduced by a reference to the Spirit, the Spirit is described as having spoken.'[14] As we read the Bible, we are not simply reading interesting historical documents. God is actively speaking, by his Holy Spirit, through the Spirit-inspired words of Scripture. Historically, Christians have held a high view of Scripture – its authority, infallibility, sufficiency and perspicuity.[15] Some have rejected the divine inspiration of Scripture; others have given greater attention to immediate revelations and words of prophecy. Historically, orthodox Christianity has always held that the Bible is God's authoritative and sufficient word for his church in every place and time, and we should give it all the attention it thus deserves.

The Jewish leaders were the people 'ever hearing but never under-standing; . . . ever seeing but never perceiving'. They were the hard-hearted, deaf and blind who had failed to turn and find healing. It was a damning verdict delivered by Paul, and we can imagine that some of his hearers would not have taken kindly to the application of Isaiah 6:9–10 to their own lives.

Luke's ending leaves the reader with a sense of both triumph and tragedy.[16] While not all had rejected (verse 24), many had turned their

---

[12] See Acts 1:3; 8:12; 14:22; 17:2–3; 18:5; 19:8.

[13] Tannehill, *Narrative Unity*, 342.

[14] Cited in Witherington, *Acts*, 802.

[15] See, for example, Westminster Confession of Faith 1.1–10.

[16] Bock, *Acts*, 749.

backs on their own Messiah, incurring God's judgment in the process. Tannehill notes that the door is not completely closed to the Jews – some of Paul's hearers were open to the message.[17] However, significant opposition remained. Recognition from the Jewish people as a whole would not be forthcoming, and any sustained ministry to the Jewish assembly would be practically impossible. While the offer of the gospel was, and is, for all, the end of Acts portrays a sobering reality in terms of the large-scale Jewish rejection in Paul's day.[18]

The use of Isaiah 6:9–10 at the end of Acts is particularly interesting. Luke, in his two-volume work, has cited key passages from Isaiah at strategic points. Yet he has reversed the order in which they appear within Isaiah's prophecy. Isaiah's commission includes the words of 6:9–10 – a prophecy of a fruitless ministry. Yet that is not the end of Isaiah's story. God will raise up a Servant who will restore Israel as a 'light for the Gentiles, that my [God's] salvation may reach to the end of the earth' (Isaiah 49:6). This Servant will bring good news to the poor, proclaiming the year of the Lord's favour (Isaiah 61:1–2).

Luke quotes all three of these key passages, but in reverse order. Pao notes the programmatic nature of the quotation of Isaiah 61:1–2 at the start of Jesus's public ministry in Luke 4:18–19.[19] Jesus is the Spirit-anointed one who will bring the good news of Yahweh's favour. In Acts 1:8 (an equally programmatic text), Jesus alludes to Isaiah 49:6 as he commands his disciples to be witnesses to the 'ends of the earth'. Paul also quotes Isaiah 49:6 in Acts 13:47 at the beginning of his own missionary journeys, referring to his own calling to Gentile mission. Finally, Paul quotes Isaiah 6:9–10 here (28:26–7), at the end of Luke's story, in the context of Jewish opposition.

Luke has arranged these three key quotations to appear at key moments. If the narrative of Isaiah is about how Israel will be restored, Luke is clearly portraying the Jewish opponents as still living in the era of Isaiah 6. Those who would be judges find themselves judged.[20] This provides

---

[17] Tannehill, *Narrative Unity*, 347.

[18] Peterson, *Acts*, 717. Some manuscripts include verse 29 at this point: 'After he said this, the Jews left, arguing vigorously among themselves.' The manuscripts that include this are later and not widely attested. This addition is not present in the earliest manuscripts and the NIV is therefore right to exclude them.

[19] Pao, *Acts and the Isaianic New Exodus*, 94–108.

[20] Marguerat, 'The Enigma of the Silent Closing', 298. Tannehill notes the contrast between the friendly and receptive Gentiles on Malta and the hostile unreceptive Jews in Rome. Tannehill, *Narrative Unity*, 342.

one final legitimation for taking the gospel to the Gentiles (verse 28).[21] God has not abandoned his people, though some of his people have abandoned him. The failure of Israel (still stuck in Isaiah 6) has led to the good news of the 'Servant' being taken to all nations. This is not the end for ethnic Jews, but it is a sobering warning for them not to reject God's anointed Messiah.

2. An unchained word • Acts 28:30–31

30 For two whole years Paul stayed there in his own rented house and welcomed all who came to see him. **31** He proclaimed the kingdom of God and taught about the Lord Jesus Christ – with all boldness and without hindrance!

Luke concludes by informing his readers that Paul spent two whole years, in his own rented house, welcoming all who came to see him.[22] Luke tells us, 'He proclaimed the kingdom of God and taught about the Lord Jesus Christ – with all boldness and without hindrance!' (verses 30–31).[23] The considerable freedom Paul enjoyed throughout this extended period again suggests his innocence in the eyes of Rome. At least he was not considered the dangerous troublemaker he had been accused of in Acts 24:5. While Paul may have had moments when he wished his circumstances were different, he was evidently determined to make the most of every opportunity right where God had placed him.

As we observe Luke's ending and his vindication of Gentile mission, it is worth noting the links between the start and finish of Luke's second volume. Just as the beginning of Acts has Jesus teaching about the kingdom of God (1:1–3), so Paul is engaged likewise at the end of Acts (28:31). Often noted are the final words of the book: 'with all boldness and without hindrance' (*meta pasēs parrēsias akōlytōs*). Paul was chained, yet at the 'ends of the earth' proclaiming and teaching about Jesus with all

---

[21] Trompf, 'On Why Luke Declined', 226.

[22] Stott says, 'The terrible verses from Isaiah 6 meant neither that no Jews were converted, nor that Jews who believed would be rejected.' The 'all' includes both Jew and Gentile. 'Nevertheless, the emphasis of Luke's conclusion is on the Gentiles who came to Paul, who were symbols and precursors of the vast, hungry Gentile world.' Stott, *Acts*, 400.

[23] This recalls the church's prayer for boldness in Acts 4:29–31. The two-year period is probably around AD 60–62. Peterson, *Acts*, 720.

boldness, unhindered (see Acts 1:8). As Stott observes, 'Together Luke's two adverbs describe the freedom which the gospel enjoyed, having neither internal nor external restraint.'[24] Luke has often given summary statements throughout Acts as to the progress of the word, and his final summary assures the reader that while Paul may be chained, the gospel is not.[25]

When we compare these final appearances of Paul with the final appearances of Peter, we can see that Luke is more concerned with the mission than the missionaries. Peter's final words come in 15:11 – a defence of Gentile mission. Before that we hear of Peter's prison escape and the soldiers' musings as to what had become of him (12:18). In Acts, we only hear about the deaths of Stephen and James. We never hear about the deaths of Paul or Peter. Christian tradition would lead us to believe that Paul was freed for a period before being re-arrested and decapitated during the persecutions of Nero.[26] Luke simply does not tell us. This is because Luke's greater interest is the progress of the mission. While missionaries may die, the mission does not, and will not because its author and director cannot.[27] As Keener notes, 'Even through the very forms of suffering that appear to destroy the gospel – such as Jesus's crucifixion and Paul's imprisonment – the living God is at work to accomplish his purposes.'[28]

Luke's sudden and unresolved ending is not unique in the ancient world. A similar phenomenon is observed in other Greek and Judeo–Christian literature.[29] Marguerat describes this narrative presentation as a 'rhetoric of silence' or 'narrative suspension'.[30] The evidence that Luke is deliber-ately using this technique is as follows: first, the preceding narrative has been leading the reader to expect Paul's appearance before Caesar.[31] The trials before Felix and Agrippa confirm Paul's destination. Second, the

---

[24] Stott, *Acts*, 400–401.

[25] Acts 6:7; 9:31; 12:24; 16:5; 19:20.

[26] 1 Clement 5:5–7; Eusebius, *History* 2.22.1–7. Peterson, *Acts*, 721.

[27] Brosend argues that by refusing to recount the death of Paul, Luke turns attention back on Jesus. Wm F. Brosend II, 'The Means of Absent Ends', in *History, Literature and Society in the Book of Acts*, ed. Ben Witherington III (Cambridge: Cambridge University Press, 1996), 361.

[28] Keener, *Acts* 4:3774.

[29] For examples of this in Greek literature, see Homer, *Iliad* 22:405–515; *Odyssey* 23:248–96; Virgil, *Aeneid* 12:952. For examples of this in Judeo–Christian literature, see 2 Kings 25:29–30; 2 Maccabees 15:25–39; Mark 16:8.

[30] Marguerat, 'The Enigma of the Silent Closing', 294.

[31] See Acts 23:11; 25:11–12, 25; 26:32; 27:24.

storm and shipwreck build suspense and, as has been argued, demonstrate Paul's innocence. Third, the reverse trial justifies Gentile mission and sets the reader up for the real trial to come, further building the suspense. Finally, after all of this, Luke's final word to his captive audience is *akōlytōs* ('unhindered'). Luke has set his narrative up such that, for the reader, silence speaks volumes.

This narrative technique affects the reader in two ways. It makes the reader look both forward and back. First, it persuades the reader that the story is not yet over; it encourages the pursuit of the story. It generates intrigue and suspense as the reader wishes to resolve the unresolved. To that end it draws the reader in to emotionally experience the story. Second, it forces the reader back, to go through the story again to look for clues as to how the story may have ended. As Chrysostom noted, long before the advent of literary theory, Luke's ending 'leaves the hearer athirst for more'.[32]

By way of contrast, the resolved story would require little of the reader. They could quietly put the book down and go on to something else. The unresolved story forces involvement or even inhabitance of the story. Kiel poignantly asks, 'Does a good ending constrict or determine the future or leave the future open?'[33] He notes that the open ending 'forces the reader/observer to interpret'.[34]

It may be objected that the open ending does not serve Luke's explicit aim to provide certainty. Yet, if the ending produces the effect suggested, is it not more likely that Theophilus may have certainty as the narrative is read, reread, inhabited and interpreted? In this way, certainty is more than merely intellectual and cognitive – it is lived out as a third volume in the life of the church and individual believers bearing witness to the ends of the earth.

Acts 27–8 vindicates Paul as innocent through his survival of shipwreck and snakebite, his bringing of salvation and healing and as he sails under the Dioscuri. In addition, Paul's 'trial' echoes Jesus's trial, providing further apology for Paul's innocence. Acts 27–8 vindicates Gentile mission by means of a 'reverse trial' in which the judges are judged, and an 'unchained word' continues towards the ends of the earth. Luke's ending,

---

[32] Chrysostom, *Homilies on Acts* 55 (*NPNF* 10:326).

[33] Micah Kiel, 'Did Paul Get Whacked? The Endings of the Sopranos and the Acts of the Apostles', *SBL Forum*, sbl-site.org/Article.aspx?ArticleID=695 (accessed 13 September 2023)

[34] Kiel, 'Did Paul Get Whacked?

as a 'rhetoric of silence', draws in the reader to inhabit and interpret the story past, present and beyond the narrative of Acts.

Luke's ending is far from incomplete, awaiting another volume; the reader *is* the next volume. The church is Acts 29. Luke is inviting Theophilus (and any other readers) to become part of the story. Luke's ending is a literary masterpiece that serves to captivate the reader, invite interaction, defend the messengers and the message, and hold out certainty regarding the things taught. Nothing can stop the progress of God's gospel – not shipwrecks, snakebites or even the full force of the Roman Empire. The word is unchained.

As Christian readers, this gives us great assurance to persevere in our own witness, confident that no obstacle can hinder the power of the gospel. As Bock notes, 'Paul suffered well. He kept the faith and continued to serve, living out his call.'[35] The risen Lord Jesus is the hero of the book of Acts. He continues to 'do and to teach' (Acts 1:1) through his witnesses, by the power of his Holy Spirit.

As Paul wrote to the Romans, 'I am not ashamed of the gospel, because it is the power of God that brings salvation to everyone who believes: first to the Jews, then to the Gentile' (Romans 1:16).

It is fitting for Luke's readership that his message should end unchained, since the risen Lord Jesus is still at work by the power of his word and Spirit, and his mission is truly unstoppable.

---

[35] Bock, *Acts*, 759.